Building Rule of Law in the Arab World

Building Rule of Law in the Arab World

Tunisia, Egypt, and Beyond

edited by
Eva Bellin
Heidi E. Lane

LYNNE
RIENNER
PUBLISHERS

BOULDER
LONDON

Published in the United States of America in 2016 by
Lynne Rienner Publishers, Inc.
1800 30th Street, Boulder, Colorado 80301
www.rienner.com

and in the United Kingdom by
Lynne Rienner Publishers, Inc.
3 Henrietta Street, Covent Garden, London WC2E 8LU

© 2016 by Lynne Rienner Publishers, Inc. All rights reserved

Library of Congress Cataloging-in-Publication Data
Names: Bellin, Eva Rana, editor. | Lane, Heidi E., editor.
Title: Building rule of law in the Arab world : Tunisia, Egypt, and beyond /
    edited by Eva Bellin and Heidi E. Lane.
Description: Boulder, Colorado | Includes bibliographical references and index.
Identifiers: LCCN 2015031367 | ISBN 9781626372788 (hardcover : alk. paper)
Subjects: LCSH: Rule of law—Middle East.
Classification: LCC KMC514 .B85 2015 | DDC 340/.11—dc23
LC record available at http://lccn.loc.gov/2015031367

British Cataloguing in Publication Data
A Cataloguing in Publication record for this book
is available from the British Library.

Printed and bound in the United States of America

The paper used in this publication meets the requirements
of the American National Standard for Permanence of
Paper for Printed Library Materials Z39.48-1992.

5 4 3 2 1

Contents

Acknowledgments   vii

1   Building Rule of Law in the Arab World: Paths to Realization   1
Eva Bellin

Part 1   Judicial Reform

2   Reforming Judiciaries in Emerging Democracies   9
Lisa Hilbink

3   A Clash of Institutions: Judiciary vs. Executive in Egypt   29
Nathalie Bernard-Maugiron

4   What Independence? Judicial Power in Tunisia   53
Mohamed Salah Ben Aissa

Part 2   Military Reform

5   Reforming the Armies of Authoritarian Regimes   67
Zoltan Barany

6   Democracy vs. Rule of Law: The Case of the Egyptian Military   89
Robert Springborg

7   Subjecting the Military to the Rule of Law: The Tunisian Model   109
Risa A. Brooks

8   The Military Balancing Act: Cohesion vs. Effectiveness in Deeply Divided Societies   131
Oren Barak

Part 3 Police Reform

9 The Politics of Police Reform in New Democracies 151
   Diane E. Davis

10 Between Collapse and Professionalism: Police Reform in Egypt 173
   Tewfiq Aclimandos

11 Dismantling the Security Apparatus:
   Challenges of Police Reform in Tunisia 189
   Querine Hanlon

Part 4 Anticorruption Reform

12 From Contention to Reform: Deep Democratization
   and Rule of Law 215
   Michael Johnston

13 Strengthening Governance and Fighting Corruption
   in the Arab World 239
   Günter Heidenhof and Lida Bteddini

Part 5 Conclusion

14 Lessons, Challenges, and Puzzles for
   Building Rule of Law in the Arab World 257
   Eva Bellin

Bibliography	277
The Contributors	299
Index	301
About the Book	311

Acknowledgments

This book was born in a moment of optimism, and it is a pleasure to thank those who enabled us to act upon that sentiment. The project owes its origins to a conference that was held at the US Naval War College in Newport, Rhode Island, on November 16, 2012. That conference brought together a group of scholars for a round of reflection on how to build rule of law in the Arab world. The talks presented at the conference, as well as the synergetic discussion that followed, gave rise to the work that forms the substance of this book.

Both the conference and the subsequent development of the volume were funded by a grant from the Naval War College Foundation made possible through the generosity of the Koret Foundation. The Crown Center for Middle East Studies at Brandeis University cosponsored the project, providing the intellectual context and research time for editor Eva Bellin to work on its development. The Crown Center also provided support for translation, bibliographic assistance, and the indexing of the volume. Two colleagues associated with the Crown Center provided invaluable assistance: Sarah Feuer artfully translated the chapter by Mohamed Salah Ben Aissa from French into English; and Suzanne Rothman helped compile the volume's bibliography, providing pivotal production support in the later stages of the project. Beyond the Crown Center, Laryssa Chomiak of the Centre d'etudes Maghrébines à Tunis stepped in with a logistical intervention that helped us vault a last-minute administrative hurdle. And not least, Frank Schwartz, as ever, delivered imperturbable calm and dry wit that helped keep the ship of revision afloat as it navigated the shoals of editing insanity. Thanks to all.

—*Eva Bellin and Heidi Lane*

1

Building Rule of Law in the Arab World: Paths to Realization

Eva Bellin

Arbitrary rule has long plagued the Arab world. Its attendant consequences—injustice, cruelty, corruption, and degradation—have cultivated a deep sense of political anger and resentment among the people of the region. In fact, outrage over such arbitrary rule proved to be one of the primary triggers for the spate of uprisings that seized the region in 2011–2012. Along with a desire for "bread" and "freedom," the people hungered for human dignity, that is, an end to the capricious and often-cruel treatment meted out by remote and unaccountable states. This desire spurred hundreds of thousands, if not millions, of citizens to take to the streets and demand political change. In the language of political analysts, the people yearned for the "rule of law." The question facing activists and analysts alike is how to achieve this objective?

In *Building Rule of Law in the Arab World* we aim to tackle this question, at least in a preliminary way. The goal of this endeavor is to get a clear sense of the institutional and political underpinnings of rule of law, consider the comparative experience of others who have wrestled with this ambition, explore the empirical foundations (and obstacles) to building rule of law in the region, and construct the analytic foundation for future research on this question. To make the project manageable, we have limited our focus to the development of four of the institutional building blocks of rule of law: the judiciary, the police, the military, and regulatory/anticorruption agencies. We draw first on the experience of specialists expressly not from the region to gain comparative analytic leverage on the means that have so far proven most effective in fostering rule of law elsewhere. Our inquiry is guided by several questions: Is there a standard menu of practices, a "toolkit" of sorts, that fosters rule of law in the given institution? What are some of the key obstacles, political and otherwise, that subvert the implementation of these reforms? What should be the timing and sequencing of these measures? And can an intrinsic relationship be identified between building rule of law and democratization such that the two must be pursued simultaneously? Or should one project logically precede the other?

To anchor this analysis in the experience of the Arab world, we have enlisted the work of specialists with expertise in the workings of the judiciary, military, police, and regulatory agencies in the region. These specialists delve into a series of case studies focused primarily (but not exclusively) on the experience of the two Arab countries at the forefront of change ushered in by the upheavals of 2011, namely Tunisia and Egypt. The goal is to highlight the specific challenges faced by these countries in building rule of law as well as to construct an empirical and historical foundation for future research in this area. The analysis makes clear some of the unique challenges faced by countries in the region just as it confirms the presence of more generalizable impediments identified by broader comparative analysis.

Defining Rule of Law

The rule of law is a capacious concept—so much so that the term's varied usages have given rise to "conceptual cacophony" (Moller and Skaaning, 2014: 173).[1] Nearly all understandings of the term embrace the notion of "restricting the arbitrary exercise of power by subordinating it to well-defined and established laws," and most definitions make gestures to such ideals as "fairness," "equal treatment," "predictability," and "transparency." But variations in both foci and remedies typically follow from the users' divergent ambitions and institutional perches. Lawyers will typically seek to end arbitrary arrests, trials without due process, and cruel or degrading punishment, and they advocate for the creation of independent and impartial judiciaries. Anticorruption crusaders will typically focus on the problems of the misuse of public funds (for private ends) and advocate for the creation of regulatory agencies with the power to monitor and punish official malfeasance. For the purposes of this book, we will embrace a slightly abridged version of the definition put forward in a report by the UN secretary-general for the UN Security Council (2004), which defines rule of law as

> a principle of governance in which all persons, institutions, and entities, public and private, including the state itself, are accountable to laws that are *publicly promulgated, equally enforced,* independently adjudicated, and which are *consistent with international human rights norms* and standards. It re-

quires, as well, measures to ensure adherence to the principle of supremacy of law, equality before the law, accountability to the law, fairness in application of the law, separation of powers, . . . legal certainty, avoidance of arbitrariness, and procedural and legal transparency.[2] (emphasis added)

The Path to Rule of Law? Different Approaches

The value of establishing rule of law seems self-evident. The path to achieving it is anything but. A rich and varied literature has developed over the years exploring the diverse routes that countries have taken to building rule of law. The actionable lessons of this research, however, are far from conclusive.

Perhaps the most august literature touching on this issue delves back into the origins of the modern state in Western and Central Europe. Building rule of law was part and parcel of this state-building process. The development of rule-governed bureaucracies, reliably impartial judiciaries, and accountable institutions of rule helped spell the distinctive success and survival of many states in medieval and early modern Europe. The historical genesis of these institutions was complex, and their creation was often the unintended consequence of competing ambitions between rulers and rivals, both external and internal. Charles Tilly (1985), for example, traces this state building to the geopolitical competition faced by European monarchs and the fiscal pressure they bore to wage war successfully against their neighbors. The latter drove the creation of rationally organized bureaucratic apparatuses capable of effective tax extraction—the institutional core of capable, rule-governed states. Joseph Strayer (1970) traces the emergence of a unified and impartial legal system in England to the political ambition of the English monarchy and the kings' desire to earn fees, build their own prestige, and undermine the authority of local lords who proffered a competing system of seigneurial justice. Thomas Ertman (1997) links the variable rise of rational bureaucratic (as opposed to patrimonial) administrative apparatuses to the distribution of medieval universities and spread of literacy (both of which shaped the supply of skilled personnel capable of manning the state). And Jorgen Moller and Svend-Erik Skaaning (2014) trace the origins of accountable government in Europe to the presence of multiple powerful and privileged groups in society (cities, churches, the nobility) uniquely equipped with long-established corporate rights and thus well positioned to demand corporate representation and consultative powers from the ruler in exchange for their fiscal support.[3]

While this literature traces European success at building rule of law to almost inadvertent institution building, another body of work focuses more on the region's distinctive cultural endowment. The role of the church was important not only because it emerged as an institution autonomous of the state and capable of limiting state discretion (Fukuyama, 2011: 274), but also because it was the propagator of a particular set of ideas, specifically the idea of human equality (Fukuyama, 2011: 324), as well as the notion that even the ruler was bound by Christian law (Moller and Skaaning, 2014: 136). Both provided ideological justification for the rule of law. The process was abetted by the Protestant Reformation, the invention of the printing press, and the development of the natural sciences, all of which undercut traditional conceptions (and figures) of absolute authority (Fukuyama, 2011: 430). And building on the classical tradition of Roman republicanism, liberal philosophers such as John Locke articulated theories of natural rights and liberties that provided the ideological foundation for placing limits on arbitrary rule—the essence of rule of law (Moller and Skaaning, 2014: 146).

A third body of literature turns away from the exceptional historical and cultural trajectory of Europe and looks instead at broader contemporary world experience and the structural variables that tend to correlate with (and perhaps cause) the establishment of rule of law. Statistical analysis suggests that rule of law, or at least some of its component parts, correlates with level of socioeconomic development, absence of natural resource abundance (of the "resource curse" variety), cultural homogeneity, degree of capitalism, and marketization of the economy, among other factors (Moller and Skaaning, 2014; Mungiu-Pippidi, 2014). The causal mechanisms linking these factors with successful establishment of rule of law are varied. Higher socioeconomic development is associated with higher rates of literacy and lower rates of economic vulnerability among the citizenry. Both of these factors discourage official high-handedness and nurture the development of countervailing power and oversight by societal groups—essential to building rule of law. Putting limits on the resources subject to discretionary distribution by the state, as in market-driven economies and where resource rents are absent, limits the opportunities for official corruption. Cultural homogeneity, as in limited sectarian or ethnic fragmentation, fosters a culture of "ethical universalism" in human exchange—another impetus to fair and equal treatment (Mungiu-Pippidi, 2014: 2).

But these three approaches, although analytically valid and rich, are discouraging to contemporary advocates of building rule of law in at least two ways. The first two approaches are focused on the exceptional experience of Europe, and indeed European countries and European settler colonies are statistically the strongest performers on rule-of-law indicators (Moller and Skaaning, 2014). This suggests that countries without European legacies are at a distinct disadvantage in building rule of law. In addition, all of the aforementioned factors—long historical trajectories, deep cultural endowment, level of ethnic homogeneity, degree of socioeconomic development—are big, slow-moving forces, beyond the near-term control of policymakers. Focusing on these factors is likely to discourage latecomers about the prospects of building rule of law in the here and now.

But counterbalancing these grounds for pessimism are reasons to believe in the possibility of purposively building rule of law. Yes, historical trajectories are important, but historical paths need not be meticulously replicated in order to emulate their outcomes. The lessons of other countries' historical accidents or cultural inspiration can be learned by latecomers; there might even be a "late-comer's advantage" as Joseph Schumpeter (1912) proposed with regard to industrialization. And yes, cultural endowment matters, and those with a long tradition of constitutionalism, republicanism, and self-governance may be advantaged in building rule of law. But cultures can change, sometimes with dramatic speed. Technology may be a catalyst here. For example, the role of social media in propelling the Arab Spring, although often overstated, certainly encouraged popular engagement and political activism in the Arab world and helped many people overcome a long-rooted "culture of fear" and political lassitude. And yes, structural conditions statistically favor certain outcomes. But these conditions are by no means deterministic. The existence of consistent "overachievers" in this domain—countries like Botswana or Estonia or South Korea that outperform the expectations set by their socioeconomic standing or cultural endowment or historical legacy—suggests the possibility of the political.[4] In each case some combination of committed leadership and mobilized civil society, motivated by crisis or proximate exemplar or contingent political calculation, and (occasionally) enabled by technological innovations or foreign assistance, or both, led to the construction of rule of law, despite the odds.[5]

Politics as Possibility or Barrier?

Mobilized political will can make this happen. But just as politics opens the door to the possibility of reform, it also erects barriers. As Thomas Carothers (2006: 4) explained, "the primary obstacle to [rule-of-law] reform [is] . . . political. . . . Entrenched elites cede their traditional impunity and vested interests only under great pressure. . . . They are reluctant to support reforms that create competing centers of authority beyond their control." The only way to overcome this opposition is to mobilize power against power and interest against interest.

This is the great insight of the "second generation" of thinking on rule of law (Kleinfeld, 2012). Earlier efforts at promoting rule of law dating back to the 1980s adopted what Carothers (2006: 21) calls a "breathtakingly mechanistic approach," one focused primarily on diagnosing a country's shortcomings in selected laws and institutions and then advocating the wholesale import of Western models—laws, institutions, and even technology—irrespective of context (Kleinfeld, 2012: 10–18). This approach yielded a proliferation of programs focused on training judges, building police academies, computerizing court systems, and rewriting laws to encourage transparency—"technocratic, cookie-cutter" programs that ended up having only a minor impact on boosting rule of law.

Why such modest returns? The problem, Rachel Kleinfeld (2012) explains, was that these programs treated reform as apolitical. The program's authors did not consider the vested interests committed to the status quo. They did not anticipate the deep resistance to change. They did not realize that to be effective, these programs needed to cultivate "an internal will to reform" and harness "local stakeholders" with extensive on-the-ground knowledge and long-term time horizons (181). In fact, to advance the rule of law, reformers are obliged to do nothing less than change the local power structure, to build up alternative centers of power (e.g., citizen committees and bar associations) capable of pressuring the government to follow the law (Kleinfeld, 2012: 163).

Going Forward in the Arab World

The goal of this book then is to take seriously the lessons of both first- and second-generation thinking on the rule of law. An institutional "toolkit" is required for anchoring the rule of law, and to determine which institutional fixes might work best, it is useful to draw on the experiences of other countries (both latecomers and veteran bearers of rule of law). At the same time, it is crucial to keep political realities in mind and consider the different strategies that might be adopted to mobilize local champions and to muster the countervailing power necessary to anchor these institutional fixes on the ground and give them local resonance. Attention to both the political experience of other regions as well as to the specific empirical realities and challenges faced in the Arab world is necessary in order to think creatively about how to build rule of law effectively in the region.

The book that follows is divided into four sections; each one is focused on a different institution that is an anchor for building the rule of law. They are, in order, the judiciary, the military, the police, and anticorruption/regulatory agencies. Each section begins with a chapter that offers a transregional perspective, presenting general lessons drawn from comparative experience about what institutional fixes are advisable and how political challenges to reform might be met. This overview chapter is followed by empirical chapters, focused primarily but not exclusively on the cases of Tunisia and Egypt, aimed at exploring the reality on the ground and the challenges faced in carrying out reform. The book concludes with some overall reflections presenting general lessons learned and future paths for research.

The challenges to building the rule of law are real. But as Daniel Kurtzer (a US diplomat long experienced in tangling with seemingly insurmountable political quandaries) once said, "political problems are man-made, and so are the solutions."[6] Deficiencies in rule of law are a man-made problem. In this book we aim to gather the collective experience and wisdom of many scholars and countries in the hopes of fostering sober reflection on this challenge as well as the will to meet it.

Notes

1. Moller and Skaaning (2014) devote the better third of their book to exploring the variety of definitions and measures used to capture the notion of "rule of law." Although the components that distinguish these different conceptions often correlate with one another, they do not uniformly do so. To manage this "conceptual cacophony," Moller and Skaaning advise that analysts always clarify their usage and explicitly "define their terms" up front. See also Kleinfeld (2006) for an extraordinarily lucid and insightful discussion of the meaning of rule of law. Kleinfeld distinguishes rule of law by identifying five ends that are typically associated with it, namely (1) government bound by law, (2) equality before the law, (3) law and order, (4) predictable and efficient justice, and (5) lack of state violation of human rights.

2. The unabridged version of this definition also includes the notion of public "participation in decisionmaking" as part of the concept of rule of law. In my mind, the right to participate in decisionmaking is more appropriately associated with "democratization" than with building rule of law. For more on the relationship between the two, see below.

3. Fukuyama (2011: 405, 333) identifies several other factors such as religion and historical experience that helped reinforce the solidarity of these social forces in their challenge to absolutist rule. For example, he argues that in the case of England "concern about being ruled by a Catholic" helped drive the Glorious Revolution and the conviction by many that government ought to be based upon consent of the governed (417). In addition, a long history of local participatory self-governance that predated even the Norman Conquest in the eleventh century predisposed many to support limits on absolutist rule.

4. And of course there are "underachievers" as well. Alina Mungiu-Pippidi (2014: 3) develops this argument cogently with regard to country performance on one component of rule of law: control of corruption. She finds that structural factors such as the level of economic development account for only about half of the variation observed among 185 cases for which data is available. This finding, she argues, "leav[es] some room for human agency."

5. Mungiu-Pippidi (2014) provides examples of each of these from cases of "overachievers" in the battle to limit corruption. Enlightened leaders committed to reform played a central role in reducing corruption in Estonia, Botswana, and Georgia. Mobilized civil society played a key role in Uruguay. Financial crisis spurred reform in Chile and South Korea. Proximity to (and emulation of) foreign models

played a role in Estonia, Georgia, South Korea, and Chile. Calculations of political advantage and specifically the desire by new political parties to distinguish themselves from the "old guard" associated with corruption drove reform in Taiwan and Georgia. Technological innovations such as "e-procurement" and online public expense tracking facilitated anticorruption efforts in Estonia as did foreign assistance from Scandinavian countries.

6. Personal e-mail communication with the author, May 31, 2015.

2

Reforming Judiciaries in Emerging Democracies

Lisa Hilbink

Judicial independence has long been recognized as a sine qua non of the rule of law. Regardless of how the rule of law is defined—in a "thin" sense, as prospectivity, stability, and predictability in the laws and their enforcement (Raz, 1979), or in a "thick" sense, imbueing it with principles of substantive justice (Dworkin, 1977)[1]—it is clear that its maintenance depends on an independent judiciary. Whereas tyranny is rule by personal whim or by fear and favor, with no constraints on how and to what ends rulers use their power, a rule-of-law regime requires that clear standards apply to the exercise of power, such that external limits, in the form of procedural and substantive rules, are placed on the actions of government officials, be they popularly elected or not.[2] Those in power are unlikely to enforce such standards and limits on themselves, however. The rule of law thus requires institutionalized mechanisms for holding government officials accountable to the rules and standards established in binding legal sources.[3] In democratic systems, regular, free, and fair elections serve as mechanisms for what has been called vertical accountability, allowing citizens institutionalized opportunities to vote perceived or proven norm violators out of office. But between election cycles, and for individual and minority claims that might never figure in electoral decisions, institutions of horizontal accountability are crucial (O'Donnell, 1999). Institutions of horizontal accountability—courts being the most obvious—are charged with ensuring that the law is being respected before, during, and after election cycles, by rulers and ruled alike, and with providing redress and sanction when it is not (O'Donnell, 1999: 39). To carry out these functions both effectively and legitimately, the officials who staff the courts and other institutions of horizontal accountability must be separate and independent from those who issue the laws or enforce orders. As Neil MacCormick (1999: 176) puts it,

> there is no security against arbitrary government unless challenges [to cases brought against citizens by the state or by private parties] are freely permitted, and subjected to adjudication by officers of state separate from and distanced from those officers who run prosecutions. In private law litigation, a similar requirement appears in the need for visible impartiality of the judge.

Taking this as its premise, in this chapter, I explore the prospects and challenges for building independent judiciaries in countries transitioning from authoritarianism, seeking to provide insights, in particular, for Arab states in transition. Following a conceptual overview of judicial independence, I offer a summary of the main judicial reforms that have been prescribed for democratizing countries over the past thirty years, explaining the logic behind them. Then, drawing on analytical works by practitioners in the international policy community, on political science scholarship on the relationship between institutional reform and judicial behavior, and on a case study of the "model" country of Chile, I identify a number of conditions that affect the success of judicial reforms, highlighting three interrelated points. First, to be successful, judicial reforms must be comprehensive, sustained, and locally adapted and supported; above all, they cannot be imposed from outside. Second, they must go beyond formal rule changes to target attitudes and practices across the legal community, and the attitudinal and behavioral changes must be bolstered by structural incentives. Third, the ultimate success of reforms lies not in technical factors but rather in social and political variables that are exogenous to the judiciary. Those who would promote judicial independence and the rule of law in any emerging democracy thus must have persuasive skill, persistence, and patience.

Judicial Independence: What and Why

The concept of judicial independence is grounded in the triadic logic of conflict resolution that can be found across human societies (Shapiro, 1981: 1). In smaller communities, conflicting parties rely on a third-party authority to serve as a go-between, mediator, or arbitrator in the resolution of their dispute. They accept the decision of the third party, who is personally known to them, because of that person's status in the community and because they accept the standards that she or he uses to resolve the conflict (Shapiro, 1981: 2).[4] In more complex societies, law and office substitute for community norms and personal "consent" to the third party. The judiciary is staffed with professionals generally not known to nor chosen by the citizens who come before them, and judges impose a preexisting rule that may or may not have been familiar to both parties at the time the conflict arose. To secure legitimacy and compliance, then, judges in contemporary societies must convince citizens that they are not predisposed to favor one disputant over another, nor that the legal rules they apply have a built-in bias.[5] In other words, citizens must recognize the judiciary as a reasonable approximation of the conventional triad and not view it as a mere façade for what is in fact "two against one" (Shapiro, 1981: 8).

Reformers seeking to build the rule of law in contemporary nation-states thus face the challenge of constructing a judiciary that will appear to preserve the fundamental triadic logic and garner the citizens' trust in a context in which it is obvious to everyone that judges are not a "disinterested third party" but are, rather, government officers who bring to bear a third set of interests: those of the state.[6] In order that citizens will turn to the courts to resolve disputes or denounce abuses and will accept as binding the rulings the courts hand down, judges must be—and, more crucially, must be perceived as being—independent from the control of government officials and other powerful actors. This independence requires not only that they be free from interference from such actors in specific cases before them, but also that the judicial ranks are not stacked in advance, through the appointment and promotion process, to reflect one particular set of interests. In other words, the judiciary must enjoy both "decisional independence" and "preference independence" (Brinks, 2005: 598–599).

This does not mean that there can be no control or oversight of the judiciary by other branches or by civil society, but rather that there cannot be unilateral control or influence over who the judges are and/or how they decide particular cases. As Daniel Brinks (2005: 600) emphasizes, "the touchstone for [judicial] independence is not lack of control, but the lack of . . . unilateral control by an identifiable faction with an interest in the outcome of a dispute" or of a general category of disputes. Most obviously, then, judges cannot be handpicked by any sitting government nor subject to threats, bribery, or other forms of unilateral influence by public or private interests. Somewhat less obviously, the judiciary must also be (and be perceived to be) representative of, transparent to, and in touch with average folk, such that citizens will not suspect judges of bias and perceive them as incapable of acting as a "neutral third" in any given dispute.[7] The demographics of the bench should approximate those of the wider society, such that no major sector of the population goes unrepresented, in an ascriptive sense, in the judiciary.[8] Moreover, courthouses and judicial proceedings should be open and accessible to the public, and judicial decisions should be clearly communicated and easily available to any interested citizens.[9]

Institutional Mechanisms to Promote Judicial Independence

What then can be done to secure judicial independence and the perceived legitimacy of the judiciary in new democracies? Over the past thirty years, in response to the third wave of global democratization (Huntington, 1991), policymakers concerned with building the rule of law have developed an extensive judicial reform toolkit and have accumulated a wealth of experience applying it in different settings.[10] In this section, I offer a summary of the variety of institutional mechanisms that reformers have advocated around the world with an eye to securing judicial independence and effectiveness. Because of my own regional expertise, I draw particularly heavily, though not exclusively, on the reform agenda from Latin America.

First, and perhaps most fundamentally, judicial reformers have targeted constitutional-level guarantees for judicial tenure, salary, budget, and jurisdiction (see Domingo, 1999; Domingo and Sieder, 2001; Hammergren, 2007; Russell and O'Brien, 2001; Shetreet, 2011). It goes without saying that if government officials can easily remove judges from their posts or reduce their salaries should they render undesired decisions, or if judges have very short appointments and must be concerned with their professional security after their terms have finished, judges will not feel very comfortable ruling against powerful interests that might retaliate against them in the short to medium term. This insight dates back to *Federalist 78*, wherein Alexander Hamilton argues that because the judiciary is the weakest branch of government, lacking the power of purse and sword, and "is [thus] in continual jeopardy of being overpowered, awed, or influenced by its coordinate branches," secure tenure "may justly be regarded as the citadel of the public justice and the public security" (*The Federalist*, 1964 [1787]: 505). Under similar logic, if sitting government officials can starve the judiciary as an institution of its operational funds by cutting its budget, or if they can, through law or decree, alter and limit the jurisdiction of the courts, diverting cases of particular interest into organisms under their direct control, judges are likely to be unwilling or simply unable to function effectively, especially in politically sensitive cases.

Second, and relatedly, reformers have focused on appointment and promotion rules, which are also frequently entrenched in constitutional documents. As noted above, in order for courts to have preference independence, judicial appointments cannot be subject to unilateral control by a particular actor or set of actors (Brinks, 2005). Institutional reforms thus frequently aim to multiply and diversify the actors and institutions that participate in the judicial appointment and promotion process, such that it is not under the unique control of a single individual or group (especially the executive). One widely embraced approach has been the creation of national judicial councils or commissions, staffed by representatives of the executive, legislature, and judiciary, and sometimes also of the bar, the legal academy, and/or the general citizenry (see Hammergren, 2002). The idea behind such councils is that their involvement in the screening and nomination process will help generate a bench that comprises consensus candidates deemed meritorious by diverse political and social constituencies or judges who, taken as a whole, represent a variety of different perspectives out of which they will build consensus among themselves on the job, since many if not most courts are collegial rather than unipersonal. In addition, such councils or commissions often operate with written requirements or informal conventions regarding ascriptive representation, such that judicial appointments reflect, proportionally, the gender, racial, ethnic, and/or religious composition of the society or of the geographic distribution of the population (Malleson and Russell, 2006). The idea here is that citizens will see people like themselves in the ranks of the judiciary and, therefore, will have greater faith that their perspectives are understood and taken into account in the judicial process (see Gargarella, 2004: 8–9; Shetreet, 2011: 8).[11]

Judicial councils have also been constructed in some countries as specialized administrative bodies, separate from the executive and/or the judicial elite, to handle matters of performance, discipline, transfer, and removal of judicial personnel. Such councils involve judges from all ranks, generally elected by their peers for a set term, in the governance and administration of the institution (Guarnieri and Pederzoli, 2002). The objective is to enhance judicial independence by preventing external control or co-optation, while also maintaining or enhancing oversight of judicial personnel. The risk, however, is that this insulation feeds a corporate mentality among judges, which may cause the public to perceive the judiciary as a whole as aloof and unaccountable. Thus some care must be taken to provide transparency in such a council's procedures, as well as mechanisms that allow public input into the evaluation of judicial services and the registration of citizen complaints about judicial misconduct (Hammergren, 2007: 254–255).

Another goal of reformers has been enhancing the professionalism of the judicial corps, on the view that highly trained and qualified judges will perform better, be less vulnerable to "improper influences" (i.e., corruption), and help to burnish the judiciary's "general institutional image" (Hammergren, 2007: 98, 106). At the most basic level, reformers seek to establish or strengthen the legal requirements for becoming a judge, as well as the formal requirements for promotion to higher courts. These requirements can include a certain age and/or number of years of experience, specific education prerequisites (basic training or subsequent professional development), and selection by a formal and rigorous state exam.[12] Increasingly, countries also stipulate that candidates for judicial posts attend a specialized judicial school and/or that they work for several years in apprenticeships before they are appointed to tenured office on the bench. Many countries have also increased incentives for specialization within the judicial career, so that judges will have greater expertise on the often-complex cases that come before them. To attract and retain the most capable individuals and to reduce the necessity to accept bribes for survival, reformers also often point to the need for providing respectable yet not excessive compensation at all levels of the judiciary (Hammergren, 2007: 108–109).

Because the power of the state is so directly implicated in the criminal justice system, and because abuse of that power under authoritarian regimes was egregious in so many countries, reformers have devoted special attention to reforms of criminal justice institutions and procedures. A first priority in this regard has been the separation of judicial and prosecutorial functions, such that judges are charged exclusively with overseeing the legality of the actions taken by those who intercept, investigate, and prosecute crime, as well as by those who defend the accused, rather than participating in these activities themselves.[13] In some countries, reforms have included the creation of an autonomous prosecutorial body, whose independent institutional status removes it from direct manipulation by the executive and, by at least some accounts, renders it more likely to pursue official abuse and corruption (Ríos-Figueroa, 2012). Another approach has been to introduce or strengthen rules that allow for private prosecutors, serving as direct representatives of victims, to participate in criminal investigations and trial proceedings. The second approach breaks the monopoly that the public prosecutor's office has on criminal prosecution and, thereby, gives citizens the opportunity to access criminal courts directly and to supplement or stand in for state prosecutors who may seem overly distant from the public and/or lacking in commitment to the pursuit of certain crimes (Michel, 2012). At the same time, criminal justice reforms have aimed to enhance public defense by professionalizing and expanding support for public defense institutions. This outcome is obviously essential to allow citizens "to challenge the allegations of fact and the assertions of law on the basis of which government agencies, of their own volition or at the instance of private litigants, threaten to intervene collectively in their lives or affairs" (MacCormick, 1999: 174). Indeed, a "vital part . . . of the rule of law is that the opportunity to mount such a challenge on fair terms and with adequate legal assistance be afforded to every person" (MacCormick, 1999: 174).

A last category of reforms includes a variety of measures that serve to increase access to and transparency of the judicial process for average citizens. These measures may include the reduction of geographic, financial, linguistic, and cultural barriers to court services; oral, preannounced, and public court proceedings; the expansion of appeals to be sure that a number of different judges review each case; the creation of mechanisms for collective and public-interest litigation; and the establishment of public relations mechanisms to communicate everything from the rules of the judicial process to the content of decisions, whether through a website or other direct media (some high courts have their own television stations) or through regular press releases to specialized journalists (Hammergren, 2007; Staton, 2010).

Caveats and Cautions from and for Practitioners

Despite the relatively broad agreement around the objectives of judicial reform and the formal institutional mechanisms that, in theory, should support those objectives, those who have analyzed the outcome of reforms in various regions warn that although institutional reforms may bring about change, they do not necessarily bring about improvement (Hammergren, 2007: 306).[14] There are several reasons for this. To begin, reformers often place too much emphasis on passing reform legislation and too little on implementation. Legislative action may be easier or harder to achieve depending on political conditions in a reforming country, but almost everywhere, implementation is much more complicated, since it requires a sustained and concerted commitment of time and resources from a variety of stakeholders, some of whom have strong incentives to delay or stymie implementation (Finkel, 2008; Salas, 2001).[15] Second, reforms are often too narrowly "'court-centered,' which is to say they do not recognize the role other institutions play in conditioning court performance," be they the police, the bar, or institutions of legal education (Hammergren, 2007: 267; see also Salas, 2001). At best, this focus results in changes that benefit judges but not the public or society as a whole (Hammergren 2007: 307). At worst, the court-centered reforms are themselves undermined by "broader environmental constraints" (Hammergren, 2007: 123).[16] Third, and connected to these first two points, the ultimate success of judicial reform— that is, its contribution to the development of the rule of law—depends on "substantial numbers of people [changing] the way they think about law" (Hendley, 1996: 176). In other words, the key to success of institutional engineering lies not in applying the correct blueprint or formula but in developing a long-term, complex, locally tailored and adaptive strategy that aims to change the attitudes, incentives, and behaviors of a variety of actors (Brinks, 2010; Hammergren, 2007: 216, 236).[17] Reformers thus need to move beyond what are too frequently "highly tactical collections of isolated interventions" to find more comprehensive approaches that involve "risks that promise largely long-term payoffs and threaten some immediate discomforts" (Hammergren, 2007: 218, 320; see also Buscaglia, 1998: 27). At the same time, they must understand that reform will only succeed if it is done *with* stakeholders, rather than imposed upon them (Salas, 2001: 45). As the failure of the law and development movement attests, when external donors and advisers parachute in to administer a seemingly foreign prescription, resistance and even backlash are likely to occur (Salas, 2001: 19–20).[18] Edgardo Buscaglia (1998: 28) notes that "the best institutional scenario ... is one in which the judicial reforms are the result of a consensus that involves the judiciary and at least one of the other two branches of government.... A further condition is that the political influence of those who hope to benefit must counter the activities of the personnel who will lose their privileges." Finally, reformers must recognize that the introduction of any new institutional mechanism carries with it a chance of producing unforeseen and unintended consequences (Meierhenrich, 2010: 324). Rather than plunge headlong into reform programs (what Stephen Golub [2006] calls a "build it and they will come" mentality), then, reformers should take the time to research approaches and outcomes in other places and, before embarking on reform projects, conduct local assessments that will inform the particular strategy to be used.[19] They should then carefully monitor the implementation of the reforms, evaluate their results, and adapt accordingly (Hammergren, 2007).

General Insights from Political Science

Just as policy analysts have recognized that judicial reforms do not necessarily lead to improvements in judicial performance, political scientists have noted a weak relationship between formal guarantees of judicial independence and actual behavioral or "positive" judicial independence, as well as between institutional independence of the judiciary and more general rule-of-law indicators (Brinks, 2005; Guarnieri and Piana, 2012). This does not simply mean that formal rules are not followed in practice, although they might not be in many countries. Rather, even where formal judicial independence is institutionalized and the formal rules are followed, judges do not necessarily engage in independent behavior on the bench, and rule-of-law indicators are not necessarily high. Scholars have thus begun to develop theories to explain when and why judges will behave independently and thereby contribute to the construction and maintenance of the rule of law.

In recent years, the literature on judicial behavior has zeroed in on two major factors that seem to be central to positive (i.e., behavioral) judicial independence: political fragmentation and professional role conceptions. The basic logic of political fragmentation theory is that judges are willing and able to take stands against powerful actors only when the political context is such that they can assert themselves without fear of retaliation (Helmke and Rosenbluth, 2009). Thus, in polities where one party dominates and has the power unilaterally to punish individual judges, to curtail the jurisdiction or corporate prerogatives of the judiciary, or simply to overrule judicial decisions, judges have no incentive to assert themselves against powerful actors. By contrast, where power is fragmented and diffused,[20] either within or between government institutions, or where alternation of parties in power is regular or anticipated, judges understand that coordination is too difficult or retaliation too costly for political actors and are hence willing and able to challenge them (see Hilbink, 2012).[21] The focus of political fragmentation theories is thus on the political configurations or contexts that, through the provision of structural incentives, constrain or enable assertions of judicial independence. In this perspective, the construction of the rule of law depends primarily on the diffusion of power in the polity and the competition that this diffusion implies between factions, parties, or branches of government; in other words, the key to the rule of law lies outside of judicial institutions and thus largely beyond the reach of judicial reformers.

The political fragmentation argument, dominant in the comparative judicial politics literature, appeals to common sense and no doubt helps account for the presence or absence of positive judicial independence in many cases. However, as Lisa Hilbink (2012) argues, political fragmentation is not sufficient or always necessary for positive judicial independence. Although judges can and obviously do in many cases assess the likely responses of actors in the other branches before asserting their authority in ways that challenge such actors, their professional role conceptions serve both to motivate (or to discourage) positive judicial independence in the abstract and to orient their assessment of the strategic environment.[22] Otherwise put, professional role conceptions, transmitted and sometimes altered through social and institutional processes, are crucial both in providing the motivation (or lack thereof) for positive judicial independence and in shaping judges' perceptions of and responses to the opportunities for and risks of such behavior. This situation suggests that judicial reformers, to the extent that they can influence professional education and socialization, might be able to enhance judicial independence.[23] However, tying in to the argument in the previous section, this kind of approach must be comprehensive, long-term, and actively promoted by domestic actors. Changes should not be expected to occur overnight and may not come to full fruition until a new generation establishes itself on the bench. And in the end, the establishment of the rule of law will depend on the willingness of local leaders and citizens to subject themselves to the scrutiny of positively independent courts (Salas, 2001: 25).

Lessons from Chile[24]

To illustrate the preceding points, I now offer a brief narrative of the judicial reform trajectory in a case often held out as a model of a successful democratic transition: Chile.[25] In 1990, an elected civilian assumed the presidency of Chile after seventeen years of repressive military rule led by General Augusto Pinochet. At the time of the transition, there was wide agreement among democratic forces that the courts had failed to defend the most basic principles of law and justice throughout the Pinochet years, despite the fact that authoritarian leaders had allowed the judiciary to function quite independently, both in terms of appointments and decisionmaking (see Hilbink, 2007, 2008). With formal democratic rule restored, then, the debate centered on what to do about this judiciary that had been so complicit with authoritarian rule. Some favored an open and thorough purge to rid the judicial ranks of Pinochet sympathizers and replace them with committed democrats. Opponents argued that such a purge would be an attack on judicial independence and would set a bad precedent going forward.[26] Others, including the first civilian president, Patricio Aylwin, recognized that a simple change of personnel would be insufficient; equipping the judiciary to serve a twenty-first-century democratic rule of law required instead a variety of changes to judicial structure, procedure, and training (Correa, 1999).

President Aylwin thus made judicial reform a top priority. His original proposals involved the creation of the multibranch, pluralistic National Judicial Council to take over administration of the judiciary from the conservative Supreme Court as well as for the establishment of a national ombudsman's office (*defensor del pueblo*), which would have provided an additional venue, outside the control of the judiciary, to which citizens might report abuses by public officials. Both met with stiff resistance from opposition legislators and from the judiciary itself and had to be withdrawn.[27] Aylwin did succeed, however, in gaining legislative approval for the establishment of the Judicial Academy judicial school (Academia Judicial) to improve the caliber of incoming judges, to promote continuing education as judges climb the hierarchy, and generally to improve the prestige of the judicial profession. The proposal even garnered support from Aylwin's opposition on the grounds that this step was important for building a judiciary that would be up to the task of adjudicating issues of central importance in a modern society and market economy. The *academia* began functioning in April of 1996.

With the experience of the Aylwin government in mind, the successor administration of Eduardo Frei, backed by the same center-left coalition of political parties, the Concertación, took a subtler and more gradual approach to judicial reform. With support from nongovernmental organizations (NGOs) that cut across the political spectrum, Frei's Ministry of Justice centered its efforts on criminal procedure reform.[28] This reform, which was finally approved by Congress in 1997, called for a geographically staged overhaul of the criminal justice system from a written and inquisitory system to an oral and accusatory one. In other words, judges in criminal cases were no longer to have both prosecutorial (investigatory) and judicial functions but would reach a decision based on the evidence and legal arguments presented by lawyers from two new institutions: an independent public prosecutorial organ and a public defense body. Moreover, criminal trials were to be conducted orally and publicly, introducing new procedural guarantees for defendants that were absent under the closed written system (Duce and Riego, 2007). Judges initially reacted negatively to the reform initiatives, but after a sustained effort on the part of the reform coalition to educate judges about the virtues of the system, a majority of the Supreme Court did finally vote to support what was billed "the reform of the century" (Correa, 1999).

Later that year, the Frei government capitalized on an alleged corruption scandal involving members of the Supreme Court to push a major reform of the court through the National Congress. Claiming that it wanted to address the root of the problem—namely, an overly autonomous, excessively insulated, and highly corporatist judiciary—and confident after its successful cooperation with the opposition on criminal procedure reform, the government seized the moment to propose fundamental structural changes to the Supreme Court. With support from the leading opposition party, the Frei administration proposed a new nomination system for Supreme Court justices. Although the court itself retained the function of compiling the five-person nomination lists to any vacancy in its ranks, the reform required that, henceforth, five posts on the court would be filled by lawyers from outside the judiciary. (This broke with a seventy-year tradition of drawing all candidates from among career judges.) In addition, the reform introduced Senate ratification, by a two-thirds vote, of any individual selected by the president from the court's nomination lists. This change effectively gave a voice in the nomination process to the opposition, which any governing administration would now have to consider in order to secure judicial appointments. The bill also expanded Supreme Court membership from seventeen to twenty-one, provided for the comfortable retirement of all judges over the age of seventy-five, and shortened the term of Supreme Court president from three to two years. Despite opposition from the judiciary, the reforms prospered and 1998 brought eleven new faces to the court, including five lawyers from outside the judicial hierarchy (Lagos, 1998).[29]

The 1998 Supreme Court reform had two immediate effects. First, it got rid of some of the oldest and most conservative judges on the high court. As Alejandra Huneeus (2006) notes, this move was "court-packing by any other name," but one that "had democratic legitimacy, not only because it was approved by an elected (mostly) Congress, but because it was a response to a court appointed [under] a dictator" (50). At the same time, it injected some new, extrabureaucratic blood directly into the Supreme Court. With five Supreme Court posts now occupied by lawyers whose legal understandings had not been forged in the judicial bureaucracy, the cupola of the judiciary was opened to fresh ideas. Although these effects were tempered by the supramajority Senate approval rule, which gave veto power of new nominees to the right-wing opposition, and by the fact that candidates for lateral entrance to the court had to be nominated by the court itself,[30] the reform nonetheless opened up new possibilities for legal interpretation.

Meanwhile, the neoconstitutionalist wave that swept Latin America in the 1980s and 1990s filtered into Chile's legal academy, gradually transforming the content of legal education away from traditional legal positivism, which cast judges as mere mouthpieces, or "slaves," of the law, to the idea of judges as guardians of a rights-based constitutional order (Couso, 2010). The new political theory of judging was transmitted from outside the country's borders through academic and professional connections. Chilean jurists trained in Spain, Germany, the United Kingdom, Canada, and the United States returned to the country well acquainted with, and often heavily influenced by, neoconstitutionalist understandings of the judicial role (Couso, 2007, 2010). Many subsequently took up teaching positions in the country's law schools and offered courses in the Judicial Academy.[31] In addition, a growing number of judges themselves began pursuing degrees in Europe and the United States (Couso and Hilbink, 2011: 107).

As a new generation of magistrates, trained in this new understanding of the judicial role, took up their posts, a second set of seemingly mundane reforms went into effect. From 1996 to 2005, a combination of reforms designed to modernize the courts—that is, to improve the caliber and the capabilities of personnel and the efficiency and effectiveness of judicial procedures—began to alter conditions for those at the base of the judicial pyramid (Vargas, 2007). These reforms included, in addition to the creation of the Judicial Academy, a substantial increase in judicial salaries, particularly at the entry level; a massive increase in the number of judges, again at the trial-court level; and a reform of the Constitutional Tribunal that transferred concrete review power away from the Supreme Court and created a new mechanism for ordinary lower-court judges to challenge the constitutionality of a law that affects a case before them (Couso and Hilbink, 2011).[32]

These reforms had three major effects. First, the increase in starting salaries, along with the competitive process established for entry into the

Judicial Academy, enhanced the intellectual and professional profile of individuals entering the judiciary. In the prereform era, it was generally not the best and brightest law students who pursued judicial careers, but rather poor to average performers who had few professional options and turned to the judiciary as a stable and respectable, but certainly not prestigious, career. They received no specialized education but were instead trained on the job. They thus tended not to have the intellectual resources and professional alternatives to support the taking of bold stands (Hilbink, 2007). The reforms changed all this. The new generation of judges is of a higher intellectual caliber, with greater formal training, and evident professional security and confidence. Hence they bristle under the pressures for unity and obedience that operate in the hierarchical institutional setting in which they work (Damaska, 1986; Sanhueza, 2011). Second, the expansion of positions at the base of the judicial pyramid, in combination with the improved salaries at the entry level, rendered ascension in the judicial hierarchy both less likely and less necessary for the career judge. Although hierarchical superiors maintain the power to evaluate, discipline, and nominate individuals for promotion, the reforms did reduce somewhat the incentives for lower-court judges to cater and conform to the views of the judicial elite. Some lower-court judges thus perceive "a space [in which to act] that wasn't there before" (Hilbink, 2012: 609). Third, and finally, the transfer of concrete judicial review powers to the Constitutional Tribunal institutionalized the opportunity for ordinary judges to raise constitutional issues directly to the Constitutional Tribunal, thus circumventing their hierarchical superiors on the Supreme Court. As Javier Couso and Lisa Hilbink (2011: 111) put it, "this new ability of lower-court judges to get around the supreme court and appeal to an external body . . . means that a lonely judge at the bottom of the regular judicial hierarchy can now (in theory) be crucial in getting a law declared unconstitutional without needing to persuade his or her superiors in the supreme court." In short, the reforms have given lower-court judges better intellectual and material resources, greater internal independence, and more opportunities to assert themselves, and propelled by their commitment to neoconstitutionalism, they have begun to do so (see Couso and Hilbink, 2011).

Chile thus appears to be a case where judicial reform has led not just to change but to improvement (per Hammergren, 2007: 306). It illustrates well points made earlier in this chapter: the need for a strategy that is long-term, complex, locally tailored, and adaptive; the value of working with stakeholders, rather than imposing reforms upon them; and the importance of changing attitudes, incentives, and behaviors of a variety of actors, not simply by replacing "enemies" with "friends" but by combining the training (and retraining) of judicial personnel with structural changes that encourage and enable new patterns of conduct. Moreover, Chile's success has been undergirded by an ideological shift regarding the proper judicial role that has inspired policymakers, informed institutional alterations, and given judicial actors both the sense of vocation and the technical tools necessary for them to engage in positive independence and to contribute to the strengthening of a democratic rule of law.[33] In sum, Chile's successful judicial reforms have involved a concerted and sustained effort on the part of mostly domestic policymakers to work with stakeholders and build political consensus across party/coalitional lines,[34] resulting in changes that, supported by a broader ideological shift, are inspiring and enabling a new generation of judges to act in ways that deepen the rule of law.

Having said that, it should be noted that Chile's successful reform experience is owed also to some broader contextual factors that may not be present in other countries. First, following the controlled transition to formal democracy, Chile was governed for twenty years by the same center-left coalition (the Concertación) that, despite some internal differences, had a generally consistent, and persistent, approach to governance and reform. In addition, this coalition had no choice but to negotiate with the right-wing opposition, to which Pinochet's 1980 constitution granted disproportionate representation and institutional voice. To be effective, Chilean governments have thus had to build consensus for almost any major policy initiative (Siavelis, 2008).[35] If, as Brinks (2010: 238) argues, "deep institutional fixes will not be forthcoming in the absence of effective political movements that mobilize for an end to the problem," then Chile seems to have enjoyed a prolonged advantage that is difficult to reproduce elsewhere. Moreover, Chile has by no means had to build up the rule of law from nothing; on the contrary, the country is known for its strong legalist tradition (see Hilbink, 2009). Formal judicial independence was firmly established by the 1930s, respected by executives even as politics polarized in the late 1960s and early 1970s, and, as noted above, largely maintained even under the military regime (Hilbink, 2007). Indeed, the Pinochet regime maintained a "dual state" (Meierhenrich, 2010), engaging, on the one hand, in massive human rights abuses that violated basic principles of law, while, on the other hand, propagating a new constitution in 1980 and creating a Constitutional Tribunal separate from the ordinary judiciary that wound up binding the government to the terms it had set for itself (Barros, 2002). In short, Chile has demonstrated long-standing commitment to governance through and in accordance with legal rules (Huneeus, 2007; Valenzuela, 1995), as well as what Marcelo Bergman (2009) dubs a "culture of compliance" in wider society.[36] The "shared mental model" of procedural legality and the expectation of compliance, cultivated and reproduced across time in Chile, facilitated cooperation between adversaries and served to generate confidence in the state, which in turn reinforced the "general commitment to a legal way of doing things" (Meierhenrich, 2010: 215, 219).[37] Such a legal tradition, as Jens Meierhenrich (2010) emphasizes, "evolve[s] and cannot be erected" (326), and "controlling and concluding [its development] is an improbable task" (325).

Conclusion

As citizens of the Arab world seek to forge transitions to stable and meaningful democracies, they must necessarily be concerned with the construction and maintenance of the rule of law, for democracy "is not only a political regime but also a particular mode of relationship between state and citizens and among citizens themselves, under the rule of law enacted and supported by a democratic state" (O'Donnell, 1999: 13).[38] In this chapter, I have argued that judicial independence is essential to the rule of law for reasons of both accountability and legitimacy. Only judges separate and independent of government officials can be expected to hold such officials accountable to external rules that may, at times, inconvenience and frustrate the pursuit of their ambitions, whether public or private. At the same time, judicial independence is crucial to public confidence in the courts as fair and unbiased sites of dispute resolution more generally. Only when judges are perceived as approximating a "neutral third," neither preselected nor unilaterally pressured or inherently predisposed to rule in favor of a particular party, will citizens turn to the courts to resolve conflicts or denounce abuses.

Thirty-some years of judicial reform experience in "third-wave" democracies have produced a comprehensive battery of reforms designed to enhance judicial independence and legal effectiveness, as elaborated above. The results, however, have often been disappointing, producing change but not necessarily improvement (Hammergren, 2007: 306). By drawing on analyses of judicial reform practitioners, the political science literature on judicial behavior, and my work on the evolving role of the judiciary in Chile, I have offered several main insights for would-be rule-of-law promoters. First, in order to succeed, reforms must be comprehensive and sustained and must actively involve, persuade, and incentivize many stakeholders. Given the suspicion of "imperialist agendas" in many emerging democracies, the most propitious context for reforms is one in which the impulse for and coordination of the effort come from local actors, with support from regional epistemic communities that are sensitive to the particular conditions in the target country. Second, and relatedly, reforms must aim not merely at changing the formal rules but at altering attitudes and practices in and around the legal and judicial system. Cultivating in the judicial corps an identification with and commitment to a shared role conception, tied to the maintenance of the democratic rule of law, appears crucial. However, this quality will likely be insufficient if such a conception of the judicial role is not shared and supported by other legal professionals. Moreover, building such a professional culture takes time and persistence; results may not become evident unless and until a new generation of legal professionals reaches positions of prominence or is otherwise granted, through structural or political changes, "room to maneuver." Third, and finally, rule-of-law promoters must be cognizant that, ultimately, the construction and maintenance of judicial independence is "likely to depend on political and historical conditions that are exogenous to the judiciary and may lie beyond reach, such as the existence of a stable, competitive, multiparty democracy" (Law, 2011: 1371). As Luis Salas (2001: 30) cautions,

> technical reforms can go a long way to making the legal system more efficient or accessible, but until the national elites see a benefit in supporting a strong and independent judiciary, [reform] projects will have little long-term impact. Hundreds of judges may be trained, for example, but the training will come to naught if, following a national election, the victorious party removes them and new judges are selected based on party affiliation.

All of this is not to say that judicial reforms should not be attempted unless political conditions are ideal; rather, I wish to emphasize that reformers must approach the enterprise of "building the rule of law" with their eyes wide open and their expectations appropriately measured.

Notes

1. For an excellent conceptual and historical treatment of the rule of law, see Tamanaha (2004).

2. "At the heart of the distinction between free and despotic governments is the idea that when governments act towards citizens, their action must be warrantable under a rule," that is, under an "explicit provision mandating, permitting, or authorizing decisions in specific terms (or involving some bounded discretion) only when certain quite clearly specified circumstances obtain." This guideline "holds good also when government . . . purports to regulate or pass judgment on claims and complaints and demands levied by citizen upon citizen" (MacCormick, 1999: 173, 172).

3. These can range from case law to statutes, codes, constitutions, and international conventions.

4. Shapiro (1981) discusses this method of arbitration in terms of consent by both parties, although the notion of consent may be easily problematized given the fundamental power differentials at work in most communities.

5. Because the focus of this chapter is limited to judicial independence and its perceived legitimacy, the related question of the perceived legitimacy of the laws themselves will not be treated, though this factor is obviously crucial to the construction and maintenance of the rule of law.

6. The bearing of a third set of interests is particularly evident for areas of

public law (criminal, political, and constitutional cases) but holds in private law, as well, where the state backs up a set of norms with force.

7. "The courts can perform their function as an institution to resolve disputes in society only if they enjoy public confidence . . . [and they] can enjoy such confidence only if they are seen as independent and unbiased, and if the process of resolving the dispute is fair, efficient, expedient, and accessible" (Shetreet, 2011: 6).

8. As will be elaborated below, this goal requires sustained efforts to train and recruit citizens of both sexes and of all races, ethnicities, religions, and regions of the country to the judiciary. While it would be difficult to achieve and maintain perfect proportionality in the judiciary as a whole, much less in any given court, it should be of particular concern at the appellate level, where final decisions are rendered.

9. For more details, refer especially to the discussion of the Chilean case below.

10. In addition to democratization and economic liberalization in Latin America, "the collapse of Communism in Europe, the economic reforms taking place in China and other Asian economies, along with the globalization of economic markets," spurred a broad "rule-of-law" reform movement (Salas, 2001: 22).

11. As another means of garnering citizen confidence, Salas (2001) endorses public (even televised) hearings on judicial nominations and open roll call votes for judicial appointment.

12. However, too much emphasis on experience or particular professional training or degrees may be at odds with diversification of the bench, since at least initially, such requirements would likely favor members of historically privileged groups.

13. Traditionally in countries of the "civil-law" tradition, judges have had a much more direct role in stages and procedures that in the common-law system are reserved for the police and the prosecution (Merryman and Pérez-Perdomo, 2007).

14. See also Guarnieri and Piana (2012: 123), who conclude that "the effectiveness of judicial reforms in supporting the development of the ROL [rule of law] should not be overvalued."

15. In addition to citizens and politicians, stakeholders include judges, state lawyers, private lawyers, and law school administrators and professors, as well as actors in any number of auxiliary institutions, depending on the specifics of the reform, such as the police, prisons, and legal nongovernmental organizations (NGOs). Some trained and vested in an existing system will view reforms as a threat to their status or power, whereas others will see opportunities for personal and professional gain in a reformed system.

16. For example, Salas (2001: 45) notes that "the experience of judiciaries throughout [Latin America] demonstrates that judicial schools can do little to create knowledgeable and efficient judges if the law graduates have serious basic deficiencies in their legal training."

17. Meierhenrich (2010: 325) writes that "the World Bank model, at least until recently, centered on (1) the centrality of legal transplants; (2) a one-size-fits-all approach; (3) top-down methods; and (4) short time horizons. . . . The problem with [this] model is that law 'is seen as technology when it should be seen as sociology or politics.'"

18. Langer (2007) argues that the success of criminal procedure reform in Latin America derives, in part, from the fact that it originated in and was diffused within the global periphery, rather than being a project conceived and imposed from the center (i.e., from the United States and Europe).

19. In other words, engagement with local actors and analysis of local conditions should reveal what the existing complex of attitudes, incentives, and behaviors is and what might be more or less likely to alter these in desired ways.

20. By fragmentation or diffusion of power, the literature generally refers to a situation in which any particular institution (e.g., the military) or political party or movement does not exercise enough control over resources to shut competitors out indefinitely. Economic resources are, obviously, crucial to the equation, but other types of resources (e.g., arms, communication, sheer numbers of followers) also come into play.

21. But see Popova (2012), who draws on Eastern European cases to demonstrate that political fragmentation and competition sometimes lead to more judicial dependence, not less.

22. For examples supporting this claim, see Nunes (2010), Ingram (2012), and González-Ocantos (2013).

23. To be sure, Guarnieri and Piana (2012: 123) contend that "identification with the institutional requirements of the judicial role" is "as important as [formal] independence."

24. In this section, I draw heavily on my previous work, one piece of which was coauthored with Javier Couso.

25. This account is stylized, leaving aside much of the conflict that was (inevitably) part of the process, and focusing on what was accomplished rather than on what remains to be addressed. For more detail on the process, see Couso and Hilbink (2011).

26. Some pointed to the "antimodel" of Argentina, where purges and stacking of the judiciary with every change of government had become an informal institutional practice that weakened the rule of law (Stotsky 1993). For a critique of this general argument, see Dyzenhaus (1998).

27. Opponents claimed these moves were an attempt to wrest independence from the judiciary, which enjoyed a significant level of bureaucratic autonomy (see Hilbink, 2007).

28. On the right, concerns about the efficiency of criminal procedure—that is, a perceived need for faster and more reliable investigations and trials to respond to crime—drove reform efforts, whereas on the left, a desire to improve due process guarantees and to fix a broken system of pretrial detention motivated reformers.

29. See Article 75 of the Chilean Constitution, as modified by this reform.

30. The court itself conducted the competition for nominations to the "external" slots, meaning they would in all likelihood choose lawyers they knew and trusted (i.e., that were similar to them).

31. Many instructors at the Judicial Academy, particularly in its early years, were experts in human rights law and gave classes that focused on the judicial duty to monitor and limit the police power of the state. In addition, the key authors of the new criminal procedure code offered seminars and workshops that placed heavy emphasis on the role of the judge as rights guarantor (Avilés, 2008; Zapata, 2009).

32. In Chile, the Supreme Court is the highest court of legal appeal, whose primary role is supposed to be clarification and uniformization of legal interpretation. From 1925 to 2005, the Supreme Court also had constitutional review power (and original and exclusive jurisdiction) in concrete cases (called the *recurso de inconstitucionalidad*); that is, it could declare null and void the application of a challenged law to a particular case on grounds of procedural or substantive unconstitutionality. The Constitutional Tribunal, which was created in 1970, suspended by the military junta after the coup in 1973 and reinstated in

somewhat altered form by the 1980 constitution, was an institution created on the "Kelsenian model," as separate from the ordinary judiciary, and with only abstract review power (that is, review of bills challenged on constitutional grounds during the legislative process). The 2005 reform referenced here altered the composition of the tribunal and, among other things, transferred jurisdiction over the *recurso de inconstitucionalidad* from the Supreme Court to the Constitutional Tribunal. Ordinary judges of all ranks may now submit constitutional questions on cases before them for resolution by the Constitutional Tribunal.

33. I owe the point about the importance of technical tools to González-Ocantos (2013).

34. Notably, under the Concertación governments that ruled Chile for twenty years after the transition to civilian rule, politics was highly consensus oriented, with administration leaders seeking to build broad support, through consultation and negotiation, for all major policies (Siavelis, 2008).

35. As Siavelis (2008: 208) notes, this approach to governance was historically rooted (though the practice broke down in polarized environment of the Cold War and was violently interrupted by the authoritarian regime) and was facilitated by "a context of strong institutions and political parties within which agreements could be structured and enforced."

36. Chile's consistently good scores in Transparency International surveys, placing it in the top category of least corrupt countries, are a testament to this culture. See http://www.transparency.org/country#CHL.

37. For a similar argument focused on the low levels of tax evasion in Chile, see Bergman (2009).

38. Voters empower individuals to represent and lead them, but whether their party wins this time around or not, they expect the government to respect their inherent dignity, that is, to show equal concern and respect for those whose lives the government can affect (Beatty, 1994; Dworkin, 1977). "For ordinary people, invoking the authority of law would be one of the most obvious ways of ensuring [that] the power of the [democratic] state would not be abused in the way which made colonial, fascistic, and communist Governments so notorious in the past" (Beatty, 1994: 3). Citizens of a democratic polity must thus have recourse to established mechanisms of judicial recourse when they feel they have been treated unjustly by power holders.

3

A Clash of Institutions: Judiciary vs. Executive in Egypt

Nathalie Bernard-Maugiron

Since the overthrow of Hosni Mubarak in February 2011, the judiciary has emerged as a central political player on the Egyptian scene. During Mohamed Morsi's year in power, members of the judiciary filled explicitly political posts in government, with prominent judges holding positions as vice president, justice minister, and chair of the Constituent Assembly. Courts increasingly weighed in on sensitive political issues, often in conflict with the executive and legislative branches. In retaliation, the executive and legislature took steps to discipline the judiciary, reduce its political influence, and even purge political opponents among them. After Morsi's ouster in July 2013, judges were accused of taking their revenge by prosecuting Morsi and his supporters. The courts cleared Mubarak and his top officials of all charges, failed to investigate members of the security forces on charges of killing protesters, and sentenced members of the Muslim Brotherhood and prominent secular opponents to jail for participating in peaceful street protests. Such rulings rendered the judges susceptible to accusations of delivering selective justice.

By taking what were considered explicitly political decisions, the courts have been accused of overstepping their authority. This perceived overreach has shaken public confidence in their standing as a dispassionate institution. In addition, the designation of the speaker of the Supreme Constitutional Court as interim head of state in 2013 (to serve until new elections could be organized) constituted a new high in the judicialization of politics or, worse, the politicization of the judiciary.[1] Furthermore, none of the regimes that have ruled the country since February 2011 have undertaken the passage of the long-anticipated reform of the judiciary.

The position of the judiciary in Egypt is thus at one of its lowest points in recent history.

The Judiciary on the Political Field

This is not the first time in Egyptian history that elements of the judiciary have been seen as being politically active. Under Mubarak, the judiciary had served as an arena for pursuing political objectives in defiance of the regime in power. The courts had challenged the authoritarian regime by issuing rulings aimed at guaranteeing a variety of political rights and freedoms (Moustafa, 2003, 2008). The courts' assertiveness led to the paradoxical outcome that under the Morsi regime judges were accused of being supporters of Mubarak and the army, whereas during the Mubarak era they were considered to be one of the few counterweights to the president's authoritarianism. Equally paradoxical, under Morsi, judges were accused of being opponents of Islamists, whereas under Mubarak, they were accused (by regime elites trying to tarnish their reputation) of being infiltrated by the Muslim Brotherhood.

Judicial Independence Prior to the 2011 Uprising

The political independence and assertiveness of the judiciary prior to the January uprising can be illustrated by several examples. The first concerns the leading role played by the judiciary in advocating for free and fair conduct of elections during the Mubarak era. Until the year 2000, state employees were assigned responsibility for overseeing the voting process in primary polling stations. Judges, by contrast, were assigned the role of monitoring general polling stations where the counting of ballots was performed. But in 2000, the Supreme Constitutional Court ruled that, in accordance with Article 88 of the constitution of 1971, the entire election process had to be performed under the supervision of members of judicial bodies.

This ruling meant that judges should supervise both general and primary polling stations. The Supreme Constitutional Court's ruling was implemented for the first time in the elections of 2000. During these elections, judges witnessed widespread fraud and irregularities and complained that they were asked to certify rigged elections.[2] They requested full supervision rights over the entire election process, from the preparation of voter lists to the announcement of the results. The battle was led by the Judges' Club,[3] ruled by the "Independent Current," a faction of judges who put forward a platform of demands for democratic reforms.

Beyond this show of assertiveness, in 2005 a number of reformist judges from civil and criminal courts launched a protest movement to advocate for free elections and real judicial independence.[4] They resorted to new means of pressure, such as making statements to newspapers, granting interviews to satellite channels, and even organizing sit-ins and demonstrations. The reformist judges also threatened to refrain from monitoring the upcoming elections and constitutional referendum unless the regime met their demands for legal reforms.

For their independence and assertiveness, the reformist judges paid a high price. Not only did the government refuse to respond to their two main demands, but the judges and their club were subject to several measures of retaliation. Several reformist judges were referred for disciplinary investigation and their immunity was lifted by the Supreme Judicial Council. Beyond that, in 2007, judges were deprived of their role of supervising the voting process. That year the constitution was amended to explicitly provide that judges would supervise general polling stations only, and henceforth, state employees, and not specifically judges, would preside over the primary polling stations as had been the case before 2000.[5]

Another example of judicial assertiveness under the Mubarak regime also focuses on the battle for free and fair elections. Besides fighting for judicial supervision of the voting process, in 2005 judges also supported the campaign by NGOs to ensure the transparency of the ballots.[6] Several human rights NGOs had submitted a request to the Presidential Elections Commission for permission to observe the elections inside the polling stations. When the NGOs failed to receive an official reply, they challenged this implicit refusal by bringing a case before the State Council.[7] In an act of surprising political independence, the State Council agreed to hear the case. (Article 76 of the constitution provided that the Presidential Elections Commission decisions could not be challenged by any other authority and that only the commission itself could examine appeals against its own decisions.)[8] After hearing the case, the court held that since civil society organizations, including human rights NGOs, were focused on reviving the idea of democracy in society and ensuring the transparency of elections, they had to be authorized to observe the electoral process, so long as they did not hinder the work of the polling stations.

But the conflict did not end there. The Presidential Election Commission challenged the State Council's competence to rule on this issue, and after appealing the decision to the Supreme Administrative Court, it had the ruling revoked. The Electoral Commission in charge of organizing the parliamentary elections then announced in a press release that NGOs and the National Council for Human Rights would be authorized to observe the parliamentary elections on the condition that they coordinate their actions and that they be "neutral" (i.e., have no political affiliation and have no members participating in the elections). But the commission refused to provide an official response to the NGOs directly. The NGOs decided to bring a suit to the Court of Administrative Litigation. On November 6, 2005, this court responded favorably to the NGOs' request. It struck down the commission's tacit rejection of the NGOs' request, maintaining that civil society organizations should be granted authorization to observe the balloting without having to coordinate with the National Council for Human Rights. The court also insisted that NGOs be present during the counting of the ballots, arguing that the role of civil society organizations was to allow the peaceful expression of opinions and participation for the political, social, and economic edification of society. The assertiveness of the courts meant that NGOs managed to have access to the primary polling stations to observe the voting process. In this case judicial independence and activism delivered a victory for more transparent elections despite the intentions of the authoritarian regime.

Interference of the Excutive Power in the Affairs of the Judiciary

These illustrations of judicial independence in Egypt are all the more surprising given the numerous laws and conventions that have long enabled the executive to meddle in the affairs of the judiciary.[9] The first of these concerns the process of judicial appointment. In Egypt, the executive is responsible for appointing the most important positions in the judiciary.[10] For example, the president, the vice presidents, and the counselors of the Court of Cassation are all appointed by the president of the republic.[11] Until 2012, the president of the republic also chose the general prosecutor among senior magistrates. The constitution of 2012 stated that he would be appointed by the president of the republic, on the basis of a selection made by the Supreme Judicial Council, for a nonrenewable period of four years or for the remaining time until retirement, whichever came first. (The 2014 constitution specified that he would be chosen by the Supreme Judicial Council and appointed by presidential decree.) The justice minister, an arm of the executive, appoints the presidents of the first instance courts for one renewable year (also subject to the agreement of the Supreme Judicial Council).[12] The justice minister also controls the geographic assignment of judges (to courts in remote areas far from the capital or not) determined once a year with the approval of the Supreme Judicial Council. The minister also plays an important role in choosing investigating judges, deciding on the transfer of members of the public prosecution, and exercising a supervisory role over the public prosecution. Overall, this set of powers gives the executive considerable influence over the judiciary.

In addition to control over the appointment process, the executive branch commands an outsize role in the Supreme Judicial Council. The council serves as the body in charge of monitoring and supervising the entire civil and criminal judicial system (nomination, judicial promotions, assignment, salaries, transfers, and disciplinary actions). It is composed of seven members: the president of the Court of Cassation, the president of the Cairo Court of Appeal, the general prosecutor, the two most senior vice presidents of the Court of Cassation, and the two most senior vice presidents of the courts of appeal. From the above it is clear that these officials owe the lion's share of their positions to executive appointment. Judicial independence is compromised by the fact that the members of the Supreme Judicial Council are not elected by the ranks of the judiciary as reformist judges have demanded.

A third means of executive interference is exercised through the Judicial Inspection Department. This department oversees the technical evaluation of judges and members of the prosecution and oversees the annual judicial "movement" project (rotation of judges). The members of this department are nominated by the Ministry of Justice, which leaves the door open to possible abuses. A judge who is diffident about ministerial instructions could be penalized by a negative evaluation that might have harmful consequences for his career or alternatively find himself posted to a court far from his family with bad working conditions.

Control over judges' delegation to other government ministries or secondment abroad is another means available to the executive to undermine judicial independence. Egyptian judges are paid low salaries, and assignment to work in a foreign country, in particular Gulf countries, constitutes a very lucrative opportunity.[13] Most of these assignments have been distributed to judges in return for attentiveness to government interests. Similarly, one of the means the regime has used to thank loyal judges is to nominate them to administrative functions in a ministry—also a financially lucrative opportunity. Such delegation creates a conflict of interest for judges since a seconded judge is likely to favor the interest of the ministry he has long served.[14] The possible reward of secondment also gives the state the means to keep control over counselors of the State Council. Of course, providing judges with salaries adequate to allow them a decent livelihood would eliminate the appeal of delegation and secondment and strengthen the autonomy of the judiciary.

The independence and autonomy of judges are also compromised by the inordinate discretionary power awarded to court presidents over judges under their jurisdiction. The presidents (appointed by the Justice Ministry) are empowered to address disciplinary warning to their judges and can propose to the general prosecutor to activate a disciplinary action against them. Furthermore, the presidents have been delegated the authority to determine the assignment of cases to specific judges, even though, in principle, the distribution of cases should be mandated according to general and abstract rules.

Finally, the executive has compromised the effective autonomy of the judiciary by selectively abstaining from the implementation of its rulings (el-Borai, 2008).[15] In addition it has routinely withdrawn sensitive cases from the jurisdiction of the regular judiciary and referred them to more reliable judges in exceptional and military courts (Abu Seada, 2008).

In the waning years of the Mubarak regime, reformist judges pressed for changes that would bolster judicial independence. Among other things they called for the election of members of the Supreme Judicial Council, higher salaries for judges, and various amendments to the Judicial Authority Law. The latter was amended in June 2006 and the amendments were partially successful in that they did diminish the justice minister's supervisory and disciplinary power over judges. They also provided for an independent budget to the judicial authority. But they did not change the composition of the Supreme Judicial Council, and thus the executive branch retained its primary mechanism for control over judicial affairs.

Judges Influence the Transition Process

After the uprising of January 25, 2011, some of the fiercest political struggles over the course of Egypt's political transition were played out in the courts. The judges emerged as central actors in this drama as illustrated by a series of signal court rulings delivered by lower and higher courts. These rulings have led to accusations that the judges were politically motivated.

Some of the earliest politically sensitive rulings delivered by the judiciary came from the administrative courts. Immediately after the revolution in February 2011, an administrative court ordered the dissolution of the former ruling National Democratic Party. In addition, the administrative court ruled to dissolve all of Egypt's local councils, which had been largely staffed by members of the ruling party. Later, the same court delivered a ruling that permitted Egyptians living abroad to vote in all elections and public referenda. The courts also cancelled the privatization of several state-owned enterprises, putting a stop to the country's economic liberalization program. But if these cases were politically sensitive, even more so were a series of cases ruled upon by the Supreme Constitutional Court[16] and the State Council.[17]

Rulings of the Supreme Constitutional Court on the People's and Consultative Assemblies

Among the most politically consequential decisions delivered by the Supreme Constitutional Court, and the ones most certain to put it on a collision course with the executive branch, concerned its rulings on the legality of parliamentary elections held in 2012. On June 14, 2012, two days before the completion of Egypt's first postrevolution presidential elections, the Supreme Constitutional Court ruled that the electoral law that had governed the election of the lower house of Parliament back in January had been unconstitutional.[18] On the basis of this ruling, the Supreme Council of the Armed Forces, which was still running the country at that time, immediately issued a decree to dissolve the assembly.

The Supreme Constitutional Court's ruling was seen by many as politically motivated, driven by opposition to the Islamist majority in the Parliament as well as concern about Islamists' controlling both the executive and legislative branch simultaneously. In addition, the court was accused of being motivated to disband the lower house of Parliament because the court was threatened by the assembly's discussion of legislation aimed at recasting the court's membership and limiting its mandate. But in fact, the reasoning of the constitutional court was not without precedent. The Supreme Constitutional Court had delivered similar rulings in 1987 and 1990 during the Mubarak era when it had declared electoral laws unconstitutional on similar grounds. But if the stance of the court was not surprising, its speed in delivering the ruling was. The the court decided this case in less than two months, despite the fact that the court had a huge backlog of cases, whereas similar rulings in the past had taken years to produce. Partisans of the Supreme Constitutional Court explained away this unusual speed by pointing to the urgency and exceptional importance of the ruling. But for nonpartisans of the court, this speed pointed to the political impetus behind the court's decision.

One year later (in June 2013), the Supreme Constitutional Court delivered a similar ruling with regard to the law that had governed the election of Egypt's upper house of Parliament, called the Shura Council. Although equally controversial, this ruling had more limited political impact. The upper house was not dissolved because the new constitution, adopted in December 2012, had expressly made the upper house immune from dissolution until new elections were held for the lower house.

The Supreme Constitutional Court and the Political Isolation Law

Another highly sensitive decision delivered by the Supreme Constitutional Court concerned its ruling on the Political Isolation Law. On June 14, 2012, the same day that it delivered the ruling declaring the election of the lower house unconstitutional, the court also ruled the Political Isolation Law unconstitutional. This law (adopted by the People's Assembly as an amendment of the 1956 law on the exercise of political rights) banned from participation in politics officials of a certain stature who had served the old regime and ruling party in the last ten years of the Mubarak era. The law had been challenged by Ahmed Shafiq, a presidential candidate deprived of his right to run because he had served as Mubarak's last prime minister. The Presidential Elections Commission referred the case to the Supreme Constitutional Court. The court ruled on the challenge two days before the second round of the presidential elections (Shafiq had been allowed to run pending the ruling of the court) and invalidated the law.

The court's reasoning behind its decision had several prongs: penal laws should not have retroactive effects; individuals should not be punished twice for the same crime; penalties should not be imposed without a court ruling; discrimination between candidates on the basis of party affiliation was illegal; and penalties should be imposed on the basis of actions taken and not on mere presumptions of behavior based on the holding of an office. Despite this arsenal of reasoning, many viewed the court's ruling as politically driven because it permitted Ahmed Shafiq, the military's preferred candidate, to remain a presidential candidate. Partisans of the court retorted that the court's decision followed the same line of reasoning that had guided its decisions in the 1980s, in particular with regard to two rulings in 1986 and 1987 that had invalidated laws depriving members of the Nasserite party and former leaders of the Wafd Party of their political rights. The court's partisans argued that the consistency in the court's approach, despite the very different political persuasions of the defendants, attested to the political neutrality of the court.

The State Council and Supreme Constitutional Court Rulings on the Constituent Assembly

The State Council, alongside the Supreme Constitutional Court, also ruled on some very sensitive and consequential political issues, most notably the composition of Egypt's Constituent Assembly—the assembly tasked with drafting the country's new constitution. The State Council declared the composition of the Constituent Assembly unconstitutional in April 2012, delaying the formulation of the document. Then, a year later, the Supreme Constitutional Court delivered a similar ruling, declaring the composition of a second Constituent Assembly unconstitutional as well. The latter ruling came five months after the new constitution drafted by this assembly had already been adopted by popular referendum and entered into force!

The logic governing the council's and the court's decisions was as follows. In March 2011 the Supreme Council of the Armed Forces had delivered a "Constitutional Declaration" calling for the creation of a Constituent Assembly. The assembly, tasked with writing a new constitution for Egypt, was to be composed of 100 members and was to be chosen by the members of the upper and lower houses of Parliament. Following the parliamentary elections, members of Parliament chose the members of the Constituent Assembly in March 2012, drawing half of the Constituent Assembly from people contemporaneously serving in the upper and lower houses of Parliament. The State Council reviewed this policy (it considered the process of composing a Constituent Assembly within its purview because it viewed the process as an administrative, not legislative, process), and it ruled that the composition of the Constituent Assembly was invalid.

What was its reasoning? The State Council argued that the language of Article 60 of the army's Constitutional Declaration was such that it required that the members of the Constituent Assembly to be chosen from outside of Parliament; that is, parliamentarians were barred from electing themselves. In addition, the State Council argued that the composition of the Constituent Assembly did not represent the entire spectrum of the Egyptian society, including too few young people, women, and minorities. The court's ruling was greeted with approval by liberals, who were especially alarmed by the preponderance of Islamist members in the Constituent Assembly. But Islamists considered this decision a politically motivated blow and argued that the State Council had no jurisdiction over the nomination decision since formation of the assembly was a purely parliamentary affair.

The issue of the composition of the Constituent Assembly did not end there. A second Constituent Assembly was formed by the Parliament in June 2012, after two months of negotiations among political forces. This time, however, its formation was challenged before the Supreme Constitutional Court. After the ruling was postponed several times, the court announced that it would decide on the case on December 2, 2012. This announcement elicited a strong response from President Morsi as well as from many of his Islamist supporters and spelled a near constitutional crisis (see below). Through some presidential high-handedness Morsi convened the Constitutional Assembly, encouraged the assembly to rush through the drafting of a constitution (delivered November 30, 2012), permitted Islamist crowds to intimidate the Supreme Constitutional Court (sufficient to suspend the court's deliberation on the assembly's legality), organized a popular referendum to approve the constitution (held December 15–22), and saw the new constitution signed into law by December 26. The court, though slow to respond, did finally rule on the issue of the legality of the Constituent Assembly a year and a half later in June 2013, declaring that the law governing the composition of the Constituent Assembly was unconstitutional. The Supreme Constitutional Court's ruling, however, had no practical impact. The Constituent Assembly had already dissolved itself in December 2012 after having finished the drafting of the new constitution. And despite the the court's ruling, the constitution drafted by this assembly remained in place because it had been adopted by popular referendum.

The Supreme Constitutional Court and the New Law on Parliamentary Elections

A fourth area of significant political contention ruled upon by the courts concerned the new constitution's law on parliamentary elections. According to the new constitution, the Supreme Constitutional Court was charged with reviewing the constitutionality of laws only after they were adopted, except in the case of electoral laws. For the latter, the court was called upon to exercise prior review; that is, Parliament was obliged to refer these laws to the court to check on their constitutionality before voting on them. If the Supreme Constitutional Court deemed the proposed law unconstitutional, it was to attach a report delineating the amendments necessary for the law to pass legal muster. The constitution, however, was silent as to whether the amended draft law had to be referred again to the court for approval before the legislature's vote.

This ambiguity set the stage for conflict between the judiciary and the legislature in 2013. In February, the upper house of Parliament sent a draft electoral law for parliamentary elections to the Supreme Constitutional Court for approval.[19] The court rejected some of the articles of the law. The upper house amended the electoral law in light of the court's rulings and then voted on it. President Morsi promulgated the new law and called for elections in April 2013. At that point a lawyer filed a case before the State Council arguing that the draft law should have been sent back to the Supreme Constitutional Court for approval of the amendments and the final version of the law. In March 2013, the Court of Administrative Litigation of the State Council decided to suspend the presidential decree calling for parliamentary elections and to refer the election law to the Supreme Constitutional Court for final review. This ruling was upheld on appeal by the Supreme Administrative Court in April 2013. The parliamentary elections were therefore postponed until the law would have been deemed constitutional by the Supreme Constitutional Court. The delay in elections was to prevent the Supreme Constitutional Court from declaring the elections invalid and once again dissolving the lower house of Parliament, as it had in June 2012.

Subsequently, the draft election law was referred to the court three times. Each time the the court found new provisions unconstitutional and the elections were postponed. Responsibility for the delay was a matter of debate. Some wondered whether the Supreme Constitutional Court was purposely impeding the process, never precisely defining the amendments necessary to make the electoral law acceptable in order to constrain the ambition of the Islamist-dominated legislature. By contrast, opposition figures began to wonder whether members of the upper house of Parliament really wanted the electoral law to be adopted and new elections for the lower chamber to be held. Members of the upper house had two reasons to delay elections. First, were a new lower house of Parliament to be elected, the upper house would lose the exceptional and temporary legislative powers that had been granted to it by the constitution so long as the lower house was dissolved (Hamzawy, 2013). Second, new elections would likely reduce the majority position Islamists held in the legislature. (The Islamist-dominated upper house had been elected with a mere 7 percent popular participation rate.) The political significance of this conflict was clear.

The Executive and Legislative Branches Push Back

The assertive stances adopted by the courts on these sensitive and highly politicized issues elicited important push back from the executive and legislative branches. At times the actions of the court pushed Egypt to the brink of constitutional crisis. They also led to reforms and decrees that impinged on the judiciary's independence and reduced the possibilities for court activism for the longer term.

The first evidence of push back from the executive branch manifested itself just a few days after Mohamed Morsi was elected president. Morsi first refused to be sworn in before the Supreme Constitutional Court (as the lower house had just been dissolved), insisting instead on taking the oath of office in Tahrir Square (to assert that his authority derived from the people, not the courts), and agreeing to appear before the court only after that event. A few days later Morsi unilaterally vitiated the court's June 14 decision to dissolve the lower house of Parliament and ordered the chamber to reconvene. The lower house of Parliament met briefly and decided to request the Court of Cassation's opinion regarding the validity of the mandate of its members. A few days later, the Court of Cassation ruled that it was not competent to decide on that case. At this point Morsi bowed to the court's authority and the lower house of Parliament was never reconvened again. But Morsi's unilateral vitiation of the Supreme Constitutional Court's decision earlier on was viewed by many as an aggression against the justice system and cast him as behaving like the head of a party, not like the president of the whole Egyptian society.

Removal of the General Prosecutor

Morsi's high-handedness toward the judiciary did not end there. Among other things, Morsi infringed on the principle of the irremovability of judges to purge those judges he considered loyal to the former regime. This intent was evident on November 22, 2012, when he unilaterally announced a "constitutional decree," firing the general prosecutor, Abdel Meguid Mahmoud, and stating that henceforth, the president would appoint the general prosecutor for a fixed term of four years.[20] This decree violated the extant Judicial Authority Law, which provided that the general prosecutor was secure in his office until the age of retirement unless removed by the Supreme Judicial Council. But Morsi was intent on getting rid of Mahmoud because he perceived him as politically unreliable. The general prosecutor had been criticized for failing to gather sufficient evidence to convict prominent Mubarak-era officials accused of attacking protesters during the January 25 revolution.[21] Furthermore, many in the Muslim Brotherhood also held the general prosecutor responsible for their years of prison and torture since he had served as a prosecutor during the Mubarak era.

In response to Morsi's dismissal of the general prosecutor in November 2012, judges and members of the prosecution suspended work nationwide, and most of them refused to supervise the constitutional referendum in December 2012. The new general prosecutor, appointed without the knowledge of the Supreme Judicial Council, was met with hostility by prosecutors who organized demonstrations to pressure him to step down.[22] In July 2013, the Court of Cassation finally ordered the return of the former general prosecutor, Mahmoud. But by that point, Mahmoud decided not to return to his post claiming that he feared he would not be able to remain impartial. Later in the month he was replaced by a new general prosecutor.

Morsi's move to fire the general prosecutor was viewed by judges and prosecutors as an attack on judicial independence. Even activists who had earlier sought the dismissal of Mahmoud on grounds of malfeasance objected to Morsi's measures. The case showed the complexity of the transition process in Egypt: Should the principle of independence and irremovability of the judiciary prevail, even to protect judicial figures suspected of violating the right to access justice and to redress grievance?

Above Judicial Review

On the same day that Morsi announced the firing of the general prosecutor (November 22, 2012), he also challenged the independence and standing of the judiciary in an even more brash way. Morsi announced that until a new constitution was in force, his decisions would not be subject to judicial review. As guardian of the revolution Morsi granted himself broad powers above the redress of the judiciary.[23] Armed with this rhetoric, Morsi encouraged the Constituent Assembly, which had been under the shadow of dissolution by the Supreme Constitutional Court (as described above), to resume the work of drafting a constitution. The drafting process was rushed through and completed on November 30. On December 2, when the court was slated to rule on the legality of the Constituent Assembly's composition, several thousand Islamist supporters of Morsi gathered outside the court's building to prevent the justices from entering and meeting. The Supreme Constitutional Court decided to suspend its work indefinitely in protest against these "psychological pressures" (BBC News, 2012). In its statement, the court added that December 2 was "the blackest day" in the history of the Egyptian judiciary (*Ahram Online*, 2012a). The Freedom and Justice Party replied by affirming the right of all citizens to peaceful demonstration. A few days later, in a statement to the foreign media, President Morsi insinuated that the Supreme Constitutional Court was an "anti-revolutionary force" (*Ahram Online*, 2012b). The court released a statement in response saying that the presidency aimed to "undermine the reputation of the court internationally without giving one piece of truthful evidence to support his allegations and claims" (*Daily News Egypt*, 2012). Shortly after the constitution was approved by popular referendum, Morsi relinquished his "above-the-law" status. But by superceding and intimidating the Supreme Constitutional Court and declaring his decisions immune from judicial review, he seriously compromised the principle of rule of law in Egypt.

Attempt to Reduce the Age of Retirement

A fourth volley in the attack on the autonomy and stature of the judiciary came from the legislative branch. Under President Morsi, the Wasat Party, a moderate Islamist party, proposed draft amendments to the judiciary laws to "rid the judicial authority from corrupt elements" (*Ahram Online*, 2013b). One of the means to achieve this objective was to lower the age of mandatory retirement for judges from seventy to sixty. The Wasat Party argued this change in law would lead to the departure of old and mostly pro-Mubarak judges and their replacement with a new generation of independent judges. The amendment, had it been passed, would have led to the departure of some 3,000 judges in one fell swoop. Notably this practice of toying with the judges' retirement age to influence the political tenor of the judiciary was not an innovation by Morsi. It had significant precedent under the Mubarak regime.[24] In the end, however, this "purge by retirement" was not carried out. The amendments submitted by the Wasat Party were referred to the legislative committee of the upper house of Parliament for discussion in April 2013. They had not been adopted before Parliament was dissolved by the military in July 2013.

Removal of Members of the Supreme Constitutional Court

Finally, the autonomy and influence of the judiciary was dealt a serious blow by the text of the constitution of 2012, which essentially decreed the "unpacking" of the Supreme Constitutional Court in a politically nonneutral way. Egypt's prior constitution (1971) did not specify the precise number of justices who were to make up the court's bench, and the 1979 law governing the Supreme Constitutional Court was hardly more specific, stating only that the number of justices had to be "sufficient." In December 2012, the court's bench comprised eighteen justices. But the constitution of 2012 specified that the bench of the Supreme Constitutional Court should be set at eleven. As a result, seven of the sitting justices had to be dismissed—the most junior ones first. Not surprisingly, last to go, according to the new threshold, was Tahany el-Gebaly, one of the most outspoken opponents of President Morsi who had stood firmly against him in favor of the army. Many suspected that the new constitutional provision had been tailored to enable Gebaly's removal.[25]

Failure to Bring Accountability and Justice

In the wake of Morsi's ouster, the courts continued to deliver highly charged rulings that tainted them with the blot of politicization. The courts were perceived as delivering selective justice. They failed to hold high officials from the old regime accountable for the death and injury of hundreds of demonstrators, and they granted these officials impunity for their misappropriation of public funds even as they condemned members of the Muslim Brotherhood, as well as political opponents of the regime of Abdel Fattah el-Sisi, to harsh sentences.

On November 29, 2014, the Cairo Court of Appeal ruled Mubarak not guilty in the killing protesters in the period between January 25 and January 28, 2011. Earlier, in June 2012, the president and his former minister of interior had been found guilty of failing to prevent the killing of peaceful protesters and had been sentenced to life in prison. The conviction had been overturned by the Court of Cassation in January 2013 on points of law and a retrial was ordered for April 2013. It ended in November 2014 with charges being dropped on procedural grounds. In January 2015 Mubarak was released, after the Court of Cassation overturned his conviction to three years in prison for embezzling public funds. A retrial was set to begin in April 2015. The cases that were brought to trial were limited in scope and all crimes perpetrated during decades of abuses remain unpunished. Almost all former government officials who stood trial for squandering public funds were also cleared. The few who had been indicted for their role in economic crimes and on corruption charges managed to negotiate financial settlements with the court.

The courts also exonerated members of security forces involved in the killing of demonstrators. Public opinion attributed this leniency to a failure of will on the part of the judiciary to punish associates of the ancien regime. Only one policeman is serving a sentence, only three years, for shooting at protesters' eyes during the January 25 revolution. Most of the police officers involved in killing protesters during the same events were not brought to trial. In the few cases where charges were brought against them, the police were acquitted on the grounds of insufficient evidence.

Only three soldiers involved in the killing and abuse of protesters during the reign of the Supreme Council of the Armed Forces (from February 2011 to June 2012) were sentenced by a military court. (They were punished with two and three years in jail.) They were charged with involuntary manslaughter for driving military vehicles into the protesters during the Maspero clashes with Coptic Christians in October 2011 (twenty-seven protesters were killed). Other police officers were set free, and the military failed to investigate incidents involving army officers. Most security forces members remained in their positions or were transferred to administrative positions.

Only four police officers were convicted for the killing of protesters in the wake of Morsi's ouster. In March 2014 one police captain was sentenced to ten years in jail, and three lower-ranking officers were given one-year suspended sentences for their roles in the deaths of thirty-seven prisoners who were gassed in a crowded police van during their transfer to a prison in August 2013. The sentence was overturned on appeal in June 2014.

Judges complain that the files sent to them by the prosecution, which investigates criminal complaints, are almost empty and that they cannot issue convictions not backed by enough concrete evidence. The prosecution accuses the police who were supposed to collect evidence of failing to gather the necessary material and blame the Interior Ministry for failing to cooperate and deliver the records of the Central Security Forces. Families of victims and their lawyers accuse the police of destroying the evidence and of pressuring and intimidating them to convince them to withdraw their complaints.

The police officers who are charged with gathering evidence belong to the very same administration as those being charged with crimes under investigation. As to members of the armed forces, they enjoy de facto immunity since they appear before military courts controlled by the military leadership.

A Selective Justice System

By contrast, the prosecution of supporters of Morsi has been much more forceful. Thousands have been arrested since Morsi's ouster and put in preventive detention pending the outcome of investigations on accusations that they took part in violent protests, belonged to a banned terrorist group, or were guilty of other charges.

Morsi and other prominent Brotherhood figures were referred to trial for escaping from prison during the opening days of the January 25 revolution and for inciting violence and killing peaceful demonstrators near the Presidential Palace in December 2012 as well as for espionage, treason, and conspiring with foreign groups to carry out terrorist acts in Egypt. He was sentenced to death in May 2015.

In separate trials in March and April 2014, a judge in the province of Minya handed down more than 1,200 death sentences for killing police officers.

> The court argued that criminal intent to kill any member of the police forces and presence at the crime scene presented sufficient evidence to convict them of murder or attempted murder. Simultaneously, courts have consistently acquitted police officers present at the scenes of protester killings, citing lack of evidence linking individual officers to protester deaths or arguing self-defense. (Egyptian Initiative for Personal Rights, 2014)

The number of death sentences in the March 2014 trial was later reduced to thirty-seven, and the other sentences were commuted to life. For the April 2014 trial, 682 death sentences were reduced to 183. Nevertheless, such draconian sentences have contributed to a loss of the courts' credibility.[26] Both trials were criticized for violating the right to a fair trial and due process. In February 2015, the Giza Criminal Court handed down a death penalty against 183 defendants on charges of killing police officers during an attack on a police station in August 2013. This ruling led to accusations of the judges sustaining a bias against Muslim Brothers and seeking revenge for their conflict with Morsi.[27]

In addition to the Muslim Brothers, secular activists, human rights defenders, and bloggers critical of the government have also been put on trial and sentenced to lengthy prison sentences and heavy fines for breaking the antiprotest law adopted in November 2013 and protesting without a permit. All these controversial rulings have led to an "alarmingly selective justice system in Egypt, which appears more intent on settling political scores and punishing dissent than establishing justice" (Egyptian Initiative for Personal Rights, 2014). Although Morsi supporters and political activists have been prosecuted and referred to trial, security forces and political officials responsible for human rights violations have walked free.

Judges: Actors in the Transition Process

Judges have been at the center of political struggles and have emerged as one of the most dynamic players in the postrevolutionary period. Their involvement in political issues can be traced to the mistakes committed by the army and by President Morsi, especially their haphazard and disorganized decisionmaking. Judges were called upon to rule by political actors who proved unable or unwilling to solve political conflicts through dialogue and consensus. Judges stepped in to fill the political vacuum left wide open by political forces who failed to be decisive. Had the leadership done its duty, the judiciary would not have carried this burden by itself.

It is true, though, that the courts could have avoided ruling on many of these issues by declaring themselves incompetent or considering the decrees under review as acts of sovereignty. However, as Sahar Aziz (2014) points out, "in light of the myriad tools used to restrain judicial independence, it is unsurprising that portions of the judiciary are cooperative in the ongoing crackdown on political dissidents. The current political climate makes it too costly for a judge to challenge the executive's core interests." Note that the courts' rulings were not criticized by other judges. The fact that judges suspected of affiliation with the Muslim Brotherhood had been subjected to dismissal may have deterred the remaining judges from speaking out against colleagues.

There is no evidence that these problematic rulings were due to direct interference from the executive authority. On the contrary, judges may have felt strong enough to let their vision of politics and society prevail in their decisions. As Ibrahim al-Houdaiby (2014) explains, "in many cases, the judiciary feels independent from the law. Judges replace their role as jurists with that of statesmen; their rulings fail to reflect prevailing interpretations of legal texts and are instead based on what they perceive as the interests of the state, based on their position in the legal structure and their own beliefs."

Most of the judges may be convinced that they are defending the stability of their country and condemning criminals that deserve such heavy sentences. Nathan Brown (2014) points out:

> The judiciary as a body shows real willingness to distance itself from the executive but little interest or willingness to distance itself from the state. And, for many judges, that state has just come under severe attack by an alien force. The invaders managed to temporarily seize the presidency; for a while key institutions of state—including, most shockingly to judges, courts themselves—were quite literally besieged by these outsiders. Of course, not all judges feel this way, but many do seem to share the sense of crisis that has led perhaps to some of the brutal efficiency displayed when trying some cases.

This politicization of the judiciary has had damaging consequences for judges themselves. The rulings led to a general perception that the courts were issuing decisions with an implicit political leaning, in conformity with the army's priorities. Under Morsi, for the first time in Eygptian experience, popular demonstrations were organized to protest court rulings and the constitutional court was even prevented from convening. The judiciary, which used to enjoy high prestige and respect within society, has seen its status diminished. Selective prosecution and sentences that target government critics and opponents contribute to a loss of the courts' credibility outside the courtroom.

The constitution of 2014 has increased judges' autonomy, enshrined by various provisions in the document. For example, the constitution declares that the Supreme Constitutional Court will henceforth appoint its own chief justice whereas the general prosecutor will be selected by the Supreme Judicial Council, not the president. As before, judges will be appointed on the basis of the recommendation of the Supreme Judicial Council and will not be removable. The budget of the judiciary will be incorporated in the annual state budget as a single figure, meaning that the judges will receive their budget in a lump sum and can transfer funds from one post to another without seeking the agreement of the Parliament. The laws on the judiciary will need a majority of two-thirds of the Parliament to be amended.

The judges managed to win more autonomy with little accountability and with very few checks on their authority. Their autonomy has increased their isolation within the state and society. No mechanism of control has been established apart from the Supreme Judicial Council and no reform of the justice system has been provided. "Some observers have argued that increasing judicial independence is a positive development. However, in a country like Egypt where courts are generally seen (with notable exceptions) as failing the people, increasing judicial independence before operating wholesale reform means that the negative practices of the past will become much more difficult to change" (Al-Ali, 2013).

The majority of judges in Egypt, though, have long been hostile to getting the judiciary involved in politics. This hostility to politics is one of the reasons why the reformists lost the elections to the Judges' Club in 2009. Many of the judges were opposed to their colleagues making political statements and taking confrontational political stands. Most Egyptian judges have a rather conservative and patriarchal mind-set (Said, 2012). They are part of the elite of society, value hierarchy, seniority, and order, and oppose radical changes in politics and society. They are trained in the faculties of law of Egyptian universities, and most see themselves as the mentors of a modern liberal state based on respect for the rule of law and the separation of powers. They are loyal to the state and apply the laws adopted by the legislative branch even if they personally disagree with their content.

The conservative bent of most judges can be traced to recruitment process used in the judiciary and the demographic selection this process imposes on the institution. The criteria for appointment to the judiciary is delineated by the judiciary law. A candidate must have Egyptian nationality and hold a law degree. He must possess a good reputation, enjoy civil rights, and present various guarantees of morality. State security agencies monitor the appointment process and investigate the social and political background of every candidate. They ensure that whoever originates from a poor social strata or has relatives known to be Islamists, criminals, or leftists will be excluded from consideration.[28] Social standing has always been a main criterion in appointment. Sons of judges have a better chance of appointment to the judiciary than other law graduates. In fact, a widespread complaint is that sons of counselors or well-known personalities close to the government manage to get hired even when their exam results at the law faculty are inferior to those of other candidates. As Sahar Aziz (2014) explains, "Egypt's politics of patronage and clientelism have further compromised judicial independence. Like other state institutions, the judiciary is wrought with nepotism, and the appointment process is far from meritocratic. Judges' family members and relations are often appointed to judgeships despite poor academic records that disqualify them."

Given this selection system, the lack of diversity found within the judiciary is not surprising. Most judges come from the middle class or elite classes of society. And until 2007, women were excluded from the courts. The Supreme Constitutional Court was the first court to include a woman judge, nominated in 2003.[29] The exclusive demographics of the judiciary mean that judges are largely conservative and accept and defend social privilege. They also explain why most judges felt threatened by the rise of Islamism in Egypt and opposed radical change and the Islamization of Egypt's law and institutions.

Conclusion

Egypt's entire judicial system is in need of structural reform. It suffers from inefficiency, slowness, notorious corruption by legal aides, and extreme case overload, particularly in the civil and criminal courts, where cases can drag on for years. Initial and continuous training of judges should be the focus of more attention, buildings should be repaired and extended, administrative personnel trained, and computerization introduced.

Reforms, however, have proven very difficult to introduce. Their cost has been deemed too high, and the system still suffers from strong inertia because of judges' conservatism. Judges by their nature oppose any radical change in their traditional working methods. All the successive governments that have ruled Egypt since the revolution of January 2011, including that of Morsi, have failed to initiate a reform of the judiciary.[30] A Justice Conference that had been scheduled to work out a reform acceptable to all sides was canceled in June 2013.[31] Any amendment to the judiciary laws is viewed as driven by a hidden political agenda. Necessary reforms to improve access to and efficiency of the judiciary are postponed for fear of a hidden agenda behind them. According to Youssef Auf, an Egyptian judge and constitutional scholar, "full reform will not unfold in the near future, since the current leadership is old and resistant to change, in addition to the fact that the current landscape in Egypt is not conducive to significant change" (cited in Atallah 2014). Any change in inherited traditions that have developed over the decades will need internal support:

> The judiciary has a perpetual sensitivity toward reform, especially when it does not come from within the judicial establishment. This leads to an important conclusion: the judiciary itself must be involved in the reform process. Otherwise, the process will be fraught with risks and prone to failure. The confrontation between the judiciary and the Muslim Brotherhood under the rule of former president Mohamed Morsi is an example of this kind of failure. (Auf, 2014)

Leading figures of the judicial independence movement, who had launched the judges' revolt under Mubarak and then participated in Morsi's government, have proved disappointing. They lost their credibility by accepting top political positions in the government and then failing to use these positions to implement the reforms they had advocated for many years prior.

Impartiality, neutrality, and independence remain the aspiration of the Egyptian judiciary. But in the absence of a political will to enforce a more democratic order, the events of the postuprising period make these components of the rule of law as elusive as ever.

Notes

1. The speaker had been elected as the new chief justice of the Supreme Constitutional Court by his colleagues in the court a few weeks before. This move marked the beginning of a total reversal of the relations between the judiciary and the executive power. If judges had been considered opponents of Morsi's regime, they were now accused of being a strong ally of Abdel Fattah el-Sisi's repressive politics toward all opponents.

2. After the constitutional referendum and the presidential elections in 2005, the Judges' Club published a report, denouncing several types of abuses judges had witnessed. A couple of months later, a female member of the Office of Administrative Prosecution publicly denounced the fraud she had witnessed in the electoral constituency where she was supervising a primary station. The Judges' Club

decided to lead an inquiry into the allegation and to interrogate judges who had supervised other polling stations in the same constituency. According to the club, 151 judges out of 160 agreed to testify, and they confirmed her testimony that the Muslim Brotherhood candidate received three times as many votes as the ruling National Democratic Party's candidate. A complaint was filed at the general prosecutor's office, but it received no response.

3. The Judges' Club was founded in Cairo in 1939 to solidify relations among judges. It has evolved into an unofficial professional association and a forum for public issues relating to the judiciary. Any member of the ordinary judiciary or the Office of Public Prosecution can join it. It has more than 9,000 members.

4. The judiciary in Egypt is divided into three sets of courts, based on the French model: (1) the ordinary courts, which deal with civil and criminal cases: Court of Cassation, appeals courts, and courts of first instance; (2) the administrative courts (State Council), which deal with litigation between citizens and a state institution or between two state agencies; and (3) the Supreme Constitutional Court, which rules on the constitutionality of laws and administrative regulations.

5. Notably, in 2009, reformist judges lost the elections to lead the board of the Judges' Club and were replaced by a more conservative, regime-allied team.

6. The judiciary had already come to the rescue of NGOs in 2000, when the Supreme Constitutional Court handed down a judgment declaring the unconstitutionality of the new Law of Associations, which NGOs had strongly criticized.

7. The State Council (or Majlis al-Dawla) is a judicial body charged with ruling on the legality of the state's administrative acts. It exercises jurisdiction over cases where a state body is a party. It includes a Court of Administrative Litigation, whose decisions can be appealed before the Supreme Administrative Court.

8. The Court of Administrative Litigation maintained that Article 76 and the Law on Presidential Elections had given an exhaustive list of the competences exercised by the Electoral Commission, which did not include the decision to prevent NGOs from accessing polling stations. The commission's decision, therefore, had to be considered an ordinary administrative decision that did not escape the control of the administrative judge.

9. For decades, Egyptian judges have been complaining of direct interference by the executive authority in judicial affairs that enabled the regime to obtain rulings in particular cases. The call for a judiciary emancipated from the grip of the executive branch was already on the agenda under former president Mubarak and even before. Judicial independence was one of the main recommendations of the 1986 Conference on Justice organized by the Judges' Club. Moreover, in 1992, the General Assembly of the Judges' Club adopted a draft law proposing amendments to the 1972 Judicial Authority Law, in order to increase judicial independence. Earlier even, in 1969, judges had already been involved in a serious conflict with the executive authority in order to keep their relative independence, a conflict that ended with the dissolution of the Board of the Judges' Club and the famous Massacre of the Judiciary (when 189 judges were dismissed from their positions and the Board of the Judges' Club dissolved, because they had refused to join the single-party Arab Socialist Union).

10. For a detailed analysis of challenges to the independence of the judiciary in Egypt, in comparison with international law, see International Bar Association Human Rights Institute (2014).

11. The Court of Cassation is at the apex of the civil and criminal court system in Egypt. It rules on challenges against decisions of the courts of appeal. Its jurisdiction bears on misapplication of the law or procedural errors, not on the facts of the case. With regard to the appointment of this court's leadership, no clear and

objective criteria guide the president's appointment. Nevertheless, the most senior vice president of the court is normally appointed by the president of the republic. Candidates for the positions of vice president and counselors are proposed by an official body of judges (the General Assembly of the Court of Cassation), and half of the candidates for the positions of counselors are proposed by the Justice Ministry (under executive control). The president makes the final call on appointments though he must seek the agreement of the Supreme Judicial Council (see below).

12. Reformist judges argue that appointment of presidents of first instance courts gives the executive authority considerable influence over the judiciary, since they have significant powers, including, in practice, the possibility to refer particular cases to particular judges.

13. Upon a decision of the president of the republic, with the advisory opinion of the general assembly of the court to which the judge belongs or of the general prosecutor and with the agreement of the Supreme Judicial Council.

14. "Judicial assignments to particular courts and cases should be done in a transparent manner based on expertise or at random in order to ensure that there can be no scope for 'fixing' the judge that is to hear a particular case. Moreover, the selection by the Minister of Justice of which judges can be transferred to a more lucrative government post, or be transferred against his will to a less attractive one, creates a system where judges have an incentive to 'please' the Minister, which also threatens independence" (International Bar Association Human Rights Institute, 2014).

15. For example the executive has failed to abide by decisions that denied certain candidates the right to stand for elections.

16. The Supreme Constitutional Court rules on the constitutionality of parliamentary laws and administrative regulations.

17. For the definition of the State Council, see note 7 above.

18. The election law allocated two-thirds of the seats to party lists and the remaining one-third to individual candidates who could be either affiliated with parties or independents. But the Supreme Constitutional Court struck the law down on the grounds that allowing members of political parties to compete with independents for individual candidate seats discriminated against independent candidates because the latter were not allowed to contest political parties' seats. That is, independent candidates saw their right to candidacy limited to the portion allocated to individual candidacy, whereas political party candidates could compete for all seats.

19. After the dissolution of the People's Assembly, and until the election of a new lower chamber, the upper assembly was in full charge of the legislative power.

20. Prior to making this decree, Morsi had tried to remove the prosecutor general by announcing that he had resigned and that Morsi was appointing him as ambassador to the Vatican. The general prosecutor, however, denied the claims that he had resigned from his position and declared that he would never leave his post.

21. According to the Judicial Authority Law, the president of the republic was appointing, by his sole decision, the general prosecutor from among the vice presidents of the courts of appeal, counselors of the Court of Cassation, and chief public attorneys or higher ranks within the Office of Public Prosecution.

22. In December 2012, he issued a very controversial decision to transfer the attorney general of East Cairo to the town of Beni Suef in Upper Egypt "in the interest of the work." This measure was considered as a way to punish him for having decided, for lack of sufficient evidence, to release more than 100 defendants that

President Morsi had described as being thugs in the aftermath of clashes at the Presidential Palace between opponents and supporters of the president. After prosecutors and judges announced their solidarity with the attorney general and threatened to suspend work, the general prosecutor reversed his decision.

23. With the lower house of the legislature dissolved and the judiciary overruled, Morsi appeared to many as seizing a "presidential dictatorship."

24. Under former president Mubarak, the Judicial Authority Law had been amended in 2007, to postpone the age of mandatory retirement of judges from sixty-eight to seventy. Reformist judges accused the government of tailoring this amendment in order to reward and keep in office some progovernment judges who had neared retirement age. These included the presidents of the Court of Cassation, the Cairo Court of Appeal, the State Council, and the Supreme Constitutional Court. At the same time, the amendment prevented younger reformist judges from occupying high-ranking posts within the judiciary. The government justified the reform on the grounds that Egypt would benefit from the experience of veteran judges, and extending the tenure of these judges would speed up the flow of court cases. Reformist judges dismissed this argument pointing to the diminished mental capacities of aged judges and the fact that most senior judges exercised administrative and leadership responsibilities and did not sit on the bench anymore.

25. Gebaly was the only woman ever appointed to the Supreme Constitutional Court. A former lawyer, after her dismissal from the court she returned to legal practice. Her six other dismissed colleagues were transferred back to their previous positions in other courts. In the past, the chief justice of the Supreme Constitutional Court has been chosen directly and freely by the president of the republic (which permitted the intrusion of political considerations into the appointment of this very powerful position in the judiciary). But in 2011 the Law on the Constitutional Court had been amended by the then-ruling military power so that henceforth the president should appoint the chief justice from its three longest-serving vice presidents and with the agreement of the general assembly of the court—an important win for judicial autonomy that was not amended again by Morsi.

26. The judge was removed from that criminal court in October 2014 and transferred to a civil court.

27. See for instance the reports of Amnesty International (2014) and International Bar Association's Human Rights Institute (2014).

28. In September 2014, the Supreme Judicial Council decided to add a new criteria in the appointment procedure: parents of the applicants must be university graduates. More than 100 candidates appointed in June 2013 were retroactively excluded from the Office of Public Prosecution because their parents lacked higher education.

29. Neither the Judicial Authority Law nor the State Council Law sanctioned any discrimination based on gender in the recruitment of judges. In 2007, after years of struggle by feminist groups and international pressure, thirty women were finally appointed as judges in the ordinary judiciary. Judges criticized the fact that they had not been consulted beforehand. According to some observers, the government used the nomination of female judges to try to divide the Judges' Club from inside and deprive it of NGO support. The constitution of 2014 stated that the state shall guarantee women's appointment in judicial bodies and authorities without discrimination. In January 2014, however, the State Council rejected again women candidates' application for membership.

30. Two conflicting draft laws amending the Judicial Authority Law were prepared under Morsi, one under the supervision of the minister of justice, and the other by the Judges' Club, but due to divisions within the judiciary and the dissolution of the People's Assembly, none of them passed. For a comparative analysis of the reform projects prepared under Morsi, see International Bar Association Human Rights Institute (2014).

31. A first Justice Conference had taken place in 1986 to discuss potential remedies to challenges the judicial system was facing.

4

What Independence? Judicial Power in Tunisia

Mohamed Salah Ben Aissa

Since January 14, 2011, postrevolution Tunisia has been searching for its path toward a democratic transition. As in comparable cases elsewhere, this search has been characterized by a persistent tension between those forces advocating a break from the past and those resisting this rupture. The degree to which the revolution's objectives are realized will depend on how this tension is resolved. In the first two years after the revolution, Tunisia's transition toward democracy remained a conflict-ridden process because a revolution does not, in and of itself, give birth to a democracy. A revolution can only steer a country toward democracy if it achieves, either in the short- or long-term and depending on local conditions, a radical rupture from the dictatorial institutions and practices of the past.

This proposition is demonstrated in different sectors of public life to varying degrees. The sphere of justice is particularly significant in this regard. Here one sees the conflict between those advocating the values and objectives of the revolution and those who, whether in or out of power, seek to delay or prevent the realization of these objectives. The primary interest of the present study is the judicial system. More than any other, this sector conjures the abuses committed under the former regime, in which the judiciary was transformed into an instrument of the dictatorship.[1] Even if an objective and nuanced approach would preclude a sweeping condemnation of all judges, most litigants recognized that the judiciary as a system enjoyed limited independence from that regime. As a result, the legal system did not enjoy the public's trust, and the judiciary was in a state of crisis. Did the revolution bring an end to this situation?

Before attempting to answer this question, one should recall that more than a year after the election of the second Constituent Assembly on October 23, 2011,[2] the Tunisian judiciary continued to be regulated by legal provisions that predated the revolution, and that had been issued in the framework of the 1959 (since abrogated).[3] These provisions were contained in Law No. 67-29 passed on July 14, 1967, concerning the organization of the judiciary, the High Council of Justice (HCJ), and the status of the judiciary—a law that was amended ten times.[4] Yet with the promulgation of Law No. 6 of December 16, 2011, establishing the provisional organization of public authorities, citizens had good reason to expect that a profound reform of the judiciary would immediately follow. Indeed, Section V of Law No. 6 is devoted to the judiciary. The two relevant articles stipulate:

> The judiciary exercises its functions in complete independence. After consultation with judges, the National Constituent Assembly (NCA) will adopt an organic law establishing a provisional, independent, and representative body, and will determine its composition and attributions . . . intended to replace the High Council of Justice (HCJ) (§1); the National Constituent Assembly will adopt organic laws concerning the reorganization of the judiciary and the supreme judicial, administrative and financial councils. It will define the principles upon which the reform of the judicial system will be based, in accordance with international standards of judicial independence.[5]

Despite the importance of these provisions, nothing envisioned in Article 22 of Law No. 6 was implemented for the first two years following the fall of the regime of Zine El Abidine Ben Ali. An organic law creating a provisional representative body to replace the functions of the old HCJ, notably those pertaining to the management of the judges' careers, was not adopted. In fact, this proposed law was rebuffed by representatives of the Ennahda party, the leading political faction in the National Constituent Assembly and coalition government.

These developments led to a serious crisis, one that was compounded by a conflict within the judiciary emanating from the existence of two institutions, each one claiming to be the legitimate representative of the judges. These consisted of the Association of Tunisian Judges (ATJ),[6] an older body with a large membership, and the Judges' Syndicate. This duality of institutions representing the judges could not be reduced to a simple matter of pluralism. Rather, an objective assessment of the positions adopted by each organization showed that the duality reflected a deep cleavage between the Judges' Syndicate—an organization prepared to accommodate the regime, as demonstrated by its pliability in the negotiations surrounding various questions pertaining to the legal system—and the ATJ—an organization that vigorously defended the principle of an independent judiciary and only reluctantly acquiesced to the regime. The

ATJ enjoyed historical legitimacy stemming from its persistent commitment to the spirit of judicial independence.

This schism within the judiciary aggravated the judicial crisis. As described below, the regime took advantage of this situation to make decisions concerning the management of judges' careers without consulting the independent provisional body called for by the law of December 16, 2011, because that body was never created!

All of this pointed to persistent political resistance to the implementation of a truly independent judiciary in the first two years following the revolution. Things proceeded in a manner that suggested that the revolution did not represent a moment of rupture. In this chapter I seek to confirm this hypothesis by linking the past and the present, and explore the past heritage of the judiciary.[7] At the same time, I will show how the problem of building an independent judiciary that evolved after the revolution in a new context characterized by the challenges of a democratic transition.

The Legacy of the Past

The refusal to elevate the justice system to the level of an independent judiciary predates the revolution. Returning to the text of the first constitution, promulgated on June 1, 1959, one sees that after independence, the Tunisian Constituent Assembly was inimical to the recognition of judicial authority. This hostility was reflected in Law No. 67-29 of July 14, 1967, concerning the organization of the judiciary, HCJ, and the status of the judiciary.

The Rejection of an Independent Judiciary in the 1959 Constitution: An Authoritarian Constitutional Doctrine

The past weighs heavily on the current legal system. In the Tunisian constitution of June 1, 1959, the Constituent Assembly adopted a conception of the justice system that precluded it from becoming a truly independent judiciary. If judicial authority means "a veritable political authority"[8] (Belaid, 1974: 301), exercising a juridical power that is "organically integrated into the structures of public authority"[9] (Ricard, 1990: 22), along with being "comparable to the legislative and executive branches"[10] (Perrot, 2006: 50), then one is forced to acknowledge that no constitutional provision established such an authority in Tunisia. Records of the preparations for the 1959 constitution, which followed debates in the Constituent Assembly, support this point. The development of Section V, containing Articles 65 and 67 regulating the judiciary, demonstrated clearly that from the outset, the Constituent Assembly adopted a minimalist conception of the judiciary, reducing it to a simple authority and refusing to elevate it to the level of an independent power. In the first draft of the constitution, Article 93 stated: "Judicial power is exercised independently by the courts of various instance," but by the second draft, a majority of representatives had abandoned the idea of an independent judiciary and voted to eliminate Article 93.[11] The revised text was limited to stipulating that "judges are independent, being subject only to the authority of the law," a formulation that made its way into the final Arabic version of Article 65 in the Tunisian Constitution and that remains unchanged to this day.[12] The judiciary is merely a public tool of the state. Unsurprisingly, Law No. 67-29 extended the power of the executive branch over the HCJ, as I will explore below.

The Executive Branch's Control of the High Council of Justice: A Circumnavigation of Justice

According to Law No. 67-29, the HCJ was to be presided over by the president of the republic; the minister of justice was to serve as the HCJ's vice president. In addition to these two leaders, the body was to comprise the following nineteen members: the first president of the Court of Cassation, the public prosecutor of the Court of Cassation, the director of judicial services, the inspector general of the Ministry of Justice, the president of the Property Court, the first president of the Court of Appeals of Tunis, the public prosecutor of the Tunis Court of Appeals, two female judges appointed by the Ministry of Justice for a term of three years, two male judges elected from each rank for three years, and eight other judiciary figures elected by their peers (one public prosecutor from an appellate court, one president from an appellte court, and two judges from each of three grades of judges).

The composition of the HCJ shows that a preponderance of members was designated by the executive branch. In fact, of nineteen members of the HCJ, eleven—roughly two-thirds—owed their position on the HCJ to the president of the republic. Thus, the representation of independently elected judges on the HCJ was extremely marginal. The same can be said for when the HJC met as a disciplinary body.

In disciplinary matters, pursuant to the modification of Law No. 67-29 by Organic Law No. 2005, the HCJ comprised two bodies: one issuing a verdict in the first instance, and another serving as a kind of appeals court. In both bodies, a clear preponderance of members was chosen by the executive branch.

Of the six members making up the body that issues verdicts of first instance, two were chosen, without consultation of the HCJ, by the president of the republic from among the judges of third rank: the first president of the Tunis Court of Appeals and the attorney general at the Tunis Court of Appeals (see Article 7b of Law No. 67-29). Two were nominated by the

HCJ and then elected by their peers, the latter of whom had already been named by the president of the republic to serve "judicial functions," so the election was a false one. These two were the first president of an appeals court outside Tunis and an attorney general at an appeals court outside Tunis.[13] The remaining two judges, one permanent and one substitute, were appointed by magistrates who had been elected by the HCJ. They were chosen from among the least senior judges of the same rank as the judge appearing before the HCJ.[14]

Of the six judges making up the appellate body, four were to be chosen, without consultation of the HCJ, by the president of the republic from among the judges of third rank. These four were the first president of the Court of Cassation, the attorney general at the Court of Cassation, the president of the Real Estate Court, and the attorney general and director of judicial services. The remaining two judges were to be elected in the same conditions as those of the first body.[15] Therefore, out of twelve members, eight were named by the president of the republic with near total discretion.

The preceding discussion makes it evident that the executive's power over the HCJ was undeniable. This domination by the executive constituted a serious obstacle to the HCJ's task of ensuring "compliance with the safeguards accorded to judges in matters of nomination, advancement, transfer, and disciplinary action," as stipulated in Article 67 of the 1959 constitution.

The revolution of January 14, 2011, and the ensuing difficulties of the democratic transition did not immediately permit a rupture with the laws and practices of the past.

The Judiciary in the Aftermath of the Revolution of January 14, 2011

In a revolution, every institution of the state is subject to tension between the need to continue functioning and the need to respond to the aspirations and hopes that fueled the revolution. The judiciary is not immune from this tension. An assessment of the relative success or failure of a democratic transition in the postrevolutionary period is an assessment of the degree to which these conflicting imperatives are reconciled. If the Tunisian judiciary is analyzed from this perspective, the greatest challenge confronting the institution is to reform itself organically. This reform concerns not only the structures of the judiciary but the judges themselves as well. In terms of structures, I am chiefly concerned with the HCJ. Since this institution is considered crucial to ensuring an independent judiciary, and given that it remained under the control of the executive for decades, studying its progression since the revolution is especially important. For this reason, I focus my analysis on this institution, which notably occupies a position of prime importance in judicial systems around the world.[16] One should take the time to ask whether the revolution enabled the HCJ to free itself from the yoke of the executive and restore its natural role, namely to safeguard the guarantees accorded to judges and to strengthen the independence of the judiciary. I am forced to admit a certain persistence of authoritarian tendencies in the first two years after the revolution. In terms of the judges themselves, the management of their careers was not made transparent, and the organic reform of the HCJ encountered serious obstacles.

But the challenges of the democratic transition are not limited to organic reforms of a country's institutions. The transition has presented another challenge to the judiciary: that of resolving disputes that have arisen from the revolution itself. And here, the judiciary has been inconsistent in its handling of these disputes.

The Persistence of Authoritarian Practices

These difficulties have been apparent in the awaited reform of the HCJ, a reform that remained blocked for two years, as well as the reform of the management of judges, a process that remained shrouded.

Two reforms were proposed. The first was a project the government put forth in 2011, which failed due to the ATJ's opposition. The second project followed the elections of October 23, 2011, and was voted down in the NCA, having failed to obtain the required majority.

Rejection of the 2011 Reform

The first reform proposed by the government included several innovations, among them the following: (1) appointment of the president of the Court of Cassation to the presidency of the HCJ, (2) the designation of the HCJ as a constitutional body endowed with legal standing and financial autonomy, (3) reorganization of the HCJ as three bodies: the High Council of Judges, the Disciplinary Council, and the General Council for Judicial Affairs, (4) the designation of the General Council for Judicial Affairs as a body to be consulted on all matters pertaining to the judiciary and the expansion of its composition to include nonjudicial professions, (5) the delegation of the HCJ's composition to election by majority vote among the elected judges, and (6) the assignment of HCJ with responsibility for the proposal of candidates to be nominated to judicial posts (including the first president of the Court of Cassation, the attorney general at the Court of Cassation, the attorney general and director of judicial services, the inspector general at the Justice Ministry, the president of the Real Estate Court, the first president of the Tunis Court of Appeals, and the attorney general at the Court of

Appeals) and to the determination of the career promotion schedule, the list of skills required to be nominated to judicial posts, and the list of skills required to be promoted to higher ranks, and, finally, oversight of the promotions, nominations, and transfers of judges on the basis of criteria determined by judges' status. The ATJ opposed this reform project, and so it failed to go forward.

Failure of the 2012 Reform

Following the elections of October 2011, the Constituent Assembly voted to adopt the constituent law of December 16, 2011, pertaining to the provisional organization of public authorities. This decision should have represented an important step in the reform of the justice system. Article 22 of Section V of that law stipulates: "After consultation with judges, the NCA will adopt an organic law establishing a provisional, independent, and representative body, and will determine its composition and attributions . . . [and this body] will be charged with implementing judicial justice and will replace the HCJ."

But for over a year this proposed reform languished. The vote on the organic law that would have created this body did not receive the required majority among the NCA's members (the final tally was 110 out of 217). From the outset, the legislative commission of the NCA confronted difficulties in working to submit a draft proposal to the entire assembly for a vote. The commission was actually presented three different proposals: one from the ATJ, one from the Judges' Syndicate, and one from the government.[17] Despite the commission's efforts to consolidate all three proposals into one draft law, the final project submitted to the plenary session of the NCA on August 2, 2012, did not receive a majority of votes. Its failure to pass was primarily due to the opposition of members of parliament that belonged to Ennahda. They were vehemently opposed to the provisions of Article 1, which granted the provisional body considerable independence: "A provisional, independent body is hereby created to replace the HCJ. The body, to be known as the Provisional Council of Justice, is endowed with legal standing and enjoys administrative and financial autonomy. It shall be headquartered in Tunis and will remain independent from the Ministry of Justice."[18]

The vote in the NCA stalled on Article 1 of the law, as the majority of members concluded that a rejection of the first article made further examination of the law pointless. The draft was sent back to the legislative commission for revision and resubmission. Between August 2, 2012, and late 2012, no new proposal was submitted to the full assembly. Thus, the reform called for by the constituent law of December 16, 2011, had not come to pass for nearly two years after the revolution. Not a single reform to the primary institution charged with protecting the guarantees accorded to judges had been made. As a result of the double failure of the reform proposals in 2011 and 2012, the executive branch, principally the Ministry of Justice, benefited from complete freedom in making decisions concerning the management of the judiciary.

The Management of the Judiciary: An Unclear Approach

Concerning the management of the judiciary, for purposes of illustration, I will focus on two significant decisions: The first one, made in a nontransparent manner, concerned the dismissal (some might say the purge) of judges mired in suspicion and implicated in corrupt practices.[19] The second one concerned the annual reshuffling of judges, particularly those which, as mandated by Article 14 of Law No. 67-29, should be examined by the HCJ before the annual judicial holiday of July 16–September 15.[20] Instead, this examination was undertaken quasi-exclusively by the Ministry of Justice.

A Purge Lacking Transparency

In the postrevolutionary period, a recurrent theme was the "purge" of professionals in various realms. In terms of the judiciary, the memory of a justice system at the mercy of the executive, and all the suspicions this situation engendered, explained the persistence of this theme, as reflected in the demands of the public and of the ATJ in particular. What the Ministry of Justice presented as a "purge" consisted of two phases in 2011 and 2012: the first was reflected in the firing of certain judges in 2011 and the second, following the elections of October 23, 2011, consisted of various dismissals of judges in 2012 undertaken by the minister of justice serving in the current coalition government.

In 2011, responding to demands for a purge of the judiciary, the successive provisional governments undertook partial and insufficient measures leading to the dismissal of only seven judges.[21] These seven were so closely associated with the former regime, their professional integrity so compromised, that rapid action had to be taken within a year after the revolution.

Then in 2012, emboldened by its democratic legitimacy, the provisional coalition government dismissed over eighty judges in a process that had its share of political maneuverings, but that nonetheless adhered to Article 44 of Law No. 67-29. That article called for the dismissal of judges, entailing a permanent end to their functions and stripping them of their status as judges. In a communiqué issued on Saturday, May 26, the Ministry of Justice announced its decision to dismiss these judges.[22] The minister explained that the decision had been made to compensate those judges who had been victims of various abuses (delayed promotions, etc.) under the former regime and to hold others accountable for undermining the honor and integrity of the justice system. According to the minister, thorough investigations had revealed that a number of judges

> continued to err and failed to take advantage of the opportunity afforded by the Revolution to redeem themselves, forcing the Minister to put an end to this abnormal situation, to all those who would undermine the honor, integrity and prestige of the justice system, and to those who would call into question the credibility of judges and the institutions of the State more generally. . . . Pursuant to the provisions of Article 44 of Law No. 67-18 of July 14, 1967, 82 judges will be dismissed as of May 26, 2012. [23]

The Justice Ministry's stance was not immune from criticism. Based on the communiqué, the judges who were targeted for dismissal were those who "continued to err"[24] after the revolution, suggesting they had violated their professional obligations. In other words, the grievances against the judges in question were of a disciplinary nature. But the law designates dismissal as a cessation of one's professional duties that is distinct from other cases of disciplinary action, particularly revocation. The ministry invoked disciplinary motives to justify its dismissals even though dismissal is not a disciplinary measure, thereby deviating from the very procedure it was supposed to follow. Instead of adopting the correct disciplinary procedure that would have honored all the necessary legal rights, most notably the right to a defense, the ministry chose the route of dismissal, which is not designed to punish disciplinary infractions.[25] In addition to this illegality, the ministry erroneously argued that if the dismissed judges had not "continued to err"—that is, if they had ceased in their violations of their professional obligations—they probably would not have been fired! Such statements suggest that the ministry assumed the task of distinguishing between those who had "continued to err" and those who had not—exercising discretion that did not conform to proper legal procedure.

The irregularities that tainted the process surrounding the dismissals, combined with the lack of sufficient communication over the motives behind these dismissals, deprived the whole enterprise, presented as a "purifying" and revolutionary endeavor, of the necessary transparency. It created serious doubts surrounding the true meaning of "purification."[26] Furthermore, the public still waited for the truth to be revealed concerning the period of Ben Ali's rule, in which the justice system was abused by the regime (*Eco Journal*, 2012).[27] This lack of transparency also accompanied the annual reshuffling of judges.[28]

The Reshuffle of Judges in 2012:
A Decision Implemented Quasi-Exclusively
by the Ministry of Justice

The failure to replace the HCJ with an independent provisional body, as envisioned in the law of December 16, 2011, on the provisional organization of public authorities, had a negative impact on the procedures for implementing the annual overhaul of judges (new appointments, promotions, transfers, and so on). These procedures were traditionally the purview of the HCJ. Ennahda's opposition to the law that would have created this body created an unprecedented situation in which the annual reshuffle of judges, normally slated to occur before the judicial holiday (July 16–September 15) pursuant to Article 14 of Law No. 67-29, was delayed until August 2, when the proposed law was voted down.

To rectify the situation, the ministry announced on September 13, 2012, that it would be assuming control of the reshuffle. The list of concerned judges (numbering roughly 750) appeared in a September 27, 2012, decree (*Journal Officiel de la République Tunisienne*, 2012),[29] invoking the need to preserve the continuity of public services and to unblock the advancement of numerous judges who had been deprived of the promotions to which they were entitled under the former regime. The ministry also stressed that the reshuffling of these judges was overseen with the participation of the old HCJ, whose three-year term (2010–2012) had not yet expired.

The ATJ criticized the ministry for handling the transfers virtually alone, since the HCJ could not possibly have reviewed more than 700 personnel files in a single meeting, purportedly held on September 8![30] The ATJ also emphasized the illegitimacy (what the president of the ATJ called the "illegality") of the HCJ in question, even if its involvement in the transfers was marginal.[31]

The deficiencies characterizing this overhaul of judges undertaken by the Ministry of Justice, and the controversy it sparked, would not have come to pass had the NCA voted in favor of the law establishing an independent provisional body in 2012. In failing to fulfill its obligation as outlined in Article 22 of the law of December 16, 2011, the NCA failed in one of its most important tasks during the democratic transition: that of endowing the country with an independent, if provisional, body garnering the trust of the judges and respecting the statutory guarantees of fair treatment owed to the judges. Thus, the NCA bore the political responsibility for delaying the establishment of a truly independent judiciary. More precisely, the parliamentary bloc headed up by the Islamist Ennahda bore direct responsibility, since Ennahda voted down the proposed law that would have created the independent provisional body.

Conclusion

The first two years following the revolution thus failed to build the institutional foundations for an independent judiciary in Tunisia. But two years later, the country seems to be on a better path. Most decisive has been the adoption of a new constitution on January 27, 2014, which represented a true break from the past. The new constitution explicitly calls for the creation of an independent judicial authority, not simply a judicial authority (as had the 1959 constitution). The independence of the judiciary is anchored in a number of important guarantees (listed in Article 102), including the immovability of judges and the nomination of judges through a process overseen by the Supreme Council of the Judiciary (rather than by the president of the republic). The independence of the Supreme Council, in turn, is shielded from executive domination by its new composition. Henceforth, two-thirds of the members of the Supreme Council are to be selected from among the country's judges and the majority of these council members are to be elected by their peers. In addition, the president of the Supreme Council is to be elected by its members, chosen from among the highest-ranked judges. These provisions constitute a revolutionary departure from the norms that prevailed under the former regime, under which the president of the republic dominated over the council.

During a period of transition, it is difficult to give a categorical assessment of the future prospects for the judiciary's independence. Everything depends on the political will of the players and the evolution of the balance of power between the partisans of substantive change and those who prefer to hold on to past practices. Nevertheless, the fundamental basis for change is written into the constitution, and this factor will make it difficult to return to former habits. That said, the independence of the judiciary is a battle that must be fought every day—a battle that must be led by the judges themselves, ahead of all others.

Notes

This chapter has been translated from the French by Sarah Feuer, a PhD student at Brandeis University.

1. See The International Federation of Leagues of Human Rights, "Instrumentalisation de la justice en Tunisie: Ingérence, violations, impunité" [The abuse of justice in Tunisia: Intrusion, violations, impunity], No. 553, January 2011. Draft-limited edition, FIDH/CNLT-Tunisia/3.

2. The first Tunisian Constituent Assembly, created by the Bey's decree of December 29, 1955, and convened on April 8, 1956, endowed the Kingdom of Tunisia with a constitution, promulgated on June 1, 1959.

3. The constitution of June 1, 1959, was first implicitly and partially abrogated

by decree Law No. 14 of March 23, 2011, establishing the provisional organization of public authorities. The 1959 constitution was formally abrogated by Article 27 of constituent Law No. 6 of December 16, 2011, establishing the provisional organization of public authorities.

4. The most recent amendment to date was introduced by organic Law No. 2005-81 of August 4, 2005 (JORT No. 64 of August 12, 2005).

5. This is a translation from Arabic of Article 22. Article 23 of the same section stipulated that the administrative court and the constitutional council would exercise their functions in accordance with the laws and regulations pertaining to their organization, their jurisdiction, and their procedures.

6. It is impossible to overstate the activism of the Association of Tunisian Judges and its efforts over the years to implement a truly independent judiciary in accordance with international standards. Under the dictatorship of Ben Ali, the ATJ opposed the regime's attempts to pack its governing structures with docile judges who would support the regime. One of the ATJ's last significant acts under the former regime was to oppose the modification of Law No. 67-29, embodied in Organic Law 2005-81 of August 4, 2005. That organic law stripped judges of their ability to go before the Administrative Court for disciplinary matters and offered insufficient protections to judges against arbitrary decisions of the regime. The conflict between the ATJ and the regime was exacerbated by decisions taken at the HCJ's annual meeting on August 1, 2005, concerning the transfer of judges. Ben Ali presided over this meeting, after which several members of ATJ's executive bureau were transferred unjustly. Among the most striking examples were K. Kannou (the current president of the ATJ), who was reassigned from Tunis to Kairouan, and Wassila Kaabi, who was transferred from Tunis to Gabès, in addition to many others. In a veritable coup against the ATJ, the minister of justice then replaced the members of the association's executive bureau with a provisional committee tasked with preparing ATJ's 11th annual congress. On September 1, 2005, this committee took possession of the ATJ's offices, and at the association's 11th congress, held on December 4, 2005, a new executive bureau was elected. The Judges' Syndicate, created during the first trimester of 2011, held its opening congress on May 22, 2011. Significantly, presiding over the Judges' Syndicate's congress was the former president of the Court of Cassation, Mohamed Ellejmi, considered a representative of the judicial hierarchy coopted by the former regime. In terms of corporate representation, the Judges' Syndicate is outclassed by the ATJ not only because the former is a more recent creation but because the latter enjoys a greater membership. It is widely believed that the Judges' Syndicate was created to counteract the influence of the ATJ, whose opposition to the regime contrasts sharply with the Judges' Syndicate's docility.

7. The focus on this link between the past and the present was suggested to us by Eva Bellin in a note concerning the objectives of this workshop: "The objective of the workshop is to examine the rule of law in Middle Eastern and North African nations *before, during and after* the transition from authoritarian rule" (emphasis added).

8. See especially Sadok Belaid, *Essai sur le pouvoir créateur et normatif du juge [Essay on the creative and normative authority of judges]* (Paris: Librairie Générale de Droit et de Jurisprudence, 1974), p. 301.

9. See Thierry Ricard, *Le conseil supérieur de la magistrature [The high council of justice]* (Paris: Presses universitaires de France, 1990), p. 22.

10. See Roger Perrot, *Institutions judiciaires [Judicial institutions],* 2nd ed. (Paris: Montchrestien, 2006), p. 50.

11. For more details, see my article "La compétence exclusive du conseil supérieur de la magistrature en matière disciplinaire 'ou' . . . quand le conseil constitutionnel brise la jurisprudence du tribunal administratif" [The exclusive jurisdiction of the High Council of Justice in disciplinary matters or . . . when the constitutional council undermines the jurisprudence of the administrative court], *En hommage à Dali Jazi* (2012), pp. 151–181.

12. Still, the French translation of the title of Section V retained the phrase "Judicial Power."

13. See decree No. 96-1011 of May 27, 1996.

14. On this point, see Article 55 of Law No. 67-29.

15. See Article 60 of Law No. 67-29.

16. This is not to suggest that the problems of the judiciary can be reduced solely to the reorganization of the HCJ. Nevertheless, the importance of such councils is broadly recognized. For evidence of the latter, see the general report of the First Study Commission of the International Association of Judges, Vienna, November 9–13, 2003, available at: http://www.iaj-uim.org/iuw/wp-content/uploads/2013/02/I-SC-2003-conclusions-E.pdf. See also the report of the French Senate, *Le Conseil Supérieur de la magistrature Italien: Symbole de l'indépendance de la justice ou instance d"autogouvernement' des juges? [The Italian High Council of Justice: Symbol of Judicial Independence or Mechanism of Judges' 'Self-Governance'?]*, http://www.senat.fr/rap/197-511/197-51113.html; and USAID, *Conseils pour promouvoir l'indépendance et l'impartialité judiciaires [Recommendations for the promotion of judicial independence and impartiality]*, May 2003, http://pdf.usaid.gov/pdf_docs/pnacp333.pdf.

17. It is worth noting that the work of the legislative commission in the NCA followed a long series of negotiations. Laborious discussions took place between the ATJ and the Ministry of Justice concerning two essential points: the composition of the provisional body and the powers it would exercise. The ATJ initially demanded that the body, when taking up questions regarding judges' careers—nominations, advancement, promotions, transfers—should only be comprised of judges; the ATJ later softened its stance and demanded that "a comfortable majority" of two-thirds be comprised of judges. The Judges' Syndicate called for merely an absolute majority of judges to sit on the body. In terms of the provisional body's powers, the ATJ demanded that it be vested with the power to make decisions, rather than being limited to a consultative role. All of these demands were rejected by the Ministry of Justice.

18. The Nahda party was hostile to the creation of an independent body. It preferred that the body be placed under the authority of the minister of justice, who was at the time a member of the Nahda party.

19. Since the revolution, the term *purge* has frequently been used to refer to the state's intervention in those sectors that had become centers of corruption under the former regime. In Arabic, the word frequently employed is *ettat'hiir.*

20. Article 38 of Law No. 67-29.

21. The seven judges who were fired on the basis of Article 46 of Law No. 67-29 were permanently excluded from the judiciary and given severance pay. They were Lotfi Daouèss, state attorney general and director of Judicial Services (decree No. 167-2011 of February, 10, 2011), Mohamed Chouikha, chamber president at the Court of Appeals in Tunis (decree No. 168-2011 of February 10, 2011), Mehrez Hammami, chamber president at the Court of 1st Instance (decree No. 169-2011 of February 10, 2011), Mannoubi Ben Hmidane, chamber president at the Court of Appeals in Tunis (decree No. 170-2011 of February 10, 2011), Zied

Souidene, investigating judge at the Court of 1st Instance in Tunis (decree No. 172-2011 of February 10. 2011), and Mohamed Amira, substitute to the attorney general of the republic at the Court of 1st Instance in Tunis (decree No. 171-2011 of February 10, 2011). To these should be added the judge of 3rd rank, Abdelmajid Ben Fraj, for whom decree No. 173-2011 of February 10, 2011 put an end to his "judicial functions."

22. On the radio and in the afternoon, no less!

23. My translation of the communiqué, published in the daily *Le Maghreb*, May 29, 2012.

24. In numerous press accounts, the minister of justice and his representatives accused the dismissed judges of corruption.

25. Aware of this significant procedural deficiency, and following criticisms from the legal professionals' representative bodies, the Ministry of Justice offered the judges in question three days to file an administrative appeal contesting their dismissals.

26. The dismissals were criticized by the ATJ and the Judges' Syndicate, but only the ATJ maintained its critical stance. The Judges' Syndicate ultimately accepted the firings. The dismissals were also criticized by numerous political parties and nongovernmental organizations, both domestic and international. Human Rights Watch, for example, reported that Judge Habib Zammali was fired on the grounds that he appeared in a photograph drinking beer. Commenting on Zammali's dismissal, Human Rights Watch (2012) noted, "No Tunisian law prohibits judges from drinking alcohol in their private life."

27. On this point, see the opinion of Samir Annabi, a lawyer at the Court of Cassation and currently the president of the Independent Authority for the Fight Against Corruption, as expressed in an interview published in *Eco Journal*, May 25–31, 2012.

28. Roughly a dozen of the judges in question chose to resign.

29. See the *Journal Officiel de la République Tunisienne*, No. 80 (October 19, 2012).

30. It seems that the files in the question were studied by a special commission within the Ministry of Justice. The list of concerned judges was later submitted to the HCJ, *a posteriori*.

31. Following an appeal by the current president of the ATJ, Kalthoum Kennou, the results of the elections for representatives of judges of second rank on the HCJ *preceding* the current one (that is, the HCJ of the 2007–2008 term), the Administrative Court annulled these elections on the grounds of significant procedural violations. See Administrative Court, 4th chamber of 1st instance, Case No. 1/17022, February 3, 2011, *K. Kennou vs. Minister of Justice*. An appeal of this decision was rejected (1st appellate chamber, No. 28719, July 5, 2010).

5

Reforming the Armies of Authoritarian Regimes

Zoltan Barany

No institution is more important to the survival of regimes than the armed forces. As the recent upheavals in the Arab world have once again demonstrated, whether states suppress uprisings or become victims to them largely depends on the armed forces' attitudes toward the protesters and the state itself. The military's role is also critically important to the transition prospects of political systems. Democracy cannot be consolidated without democratic armies: in the absence of armed forces supportive of the principle of democratic governance, not one political force or another, democracy cannot survive. In fact, the generals' backing is an indispensable prerequisite of regime consolidation for polities of all types, regardless of whether they are democratic. In other words, the new regime needs the military establishment's support. Furthermore, rule of law cannot exist if the armed forces remain outside of the control of the civilian legal authority.

No mystery exists about the key attributes of democratic civil-military relations. What does make a great difference, however, is the starting point of defense reform. What reforms need to be implemented in a political system just emerging from military rule or socialism, from a major interstate war or civil war, or perhaps from a colonial past? Owing to the large disparities in these contexts, the tasks of army builders and the manner in which reforms are implemented are going to be rather different as well. Nevertheless, the goal, the establishment of a democratic army, is similar in all of them.

My aim in this chapter is to answer a fundamental question: How does a newly democratizing country build an effective, cohesive, and accountable military? Because this book is about the Arab world where to date no democracy has been consolidated, I will cast my net wide and discuss the reform of civil-military relations not only in cases of democratic transition but also in settings where an authoritarian regime is supplanted by another, albeit different kind, of authoritarian polity.

The chapter will proceed as follows. In the first section I will explain *what* specifically should be reformed as I consider components of a reform package democratizing states should consider. In the next part my attention shifts to *how* defense reform should be conceived and conducted. Finally, I will identify special areas of concern and opportunity for the military establishments of four Arab republics: Egypt, Libya, Tunisia, and Yemen.

What? Components of Defense Reform

Crafting democratic civil-military relations is an endeavor that is largely determined by the context in which it is pursued. Let us discuss the main components of the reform program that need to be implemented in virtually all political systems transitioning toward democracy.

Minimizing the Military's Prerogatives and Political Activism

The international relations scholar Hans Morgenthau writes that "a completely neutral armed force within the state is a contradiction in terms" (as cited in Lang, 2004: 76). In fact, a democracy should not aspire to a politically neutral military but to one that is firmly committed to democratic governance. The armed forces must be depoliticized, and their members must not play any political role other than exercising their civic right to vote. Active-duty military personnel must not run for, accept, or hold political office and should not appear at political rallies in uniform. The selection and promotion of the top military leadership must be controlled by the civilians, ideally by some combination of officials from the executive and legislative branches and, again, ideally (but not necessarily) following consultation of leading generals. One related issue is the need to codify the political institutions' areas of responsibility over the armed forces for all potential scenarios (peacetime, emergencies, war).

In most democracies, the head of state is the military's commander in chief, and a civilian minister of defense is responsible for the army's day-to-day operations. Selecting a defense minister who possesses a measure of expertise or at least some demonstrated interest in defense-security matters and international affairs signals to the armed forces that the state takes them seriously. Ideally, the defense minister and his or her ministry are integrated into the governmental power structure, enjoy the confidence of the president or prime minister, and are willing to defend the legitimate professional interests of the military. Chains of command within the armed forces must be clearly spelled out, and potential ambiguities need to be eliminated. The top-ranking uniformed person of the military—the chief of the general staff or whatever designation that person may hold—should be subordinated to the civilian defense minister, a cabinet member who represents the government in the armed forces and the armed forces in the cabinet.

In virtually all authoritarian systems, military officers enjoy numerous political or socioeconomic perquisites. The aim of democratizers is to "roll back" the army's privileged status and establish armed forces that are reliable, capable, and also valued and respected servants of the state and its citizenry. The military must become accountable before the law, obedient to and supportive of the democratic polity, and its professional responsibilities must be constitutionally regulated. The armed forces should be staffed by the kind of individuals who are inclined to obey, and the state should adjust the incentives of the military so that, regardless of their nature, they would prefer to obey (Feaver, 1999: 226). Enforcing the retirement age (say fifty-five) for officers in postauthoritarian contexts may effectively serve the purpose of getting rid of troublemaking generals. Establishing a pay scale for military personnel that corresponds to the salaries of civil service employees on appropriate levels helps to create a culture of transparency and enhances desirable relations between the armed forces and society.

All too often the elites of newly emerging democratic regimes have little understanding of and/or interest in learning about the military as a professional organization. This mistake is a costly one because it is in the direct interest of the state to maintain armed forces that are not only supportive of democratic governance but also capable of executing the missions politicians assign to them. It is important not only that the military stay away from politics but also that it is content with the conditions of service. Although in a democracy the army should not have to be bribed or appeased, if at all possible, the state ought to extend the armed forces high professional status through the provision of up-to-date equipment and decent salaries and benefits; raise the social esteem of the military profession; avoid intruding in the army's internal affairs—such as training and routine promotions—and, by all means, avoid using the military as a tool in domestic political competition. A democratic state must honor the military's esprit de corps while preserving democratic values and respect for human rights within the military culture (Young, 2006: 22).

What has been the experience of reducing military politics and removing the armed forces from politics around the world? The answer depends largely on the amount of leverage the armed forces possess at the time of regime change. Ordinarily, military elites that enjoy little leverage and retain modest societal support at the time of regime change are easily extracted from politics and are not in the position to effectively oppose the reduction of their privileges by the new democratizing regime. The best examples of this scenario are Greece and Argentina after military rule (1967–1974 and 1976–1983, respectively). In contrast, where the armed forces maintain significant public support at the end of their rule—Chile comes first to mind—democratizers need to be far more careful to treat the military in a way that tends to preserve some of their privileges and political clout, at least in the short run (Barany, 2012).

The situation is rather different in postsocialist states. In communist regimes the communist party controls the armed forces through a variety of institutions and agencies. The party is an organic component of the military itself: party organizations can be found from the top echelons of the armed forces all the way to the platoon level. Much of the time of armed forces personnel is taken up with ideological indoctrination and training and ensuring that soldiers and their commanders remain good communists vigilantly protecting the regime, rather than the nation. After the fall of state socialism, then, the main task of democratizers is not to take the military out of politics, as in postmilitary regimes, but the opposite: to take the politics out of the military, that is, to abolish party organizations and party influence over the armed forces (Barany, 1997). Getting the military to accept a reduction in their privileges is seldom difficult in postsocialist regimes, because the armed forces are under firm civilian control in communist states.

Eliminate the Military's Domestic Missions

Since a principal objective of civilian leaders is to prevent the armed forces from interfering in domestic politics, the conditions under which the military may be used internally must be specified by law. Generally speaking, in the modern democratic state the only legitimate internal role for the army is to provide relief after natural disasters. The military is ideally positioned to fulfill this goal, which can also increase its societal esteem, given its manpower, transportation capability, and equipment (e.g., heavy machinery for tasks like bridge building and infrastructure reparation). The military should not be used to quell domestic disturbances or to perform crowd control and other security functions that should be the responsibility of the police and other domestic security organizations. In particular, the armed forces should have no role in combatting drug trafficking or manufacturing because such activities inevitably increase the likelihood of corruption; besides, these tasks should be part of an internal security forces' professional portfolio. In a similar vein, ideally soldiers would not participate in domestic programs such as rural infrastructure development that might foster their politicization. States that maintain paramilitary organizations, gendarmeries, militias, national guards, and so on, must clearly regulate the use of those organizations. The constitution must be clear about both the sort of domestic tasks permissible for the armed forces to take on and the conditions necessary for their deployment.

A number of states can be found with otherwise appropriate civil-military relations where the military is asked to fulfill functions that should not be its responsibility. One example is the Indian armed forces' continued involvement in the suppression of domestic conflicts. This function constitutes such a troubling aspect of Indian military politics that according to Stephen Cohen (2001: xv), "India is not a democracy in many of its districts where the army and the paramilitary forces supplanted the judiciary, the civil administration, and the ballot box as the ultimate arbiter."

In a democratic state the wartime use of the military must also be unambiguously regulated in the constitution. Ordinarily, the power to declare war and states of emergency rests with the legislature, or at the very least, the executive must obtain parliament's approval. The deployment of troops with or without a formal declaration is an important constitutional issue pertaining, in particular, to presidential powers and has been widely debated. In the United States, for instance, this issue was settled only in 1973 with the War Powers Resolution, which clearly defined how many soldiers could be deployed by the president of the United States and for how long without legislative approval. In Canada, however, the declaration of war is still entirely an executive prerogative; although Parliament has been consulted, it has never claimed the right to declare war or to say when it has ended or how it should be conducted (Dunn, 2007).

Eliminate the Military's Role in the National Economy

The armed forces should not be involved in the economy. Business activities distract soldiers from their primary mission—the defense of the homeland—and create conditions for corruption and negative interservice or interunit rivalry. These activities harm both the professionalism and the societal prestige of the military establishment. China is one of the major powers where the political leadership finally recognized the negative effects of decades-long and perfectly legal economic activities by the People's Liberation Army. In the late 1990s the leadership of the Communist Party of China debated the issue and in 1998 promulgated the Divestiture Act, which banned the People's Liberation Army from all commercial activities. Recent analyses have confirmed that the new policy has contributed significantly to the growing professionalism of the army (Kiselycznyk and Saunders, 2010; Lee, 2006; Li, 2010). The detrimental consequences of the armed forces' economic role have been acknowledged in other states that cannot compete with the Chinese state's financial resources to make up the losses from the defense budget that the military would suufer by ending its business endeavors. For instance, Indonesian president Susilo Bambang Yudhoyono promised to drastically scale down the armed forces' involvement in the national economy, and in 2004, a law was passed by the Jakarta legislature to enforce this policy. Although the results have left a great deal to be desired—the Indonesian state, unlike the People's Republic of China, has no way of compensating the armed forces for their lost revenues—the intention alone speaks for itself (Crouch, 2010: 161–169).

Strengthening Legislative Involvement

Military politics is played out among the triangle of the state, the armed forces, and society, with the executive branch dominating the state and the legislature enjoying far less coult. An important criterion of democratic governance is that civilian control over the armed forces be balanced between the executive and legislative branches of government. As Robert Dahl (1989: 235) writes, "the civilians who control the military [and police] must themselves be subject to the democratic process." The legislature debates foreign policy and defense issues and ought to have the power to call on members of the executive branch and the armed forces to testify before it in open or closed hearings. Nevertheless, in many democracies legislators do not play an independent role in overseeing the armed forces owing to limitations on their space of action, a lack of expertise or interest in defense matters, or insufficient access to objective data and information. Inadequate legislative involvement in the defense-security domain is a shortcoming in numerous states that otherwise have overwhelmingly positive civil-military relations, such as Botswana, Greece, and Japan.

In only a few polities does the legislature play the kind of role necessary for substantively balanced civilian control of the military. This role comprises not just debating and passing defense-related bills but, crucially important, taking an active part in three aspects of the armed forces fiscal affairs. First, parliament determines the process of how defense budgets are devised, including the questions of what institutions (such as general staff, the defense ministry, governmental advisory bodies, NGOs, the prime minister's office, or the parliamentary defense committees) are involved and in what sequence. Second, the deputies participate in the formulation of the actual defense budget. And third, members of parliament maintain oversight of the disbursement and implementation of defense outlays. Countries with a long-term record of active and vigorous parliamentary oversight are rare; of those with post–World War II transitions to democracy, Germany and Spain are particularly prominent.

It is worth noting that the effectiveness of both Germany and Spain as active members of the North Atlantic Treaty Organization (NATO) is compromised but not because their armies lack professionalism. Rather, politicians in Berlin and Madrid are loathe to send their armed forces to participate in NATO operations, and when they do, German and Spanish units operate under restrictions that limit their usefulness. There seems to be a positive correlation between legislative authority and lacking enthusiasm for foreign military deployments. One might argue that parliamentarians enjoy a more direct link with the society that ultimately spawns soldiers than members of the executive branch, the policymakers who are more involved in decisions regarding military engagements (Barany, 2012: 352).

In short, there is a direct correlation between democratic civil-military relations and robust parliamentary participation in defense-security affairs. Consequently, enhancing the legislature's clout, by increasing the authority of its defense committees and requiring its substantive contribution to procedures and deliberations pertaining to the armed forces, should be a priority for democracy activists.

Bringing Society In

Independent civilian defense experts, NGOs, and journalists focusing on security issues can play an important role in advising elected officials and the public about military affairs. Their involvement can encourage transparency and promote confidence between state, society, and the armed forces. Introducing defense-related courses at universities, allowing civilians (journalists, bureaucrats, politicians, and so on) to enroll in appropriate programs at military academies, and providing some public funding on a competitive basis to NGOs studying defense issues all contribute to the overall improvement of democratic civil-military relations. In sum, in a democratic state, the public has easy access to balanced, objective information regarding defense and national security matters. NGOs, the media, and civilian defense experts are the sources of that information not just for society at large but also for political parties and members of the legislature.

Democratic civil-military relations should be taught in military colleges and academies and must be a major component of the education of armed forces personnel. Instruction regarding the proper role of the military in a democracy ought to be a part of the curricula in the public school system so citizens can learn from an early age about the military's position in the state.

Using the Military's Expertise

States and societies make considerable financial and other sacrifices to educate, train, equip, and otherwise maintain their armed forces. Marginalizing military officers by not asking for their advice in the process of devising defense and foreign policy let alone military strategy is irresponsible public policy and wasteful of public resources. In other words, officers acquire their specialized knowledge at a significant cost to taxpayers, who should get some return on this investment. Using the military's expertise does not mean that politicians are obligated to listen to members of the military and adopt their recommendations. But forgoing the opportunity to quiz expert military officers about issues they likely know better than anyone else—their own and other armies' strategies, tactics, weapons system, capabilities, combat readiness, and so on—is clearly unwise. Furthermore, the practice of regularly requesting that officers share their knowledge with their civilian masters is also beneficial for overall civil-military relations because it makes the military feel useful, important, and relevant and more vested in the success of the regime.

One would be hard pressed to find a case more illustrative of how things go wrong when the armed forces are ignored or marginalized than under presidents Néstor Kirchner (2003–2007) and his wife, Cristina Fernández de Kirchner (2007 to the present), in Argentina. In 2005, Néstor Kirchner appointed Nilda Garré, a former leftist militant, to lead the defense ministry. During her term as defense minister, Garré showed nothing but contempt and disdain toward the armed forces as an institution. She displayed leftist posters and mementos in her office that were calculated to irk military personnel, and since she was said to be allergic to uniforms, active-duty officers did not dare to wear them in her presence. Garré and the all-civilian defense ministry leadership did not ask for the generals' advice and seldom met with the service chiefs. The ongoing tension between the ministry and the military benefited neither (Barany, 2012: 164).

Identifying New Missions

In numerous countries experiencing democratic transitions, the obvious question of "What do we need armed forces for?" has been the subject of public debate. "Why maintain an expensive army?" people in the Czech Republic and Slovenia asked in the absence of any real security threats or troublesome neighbors (Barany, 2003: 97, 106). In Argentina and Chile, too, journalists and pundits frequently question the utility of the armed forces. Nonetheless, the military has very real uses even in the post–Cold War world. A state ought to have the capacity to protect itself from potential foreign threats to its security and to make contributions to military alliances according to its ability. Armed forces are also needed, for instance, to defend a country's airspace from unauthorized air traffic and to repel illegal fishing vessels from its coastal waters. The conventional armed forces also have the unique skills and equipment to provide help in natural disasters.

Samuel P. Huntington (1991: 252) writes that policymakers should equip their armies with "new and fancy tanks, planes, armored cars, artillery, and sophisticated electronic equipment," in other words, "give them toys" to keep them happy and occupied. But most states do not enjoy the resources necessary to take this advice, so what should they do? One important part of the solution is to search for new missions for the military. For instance, the government could sign up the armed forces to participate in international peacekeeping operations. These activities will make soldiers feel useful, enhance their own prestige as well as international regard for their country, and might even be a significant source of income for military personnel in poor states. In addition, the special skills and training that peacekeepers require creates the need for international peacekeeping centers, conflict prevention, management, and resolution programs that boost international cooperation and improve the army's public image at home.

Alternatively, the armed forces could also be trained to provide humanitarian assistance and disaster relief abroad. Such a strategy would ordinarily require enhancing the military's airlift and transportation capabilities though such services might be provided by another nation. Another worthwhile objective might be to prepare specialized military units for counterterrorism operations. The military should participate in these sorts of missions abroad, within the framework of international operations. Domestic counterterrorist activities that might involve the generals in politics should be avoided and left to the police, intelligence, and paramilitary organizations. In general, a sensible government would seek to design and build an increasingly outward-looking military establishment.

Participation in internationally sanctioned operations has especially benefited the soldiers of poorer countries. For instance, the Bangladesh Armed Forces have been heavily involved in UN peacekeeping activities. In the Bangladeshi case these operations have constituted a major source of domestic and international prestige and much-needed resources for the military (Krishnasamy, 2003). Involvement in peacekeeping activities can also serve as a means to domestic and international "rehabilitation" for armed forces in need of an image boost. Both the Argentine and Chilean armies have participated in numerous UN-sanctioned international peacekeeping operations. Argentine president Carlos Menem (1989–1999), especially, was a strong advocate of such endeavors believing that they would promote Argentina's readmission into the international community as a reliable partner after years of military rule and would also help create a new identity for its armed forces (Worboys, 2007).

Limiting the Influence of Retired Generals

In many countries, including some liberal democracies such as the United States, high-ranking officers accept lucrative jobs as lobbyists, consultants, and military advisers as soon as they retire. Former generals who are hired by defense contractors turn into acquisition consultants whose influence is often used to serve the interests of their employers while contravening the interests of the public. This practice is unethical and harmful to civil-military relations (Moten, 2010). South Korean law prohibits the employment of officers by defense firms for five years after their retirement, providing an excellent example of an important lesson that long-consolidated democracies could learn from relative newcomers to their ranks.

How? Thinking About Implementation

The objectives of postauthoritarian defense reform can be well conceived, but a crucial part of the reform program is the manner in which it is put into practice. Especially in cases where the military had retained some leverage following the fall of the old regime, *how* reforms are implemented can be a very sensitive issue. Let us briefly consider three principles of how to properly carry out military reforms.

Clarity

Given the high stakes involved, that is, the military's ability to overthrow the state, is essential to provide the armed forces with as unambiguous a political environment as possible. Constitutions should be clear about the chain of command in peacetime, wartime, and cases of national emergencies. What is an acceptable political role to be played by active duty, reserve, and retired armed forces personnel? Should they be able to vote, join parties, appear in uniform at political rallies, or run for office? The answers to these questions must be explained and backed up with regulations, and the consequences of noncompliance should be clear and consistently applied.

In its dealings with the armed forces' leadership, the government should strive for transparency. If at all possible, political leaders should explain to the top brass, for instance, the political, social, and economic justifications for the defense budget, why the promotion of General X was vetoed by the prime minister, or the reasons for the party debates regarding the abolition of universal conscription. Such transparency reduces insecurity, builds trust, and helps eliminate rumors.

Just how important clarity in regulations and lack of ambiguity in laws are has been demonstrated by the murkiness in the 1992 Chapúltepec Peace Accord that ended El Salvador's civil war. According to the Chapúltepec accord, the Armed Forces of El Salvador are constitutionally limited to performing external security operations (defense from external threats) and providing help in national emergencies. Importantly, the idea of "national emergencies" was to denote—but did not specify—natural disasters. Nevertheless, already by 1994 nearly 7,000 soldiers were deployed in the countryside, ostensibly to make up for the vacuum created by the layoff of corrupt counternarcotics agents. When opposition politicians raised the issue, the government responded that the operation was legitimate because crime in rural areas had reached "emergency proportions" (Macías, 1999: 7).

Gradualism and Compromise

In many cases when democratic transition follows authoritarian regimes and the military enjoys an influential political role, swift and drastic changes are inadvisable because they might unnecessarily provoke the ire of the soldiers for whom regime change signifies the loss of their power and privileges. Following a gradualist approach that places emphasis on coalition building and willingness to make acceptable compromises is usually a prudent way to proceed.

A fine example is the record of Adolfo Suárez, Spain's first democratically elected prime minister (1976–1981). Intent on radically transforming the Spanish defense establishment, Suárez moved prudently. He first sought and obtained the collaboration of people in influential military circles who were concerned primarily with the future of the armed forces. Only afterward did Suárez approach the confirmed democrats in the officer corps who might have been objectionable to the former group (Rodrigo, 1991: 65). He implemented further reforms with the coordination of the service branches and only after prior consultation with them. According to some observers, the "most prominent trait of the political transition from dictatorship to democracy in Spain is the peaceful manner in which the armed forces abdicated their powerful formal position in institutions and political life, accepting the normative establishment of civil supremacy" (Bañón Martínez, 1988: 311).

South Korea's first truly civilian president in three decades, Kim Young-sam, took a page from Suárez's playbook by contacting top generals to discuss his reform proposals and, in the process, gaining their support. In the end, Kim succeeded in democratizing South Korea's military elites by cleverly neutralizing potential military opposition and by relying on generals from his native Busan and South Gyeongsang region, capitalizing on existing regional sentiments in the armed forces (Woo, 2011: 111–112).

In countries where the armed forces retain some political clout and public esteem after withdrawing from power, it is especially important not to needlessly antagonize them by putting in place overly rapid reform programs designed to reduce their autonomy and privileges. The inability of politicians to compromise when necessary or to cut some slack to the generals on issues of minor importance might easily serve to alienate people who would be otherwise willing to subordinate themselves to civilian control. In other words, strategic compromises can enhance the prospects of successful democratic consolidation and cement civilian control over the armed forces. An apt example is Chile under its first president after Augusto Pinochet, Patricio Aylwin (1990–1994). At first, Chile's democratic reformers were forced to trade off civilian control of the armed forces for short-term regime survival (Trinkunas, 2005). The military was still powerful and retained the approval of a large segment of the population, and all Aylwin and his government could do was try to consolidate and expand presidential and state power over the generals. Although his elbow room was admittedly limited, he still accomplished many objectives. More important, Aylwin established the Commission on Truth and Reconciliation to search for the truth, identify victims, and investigate accountability. The government's action amounted to moral reparation and monetary compensation, even if the armed forces' leadership, insisting that its 1973 intervention was a "patriotic mission," refused to apologize at this point. Aylwin's main objective was to begin a process of democratic consolidation that could only succeed if soldiers returned to their barracks and stayed there (Silva, 2002: 378). In other words, the compromise lay in understanding that even though the military would not be "divested" of its privileges, it acquiesced, willy-nilly, to the establishment of the commission.

In Indonesia President Susilo Bambang Yudhoyono (2004 to present), a former military man himself, has almost instinctively understood how far he could pressure the armed forces' internal reform program and at what point he should pull back and make a compromise. Indonesia's financial limitations ought to be taken into consideration when discussing the evolution of its civil-military relations. This country of 245 million people is living on 735,358 square miles, but its defense budget is smaller than that of Singapore, a 274-square-mile city-state with 5.3 million inhabitants. So although Yudhoyono has repeatedly urged the armed forces' leadership to find ways to stretch the defense budget allocated to them, he has stopped short of taking radical measures to enforce their complete withdrawal from the civilian economy.

Sequencing and Interference

Individual settings require different types of defense reforms. The main tasks for democracy builders range from having to build new independent armies on the shaky or absent foundations left behind by imperial powers all the way to drastically reducing the autonomy, privileges, and size of the armed forces in postpraetorian environments. A thoughtful sequencing of defense reforms can be exceedingly important in ensuring the military's compliance and cooperation. Consulting with democratic-minded military officers regarding the details and order of reform usually signals the state's willingness to consider the perspectives of the armed forces and can be expected to foster an agreeable interinstitutional climate. For instance, civilian authorities, especially in countries just emerging from military rule where uniformed officers tend to monopolize defense-related expertise, might not be aware that certain army units can only be upgraded or decommissioned if their place in the battle order of the entire armed forces is previously reassessed. Recommendations of the top brass should also be sought out relating to the most efficient way of spending the armaments acquisition portion of the defense budget *prior* to the implementation of the army's internal organizational reform. Such discussions do not mean, of course, that the government is obligated to take the generals' advice, but as the Spanish case suggests, the recommendations of the generals are helpful in finding out the military's preferences and they usually benefit both sides.

The state should embrace numerous other measures. It should follow Samuel Huntington's (1991: 252–253) advice and decrease the military's presence in the capital city and other political centers, as well as develop political organizations capable of mobilizing throngs of supporters to help avert potential coup attempts. A more unusual but eminently sensible Huntingtonian advice to civilian rulers is to identify themselves with the armed forces, attend their ceremonies, award medals, and praise the soldiers as exemplifying the most noble virtues of the nation (Huntington, 1991: 253). To illustrate the good sense this point makes one needs to look no further than post-military-rule Argentina. President Carlos Menem significantly reduced the military's political autonomy and budget and yet was held in high regard by the officer corps due to his numerous positive deeds signaling his appreciation of the armed forces. In contrast, Presidents Kirchner and Fernández have alienated the military through a number of humiliating and unnecessary gestures creating an extremely unpleasant nexus between the executive branch and the armed forces.

Ideally, the army's involvement in the economy should be terminated. At the same time, sequencing is critical: practical issues must be considered before hastily outlawing the military's commercial pursuits. For instance, if the resources the military gains from its business activities are used for vital operational expenses, where will the funds to cover those costs come from? If no satisfactory answer can be given to this dilemma, a timetable should be set for the military's gradual withdrawal from the economy during which time the state must find the resources to compensate for the lost revenue.

The state should have the ability to oversee the promotion of the most senior members of the armed forces. (In small- and medium-size armies, promotions over the rank of colonel should be approved by appropriate civilian officials; in a large army, the same approval should be reserved for individuals subject to promotion beyond the level of two-star general.) At the same time, the politicians should make sure that if they do veto promotions, their reasoning is based on solid evidence regarding the objectionable candidate's professional incompetence or political attitudes incompatible with democratic civil-military relations. Politicians should not interfere in the routine promotions of lower ranks nor should they get in the way of military education, training, and professional concerns unless those are in conflict with fundamental democratic values. When they do interfere, trouble tends to follow.

A fitting example is the way in which Thaksin Shinawatra, a Thai prime minister (2001–2006), frittered away his once considerable leverage over the armed forces. Notwithstanding his many conciliatory gestures toward the Royal Thai Armed Forces, which included steering his cabinet away from meddling in the army's internal affairs in his first couple of years in power, Thaksin enraged the top brass by repeatedly interfering in the army's promotion procedures in order to solidify his support base. Not discerning or choosing to ignore the signals of the deep-seated displeasure his actions provoked among the generals, he continued to appoint supporters and even family members to top military posts. These dangerous measures ultimately sacrificed not only Thaksin's own regime but, more broadly, civilian rule in Thailand (Barany, 2012: 195).

Defense Reform in the Arab Republics

Without establishing democratic civil-military relations, democracy cannot be consolidated. All of the Arab states that experienced uprisings in 2011 are currently far from democratic consolidation, and in fact, it is unclear whether their political elites even desire democracy. Nevertheless, reforming military politics and defense-security establishments ought to be an important priority, even if all the Arab states experience transition from one authoritarian regime to another.

In this section I focus on four Arab republics where uprisings in 2011 led to the fall of authoritarian regimes: Tunisia, Egypt, Libya, and Yemen. I will not address Syria, where, at the time of this writing, civil war continues to rage unabated more than two years after the revolution there began. I also leave Bahrain out of this discussion. Notwithstanding the major demonstrations, violence, and the ongoing protests it has witnessed, Bahrain remains an absolute monarchy where the chances of regime change appear to be close to nil in the foreseeable future.

As I noted above, the starting point of countries prior to defense reform is crucially important to consider because it has a strong effect on the reforms to be implemented and the manner of implementation itself. The four countries are in very different positions. Egypt's civil-military relations in many respects are similar to those of a country just emerging from military rule. Libya and Yemen, on the other hand, should be thought of as post–civil war cases. Finally, Tunisian military politics may be compared to those of a country after the fall of one-party rule, where the military did not play more than a relatively passive supporting political role. Let us see what lessons could be learned by these four republics from the experiences of earlier transitioning states in shaping new civil-military relations.

Tunisia

From the perspective of civil-military relations reform, Tunisia is in an enviable situation indeed. The biggest task for reformers in polities that follow a regime like Zine El Abidine Ben Ali's in Tunisia (i.e., one similar to one-party rule) is to reduce the political influence of the former elites in the military. But Tunisia's armed forces were highly unusual in that the old regime marginalized them and did not require soldiers to continually demonstrate their overt political support. In fact, Tunisian professional armed forces' personnel were not even allowed to vote. Moreover, the military had a relatively small budget, corruption in the army was not a serious problem, and the institution had played no role in the national economy (Barany, 2011: 27).

Tunisian military leaders have repeatedly expressed their willingness and even enthusiasm to work with the new regime in establishing democratic civil-military relations. They have declared that their extant arsenal and equipment were sufficient to fulfill their mission—a rather unusual opinion to hear from high-ranking soldiers (Hanlon, 2012b). The Ministry of Defense is mostly staffed by civilian personnel and is led by a civilian minister. One important task for Tunisia is to increase the legislature's involvement in defense matters. Tunisian political elites might want to follow the blueprint of the new democracies of southern and eastern Europe, where the legislature took on this role. One should note, however, that even in Spain, perhaps the quickest and most successful case of military transition in the region, the road to success was neither linear nor without difficulties (Agüero, 1995). The key is to promote legislators' interest in defense issues and to provide them with the unbiased civilian expertise they need—access to experts on military-security issues and relevant NGOs—to allow them to make informed decisions. All signs suggest that the legislature in Tunis will have an entirely accommodating group of generals to work with.

Egypt

Every Egyptian leader since the monarchy fell in 1952 has been a military man with the exception of the recently deposed president Mohamed Morsi, whom the military could tolerate for no more than 368 days (June 30, 2012–July 3, 2013). In many ways the position of Egypt's military is akin to an army emerging out of military rule possessing plenty of leverage. To be sure, this analogy is somewhat misleading; after all, the Egyptian Armed Forces were less politically influential in the last couple of decades of Hosni Mubarak's thirty-year reign than the internal security apparatus. Nevertheless, their significant remaining political clout, their deep involvement in the national economy, and their high societal prestige, which only increased following the revolution, render them, along with the Muslim Brotherhood, one of the two most important political players in the country (Kandil, 2012). If Egypt were on course to a democratic transition—something I am rather skeptical of—its leaders would have a lot to learn from earlier democratization experiences. Although several ways can be found to improve Egyptian civil-military relations, the strong position of the Egyptian Armed Forces tempers optimism about how many of these reforms can be or will be implemented. But let us cast our doubts aside for the moment and see what could be done in an ideal world.

The new Egyptian legislature should certainly gain more voice in defense matters by actively involving itself in debates regarding defense budgets, the use of monies, and the manner in which they are distributed, along with calling leading officers to provide parliamentary testimonies. An example that might be instructive is Indonesia, where after Suharto's fall, a gradual transition has taken place that culminated in something approximating democratic consolidation in the past decade. Parliamentary seats assigned to military officers were first decreased, and then the entire practice of military "safe seats" was eliminated. (The armed forces also received such political privileges in other current or former Asian praetorian regimes such as Thailand, though, importantly, not in South Korea.) The parliament in Jakarta does have a significant say in controlling the defense budget; it even has the right to change specifications of procurement items. Overall, however, Indonesian parliamentarians still exercise little oversight outside of budgetary matters, which are, admittedly, one of the most important areas to oversee (Barany, 2015). The reason is that many legislators lack the expertise or interest to ask the right questions, and they don't have the support staff to prepare them properly. The expansion of parliament's role has gone hand in hand with a number of new laws narrowing military prerogatives, creating the powerful Constitutional Court, and gradually increasing the clout of civilian political institutions (Mietzner, 1999: 329–360). Given that the state religion in Indonesia is also Islam, its overwhelmingly successful experience in transforming civil-military relations should be closely followed by Egyptian democratizers. In my view, it is quite doubtful that this incrementally implemented reform will take place in Egypt. The crucial two ingredients that Indonesia possessed during its most successful reform periods—a military establishment amenable to the diminution of its political privileges and a unified political opposition—seem to be missing in Egypt.

Another case that Egyptian democratizers might study with profit is Turkey during the now decadelong prime ministership of Recep Tayyip Erdoğan (2003 to present). There the military's power has been gradually diminished by political elites through the diminution of the army's representation in central institutions and the slow but steady expansion of the legislature's involvement in defense affairs (Aydinli, 2009; Gürsoy, 2011). Although in terms of political, economic, and social development, Turkey is far ahead of Egypt, its experiences in the last decade demonstrate the continuous gains a moderate Islamist state can make in limiting the political influence of a previously seemingly omnipotent military establishment. To be sure, not everything in the Turkish experience is worthy of admiration—the recent judicial campaign against leading generals is a case in point—but Egyptian reformers would have much that is progressive to consider (Gümüşçü, 2010, 2012).

Another important area of concern for Egyptian reformers is the army's deep involvement in the national economy. As I noted above, in recent memory only the Chinese government has eliminated the military's previously significant economic role. In contrast to Egypt and Pakistan, where the army has also carved out for itself a substantial economic presence, China possessed the financial resources to complete the army's transitioning out of the economy without experiencing a corresponding shock on the defense budget (Siddiqa, 2007). Moreover, unlike in Egypt and Pakistan, where the armed forces play critical political roles in the state, the Communist Party's control of the Chinese military is not challenged (Lee, 2006). Any serious contemplation of a forced reduction of the army's political role can only begin once the state is firmly in control of the armed forces, something that seems not to be the case in present-day Egypt. One should also be aware of the coup-proneness of military elites during the diminution of their political influence, as for, instance, Argentine, Russian, Spanish, and Thai postauthoritarian transitions (some successful, others not) show.

Libya and Yemen

Although Yemen is far poorer than oil-rich Libya, the two states share many similarities, among them low levels of institutional development and towering corruption. These two countries had no public institutions capable of operating independently of Ali Abdullah Saleh and Muammar Qaddafi. Libya had not had a constitution since 1951. Corruption is rampant in both countries, but the government in Sana'a "makes even the Karzai regime, in Afghanistan, seem like a model of propriety" (Filkins, 2011: 42). Tribal affiliations, of relatively little consequence in Tunisia and Egypt, are of foremost importance in Libya and Yemen. In each country, but particularly in Libya, the military and security establishment was divided into numerous organizations that had little contact with one another. The regular military was ostensibly charged with the external defense of the country whereas the security forces were supposed to protect the regime, though in practice ensuring regime survival was the main mission of all these forces.

Another important characteristic Libya and Yemen share is that both should be considered as post–civil war settings. What are the most important tasks of reformers in these contexts? What can Libyan and Yemeni reformers learn from the experiences of post–civil war countries elsewhere? In every post–civil war situation the building or rebuilding of a *national* army is a critical component of the reconstruction program. In such environments, the demobilization of forces and the reintegration of erstwhile combatants into civilian life are two of the most pressing undertakings. The collection and destruction of excess weapons and ammunition are related tasks that, as can be seen in the cases of post–civil war Bosnia, El Salvador, and Lebanon, are often very contentious. Owing to the lack of trust between former enemy forces, unsurprisingly, they generally want to retain some strategic advantage or security guarantee that will enable them to resume fighting if necessary. Therefore, promoting transparency and building trust between the different sides through a variety of confidence-building measures implemented by impartial security institutions is critically important for long-term stability.

In post–civil war environments, it is imperative to balance public sector positions of all ranks between the various former enemy communities assumes great significance. Quotas are advisable, based on whatever issue divided the population and led to war, whether it was religion, ethnicity, regional origin, or social class. Apportioning jobs on the basis of identity may generate corruption, often dilutes the merit principle, and might create jealousies and inefficiency but, more important, it will likely to go far in preserving peace (Gaub, 2010: 14–16). In the military realm, putting ethnoreligious or tribal quotas into practice is a similarly difficult endeavor that can be accomplished according to different methods and with varying levels of success. Nonetheless, fostering the creation of a truly national identity, particularly in the armed forces, is an important long-term objective.

Of course, failing to bridge ethnic divisions can have severe consequences. In Bosnia, the unusual strategy of keeping soldiers in units segregated by religion may have been in large part responsible for the preservation of divisions, aversion, and distance between different ethnic communities in the military long after the end of hostilities (Alexa and Metzsch, 2003). The Lebanese Armed Forces—like most postconflict armies such as those of Guatemala, Mozambique, Nicaragua, Nigeria, Sierra Leone, and South Africa—have been fully integrated and have not experienced any major sectarian problems. In Salvadoran army units, too, former guerrillas and government soldiers have quickly found a way to put the past behind them and concentrate on their tasks. As in many other settings, regular and intensive training together helps not just the army's professionalization but also deepens its esprit de corps and common purpose (Gaub, 2011: 22–27). Ejecting the most radical members of both the former guerrilla force and the government's army—that is, individuals the erstwhile combatants find most objectionable—from the new integrated military clearly serves both the purposes of reconciliation and building a cohesive army. Another policy that has paid dividends in El Salvador has been the granting of government or private charitable aid to families of fallen or wounded guerrillas. This has created goodwill toward the new regime and eased the way into the new army for the former opponents of the regime.

Gradualism is particularly important in post–civil war reform implementation. Given that in civil wars, by definition, the warring sides know one another, healing the rift between them is likely to take far longer than between strangers after a war between different states. For starters, the amount of time between the realization of opposing sides that a cease-fire and peace settlement are desirable and the actual signing of a peace agreement may be considerable. True reconciliation between the erstwhile antagonists is nearly always a long process; indeed it might take generations. At the same time, it must be relentlessly pursued because as long as politics is about identity rather than issues, nationalist and extremist parties will enjoy an influential political role at the expense of political organizations with more substance-oriented agendas. In armies divided along ethnic, religious, or tribal lines, one's group membership is likely to trump all other loyalties, though in time, particularly given favorable political and socioeconomic developments, commitment to democracy may become more robust and, eventually, might even dominate other forms of identity. The need for gradualism, power sharing, and ethno-religious accommodation all suggest that post–civil war environments require a delicate balancing act between all these and often some additional factors. Bringing former warring parties back together and then moving forward as one is what post–civil war settings are all about.

Reconstructing the security sector may be the most important undertaking of the Libyan and Yemeni regimes. In the former, hundreds of rival militias represent different tribes from different regions of the country. Most of them need to be disarmed and dispersed although some could be integrated into a new national army. But, as is clear from the foregoing, which militias to disarm and break up and which ones to include in the new national force is, indeed, a tremendously complex and politically sensitive undertaking (Kadlec, 2012; Lacher, 2013). Even prior to the Arab Spring, Yemen had more guns than people; bringing normalcy to the country, which is now more extensively armed, particularly with two insurgencies continuing (the Houthi rebellion in the north and the separatist conflict in the south) will be exceedingly difficult.

Conclusion

Reestablishing security and creating or re-forming a unified national identity are some of the indispensable tasks that must be high on the agenda of Arab reformers in the wake of the recent uprisings. Several weighty issues are common to all of them. Improving the effectiveness of the armed forces is just as important in Egypt, where the bloated military has been frequently described as lacking professionalism (Kandil, 2012: 192; Sayigh, 2012: 9–10), as in Libya and Yemen, although as in so many respects, Tunisia is an exception. To appreciably raise the level of professionalism, however, the state needs to be both willing and able (i.e., in control of the military) to drastically transform the armed forces, and the generals must be amenable to change long-ingrained routines. These conditions have seldom been present at the same time elsewhere, unless the military was built from the bottom up following catastrophic defeats (as in post–World War II Germany and Japan).

Another concern that is likely to change all of these military establishments is the creeping Islamization of their respective polities. Prior to the Arab Spring, these armies were dominated by secularist or moderate Islamist cadres, given the political elites' deep suspicions of, or overt antagonism toward, religious extremism. Just how they are going to respond to the growing influence of Islamists in the new governments will depend primarily on the manner and directness with which religious currents are going to affect them. The gradual but unrelenting Islamization of the Pakistan Army, which started during the presidency of General Muhammad Zia-ul-Haq (1978–1988), is an illustrative example (Fair, 2012; Nasr, 2004). For another set of examples one might look at the experiences of Eastern European countries that were suppressed by the Soviet Union following World War II; their armies underwent a forced transition to a culture dominated by Marxist-Leninist ideology (Jones, 1981).

In sum, defense reform is an important and urgent task for the Arab republics with the notable exception of Tunisia. The conceptualization and preparation of these reforms are complex and difficult projects in themselves; implementation will be even more so. The fundamental prerequisite to these undertakings is the establishment of governments interested in and capable of pursuing them. The governments also must have enough leverage over the military to get the generals to accept and, ideally, embrace defense reform. These endeavors, as I have attempted to outline, have been beset by many obstacles in settings far less challenging than those of the contemporary Arab republics.

6

Democracy vs. Rule of Law: The Case of the Egyptian Military

Robert Springborg

As Nathan Brown (1997: 241–242) astutely observes, Egypt has had rule by law, not rule of law. The legal system has served less to constrain than to legitimate authoritarian government and to facilitate its rule. The "coup-volution" of February 2011 raised hopes for a democratic transition in Egypt, of which the transition from rule *by* to rule *of* law would be a vital component (Toronto, 2011).[1] Subsequent events have eroded those hopes, if not dashed them altogether, raising the questions of why the bright prospects for a democratic transition propelled by a mass mobilization not witnessed in Egypt since 1919 dimmed so profoundly, and what the outlook is for a resurgence of those prospects.

The answer to both queries lies primarily with the power and preferences of the two principal political actors spawned by more than half a century of authoritarian rule—the deep state, at the heart of which is the military, and the Muslim Brotherhood. Democracy requires that a broader range of actors compete for and indeed share political power, and that acting collectively through constitutionally empowered institutions, they control the armed forces. After January 2011, the military and the Brothers both sought to construct new, noninclusive political orders over which they would preside without serious political, constitutional, or legal constraints. Ultimately the military won that struggle for power by staging a coup against the Brotherhood government in July 2013. It immediately sought to exterminate the Brotherhood, assert direct control over the civilian state, and emasculate both civil and political society. Almost two years later it had partially achieved those objectives, although a simmering quasi insurgency, stagnating economy, repeated postponement of parliamentary elections, manifestations of popular discontent, and ever-increasing violations by the military-dominated government of human, civil, and political rights indicated at the very least that its grand project of subordinating the country to its will was still a work in progress.

Included in the collateral damage to the country's institutions has been the effectiveness of the military itself. The combination of its confrontation with a near-insurgency for which it is woefully unprepared and the overall mission creep implied in its running of the government and the economy while trying to organize a new polity has undermined what relatively little combat effectiveness it possessed under Hosni Mubarak. The winner-take-all strategy pursued by the military has thus eroded its own capacities, vitiated what little rule of law prevailed under the Mubarak and Brotherhood regimes, and as yet failed to bring about the military's primary objective of building a corporatist "military society" as Anouar Abdel-Malek (1968) labels the predecessor regime headed up by Gamal Abdul Nasser. The country's political community has been eroded and its national institutions degraded, rendering achievement of the military-led project all the more difficult. The tale of the winner-take-all contest between the military and the Brotherhood and assessment of its consequences are thus interesting, even if disappointing, additions to the literature on failed democratic transitions.

The Odd Couple: Cohabitation of Regime and Brothers

Political cohabitation of the military with the Muslim Brotherhood was not novel after the fall of Mubarak. Indeed, it is deeply rooted, albeit intermittent, in the political dynamics of twentieth-century Egyptian politics. The military was not even a semiautonomous actor under Kings Fuad and Farouk, monarchs who utilized the Brothers as a political and ideological counterweight to the secular nationalist Wafd Party. For their part the Brothers played both ends against the middle, seeking covert royal patronage while simultaneously conspiring with the military against the king and the British. Following the July 1952 coup, the Free Officers and the Brothers "cohabited" for almost two years before Nasser embarked on an ultimately vain effort to liquidate this last viable civilian political organization (Kandil, 2014).[2] During that tumultuous period, Nasser laid the tripartite foundations for the deep state, consisting of the military, the security services, and the increasingly overgrown presidency itself, including the Republican Guard attached to it (Kandil, 2012; Sirrs, 2010).[3]

The strength and political ambitions of the military, the most powerful institution within the deep state, compelled Nasser and his successors continually to upgrade the security services as a counterbalance, while also implementing various strategies to subordinate the military to their personal control. Nasser finally purged his nemesis Field Marshal Abdel Hakim Amer in the wake of the 1967 war, before then turning effective command of the military over to Soviet advisers, who busied their protégés with preparations to regain the Sinai. Anwar Sadat employed a strategy of limited war in his October 1973 campaign so the military could not be seen as the liberator of Sinai, a title he sought for himself through his egotistical, personal diplomacy conducted in tandem with Henry Kissinger. The "Hero of the Crossing" then began a continual purge and churning of the officer corps, ensuring that none of the real military heroes of the 1973 war or any other officer would be in a position to challenge him. Humiliated and resentful officers are alleged in fact to have been the prime movers in his assassination in 1981. Mubarak ultimately finished Sadat's removal of potential challengers when he purged Field Marshal Abd al Halim Abu Ghazala in 1989, replacing him after a brief interval with the lackluster Muhamed Hussein Tantawi. Mubarak, however, relied less on manipulation of individual officers than on an across-the-board strategy of enriching the corps in order to retain its loyalty. To that end he resisted internal and external pressure to reap a "peace dividend" by downsizing the armed forces, which he retained at some half a million men. He dramatically increased the comparatively small military economy he inherited from Sadat in 1981, and he broadened the access of officers to civilian employment in the state administration and public sector. General Tantawi became in effect the chief executive officer of "Military, Inc.," the soft cop in Mubarak's strategy for control of the armed forces, whereas General Omar Suleiman, Mubarak's trusted and ruthless head of the General Intelligence Directorate, was the hard one (Siddiqa, 2007).[4] The officer corps, in effect, was partitioned off from the political system, a status it was willing to accept as the corollary of its enrichment.

Preoccupied with control of the military, the primary threat to their rule, Egypt's presidents have paid much less attention to the Muslim Brotherhood, the only civilian political organization capable of posing a challenge. Nasser sought unsuccessfully to destroy it, his failure explaining in part his successor's restoration of the previous policy of cohabitation, which had been abruptly terminated in 1954. The inherent precariousness of a tacit alliance between two authoritarian actors with profoundly different agendas, however, resulted in its breakdown as the Brothers' political base proved threatening to a president intent on reaching a peace treaty with Israel. Mubarak, not threatened by organized leftist forces as his predecessor had been, had less need to empower the Brotherhood as a counterbalance, but he nevertheless crafted a cohabitation strategy that was intended to cause the Brothers to serve his political purposes. Theirs was, however, a more complicated, even contradictory relationship. On the one hand,

Mubarak sought to use the Brotherhood as a counterbalance to secularists, whereas on the other hand, he needed it for the demonstration effect it would have on those who feared Islamists, both domestic and foreign. So the relationship zigzagged throughout the Mubarak era as one or the other need took precedence and as he had to permit greater or lesser political freedom, primarily as a result of US pressure.

By 2011 then both the deep state and the civilian political system had become misshapen. The military had grown fat and lazy; at the same time, the muscular security forces under the Ministry of Interior were working overtime to contain the opposition, secular and Islamist. These two coercive state institutions, always competitors, came to resent one another profoundly. As if this situation were not enough threat to the coherence and stability of the deep state, the presidency had been harnessed to the cause of implementing a Mubarak family succession, thus alienating both the military and at least some in the security forces. Weakened by these internal tensions, the deep state confronted a population that was profoundly disenchanted with the political status quo but lacked any strong political organization other than the Brotherhood.

So when the populace arose to challenge the Mubarak regime, the deep state, unable to act coherently, collapsed after eighteen days, leaving its military core in place, the security services in shambles, and Mubarak in jail. For their part the Brothers emerged as not only the sole political actor with a popular base but one with a hierarchical organizational structure akin to a military command and control system. From the military's perspective, therefore, the Brothers were ideal civilian partners. They could not only deliver the "street" but do so in authoritarian fashion, enabling the military to cut clandestine deals with a leadership that had the capacity to implement them forthwith rather than haggle over them publicly. By contrast, secular "revolutionaries" lacked both mass organization and elite decision-making coherence, rendering them far less attractive to the military as collaborators in reimposing order. Moreover, the long, if checkered, history of political cohabitation by the military and the Brothers had accustomed them to dealing with one another. For their part the Brothers had always sought the relationship out of their need for access to and protection from the state. As for the military and the regime for which it provided core support, the Brothers had provided a political counterbalance, a connection to street-level politics, and, as the years passed, social services in the wake of the state's steady retreat from the Nasserist social contract. So the political logic of a revived or altogether new military-Brotherhood cohabitation, at least as a temporary arrangement as both struggled to subordinate the other, was apparent and appealing to both parties.

The devil of a reconfigured cohabitation deal was truly in the details, however, for no obvious, clear line could be drawn between civilian and military authority and responsibilities. Previous partitioning had been based on a vastly disproportionate balance of power between the two sides. The line of authority had left little space for the Brothers, limiting their operations almost entirely to the realm of civil society rather than within the state. Now, however, the Brothers aspired to exercise power within the state itself, so a new partition line had to be drawn. The most obvious line was that which separated national security from other governmental functions. The military under General Tantawi, however, was unwilling to cede that much space, for such relinquishment would threaten military interests in the economy and indirect control over much of the state structure itself. For their part the Brothers saw an opportunity not only for marginal gains within state institutions responsible for low policy but for real and substantive ones in high-policy areas including finance, foreign policy, domestic security, and even some areas of external national security, especially that related to the Israel-Palestine conflict. The Brothers also entertained the hope that they, rather than the military, would end up as the senior partner in the new cohabitation agreement. But that they could even aspire to do so in less than two years was probably beyond even their most optimistic appraisals. How the Brotherhood, which for decades had played the cobra against the military and regime's mongoose, managed to even try to reverse the roles so quickly is a question worth a brief attempt to answer.

The Odd Couple: Redrawing the Partition Line

The military emerged from the coup-volution with its reputation intact, if not enhanced. The forces mobilized onto Egypt's streets were reformist rather than revolutionary in that they sought only the removal of the Mubaraks and those cronies implicated in their alleged misdeeds, not the destruction of the deep state and its military foundation. The slogan "the army and the people are one hand" reflected the limited objectives of the reformers and served to ensure that the military not become collateral political damage of the attack on Mubarak. The armed forces emerged from the coup-volution with their command structures intact and with few desertions in the face of protests, reflecting the fact that they were not the protesters' target and suggesting comparatively little intrainstitutional tension and conflict (*Al-Ahram Weekly*, 2013b).[5] Even before Mubarak fell, the military high command reconstituted itself as the Supreme Council of the Armed Forces (SCAF), its eighteen or so members representing all branches of the armed forces and the chief intelligence and combat commands. The game of reconstituting the political order, therefore, seemed to be the united military's to lose.

Closer consideration of the SCAF and the broader military, however, reveals some internal weaknesses and an environment not necessarily conducive to its political aspirations. The officer corps had grown comfortable in its convenient, nondemanding, subterranean role in a deep state headed by a president from its own ranks who asked only for loyalty, not for performance. Its leadership was old, with Tantawi himself in his upper seventies. He and his closest colleagues were discredited by rumors of corruption and by their close association with Mubarak. It was common knowledge within the officer corps that young, ambitious officers with US training were systematically sidelined, the entrenched high command seeking compliance and lassitude, not ambition, energy, and professionalism. The SCAF was therefore vulnerable to dissatisfaction within the officer corps; it had indeed been subject to continuing and intense pressure from the street. Additionally, the high command was unaccustomed to the give-and-take of politics, of which it had no previous experience, unlike the Ministry of Interior's security agencies, which were the regime's primary tools with which to manipulate and control political forces.

Besides its own weaknesses, the military also confronted a more difficult challenge to reconstituting a political order than was first apparent. General Tantawi's political trial balloon in the form of "casual" but media-choreographed appearances in downtown Cairo was immediately deflated by negative popular reaction. Hence, the option of direct rule, at least by General Tantawi, was rejected. Tantawi was personally ill suited to a political leadership role, so he had to find a replacement from within the military who could secure its loyalty and cohesion, achieve popularity, and not trigger an immediate, negative reaction from the increasingly powerful Brothers. A further challenge faced by the high command was that the United States was actively counseling against direct military rule. As for coalition options, the military distrusted secular revolutionaries both because some demonstrated an interest in subordinating the military to civilian control and because they lacked a strong political base and political experience. They were, in sum, too much of a threat and promised too little deferential political assistance to be attractive to the SCAF. So the military was left with no alternative to the Brotherhood to serve as its civilian partner in a reconstituted polity that would preserve military powers and privileges, while at least appearing to empower civilian forces unleashed by the coup-volution. The military thus set itself the task of crafting a partition plan that awarded it the predominant political space but would nevertheless be accepted by the ever more powerful Brothers and public opinion more generally. Having rejected the obvious alternative solution, which was to orchestrate a democratic transition that would empower secularists as a counterbalance to the Brothers, but at the potential cost of some civilian oversight and reduction in privileges, the military lent its weight to the Brothers.

The military was thus dealing with the Brothers from a position of at least temporary weakness, a situation that became manifest in June 2012. In the wake of the Brotherhood's victory in the presidential election, for which the SCAF was ill prepared in part because of the Brother's adroit political maneuvering, the panicked SCAF decreed new constitutional provisions that would severely curtail the powers of the new civilian president. The SCAF relied upon allies in the Supreme Constitutional Court to craft those provisions as well as to rule in the SCAF's favor upon them. This was a hasty, even desperate measure reflecting General Tantawi's political ineptness and fear of the military's political marginalization. The Brothers sensed they now had the upper hand and could undermine the SCAF rather than having to accept its dictates. The SCAF decree had left them little choice, for it targeted both the legislative and executive branches, which the Brotherhood controlled, and, implicitly and subsequently, their dominant influence on the street.

So by midsummer 2012 the SCAF appeared to be in a possibly terminal political decline. It had squandered much of its original popular support, even among secularists, who in large numbers voted for the Brotherhood presidential candidate, Mohamed Morsi, rather than the SCAF's "nominee," Ahmed Shafiq. Having ordered inept and brutal military police to contain demonstrators in front of the Cairo broadcast headquarters at Maspero in October 2012 and then in November on Muhammad Mahmoud Street leading to the Ministry of Interior and the Parliament, the SCAF's claim that the military was one with the people had lost credibility. Its politically costly attempt to regain control of the street had been necessitated by its distrust and contempt for the Ministry of Interior's riot control forces, thereby necessitating the use of military troops. The internal, subterranean politics of the deep state seemed to have been carried over inappropriately into the new era by a military leadership unable to grasp the significance of the changed political context. The SCAF's collaboration with *fulul*, "remnants" of the ancien regime, most notably presidential candidate Ahmed Shafiq as well as judges, further demonstrated its backward-oriented political vision, thereby diminishing its already tarnished reputation yet more. Washington's position was implicitly to support the Brotherhood in opposition to the SCAF, as evidenced by its criticism of the June constitutional decrees (Eleiba, 2013b).[6]

In the face of these setbacks, Tantawi and his closest colleagues on the SCAF apparently decided that they had to prepare for a transition of military leadership to a younger generation that was not tainted by direct association with the Mubarak regime. This new military leadership also had to avoid the appearance of a mortal threat to the Brotherhood, now consolidated in the presidency, the upper house of Parliament, and the committee established to draft the new constitution. The key figure in this regard was

Tantawi's handpicked successor, General Abdel Fattah el-Sisi, at fifty-seven the youngest member of the SCAF. His last-minute recruitment into the SCAF, presumably intended to provide him the key platform from which to make his and the high command's bid for power, was justified on the basis of his position as chief of military intelligence, a position that gave him some responsibility for monitoring Islamists and put him in direct contact with the Brotherhood's leadership.[7] General Sisi, who had ordered "virginity tests" on female demonstrators arrested by military police and held in military custody, did not hide his views that Islam provided a comprehensive framework not only for personal life but also for constructing and operating the political system (el-Sisi, 2006).[8]

When the military bungled a security operation in the Sinai in August 2012, the occasion provided justification for President Morsi to move against Tantawi and his allies in the SCAF and key operational commands, installing General Sisi in his place, presumably just as Tantawi had anticipated. Quickly promoted to minister of defense, Sisi, who had ranked number 67 in seniority in the army, then retired off another hundred or so officers but left in place several key Tantawi loyalists and rewarded Tantawi himself and other notable retirees with honors and, in some cases, new posts in the military economy. So Sisi established himself as the undisputed head of the military, with the blessing of both that institution and its chief rival, the Brotherhood (Hessler, 2013: 24–30).[9] The way had been cleared for redrawing the partition line between the military and the Brothers, with the latter believing they had the chalk in their hands, when in reality the newly reconstituted high command was preparing to remove them.

The task of completing the repartition proved to be remarkably easy. The SCAF had made clear the military's red lines in the "constitutional principles" document issued by Ali al Salmi, the minister of "democratic transition," in November 2011. It assigned the military the exclusive right to "revise and supervise" all that is related to the armed forces, including its budget, which was to be presented as one number in the state's finances. The military was also to have veto power over a declaration of war issued by the president (el-Ghobashy, 2012).[10] These and associated demands from the military were incorporated into the new constitution written and promulgated under the Brotherhood's supervision in a matter of weeks at the end of 2012.[11] The key articles provided for national security policy and oversight of the military to be vested in a National Defense Council (a majority of whose members were to be drawn from the military), for the minister of defense to be an active-duty military officer, for a continuation of conscription, and for the preservation of a separate military legal system with jurisdiction over civilians (M. S. El-Din, 2013).[12] The Parliament was thus denied any constitutional power to oversee the military and its budget, while Military, Inc. was guaranteed a steady flow of quasi-slave labor in the form of conscripts. Ostensibly then the military emerged from the constitution promulgation phase of the transition with the scope of its authority enhanced rather than diminished (Ibrahim, 2012a).[13] No previous constitution in independent Egypt, dating to the first in 1923, had awarded the military such specific, wide-ranging powers (Ashour, 2012).[14] Egypt's new order, however, like the old one, was not constitutional in the sense that this document did not underpin the rule of law by providing definitive and enforceable norms and procedures. In the first instance, the manner of drafting and ratifying the 2012 constitution detracted from its legitimacy, whereas in the second, the combination of its loose wording and the pattern of manipulation by the Brothers suggested that the promulgation of the constitution signaled an intensification of political struggle toward victory by any means, rather than the structuring of it clearly and precisely within a consensual, democratic constitutional framework. So the key political actors, the Brothers and the military, were left to define the borders between their respective spheres of power through a winner-take-all battle for power.

Tensions in the Brotherhood-Military Relationship

No sooner had the constitution been ratified than signs of tension between officers and Brothers began to emerge, including in the area of greatest sensitivity in the overall relationship, that of control of the means of coercion, including the military itself. Since the Nasser era, known members of the Brotherhood and even those with close relatives as members have been denied access to the military and police academies, in effect the only pathways into the respective officer corps. Conscripts in both have also been screened for Brotherhood membership, although this filtering process has been less rigorous than that for the academies (Aclimandos, 2012). So in the wake of the Brotherhood's ascension to legislative and executive power, the question immediately arose as to whether its members would continue to be denied access to the military and security forces. The Brother's supreme guide, Mohammed Badie, seemed to weigh into what had up to that point been a largely subterranean dispute, when in an interview he alleged that the principal reason for the poor performance of the military and Ministry of Interior forces in dealing with security challenges was the lack of appropriate motivation on the part of its members. Badie's allegation was immediately interpreted as meaning that he believed Islamism was the appropriate inspiration for such motivation or, in short, that he was demanding access for Brothers to the armed forces (Eleiba, 2012c).[15] Against the backdrop of extensive discussion in the media as to whether the Brothers would seek *akhwanat* (instrumentalization or monopolization) of those forces by subjecting them to their will and mission, Badie's remarks stimulated an immediate, negative reaction from the Ministry of Defense (Eleiba, 2013a).[16]

Although the specific issue of recruitment of Brothers into the armed forces remained unresolved, the Brothers moved on another front to assert themselves over the Ministry of Interior. In the so-called Ittihadiya demonstrations, being those in early December 2012 in front of the presidential palace in Heliopolis, Central Security Forces riot control troops did not prevent protesters from reaching the walls of the palace itself, apparently because commanding officers sought to embarrass the president therein (Eleiba, 2013a).[17] Similarly, Republican Guard forces, whose command is shared between the minister of defense and the president, also stood aside (Hessler, 2013).[18] Morsi and his fellow Brothers were outraged, deeming the lack of protection an attempt by the leadership in the Ministry of Interior to bring the Brothers down and by the minister of defense to portray the army as "neutral" rather than allied with or subordinate to the Brother president. Not strong enough yet to attack the Ministry of Defense, Morsi went after the Ministry of Interior. In the immediate wake of the ratification of the constitution, Morsi carried out a cabinet reshuffle, replacing Ahmed Gamal El Din with Mohamed Ibrahim. The latter quickly retired off senior officers close to his predecessor.[19] In this cabinet reshuffle only one portfolio other than that of defense (civil aviation) was awarded to a military officer. Coupled with this reshuffle was the announcement of eight new appointments to the key security positions of provincial governor. These are cabinet-level positions but they report operationally to the Ministry of Interior.[20] Under Mubarak the majority of governors had been military or police officers. Morsi's appointees, by contrast, were active members or sympathizers with the Brotherhood, typically with professional backgrounds. The newly appointed minister of state for local development was Muhammad Bashir, a senior member of the Brotherhood's Guidance Bureau and professor of electrical engineering at Cairo University. This post, along with the governorships, is vital in the political control of rural Egypt, for it commands the sprawling network of local government employees and also has influence over governors themselves. Almost simultaneously, the announcement was made that the prohibition on policemen having beards, which was challenged by the Brothers shortly after the coup-volution, had been rescinded. Sources in the Brotherhood also floated a proposal that noncommissioned police officers, *amin shurta*, be permitted to immediately apply to join the ranks of commissioned officers, as opposed to having to wait twenty-four years as previously had been the case prior. Incumbent officers registered their disapproval, interpreting the proposal as an attempt to "encourage the rising of a new, low-skilled class of subordinates devoted to the cause of the Muslim Brothers" (Aclimandos, 2012: 11).

The Brothers thus made more progress in asserting themselves over the weaker of the two state institutions of coercion, but the one that nevertheless then had primary responsibility for controlling the street. The Brothers were thus busily drawing the partition line with the Ministry of Interior on their, rather than the military's, side.[21] The army's disdain for the Ministry of Interior's security forces and its unwillingness to initiate a reform of these forces when the SCAF was in the driver's seat was thus a strategic blunder on which the Brothers sought to capitalize. Also worth noting is that President Morsi was careful to avoid any criticism of the military. Indeed, after becoming president he continually heaped praise upon it (Ibrahim, 2012b).[22]

Jousting over control of national security policy proceeded behind the scenes as Morsi was maneuvering to gain control over the Ministry of Interior. On December 26, 2012, Minister of Defense Sisi issued Armed Forces Decree 203/2012, which banned foreign ownership of land in the Sinai Peninsula (Ibrahim, 2012c). Eyebrows were immediately raised at this apparent impingement on presidential powers. The Ministry of Defense justified the move by saying that the Sinai is a military zone, thus under its minister's jurisdiction. Security concerns, according to its spokesperson, necessitated that radical elements, including Palestinians, not have ownership in areas bordering Gaza and Israel. Independent speculation suggested alternative or additional motives. Most notably General Sisi was claimed to fear the consequences of Qatari money being used, with the full knowledge of President Morsi, to facilitate purchases by Palestinians and Islamists of those border areas, thus providing a means for leverage by Morsi, backed by the Islamist-sympathizing Qataris, over Gaza and the Israelis (Ibrahim, 2013).[23] This interpretation suggested that the military remained intent on pursuing a cautious approach to the Palestinian-Israeli conflict, whereas Morsi was seeking to lay the groundwork for an intensification of pressure on the Israelis and influence over the Palestinians, all with the backing of funding from a sympathetic Gulf source. This interpretation, which subsequently was confirmed by Sisi's military government, was further supported by reports that the Brothers sought to appoint Rifaat Muhammad Tantawi as foreign minister in the January 2013 cabinet reshuffle because he was perceived as a strong proponent of strengthened Iranian-Egyptian ties and a strong opponent of the peace treaty with Israel. According to Eric Trager (2013), the military "prevented his appointment." So during the year in which the Brothers and the military "cohabited," the military retained the upper hand in the formation and implementation of the external aspects of national security policy, although it was under sustained pressure from the Brothers.

The Gulf featured in another shadowy event that suggested tension between the armed forces and the president. On January 8, 2013, the *Lon-*

don Times alleged that the commander of the Quds Brigade of the Iranian Revolutionary Guard Corps, General Qassem Suleimani, had visited Cairo for two days in December on the invitation of the government of Egypt and the Muslim Brotherhood. Egypt's ambassador to the United Kingdom immediately challenged the veracity of the report. His source was likely from within the Egyptian Ministry of Defense, which was obviously displeased with Morsi's attempt at reconciliation with Iran (Sultan, 2013). Whatever the truth regarding this alleged visit, subsequent events clearly demonstrated Morsi's intent to move closer to Tehran. Later in January he received Iranian foreign minister Ali Akbar Salehi in the presidential office, at which time he extended an invitation to Iranian president Mahmoud Ahmadinejad for an official visit (*Al Quds al Arabi*, 2013).[24] With longstanding strategic and operational relations with Saudi Arabia, the Egyptian military was wary of all such efforts, including the proposal by President Morsi for Iran to be included in a quadripartite effort to resolve the Syrian crisis, a proposal immediately rejected by Riyadh. Again the evidence indicates that Morsi was seeking to reorient Egyptian national security policy, which the military resisted.

The public images of the heads of state and the military were also subject to competition. As the conflict between the Brotherhood and secularists over the drafting and ratification of the constitution intensified, General Sisi sought on December 11, 2012, to defuse it by proposing a national dialogue between Islamists and secularists to commence the following day at the Olympic Village, over which he would preside. This proposal brought an immediate rejection from the president's office, suggesting that Morsi did not want to appear subordinate to Sisi, nor to place himself on par with his secular challengers by accepting to negotiate on neutral territory rather than in the president's office.[25] Sisi was thus placed in the embarrassing position of seeing his invitation dismissed, suggesting that Morsi considered him and the military not to be his equals but his subordinates. How Sisi felt about this loss of political face is unknown, but presumably he took it as an insult to him and the institution he commanded (Ezzat, 2012).[26] His manifest interest in projecting a positive image of the military was reflected in the public relations campaign that he launched shortly after taking over as minister of defense. On the thirty-ninth anniversary of the 1973 Arab-Israeli War, for example, the Armed Forces Morale Affairs Department organized a three-day festival "where the public will be invited to attend a military show . . . [and] attendees will receive free gifts dropped by aircraft." That department also announced it had produced six new films of up to three hours in length to "acquaint the new generation of young military officers with the lessons of the October War" (Ibrahim 2012a). Those lessons included veneration of the roles of Generals Saad el-Shazly and Mohamed Abdel Ghani el-Gamasi, then chief of staff and chief of operations, respectively, both of whom Sadat had removed. The army simultaneously unveiled its new uniform, implying that this venerable institution remained in the vanguard (Ibrahim, 2012a).

The Brotherhood demonstrated its ascendancy over the military in matters of domestic politics during the January 2013 drafting of the new election law by the Shura Council (Maglis al Shura), the upper but only functioning house of Parliament. The military's allies within the Shura Council unsuccessfully opposed an article that extended the franchise to citizens who have not performed military service (G. E. El-Din, 2013). Almost simultaneously President Morsi's fact-finding committee investigating killings of protesters during and after the January 25, 2011, uprising issued a report alleging that "security officials and the military used live ammunition more than once" (Abdel-Baky, 2013). It also condemned the abuse of female protesters, including so-called virginity tests that were ordered by General Sisi. The report called upon Parliament to amend the military code to permit investigations of army officers implicated in killings and rights abuses. The committee's report appeared to be an effort to sully the reputation of the military, possibly including General Sisi, while also raising the threat of prosecution (Abdel-Baky, 2013). The military's reputation was further damaged in early 2013 when ten crewmen vanished from a fishing boat off the northwest Mediterranean coast. Relatives of the victims stormed the Alexandria naval base and set several buildings alight in protest against the navy's alleged failure to respond quickly and effectively to the vessel's distress calls (*Ahram Online*, 2013a). Morsi also achieved a symbolic advance against secular traditions in the military and security forces when he had the incoming head of the General Intelligence Directorate, General Mohamed Raafat Shehata, take a newly worded oath that commenced with "I swear by the greatness of Allah and his Holy Book to be loyal to the Arab Republic of Egypt" (Abdel-Baky, 2012a). This first-time reference to Allah and the Quran was interpreted as "a step in the Muslim Brotherhood's plan to tighten its grip on state institutions" (Abdel-Baky, 2012a). In early October 2012, President Morsi suddenly announced that Egypt's chief administrative watchdog, the head of the Central Agency for Organization and Administration, Safwat al Nahas, a former military officer who had held the position since 2004, was to be replaced by a woman who had no connections to the military (*Ahram Online*, 2012a).

Finally, key material interests were at stake in the increasingly tense relationship between the Brothers and the military. The presidency and the military have long contested control over the lucrative energy sector. This tension had been reflected in the drawn-out battle over the contract to export gas to Israel during the Mubarak era. That battle had finally been won by President Mubarak in league with his close ally, former intelligence officer Hussein Salem. Active duty and retired officers were sprinkled into state-owned and private oil and gas companies. The entire sector operated off budget, not subject to oversight by the Central Auditing Agency or any other governmental regulatory body. In addition, the military and officer economies steadily expanded into energy-intensive industries, such as cement, steel, fertilizer, and ceramics, the profits of which were underwritten by rents in the form of subsidized energy inputs (Abul-Magd, 2011, 2012a; Marshall, 2012; Marshall and Stacher, 2012).[27] With Mubarak gone, the reallocation of these energy rents was on the table and this became a cause of additional tension between Morsi and the military. The government was under pressure from the International Monetary Fund to reduce energy subsidies as a condition for a standby agreement. Moreover, gas production was rapidly falling behind demand, forcing Egypt to seek gas imports from Algeria and Qatar. In late 2012 the government announced small price increases for gas and electricity provided to industry, but some question seemed to remain as to the timing and extent of their application, possibly because of push back from the military. Given suspicion within the military of Qatari motives, there may also have been hesitation on its part regarding gas supplied from that country, which would have enhanced its leverage over Morsi and Egypt as a whole. Both material and strategic interests, therefore, placed Morsi and the military in different positions on energy issues. Even though such differences were manageable under Mubarak because of the relatively well-established spheres of influence of the two parties, they were more difficult to contain in the context of uncertain jurisdiction and power that prevailed when Morsi was president.

Tensions between the military and the Brotherhood suggested that the two were on a collision course, a conclusion that President Morsi hesitated to draw virtually until the coup unfolded on July 3, 2013. He and his organization were so intent on asserting control over the entire state, including its coercive arms, and apparently so convinced of Sisi's loyalty, that they were oblivious to the mounting threat. For its part, the military had four choices in the wake of the coup-volution. It could have submitted to the Brotherhood's efforts to instrumentalize it as an Islamist force, akin in some ways to what happened in Iran. Alternatively, it could have sought to hold the partition line as close to the preexisting demarcation under Mubarak as possible, whereby influence over state institutions, the economy, and national security policy was shared in some mutually agreed fashion, trusting that over time a stable modus operandi, as with Mubarak, would be established. A third possibility was to decide that the Brothers posed a mortal threat to the military's and nation's interests, so stage a coup against it, seizing and exercising power in its own right for at least some time, possibly then seeking another civilian partner either with which to cohabit or to subordinate to the military's political will. Finally, the military could have chosen democracy as the preferred alternative. This last would have required it to dig in against the Brothers, defending constitutionalism and the rule of law while doing all possible to enhance the power and capacities of political actors who could serve as counterbalances to the Brotherhood. In the end the military chose to go it alone, crushing the Brotherhood while constructing a transparent political façade over its own rule, thereby raising the question of why it rejected so utterly and completely the democratic option.

Why the Military Did Not Choose or Was Forced to Accept Democracy and the Rule of Law

The key reason why the military did not opt for democracy as a better alternative to a marriage of convenience with the Muslim Brotherhood or to its own direct rule is that democracy would have demanded reform of the military itself, not just reform of the polity. Because the Egyptian military is so bloated, so ill prepared to discharge the increasingly wide range of national security duties, so poorly trained and its officer corps so enriched through corrupt practices, it simply could not afford to allow the nation to know these unpalatable truths (Fomby, 2006; Springborg, 2013: 93–109).[28] If Egyptians were aware of how fundamentally incompetent, expensive, and corrupt their military is, demands for its subordination to civilian control would surely intensify. Voices would be raised for it to be shorn of its economic largesse and for the dismantling of the "officers' republic," as Yezid Sayigh (2012) has so aptly dubbed military control over the state apparatus. The military, in sum, would wilt in the sunlight of transparency, an inevitable component of democracy.[29]

The military high command thus would have had to be willing to surrender the institution's political, economic, and even social power to the unknown, untested political forces that would compose a new democratic order. The latter would very likely challenge the military's economic, administrative, and political roles. Further barring the democratic option was that the officers not only disagreed over which civilian political forces should prevail but also shared a general contempt for civilians and were persuaded that the military was the rightful and only effective guardian of the nation. The officers have been indoctrinated with the view that they can do it better, whatever the "it" is, ranging from managing economic enterprises, to directing state instrumentalities, to fielding sports teams.[30] So only brave or foolish officers would seek to convince their colleagues that the military should serve as the midwife of democracy, handing their institution's power and privileges over to a mixed bag of civilians. The quasi insurgency that erupted in the wake of the July 2013 coup reinforced the belief that only the military could be trusted to guide the nation in such parlous times.

The chances of the military choosing democracy are thus slim, but what about its being forced to accept it by energized and effective civilian political actors united in that aim? Contemporary prospects for such a broad-based coalition, which would have to include Islamists of various persuasions as well as their traditional opponents among liberal secularists, Christians, women, and others, remain as remote as they had become by 2012 when the Brothers overreached and by so doing destroyed what remained of the "revolutionary" coalition of 2011. Persistent resentment of the Brotherhood, combined with security fears intensified by the quasi insurgency, has caused most non-Islamist political actors to accept military rule as the least bad alternative, if not actually to endorse it.

A "pacted" agreement to democratize, which would necessitate imposing civilian control on the military, is thus unlikely in the absence of another major crisis, whether of a political or economic nature. Such a crisis, moreover, might pave the way not for democracy but for systemic collapse or some other cataclysmic outcome. The 2011 coup-volution was in effect a reform movement led by the urban middle class, which felt economically and politically marginalized. Since then the economy has further deteriorated as population growth has intensified. Dramatic increases in poverty and unemployment have been coupled with ever more frequent and widespread breakdowns of public services including electricity, water, sewerage, and public health. The military has assumed ever more direct control and responsibility for those services and for running the economy as a whole. This control has placed it potentially in direct conflict with an increasing proportion of the economically deprived and politically powerless population. Such conditions foster revolution, not reform, or at least widespread mobilization of those below middle-class status. In that event, the people and the military would not be "one hand" but would contest openly and violently for power. Although ultimately this path could be one to democratic control of the armed forces coupled with the establishment of rule of law, that path is clearly lengthy and strewn with innumerable obstacles. In the meantime, Egypt's military rulers remain unconstrained by a constitution or laws, without a judicial system enforcing them or a parliament making them. Increasingly their rule is based on sheer coercion and intimidation, thus taking Egypt back to the darkest days of repression in the Nasser era.

Notes

The author would like to thank his colleague Thomas C. Bruneau for his comments on an earlier draft of this chapter. The views expressed are those of the author and not necessarily those of the US Department of Defense.

1. The term *coup-volution* was coined by Nathan W. Toronto (2011).
2. On the Brotherhood's political maneuvering, see Kandil (2014).
3. On the origins and evolution of the deep state and relations within it, see Kandil (2012). On the historical development and contemporary roles of the various intelligence agencies in Egypt, see Sirrs (2010).
4. The term *Military, Inc.*, coined by Ayesha Siddiqa (2007) in reference to Pakistan, is very applicable to Egypt.
5. Some thirty officers joined protests against the Supreme Council of the Armed Forces–dominated government in April, May, and November of 2011. All were ultimately arrested and imprisoned, with the maximum sentence handed down being thirteen years, subsequently reduced to three. Most or all of the imprisoned officers were released by January 2013. The highest ranking among them was Captain Muhammad Wadi'a. See *Al-Ahram Weekly* (2013a).
6. The Obama administration persisted in its policy of signaling support for the Brotherhood even after it had crafted and promulgated an antidemocratic constitution, as suggested by the dispatch of 20 F-16 fighter planes and 200 tanks in January 2013, a move widely viewed in Egypt as Washington's endorsement of President Morsi, primarily for having maintained the peace treaty with Israel. See for example Eleiba (2013b).
7. According to one Brotherhood source, "General Sisi was in contact with the president following most SCAF meetings. He was known to us as the General." According to this source, Sisi acted as the intermediary between Morsi and Tantawi in negotiating the latter's departure. See Eleiba (2012b).
8. General Sisi, for example, commences a paper on "Democracy in the Middle East" with the observation that religion is essential to politics in the Middle East and goes on to argue that democracy must "show respect to the religious nature of culture" and if democracy is presented as "a secular entity," it will fail and society will be fractured. Moreover, he claimed, democracy in the Middle East should be based on Islamic concepts, such as the caliphate, *baya* (consensus), and *shura* (consultation), not on the separation of powers between the executive, legislative, and judicial branches (el-Sisi, 2006).
9. Telephone conversations with Peter Hessler, December 2012.
10. For a review of the document and steps leading up to it see el-Ghobashy (2012).
11. For a comparison in Arabic of Article 196 of the final constitution and the relevant Articles 9 and 10 of Ali al Silmi's document, see http://www.facebook.com/photo.php?fbid=10151255367310211&set=a.420084860210.213239.523705210&type=1&theater.
12. Although the first three of these constitutional provisions defend the military from civilian oversight, the final one empowers the military over civilians. The extent of that empowerment is suggested by the fact that 12,000 civilians were subject to military trials during the reign of the SCAF. For examples of how the armed forces have utilized this power in specific cases, see Mai Shams El-Din (2013).
13. Reports at the time nevertheless indicated that the military's representatives in the Constituent Assembly "appeared not to be satisfied with many of the articles" (Ibrahim, 2012d). The key issue apparently turned on the creation of a National Security Council, which would have had responsibility for handling crises and which would have provided the presidency and cabinet ministers some measure of civilian control over the military in emergency situations. Such a council had been created during the Sadat era, but the military had essentially ignored it. The 2012 constitution provided for both a National Security Council as well as a National

Defense Council. The latter, the senior of the two bodies, was to be dominated by the military and was presumably created by the Muslim Brotherhood to mollify the military. The National Security Council, which had significantly more civilian members, was retained to provide some leverage for the Brotherhood over security issues. See Ibrahim (2012d).

14. Article 20 of the 1954 draft constitution, for example, strictly prohibited the prosecution of civilians in military courts, whereas Article 198 of the 2012 constitution allows military trials for civilians "when a crime harms the armed forces." For an overall comparison of the 2012 to earlier constitutions, see Ashour (2012). That the military intends to use these powers was demonstrated early in 2013, when it arrested the owner of a computer shop on the grounds that he possessed classified information on an army unit. Sent to a military trial, he argued that he worked as a computer technician and his customers were officers who kept their personal information on his computer while he fixed theirs. See *Al Masry al Youm* (2013a).

15. For an account of this affair, including Badie's statement, see Eleiba (2012c).

16. For the Brotherhood's view of these events, see the interview with Mahmud Husayn, the secretary-general of the Muslim Brotherhood, by Eleiba (2013a).

17. This interpretation is offered by Mahmud Husayn in his interview with Eleiba (2013a).

18. For an eyewitness account of this demonstration and reaction to it by Ministry of Interior and Republican Guard officers, see Hessler (2013).

19. Prior to the removal of Gamal El Din, the Brotherhood had pressured him to appoint sympathetic officers to key positions in his ministry, including Khalid Tharwat, who in October 2012 was promoted to director of the Egyptian Homeland Security department, which had been created in May 2011 to replace the notorious State Security Investigations Services, the principal political security force under Mubarak. Tharwat was selected because, atypical for a former officer in the State Security Investigations Services, "he had never been involved in interrogating or torturing members of Islamist groups." See Abdel-Baky (2012b).

20. Of the eight appointees, seven were affiliated directly or indirectly with the Brotherhood or the Salafis, while one, in the remote New Valley Province, was General Sisi's nominee (*Al Masry al Youm* 2013b). The cabinet reshuffle resulted in the Brotherhood's Freedom and Justice Party holding nine portfolios. The supreme guide, Mohammad Badie, as well as the Salafi leader Hazim Salah Abu Ismail, personally attacked Minister of Interior Ahmed Gamal El Din just prior to the reshuffle (el-Bey, 2013).

21. The continual criticism of the Ministry of Interior by high-ranking Brothers as being a tool of the ancien regime hostile to the president and the Brotherhood more generally is suggestive of their persisting desire to bring the ministry under their control. See, for example, the comments by one of Morsi's key aides cited by Dina Ezzat (2013).

22. His positive statements about the military even extended to former SCAF leaders General Tantawi and Sami Anan, whom he referred to as "great commanders" who did "a great job in protecting the revolution." See A. Ibrahim (2012b).

23. For interpretations of General Sisi's motives in issuing Decree 203, including that of protecting the material interests of officers involved in the smuggling trade, see Ibrahim (2013).

24. For an analysis of the warming of Egyptian-Iranian relations, see *Al Quds al Arabi* (2013).

25. General Sisi's statement called for a meeting of "national unity for the love of Egypt to bring together partners of the country in the presence of the president of

the republic," while observers interpreted it as a "warning to Morsi and his Islamist supporters" (Ibrahim, 2012e).

26. Reporter Dina Ezzat (2012) notes that this rebuff of Sisi's initiative resulted from Supreme Guide Badie overruling President Morsi's initial acceptance of the proposal by Sisi. She observes that "this is not the first sign of tension between Morsi and al Sissi," and that "new tensions in relations between the president and the army add to existing unease and even anger between the presidency and both police and intelligence."

27. On the various elements of the military economy, see Marshall and Stacher (2012), Marshall (2012), and Abul-Magd (2011, 2012c).

28. For frank assessments of the Egyptian military, see Fomby (2006) and Springborg (2013).

29. This is not to say, however, that awareness of the need to reform the military is completely lacking. Indeed, since the appointment of General Sisi as minister of defense, various official statements have been issued stressing the need for the armed forces to "operate professionally," to "improve combat efficiency of its officers and soldiers," and to "have nothing to do with politics" (*Al Masry al Youm* 2013d). At a military exercise in October 2012, General Sisi proclaimed that "we are determined to exert all possible efforts to improve our army's capacities and combat readiness, to protect and develop its equipment, and to preserve the efficacy and morale of the troops" (Eleiba, 2012a).

30. This interpretation is based on the author's interactions since 1965 with Egyptian active-duty and retired officers.

7
Subjecting the Military to the Rule of Law: The Tunisian Model
Risa A. Brooks

Establishing democratic control of the military is a fundamental task facing citizens and political leaders who seek to build the rule of law in postauthoritarian states. It is also a task fraught with challenges. Democratic control redefines how decisions are made about the most elemental aspects of a military: its mandate, regulation, and resources. It entails subjecting a constituency with substantial manifest or latent political power to public accountability. Militaries, even those that have long been subjected to civilian control by an autocratic leadership and proven compliant to political authority, must be transformed so that that they act at the behest and behalf of the public in a manner that is transparent and respectful of civil rights. Indeed, the more one understands the magnitude of the challenges involved, the clearer it becomes that democratic control of the military is essential to the development of the rule of law and the advancement of its core principles.

In this context, the Tunisian military is, by many accounts, exceptional in its readiness to adapt to the principles and institutions of democratic control. Although establishing such oversight of the military is commonly viewed as a formidable, if not an insurmountable, challenge in transitioning states, it is often portrayed as unproblematical and straightforward in Tunisia (Hanlon, 2012a; Sayigh, 2011).

Less understood, however, is why the Tunisian military may be prepared to subject itself to democratic control. If the Tunisian military will readily accommodate democratic control, what quality or qualities precisely explain its willingness to do so? Answering this question helps explain the

Tunisian case but also potentially sheds light on the factors that more broadly may affect a military's receptivity to fundamental reform.

In this chapter, I provide an explanation for why the Tunisian military may be receptive to democratic control. I argue that the willingness is largely shaped by the legacy of the political strategy of control of prior authoritarian regimes, specifically, the country's former political leaders, Habib Bourguiba and Zine El Abedine Ben Ali, who employed a strategy focused on marginalization and exclusion. This strategy relegated the military to the periphery of the regime, allowing a strong corporate identity to flourish while habituating its leaders to civilian authority and legal and regulatory control. In addition, this strategy militated against the military developing a corporate investment, or its officers a personal stake, in the authoritarian status quo. Together these factors help explain why the Tunisian military does appear to be well positioned to submit to democratic control.

To advance this argument, I begin this chapter by defining and discussing key indicators of democratic control of the armed forces. I then develop the concept of the strategy of exclusion and marginalization. I discuss the experience of political control under Bourguiba and Ben Ali and argue that a combination of historical conditions along with deliberate choices made by the leaders led to the adoption of this strategy of marginalization and exclusion. I explain how this strategy renders the Tunisian military well positioned to adapt to institutions essential to the rule of law. As such in this chapter I hope to illuminate the Tunisian experience but also shed light on possibilities and constraints governing the process of bringing militaries under democratic control in general.

The Meaning of Democratic Reform of the Military

Advancing democratic control of the military involves the establishment of formal and informal institutions that promote the military's accountability and transparency (McFate, 2008).[1] Examples of such reform include (1) the establishment of a civilian secretary or minister who exercises final authority over both the military's administrative and personnel matters, (2) the establishment of institutional mechanisms through which democratically elected leaders in the legislature and executive can request and review information about the military's organization and related matters, (3) the conferment of powers of appointment and dismissal to the political leadership that enable them to hold military leaders accountable, and (4) the assignment of budgetary control over the military to the political leadership. Scholars commonly identify these institutional changes with the enhancement of democratic control and view the military's ability to obtain or retain or prerogatives in these areas as symptomatic of military leaders' reserving power over their own affairs (Pion-Berlin, 1997; Stepan, 1988).

Democratic control of the military implies institutional and organizational changes that are distinct from the attainment of civilian control of the military. Empirically and analytically, civilian control can occur in the absence of democracy and is often observed in autocratic states where political leaders dominate procedural and policy decision. By contrast, to achieve democratic control, the political leadership must be both civilian and democratically elected, and it must possess oversight powers that enable it to regulate the military in an open and transparent manner. The distinguishing feature of democratic control is public accountability, which requires institutional mechanisms that enable the monitoring of the military and the provision of checks and balances on military behavior. It is in this regard that democratic control is integral to the establishment of rule of law and also why it amounts to such a substantial paradigm shift in civil-military relations for postauthoritarian states.[2]

The Prospects for Democratic Control:
The Centrality of Past Strategy of Political Control

Here, I argue that Tunisian military's acceptance of democratic oversight was shaped by the "strategy of political control" employed by the country's former autocratic leaders. By "strategy of political control," I refer to the approach that political leaders in an authoritarian state employ to accommodate the military to their rule. The underlying assumption is that in a political system in which coercion and repression play a significant role in maintaining the status quo, the military serves as the regime's protector of last resort. This role imbues the military with latent or manifest political power. Such power presents a fundamental governance dilemma for the political leadership: How to guarantee control of the military and ensure that it will act to safeguard the leadership's position and policy preferences?

Especially important in understanding the Tunisian case is the development of what I call a strategy of control through exclusion or marginalization. This strategy entails circumscribing the military's bargaining power in the regime so that it has little leverage to pursue its own ends. This is accomplished through a number of means: carefully regulating the military's size and budget, isolating the military and limiting its access to core centers of power in the regime, and empowering other actors to balance its centrality in the regime (e.g., developing alternative forces such as paramilitaries and interior ministry forces to handle domestic policing and to supply security in the capital and other sensitive areas). The military is largely kept at a distance from the politics of the state: it is not treated as empowered third party but as a resource-constrained constituency. These measures limit the military's political leverage as well as its organizational capacity to act against the regime or challenge the political leader's position or policies.

In summary, marginalization achieves the twin objectives at the heart of autocratic governance of the military: (1) it limits the political influence of the military and its capacity to extract concessions and exercise pressure in policy decisions, and (2) it complicates the effort to remove a leader from office by limiting the military's capacity to do so, by circumscribing its size, mandate, and equipment and providing well-resourced opponents to defend the regime.

Given these benefits, marginalization would seem an obvious strategy of choice for autocrats as they aim to control the military. Yet as the Tunisian case highlights below, the strategy is not without its drawbacks.[3] Marginalizing the military mitigates the risk facing autocrats that an empowered military will use its power against them, as outlined by Milan Svolik (2012). Yet it invites another potential problem: a military with little investment in the regime will also have little incentive to come to its defense. In the case of Tunisia, Bourguiba and Ben Ali hedged against this threat to regime survival by building up regime "insurance" in the form of skilled security forces under the Interior Ministry as well as a presidential guard and private militia.

A second reason why leaders may "choose" to refrain from a strategy of marginalization is that not all strategies are equally available to every autocratic regime. Structural and historical factors shape the context in which political leaders then make choices that sustain or subvert a particular pattern of civil-military relations. Attention to the historical circumstances of the Tunisian regime and its evolution, as described below, is central to understanding why, for example, the military was controlled with a strategy of marginalization and exclusion.

Control Through Exclusion: Implications

The strategy of political control employed by a leader determines the likely response of the military to the prospect of reform by shaping its material incentives and organizational culture. Below I discuss the way a strategy of marginalization and exclusion may shape the character of the military generally. In subsequent sections, I discuss the implications for the Tunisian military specifically.

Organizational Culture

One of the most important ramifications of a strategy of control through marginalization and exclusion is how it shapes the organizational culture within the military, most specifically, its "corporateness" and "role beliefs." I use the term *corporateness* to refer to the degree to which (1) officers and leaders within the military identify with the military as an overarching organization, and (2) whether or not their affiliation with the organization trumps other affiliations. Although officers may have specific organizational identities (conventionally, by service branch or combat arm), there is a larger organizational identity that supersedes these subordinate affiliations. A military that is "corporate" is dominated by military officers who see themselves as part of a strong internal hierarchy in which the organization is distinct from other institutions in the state; they identify strongly with the missions and roles of that institution above all else.

In using the term *role beliefs*, I follow work by Samuel J. Fitch (1998), David Pion Berlin, Diego Esparza, and Kevin Grisham (2014), and Brian Taylor (2003) in emphasizing what military officers view as their "appropriate role or mission in the state." The emphasis here is on the particular historically and structurally based organizational culture that has emerged within a military (Kier, 1997). This culture is shaped by daily roles and missions and is reflected in documents and regimens. Different forms of political control may also shape military culture (e.g., norms of professionalism) as well as the military's corporate identity (Bellin, 2004, 2012; Huntington, 1957).

The strategy of marginalization and exclusion is likely to have significant implications for corporateness and role beliefs. Consigning the military to the periphery of the state creates space for the military to develop a separate, overarching identity, which can be reinforced through education, service, and doctrine. In addition, peripheralization insulates the military from the cross-pressures of the regime's internecine politics; officers do not have to accommodate the competing identities that may emerge when military leaders are engaged in the politics of the civilian state. In short, this structural situation can provide the framework in which corporateness can flourish (Bellin, 2004, 2012).

Marginalization may also foster and reinforce specific beliefs among military officers about the "appropriate" boundaries for their participation or intervention in politics. Since very little of what the military actually does on a daily basis has to do with engagement in politics or the civilian sphere of the state, one by-product of this strategy over time may be that the military leadership comes to see intervention in domestic politics as beyond its mandate (Pion-Berlin, Esparza, and Grisham, 2014; Taylor,

2003). The military's exclusion from politics means it is apt to view such activities as outside its normal role and identity.

These militaries also do not face the same internal pressures for politicization that are often observed in other autocratic regimes. For example, in Egypt, political concerns permeated the military and affected its management by senior officers; military leaders policed the ranks to ensure that junior officers were politically palatable and would comply with the accommodations made to the country's political leaders (the patrons of the senior officers) (Bou Nassif, 2013; Sayigh, 2014). Such politicization is not the case where the military is kept at an arm's length from politics.

Material Interests

In addition to these ideational effects on corporate identity and role beliefs, this strategy of control has important implications for the material interests of the military and consequently for the military's investment in sustaining the institutions of the autocratic regime. The strategy of marginalization denies the military, and more importantly its officer class, special perquisites or elevated salaries. It also denies them an arms industry or a private industrial economy. In addition, this lack of economic status may be paired with a deficit in what might be called regime "respect." The political leadership may not engage in symbolic acts recognizing the status and prestige of the military such as trumpeting the armed forces in public propaganda or attending signature military events. Even more pointedly, the regime may be disparaging to officers and leaders (as in the case of Tunisia). Consequently, the officer corps, either as individuals or as an organizational whole, lacks any substantive interest in sustaining the autocratic status quo.

Notably, the lack of investment in the autocratic status quo does not guarantee that the military will favor the political system's replacement with a democratic regime. The military's willingness to defect from the status quo might just as easily lead it to support the replacement of one autocrat with another or for the reformulation of the autocratic regime in ways that deliver improved status to the military. In the Tunisian case, the military's "defection" from Ben Ali during the 2010–2011 protests did not necessarily imply a commitment to democratic institutions.

Nevertheless, the military's marginalization under this system of control means that democratic transition does not appear potentially injurious; it does not raise the specter of a decline in the economic and political status for the military. The marginalized military has less to lose from the establishment of institutions that promote public accountability over its affairs because the military has not been a principal beneficiary of the autocratic state. In fact, it may experience an elevation in status and an improvement in resource allocation when placed under the control of a popularly elected legislature.

Social Standing

A strategy of marginalization strategy may also have an indirect effect on the military's social standing, principally because it leaves the military out of domestic policing. The military is not "sullied" by involvement in the harassment and persecution of the country's citizens; rather, the interior ministry or other security forces are charged with that task. By not being identified by the mass public as the agents of the oppressive regime, the military preserves its status and may be viewed if not positively, at least neutrally by the population.

Analytically, the impact of the military's social standing in shaping its attitude toward reform is contingent on other variables. For example, in the case of Chile after the rule of Augusto Pinochet ended, the military's ability to draw on public esteem enabled it to resist efforts to impose democratic oversight on the armed forces. Nevertheless, public esteem for the military removes a crucial obstacle to reform: it means that the military faces fewer risks in submitting to institutions that subject it to public control. The public is not necessarily seeking revenge against the military, either in the form of withdrawing resources or engaging in harsher retributive measures. In other words, democratic reform may be seen as less risky by military leaders if the demos views the armed forces favorably.

Political Control in Tunisia

As I describe below, Tunisia's leaders employed tactics that resemble a strategy of control through marginalization or exclusion. In this section, I discuss structures of political control first under Bourguiba and then under Ben Ali.

The Bourguiba Legacy

Although this chapter is principally focused on the implications of marginalization for the Tunisian military's actions in the 2010–2011 uprising and beyond, it is worth briefly considering why a strategy of marginalization originated and was initially employed by Bourguiba. One important factor is the formative events of the regime's origins. In contrast to the Egyptian case, in which the military installed the regime of Gamal Abdul Nassar through a coup, or the Algerian case, in which Algerian forces fought the French for independence, the Tunisian military did not bring the Bourguiba regime to power in 1956. Consequently, in contrast to its neighbors, the military in Tunisia did not play a vanguard role as a symbol of revolutionary change in a newly established republic, nor did it enjoy substantial political power upon independence. Bourguiba was a civilian politician, nationalist, and leader of the Neo Destour movement who, through political pressure and coercive methods (bombings and attacks on colonial forces and facilities), eventually pressured France into granting Tunisia's independence. The army was created in 1956 with Tunisians who had served in the French army and the Beylical Guard under French administration (Jebnoun, 2014). As James Gelvin (2012: 68) aptly captures it, "the Tunisian army is the product of independence, not the progenitor of independence." In short, the military lacked the power to shape the terms of its accommodation to the newly established Bourguiba regime.

In addition, Bourguiba's own preferences and political worldview seemed to play a role in his embrace of the marginalization strategy. Bourguiba was a committed Francophile and lawyer who apparently was influenced by French civil-military relations (Lutterbeck, 2012: 5). He also mistrusted the military (Bou Nassif, 2015). When he became the country's first president, he did so with a very particular conception of the military's role in the state in which it would only play a small role in politics (Lutterbeck, 2012).

Finally, also worth noting is that despite tensions at times with its neighbors, Libya and Algeria, Tunisia has historically not fought large wars or faced significant external and internal threats (with the exception of the contemporary threat posed by insurgents based in the country's mountainous border area with Algeria). Marginalization was facilitated by the absence of serious external challenges, making it easier to maintain a small and under-resourced military.

Once in power, Bourguiba organized civil-military relations to sustain the military's minimal role in politics, establishing routines and institutional roles accordingly. For example, he disenfranchised the military politically. The officer corps was denied the right of political association. Officers were prevented from playing a role in the ruling party. Bourguiba also deliberately distanced the military from daily policing and coercive functions, assigning that role to the Interior Ministry and the collection of police, security, and paramilitary forces under its control (Ware, 1985).

So enduring was the marginalization of the military from regime politics that when Ben Ali became minister of the interior in 1986 under Bourguiba, he was the first career military officer to be appointed a cabinet-level post (Gassner, 1987). Ben Ali had attended the Saint-Cyr Military Academy in France and also received intelligence and security training as a young officer in the United States. Early in his career, he served in military intelligence. Later, when serving in the Interior Ministry, he helped coordinate security in the aftermath of the bread riots that occurred in January 1978. After a stint as Tunisia's ambassador to Poland, he returned to the Interior Ministry, moving up through its leadership ranks. Finally in April 1986, he was appointed interior minister (Gassner, 1987; Jebnoun, 2014; Murphy, 1999; Ware, 1985). Ben Ali also retained that portfolio when in October 1987 he became prime minister. One month later he maneuvered Bourguiba, whose health and erratic behavior had become increasingly serious, out of office through a bloodless coup (Borowiec, 1998).[4]

Political Control Under Ben Ali

When Ben Ali assumed power after Bourguiba's ouster, he inherited the structures and methods of political control established by his predecessor. Ben Ali innovated within the parameters of these extant structures. His method of political control represented a variation rather than a dramatic departure from the broad framework of political control established under Bourguiba.

In contrast to the armed forces in most Arab countries, the military in Tunisia was deliberately limited in size, resources, and mission. In 2011, the regular armed forces included a 27,000-strong army (of which approximately 20,000 were conscripts), a navy with 4,800 personnel, and an air force of 4,000 (IISS, 2012). The military's budget was set at approximately 1.4 percent of Tunisia's gross domestic product (GDP), placing Tunisia 109th in world rankings in terms of percent of GDP devoted to defense expenditure. This low ranking contrasted sharply with that of other states in the Arab world. Denied funding for major arms purchases, the military was often supplied with surplus equipment that was donated by foreign allies. In many cases the military lacked the resources to maintain what it did manage to acquire (Lutterbeck, 2012: 7).

In addition to keeping the military small, Ben Ali limited its role within the Tunisian state. The operational responsibilities of the military were circumscribed; the military played a role in infrastructure development, disaster relief, and humanitarian assistance. Moreover, the army operated alongside the Tunisian National Guard (a 12,000-strong paramilitary force under control of the Ministry of Interior) in border control and alone in southern parts of the country.[5] A central aim of these efforts was to tie down resources and keep the military occupied and distant from the capital (Jebnoun, 2014). The army also traditionally participated in regional peacekeeping missions.

Importantly, the military did not engage in policing and monitoring the civilian population. The military did not even operate in Tunis, a fact that reflected both its circumscribed mandate in the autocratic regime and also the regime's desire to limit the military's operations to outside the capital. Security in Tunis and other major cities was provided by the police and various forces controlled by the Interior Ministry. Outside of Tunis, in the countryside and smaller cities, the National Guard played the primary policing role. Hence, Ben Ali's deployment of the army to the capital on January 12 during the 2010–2011 uprising indicated the severity of the situation facing the regime (*Maghreb Confidential*, 2011a, 2011b). The Tunisian military had only rarely been called upon to actively participate in repressing political activity and reportedly disdained such roles.[6]

Whereas the military was kept on the sidelines, in contrast, Ben Ali sponsored a significant expansion of security forces housed in the Ministry of Interior.[7] Ben Ali's long career in intelligence and the security services meant that he favored these arms of the state over the military. After all, the forces of the Interior Ministry were the ones who initially assisted Ben Ali in his ouster of Bourguiba (Jebnoun, 2014: 300). Despite his military background, Ben Ali did not come to power at the behest of, or with the backing of, the military (Penner Angrist, 2013: 550).

Beginning in the 1990s, the size of the police and the nonmilitary security forces grew substantially, by some accounts quadrupling. These included forces under the formal control of the Interior Ministry, in addition to militias that were directly accountable to the president.[8] Indeed, the police were so omnipresent that at the time of the revolution, they were estimated to number between 120,000 and 200,000—an astounding figure for a country of 10.5 million (Lutterbeck, 2012: 9; Erdle, 2004; Goldstein, 2011; Henry and Springborg, 2011). As Christopher Alexander (2011) writes, "the police force, uniformed and plainclothes, became the regime's praetorian guard." Under Ben Ali's rule, the status and political importance of the security forces grew, overshadowing the military.

Within the Interior Ministry were several well-equipped and well-trained specialized forces. These included the Public Order Brigade (Brigade de l'Ordre Publique) or riot police, which played an important role in the regime's efforts to repress the 2010–2011 uprising (Amnesty International, 2011). In addition, the State Security Department was especially dreaded by the population and formally abolished in March 2011. Also important were the elite units of the the Interior Ministry's Intervention Forces, including the Rapid Intervention Response Brigade, the Anti-Terrorism Brigade, and the National Guard Special Unit, an elite tactical unit of the Tunisian National Guard. These units benefited from professional training and equipment and were known for their skill and specialization.

Also central to Ben Ali's security forces was his 5,000–6,000-strong Presidential Guard, which played an important role as protector of the regime. The Presidential Guard was notable both for being well equipped and well treated under Ben Ali.[9] Consequently, it remained loyal to the autocrat even as the protests escalated in January 2014. Immediately following Ben Ali's departure on January 14, the army (in combination with some segments of the police) was forced to conduct fierce gun battles around the capital, including at the presidential palace in Carthage and at the Interior Ministry, against remnants of the security forces who remained loyal to Ben Ali. These included members of the Presidential Guard and private militia recruited and directed by Ben Ali (Kirkpatrick, 2011b; Walt, 2011).[10] In contrast to the Tunisian military, these elements of the security forces enjoyed privileged status and access to the presidency and hence had a much larger stake in sustaining the autocratic regime.

Another tactic employed by Ben Ali to contain the military was to place it under the oversight of a civilian. In contrast to many other autocratic regimes, Tunisia had a civilian-led Ministry of Defense that placed civilians in charge of formulating and implementing decisions about the policy and administration of the armed forces. In a structure somewhat similar to that found in many democratic states, the chief of staff of the armed forces played the role of chief adviser to the minister of defense, managing coordination with the heads of the various service branches (Hanlon, 2012b).

At the same time, Ben Ali kept a tight grasp on promotions in the military and limited the number of general officers. In addition, prior to the appointment of Rachid Ammar in April 2011, Tunisia did not have a Joint Chiefs of Staff with a chairman designated to lead it, which prevented the emergence of an influential chief of all the armed services. General Rachid Ammar, the chief of staff of the army at the time of the uprisings, was not a prominent figure, consistent with the military's general reputation as the La Grande Muette ("the big silent one") (Sayigh, 2011).

In summary, Ben Ali's formula for keeping the military subordinate had been largely one of control through exclusion. The military was kept at a distance from the regime, both literally and figuratively, and its influence was balanced by a large police and security apparatus. Ben Ali's approach to controlling the military, moreover, contrasts with his approach to managing the regime more broadly. He ruled through direct control and management of a small cohort of elites who rotated in and out of government institutions, as well as through a clique of presidential advisers operating out of the palace. Power was increasingly concentrated in a narrow cohort with Ben Ali at the center (Erdle, 2004; Murphy, 2002; Penner Angrist, 2007).

Implications of Political Control: Explaining the Character of the Tunisian Military

The character of political control sustained by Tunisia's autocratic regime played a central role in shaping the military's receptivity to reform in the postauthoritarian period.

Corporate Ethos and Role Beliefs

As the argument above suggests, the isolation and marginalization of the Tunisian military during the reigns of Bourguiba and Ben Ali provided the foundation for the development of its organizational culture.[11] The relegation of the military to the periphery of the regime effectively granted the military significant organizational autonomy. Consequently, the military was able to sustain a corporate ethos that prioritized cohesion and meritocratic traditions within the officer corps and the institution generally (Gaaloul, 2011). In addition, the military's limited mandate, focused primarily on defense of the country from external threats, border control, and participation in peacekeeping missions, reinforced the military's role as the protector of state from external and radical threats rather than the protector of the state from its own citizens. Equally important, the limited budget allocated to the military meant that it performed these tasks with limited resources, thereby preventing the self-aggrandizement common among autocratic militaries that enjoy bloated budgets and inflated status.

Exclusion from political institutions also limited the vulnerability of the military to the mixed incentives and distortions that can result from participation in elite politics and patronage networks within the state. Temptations to become drawn into distributional conflicts were thus limited.

In this way, the military developed a strong corporate ethos in which officers identified with the military as a cohesive, distinct, and esteemed institution that operated apart from other institutions in the state. In addition, military officers developed what some analysts called a "republican" ethos. The military came to see its primary mission as safeguarding and abiding constitutional processes and procedures. As Yezid Sayigh (2011) writes, the Tunisian army was notable for its "adherence to the republican system, in particular the constitutional order and the pre-eminence of civilian control." This commitment to constitutionalism distinguished the Tunisian military from that of other republican regimes of the Arab world, and many analysts conclude that this particular quality made intervention in politics less likely. Such intervention was seen as outside the military's mandate and mission.

The military's republican culture may have also been reinforced by its relations with foreign military counterparts, especially those in the United States and France (Arieff, 2011: 21; US Embassy Tunisia, 2008). The United States, for example, had long cultivated military-to-military relations with Tunisia. The forces participated in annual meetings of a joint military commission and engaged in regular joint training exercises. Moreover, the Tunisian military benefited from two programs sponsored by the US Department of Defense, Foreign Military Financing (FMF) and International Military Education and Training (IMET), which in 2011 amounted to approximately $17 million and $1.7 million worth of aid, respectively.[12]

These activities facilitated interaction with officers in the US military and exposed Tunisian officers to norms of prioritizing professional expertise and protecting the integrity of the military institution. To the extent that these socialization processes matter, they may have served to reinforce meritocratic norms and support the conception of the military as operating outside of politics. This does mean that the military had a normative commitment to "democracy"; nor does it mean that its actions were not politically minded or lacked political implications (see the discussion of Rachid Ammar below in the days following Ben Ali's ouster). But the military did not see its role as that of an overt actor in the political process itself, no doubt a consequence of the military's socialization process, reinforced by its structural isolation from politics.

Clarifying the Importance of the Specific Character of the Tunisian Military: Beyond "Professionalism" and an "Apolitical" Military

The Tunisian military's corporate ethos, its apparent regard for constitutional processes and "republican principles," and its professionalism in its skill and training do not mean that it was inherently and reflexively "apolitical." Many scholars have used that terminology as shorthand to explain its decision not to use force to defend the Ben Ali regime during the 2010–2011 protests.[13] Two issues merit consideration in this regard.

First, even though the military may be lauded for not using force during the uprising, its actions were not apolitical. In fact, by not defending the regime, the military was playing an ineluctable, if not especially self-conscious, political role, both before and during the uprising (Penner Angrist, 2013). Admittedly, the Tunisian military did not actively oversee the removal of the president nor seize power after the transition as did the military in Egypt. Still, by refusing to use force to disperse the protestors and by standing by a stated mandate to protect state institutions, the military leadership was making a political decision—to not safeguard Ben Ali's position in power.[14] In other words, doing nothing may have been justifiable within the scope of the military's republican traditions, but that does not mean that doing nothing was not a political decision.[15] Given the centrality of the military as the coercive force of last resort in autocratic regimes, not stepping up in defense of the Ben Ali regime was a decision that was intrinsically political.[16]

Second, the decisions made during the final days of the uprising were also political in the sense that they meant the army, in particular, its leader, General Ammar, was de facto the key power broker in the country—a role that in the weeks following the protests became manifestly clear. Not only had the military refrained from defending Ben Ali, precipitating his departure from the country, but it also subsequently played a vital role in reestablishing control under a new government in the days that followed. Military personnel participated in the arrest of key officials and provided essential backing to the interim government led by Ben Ali's longtime prime minister, Mohamed Ghannouchi. In turn, it defended the government from threats posed by Ben Ali loyalists by engaging in a series of street battles with members of security forces allied with the leader.[17] In short, when General Ammar famously stated that "the army will protect the revolution," he was essentially admitting to the military's fundamental role as power broker (Kirkpatrick, 2011e). What is important in this context is how the military saw its appropriate role within democratic society—not that its leaders were somehow immune to political engagement and decisionmaking.

Role Beliefs and Socialization to Civilian Control

The Tunisian military's role beliefs can also be traced to Tunisia's long tradition of a civilian-led Ministry of Defense.[18] The minister of defense in Tunisia was not just the nominal leader of an otherwise military-dominated ministry; he was always a civilian who commanded significant authority (Lutterbeck, 2012).[19] This norm is crucial because it meant that the practice of civilian control of the armed forces was in place long before Ben Ali's departure. Under Ben Ali, of course, the civilian defense minister was part of the regime and answerable to the ruling autocrat. This situation was quite different from accountability to a democratically elected parliament. However, the structure of civilian oversight was in place, which appears to have prepared the Tunisian military, culturally, to accept constitutionally mandated oversight.

The Tunisian military's deference to political control by civilians was evident even during the tense days of protest in 2011 and, in particular, during the final days of the Ben Ali regime.[20] Noureddine Jebnoun (2014: 303–314) describes several incidents in which General Rachid Ammar refrained from overtly challenging decisions and orders from the Ministry of Defense and political leadership at this time. Instead the general limited himself to subverting or altering the implementation of these orders with the goal of diluting their significance. In one incident, for example, Jebnoun reports that Ammar was ordered to have the army officers remove their helmets so that they would resemble the National Guard (an Interior Ministry force). Ammar complied but had the army soldiers put on red berets to distinguish them so they would not be implicated in the violent suppression of the protests. Similarly, on January 13, 2011, Chief of Staff General Rachid Ammar was sent by the minister of defense to the Interior Ministry to help coordinate efforts to respond to the protests. At this point the army had deployed to the streets and was guarding government buildings. The fact that General Ammar reported to the ministry and thus did follow orders, even during a moment of intense stress on the regime, demonstrates that the routines and structures of civilian control were intact and entrenched.[21]

Material Interests in Sustaining an Autocratic Regime

The Tunisian military's receptivity to democratic transition and control was also a consequence of its material interests and its lack of investment in maintaining the autocratic regime of Ben Ali. This stance was in large part due to the material deprivation the military experienced under his watch. As discussed above, military leaders and officers were not well compensated, and the military was not well funded during the reign of Ben Ali. Hence neither the leadership nor the organization had any financial incentive to keep the existing political structure intact.

In addition, status issues turned the military against the autocratic regime. Ben Ali privileged the police and the Interior Ministry in the distribution of resources and status. By some accounts, this favoritism created resentment and dissatisfaction within the conventional armed forces (Erdle, 2010). As Querine Hanlon (2012a) reports, military officers were "at the bottom" of the hierarchy of security institutions. As one officer put it, "We were always last . . . [because] the regime did not like us" (4). Hence, the military risked no loss in privilege by abandoning the old regime.

The military's estrangement from Ben Ali's regime, however, went beyond the damage to its material status and prestige. There is evidence that the Ben Ali regime also purposely sought to humiliate and subordinate the military leadership. This humiliation occurred, most notably, in an incident in May 1991 referred to as the "Barraket Essahel Affair." Presumably, in order to provide a rationale for a purge of the military, the regime fabricated a coup attempt by military leaders. Up to 200 officers were taken to the Ministry of Interior, and some were submitted to torture and forced confessions. The regime maintained the coup plot was real, and only in the aftermath of Ben Ali's departure did the regime's treachery become known. The incident spoke to Ben Ali's approach to the military and the underlying divide between him and its officers.[22] More recently, some have speculated that Ben Ali may have played a role in the downing of a helicopter in 2002, a crash that killed General Ammar's predecessor and twelve other senior officers and personnel; the incident, if true, would have indicated further the estrangement of the military and the regime. Even if Ben Ali's role had only been indirect (in the sense that he refused to supply sufficient funding to ensure aircraft were adequately maintained), this behavior no doubt caused tension with the military (Jebnoun, 2014: 302–303).[23] In short, the military had many reason to lack attachment to the autocratic institutions of Ben Ali's regime.

Social Esteem

The relative social standing of the Tunisian military and the esteem it commanded in society are together another factor explaining the military's willingness to abandon Ben Ali's autocratic regime and bow to democratic controls. Thanks to its marginalization under Ben Ali, the military was left out of daily coercive functions and the policing of the population. Accordingly, it was not implicated in those detested policies when Ben Ali was ousted. The military was also not viewed as a principal beneficiary of a regime whose corrupt institutions delivered substantial perquisites to the ruling autocrat's family and cronies. Hence the military enjoyed substantial social standing and popular support in the wake of Ben Ali's fall. The military faced the prospects of democratic transition unclouded by a mistrustful population and an unsavory legacy of having acted as the coercive arm of a corrupt and brutal state. Submitting to democratic controls thus did not threaten the military with vulnerability to popular calls for retribution and dismantlement. As such, the military leadership could more easily submit to the authority of institutions that would make it accountable to the public.

In sum, these factors are critical to understanding the contemporary Tunisian military and its receptivity to efforts to assert civilian control over the military through parliamentary institutions. Material interests coincide with and reinforce a corporate ethos in which the military's roles and missions are conceived as limited to a narrow mandate to safeguard national security. Without a prominent role in bringing the regime to power and subjected to the politics of exclusion and marginalization, the military's regard for procedure and republican constitutionalism appear to have flourished.

In fact, by providing protections from the arbitrariness of the autocratic regime, the military may stand to gain under institutions that provide transparent and consistent oversight. The military may also benefit from democratic control if funding increases and better equipment is secured as a result. In this context, democracy could afford some protections and improvements in the organizational status and resources of the military that were absent under Ben Ali.

The Military and Democratic Reform: Preliminary Evidence

In the years since the revolution in Tunisia, the military appears to have accepted the principle of democratic oversight and civilian control despite facing significant challenges and considerable opportunities to intervene in politics and enhance its prerogatives. The authority of the president and civilian defense minister remained publicly uncontested by the military. The fact that elected political leaders and their civilian appointees remain in charge is notable (even if, at this point in the transition, the government falls short of providing comprehensive democratic control in the form of public accountability).

Especially significant is the fact that the military's political restraint persisted despite the challenges and humiliations it experienced. These have included the failure of the country's political leaders to comprehensively reform the Ministry of Interior, which in turn has burdened the military with significant responsibility for maintaining law and order (Sayigh, 2015; Tusa, 2014). Also challenging to the military has been the increasingly violent insurgency, including attacks by militants in July 2013 and July 2014 that left eight and fourteen soldiers dead, respectively (Tajine, 2014).[24] The military also has been humiliated by sharp criticism voiced by civilian politicians regarding its ineffectiveness (*Asharq Al-Awsat*, 2013). It has also endured the resignations of General Rachid Ammar in June 2013 and Ammar's successor, Brigadier General Mohamed Salah Hamdi, in July 2014 under the cloud of questions about their competency in managing the battle against the militants (*Asharq Al-Awsat*, 2014).

Tunisia has also experienced serious political crises, especially in 2013, in the aftermath of the assassinations of two opposition politicians in February and July, which caused dramatic strife and fears for the future of the transition. Although the crisis was ultimately resolved with the leader of the Islamist party agreeing to the creation of a "technocratic government," the resolution was preceded by several months of uncertainty and tension. This crisis alone might have justified an enhanced political role by the Tunisian military. In fact, the success of the Tamarod ("rebel") movement in Egypt in provoking military intervention against President Mohamed Morsi in early July 2013 prompted calls by the opposition for the Tunisian army to follow suit and oust the elected government (*New Zealand Herald*, 2013).

Most remarkable is the fact that throughout the transition, the Tunisian military has remained popular, with a Pew Global Survey from October 2014 reporting that 95 percent of respondents felt the military was having a "good influence" on the "way things are going" in the country (Pew Global, 2014). Had the military sought to play a more visible role in politics and to leverage that influence to enhance control over its own affairs, it clearly had opportunities to do so. Its reluctance raises a provocative counterfactual: had the military not been shaped by the legacy of marginalization, with the combined ideational and material implications of that strategy, might the Tunisian military have sought to insulate itself from civilian oversight, increase its resources, and assure its own prerogatives on the grounds that doing so was essential to safeguarding national security, if nothing else?

Tunisia's 2014 constitution is notable for the democratic oversight it imposes on the military. A comparison with the recent constitutions drafted in Egypt is instructive in this regard. Egypt's 2012 constitution, for example, provided that the minister of defense should be an officer, not a civilian, and allocated control of the budget to the National Defense Council, which in turn was to be dominated by members from the military.[25] The document also required the National Defense Council be consulted on any decision to deploy forces or declare war. Egypt's 2014 constitution went even further, assigning the Supreme Council of the Armed Forces the power to appoint the defense minister from within the military and adding the stipulation that the general officer appointed must have served five years in a major service branch.

This comparison sets into sharp relief the democratic parameters imposed on the armed forces by the Tunisian constitution of 2014.[26] According to the document, the elected president retains the powers of appointment and dismissal over military officers, serves as commander in chief, and is empowered to declare war and make peace agreements. The Tunisian armed forces are deemed a "republican army" that is "composed and structurally organized in accordance with the law" and must "remain entirely impartial." Although the constitution could have been more detailed in its delineation of the means of legislative and executive oversight, this failure seems largely due to the lack of expertise in specifying such matters by the civilians involved in the drafting process (Roach, 2013). At the least, the Tunisian constitution sets the stage for the development of such oversight.

All these reasons for optimism, however, do not mean that all is resolved regarding democratic oversight of the Tunisian Armed Forces. One shortcoming concerns legal provisions that continue to permit the trial of civilians in military courts and make criticism of the military a prosecutable offense. In January 2015, for example, a Tunisian blogger who posted about potential corruption and financial irregularities within the military was sentenced to prison under Article 91 of the Code of Military Justice, which renders "defam[ing] the military" illegal (Al Jazeera, 2015). Amendments to autocratic laws such as this one are essential if democratic reform is to become a reality.[27]

Conclusion

There is sound reason for optimism that the Tunisian military will continue to acquiesce to parliamentary oversight and democratic controls. Such optimism is rooted in the military's history, its structural role, and the methods of political control employed by the Bourguiba and Ben Ali regimes. These factors have shaped the military's organizational culture, which appears amenable to constitutionalism.

The Tunisian case, although unique in some ways, offers a number of lessons for scholars and practitioners. The first lesson of the Tunisian case is the fact that an autocracy's strategy of control, and specifically the adoption of military marginalization, can yield unanticipated consequences for the autocrat and even hasten his or her ouster. Many scholars have studied the variety of coup-proofing tactics available to dictators, which encompass everything from developing overlapping security services, to relying on favored minority groups in promotions and key appointments, to providing perquisites to officers along with equipment and resources to the military as a whole, to centralizing commands, to creating shadow commands and attaching political officers or commissars to them to monitor units (Biddle and Zirkle, 1996; Brooks, 1998, 2004; De Atkine, 1999; Picard, 1990; Quinlivan, 1999). What the Tunisian case suggests is a slightly different logic of control that involves disenfranchising the military politically and organizationally within the state. By minimizing the military's political roles, status, and resources, and balancing it with interior ministry forces, the political leader maintains control through exclusion or marginalization. The problem for a dictatorship, of course, is that marginalization of the military also means the military lacks investment in the status quo, either as individual officers or as an organization. This lack of investment shapes the military's calculations in deciding whether to revert to costly and normatively negative uses of force to defend the regime from civilian uprising. Such calculations may spell the downfall of the regime.

More broadly, the Tunisian case raises questions about the concept of military "defection" from political rule. It suggests that the specific method, or mechanism of coup-proofing, shapes the military's incentives to defect (McLauchlin, 2010). Rather than conceptualizing methods of political control as a list of interchangeable tactics, scholars might consider conceptualizing alternative systems of control and identifying empirical variants of these systems. One method may involve control through divide and rule (think Syria) versus control through a grand bargain between the political and military leadership (Egypt) versus control through marginalization (Tunisia). Each method of political control has different implications for how the military will respond when faced with challenges, such as the popular uprisings these states experienced in 2011.

A second lesson that might be drawn from the Tunisian case concerns the concept of "professionalism." Professionalism as a concept alone has limited explanatory power to account for Tunisia's positive trajectory, especially when the political roles played by other "professional" militaries in the region (e.g., Egypt) are taken into consideration. The Tunisian case instead points to the particularities of the corporate ethos or specific organizational culture of the armed forces, which is historically and structurally bound.[28] That the Tunisian military appears to be receptive to accommodating democratic institutions is a reflection of a lack of material investment in the former autocratic institutions of the state, as well as the military's particular organizational culture and its role conception in the Tunisian state. The particularities of the military in question, in turn, are likely critical to understanding its adaptation and willingness to abide by rule-of-law institutions and accommodate democratic control of its organization. For those seeking to advance the rule of law, understanding the character of the military in question, as it has been shaped by the history and choices of former political leaders, is crucial.

Notes

1. An alternative approach might stress the impact on actual security outcomes, such as the protection of personal and human security, which is often associated with "effective" security sector reform, but I choose the more proximate outcome of looking at the changes in institutions.

2. Conceived this way, "democratic control" is a continuous variable, in which different levels of control are observed not only in transitioning states but in consolidated democracies as well.

3. In fact, by keeping the military small and depriving it of status in the regime, the autocrat may foster the rationale or incentive for the very military intervention he seeks to preclude; a principal grievance in coups over time is deprivation and suppression of officers' prerogatives and the military's organizational interests (Nordlinger, 1977). According to Lutterbeck (2012), the military in Tunisia, for example, greatly resented its state of "beggardom" (7).

4. According to Borowiec (1998), Ben Ali relied on forces from the National Guard and not the regular army to deploy to key sites in the capital setting the stage for the bloodless coup that ensued. Also see Cody (1987).

5. See the description, for example, offered by the minister of defense to US Embassy officials and leaked by Wikileaks (Wikileaks cable/09TUNIS506).

6. Exceptions include the 1978 and 1984 bread riots (Kamm, 1984). In 2008, the military had been called in to provide reinforcements during in the Gafsa region (BBC Monitoring [Middle East] 2008). Also see Amnesty International (2009).

7. On this tactic of political control, see Quinlivan (1999), De Atkine (1999), Picard (1990), Biddle and Zirkle (1996), Brooks (1998), and Belkin (2005).

8. The police numbered 40,000 under Bourguiba according to Kallander (2011); also see Alexander (1997).

9. Many rank and file in the national police by contrast were poorly paid and equipped, possibly because employment in the police force apparently doubled as kind of jobs program under the regime (Amara, 2011a; Daragahi, 2011; Kallander, 2011).

10. These forces engaged in looting and violence, which appeared to have been part of a strategy to sow chaos and lay the groundwork for Ben Ali's return to the country, forcing citizen patrols to mobilize to protect their neighborhoods (Al Jazeera, 2011a).

11. On the importance of how military organizations understand their appropriate roles and missions in society and the state see Taylor (2003) and Pion-Berlin, Esparza, and Grisham (2014).

12. In 2009 total FMF aid was $12 million, and $17 million in 2011. Tunisia relied on FMF to maintain its 1980s- and 1990s-era US-origin military equipment, which accounts for 70 percent of its total inventory. Since 1994 Tunisian has been one of the top-twenty recipients of IMET, which was close to $2 million in 2011. In addition, Tunisia in 2011 received $20 million in Section 1206 funding, which provides US Department of Defense funds for use in training and equipping the military's maritime security capability to aid counterterrorism. The US-Tunisian Joint Military Commission meets annually, and joint exercises are held regularly (Arieff, 2011).

13. References to the apolitical nature of the Tunisian military are often used as a shorthand explanation for why the military acted as it did in January 2011. What precisely is captured by that concept, however, is rarely explored. For a discussion of events that underscores the military's role as power broker, see el-Amrani (2011), Murphy (2011), and Cockburn (2011).

14. Granted this position was one that Tunisian military officers could argue accorded with the military's constitutionalist role to uphold the republic. See the interviews of Tunisian senior officers cited in Bou Nassif (2015) that show how military officers justified their actions as consistent with their republican ethos. As he observes, all the officers had to do was to stand by and let the status quo fall apart during the uprising. Such a stance is different from engaging in a coup, which would have been contrary to the noninterventionist tradition.

15. Some ambiguity remains over what Ben Ali explicitly ordered Army Chief of Staff General Ammar to do and whether he told him overtly to fire on protesters, and if so, the manner in which the orders were conveyed. A lengthy investigation by Al Arabiya (2012) suggests that no such order was given, a position that is supported by solidly researched scholarship by Bou Nassif (2015) and Jebnoun (2014). Bou Nassif (2015) links the origins of the story that Ammar refused orders to fire to a Tunisian activist who was trying to split the military from Ben Ali. The fact remains that the military did not step up in defense of the regime and aid what was clearly a faltering, if not doomed, effort by the police to contain the protests. Whether or not Ben Ali explicitly ordered the use of force, or the military simply refused to entertain the idea itself, it is clear that force was not used by the military in defense of the regime. No evidence exists that the army used live ammunition in cities where it was deployed; to the contrary, reports surfaced that soldiers were interposing themselves between police and protesters to try to protect the latter and calm the situation. See Kirkpatrick (2011a, 2011b, 2011c), International Crisis Group (2011), and Africa News (2011).

16. Pachon (2014) has also recently made the argument that the military was not asked to fire (or that some uncertainty exists about interactions between General Ammar and Ben Ali), but he pushes further, concluding that this lack of confrontation meant that there was no "defection" from the Ben Ali regime by the military. But this conclusion misses the point. Key to keep in mind is the coercive foundation of an autocratic regime, in which the armed forces are the protector of last resort—the ultimate enforcer and safeguard of the regime. Whatever the precise details, and regardless of whether and how Ammar explicitly defied any orders by Ben Ali to fire on protesters, by January 11 the situation had become dire. The regime's future was seriously in question. By deploying to the streets ostensibly to provide public order without protecting the regime (as would the militia and elements of the Presidential Guard in the aftermath of what appeared to be Ben Ali's temporary trip to Saudi Arabia), the military failed to fulfill its implicit mandate to protect the regime. In the deeper and important sense then, it defected.

17. According to the prime minister, the army was acting in accordance with the constitutional state of emergency declared on January 14 (BBC Monitoring [Middle East], 2011).

18. On the significance of a civilian defense minister, see Stepan (1988).

19. The utility of the defense minister as a method of control for Ben Ali is illustrated by the fact that, after first taking power and shuffling the government, Ben Ali assumed the position (along with the presidency), according to some in order to exert direct control over the military during the transition period. The Ministry of Defense was subsequently subjected to oversight by the Ministry of Interior, and the civilian defense minister was made accountable to the interior minister as a form of oversight by the trusted Ministry of Interior. On these issues, see Bou Nassif (2015). Consistent with this hierarchy is that during the uprising Ammar was told by the minister of defense to go to the Ministry of Interior, presumably so that that ministry could oversee the response to the protests. See Al Arabiya (2012) as well as the discussion below.

20. For details on the protests see Amnesty International (2011) and Chomiak and Entellis (2011: 13–15).

21. See the extensive exposé in Al Arabiya (2012) on these events.

22. For an account of the affair, see Klaas (2013). Also see the lengthy discussion in Bou Nassif (2015) and in Jebnoun (2014).

23. See BBC News (2002). There were also indications of growing tensions between the regime and the military before the protests (Kallander, 2011).

24. The military retains a significant stake in decisions by the civilian Ministry of Defense about resources and counterterrorism policy since these decisions affect the efficacy of its efforts to battle the militants.

25. The December 2012 constitution was passed under President Mohamed Morsi, and the January 2014 constitution was passed under the appointed president, Adly Mansour, at the behest of the Supreme Council of the Armed Forces. For a copy of the 2012 constitution, see Youssef (2012). The 2014 constitution is available at http://www.sis.gov.eg/Newvr/Dustor-en001.pdf.

26. An unofficial translation of the Tunisian constitution is available at http://www.jasmine-foundation.org/doc/unofficial_english_translation_of_tunisian_constitution_final_ed.pdf.

27. Other similar sentences have been given to other bloggers and critics of the military. See Amnesty International (2015).

28. On the importance of a military's organizational culture and unique conception of its roles and missions, see Taylor (2003), Pion-Berlin, Esparza, and Grisham (2014), Kier (1997), Farrell (2005), and Feaver (1999).

8

The Military Balancing Act: Cohesion vs. Effectiveness in Deeply Divided Societies

Oren Barak

In order to be successful, building the rule of law in the Arab states requires building legitimate law enforcement agencies. However, since most Arab states in the Middle East are composed of divided societies, building security sectors that are acceptable to all constituent communities poses a perennial challenge.[1] In this chapter, I consider how to build legitimate security sectors as part of building the rule of law in those Arab states that are divided societies. I make a twofold argument: First, the legitimacy of the security sector in divided societies hinges on the sense of ownership that members of the diverse communities in society feel toward that particular sector and the agencies that it comprises. Second, in order to produce this sense of ownership, the security sector must sometimes sacrifice at least part of its professional ethos. In short, in forging a capable security sector in a divided society there is an inherent tension between cultivating the security sector's legitimacy, that is, the extent to which citizens regard it as proper and deserving of their support,[2] and cultivating the security sector's effectiveness, that is, its power to achieve results that correspond to its professional ethos.[3] As I suggest below, only by reframing the role of the security sector and reconceiving its contribution to building stability and rule of law in these contexts can this inherent tension be resolved.

As is well known, for many decades the security sector (especially the military), played a significant, and often the dominant, role in many Arab states, not only in the area of national security but also in the political and economic spheres (Owen, 2000). The military played this role not only in the region's authoritarian regimes but also in those states defined as partially or formally democratic.[4] Over time the security sector witnessed important changes in its role. If in the early decades of independence, the security sector (again, especially the military) was a source of instability in many Arab states, mainly in the form of repeated military coups, in subsequent years, the security sector, including the military but also other security agencies, became one the most important forces for, and one of the major beneficiaries of, political stability in these states (Bellin, 2004; Picard, 1990; Quinlivan, 1999). Security forces in a number of Arab states also distinguished themselves by investing considerable efforts toward garnering popular support, whether by portraying themselves as the defender of the state against foreign aggression or as the state's foremost protector against terrorist plots from within, or at times, by referencing both of these roles.

Until the outbreak of the Arab Spring, the Arab security sector was a relatively understudied topic, particularly when compared to other issues relevant to the region such as civil society and radical Islam.[5] But in the wake of these dramatic events, the Arab security sector began to receive more attention. Those interested in the Arab security sector today include scholars and practitioners from the region and beyond, who acknowledge its pivotal role in politics and would like to see it play a constructive role in political reforms there, particularly in shepherding states through a peaceful transition from authoritarian or partially authoritarian regimes to effective democracies.[6]

One of the most important issues related to the security sector in divided societies is its complex relationship with the pattern of intercommunal relations in these states (Enloe, 1980; Horowitz, 1985). Since the majority of states in the Arab world rule over divided societies that are composed of different communities (Esman and Rabinovich, 1988; Ibrahim, 1998), this relationship is of particular relevance not only when trying to comprehend past and current developments but also when contemplating political—especially democratic—reform.

In this chapter, I focus on the relationship between the security sector and the pattern of intercommunal relations in the Arab states that govern divided societies. First, I explain what divided societies are and identify the major patterns of intercommunal relations associated with them. Second, I discuss the main dilemma of building a capable security sector in divided societies, particularly the above-mentioned "trade-off" between the security sector's effectiveness and legitimacy. Third, I explore the association of different patterns of intercommunal relations with different models of security sector organization. To illustrate the trade-offs associated with each model, I draw on illuminating cases from the experience of Lebanon. Finally, I reflect on the need to reframe the role of the coercive apparatus in order to reconcile the dual objectives of creating a security sector that is both effective and legitimate. This analysis should prove instructive for those focused on building capable security sectors in other divided Arab societies in the wake of the Arab Spring.

A word on case selection before proceeding: I use the case of Lebanon to explore alternate models of security sector organization in divided societies for three reasons. First, Lebanon is the quintessential case of a divided society in the Arab world, composed of about twenty different communities (or ethnic groups), not counting powerful region- and clan-based identities (Hanf, 1993; Hudson, 1968). Second, Lebanon has witnessed considerable changes in its pattern of intercommunal relations and in the organization of its security sector since gaining independence in the 1940s. This internal variation provides considerable analytic leverage on the question at hand. Finally, the civil war in Lebanon came to an end more than two decades ago, and as such it provides significant historical perspective on how to promote security in the wake of deep societal division, which is relevant to other countries facing similar challenges today.

Patterns of Intercommunal Relations in Divided Societies

In this section, I explain what divided societies are and what major patterns of intercommunal relations can be identified in them. Then, in the next section, I discuss the major roles and dilemmas of the security sector in these contexts.

Divided societies are societies composed of diverse communities—mainly defined along ethnic (including religious) or national lines—where communal identities and divisions are extraordinarily salient politically. In divided societies, the communal considerations dominate all public spheres, including politics, society, the economy, and culture and, as such, assume precedence over all other issues and concerns.[7]

Divided societies are susceptible to instability and violence; hence, the major challenge they face is the construction of political institutions that will deliver civil peace and stability. Different patterns of intercommunal relations are possible, distinguished by (1) the degree to which the state and its institutions are dominated by one community and (2) the degree to which violence is integral to the strategy of governance. Four patterns of intercommunal relations are salient in the Arab world and in the Middle East in general.

The first pattern, power sharing, consists primarily of a "grand coalition" that includes members of all major communities in the governance of the state. This arrangement is complemented by three supporting mechanisms: proportionality in the allocation of funds and government posts, mutual veto over decisions that offend certain communities, and autonomy for all communities (Hartzell and Hoddie, 2007; Lijphart, 1977, 2004; McCulloch, 2014; O'Leary, 2013; Sisk, 1996). Power sharing is supposed to prevent intercommunal violence, and ideally it is not created through violence. However, within communities, violence is sometimes observed in competition between elites and in political leaders' attempts to enforce their control over their followers (Barak, 2002).[8]

The second pattern, control, is defined as "the emergence and maintenance of a relationship in which the superior power of one segment" of the divided society "is mobilized to enforce stability by constraining the political actions and opportunities of another segment or segments" (Lustick, 1979: 328). Like power sharing, control is not sustained through violence, though one can argue that some of the measures that the dominant community employs in order to get its way vis-à-vis the subaltern community (or communities), such as the appropriation of land or other resources belonging to a subaltern community by the state's institutions, which are presided over by the dominant community, are, at least implicitly, violent.

The third pattern of intercommunal relations, repression, occurs when the dominant community uses massive violence against other communities, thereby asserting its central position in the state. James Ron (2003: 5–8) observes that various types of regimes exhibit important variations in the level of state repression.

Finally, the fourth pattern of intercommunal relations is a stalemate, during which a violent struggle is waged between some or all of the communities in the divided society but no single community is capable of dominating the country (Luttwak, 2013).

These four patterns of intercommunal relations in divided societies are presented in Table 8.1 below, though I should immediately add that that these are, essentially, ideal types and that, at least with regard to repression

Table 8.1 Patterns of Intercommunal Relations in Divided Societies

	No one community is dominant	One community is dominant
No explicitly violent	Power sharing	Control
Massively violent	Stalemate	Stalemate

and stalemate, distinguishing between them is sometimes difficult, and one can find cases that fit into both categories. A noted example is Syria since 2011, where the uprising against President Bashar al-Assad and his Alawite-dominated regime has oscillated between repression and stalemate. Thus, these two patterns will be dealt with together in the next sections.

A cursory glance at the Middle East in general and the Arab states in particular suggests that all major patterns of intercommunal relations have been represented in the region both before and since the beginning of the Arab Spring. But what role does the security sector play in these contexts, and how does that role relate to the pattern of intercommunal relations in the state? In order to answer these questions, let us first elucidate the major roles of, and dilemmas facing, the security sector in divided societies.

The Security Sector in Divided Societies: Major Roles and Dilemmas

What role does the security sector, and especially the military, play in divided societies? One community's domination of the security sector is liable to reinforce that community's hegemonic position in the state. By contrast, lack of such communal domination of the security sector can help buttress a more balanced intercommunal relationship. The communal character of the security sector, in other words, is politically fraught in states that govern divided societies.[9]

This tension was evident in the case of Iraq after the US-led invasion in 2003 when the country faced the reconstruction of its security apparatus. As explained by Major General Najim Abed al-Jabouri, a former high-ranking Iraqi officer, the challenge of dismantling the old Iraqi military and replacing it with the new Iraqi Security Forces was perceived as "the battleground in the larger communal struggle for power and survival" in the country. He added, "He who owns the security forces, owns the politics" (quoted in International Crisis Group, 2010: 18; see also Barak, 2007).[10] As will become evident, this situation is not unique to Iraq.

In divided societies, then, the communal character of ostensibly nonpartisan and professional institutions such as the security sector is an extremely political matter, no less than the communal character of the state's "explicit" political institutions such as the presidency, government, parliament, and political parties. Most importantly, if the security sector in these societies is not owned by all communities, its legitimacy in the eyes of members of the subaltern communities is impaired.

How can a sense of ownership toward the security sector in divided societies be acquired? First, it matters a great deal who serves and who does not serve in—that is, who is excluded from or refuses to join—the security sector and its various agencies, especially the military. When examining this question, one should focus on the security sector's recruitment policy and how it affects the composition of the security agencies (Cf. Enloe, 1980; Krebs, 2006; Peled, 1998).

The second relevant issue is, who commands the security agencies, who are the civilian officials that exercise control over them, and are these security and civilian officials members of one or all major communities in the state? These questions are important because the rank and file of the security sector may be heterogeneous; that is, they may be drawn from all or most communities in society. However, if only one community "calls the shots," then the security sector will not be seen as owned by all.

The third and fourth factors that determine whether there is a sense of ownership of the security sector in divided societies concern the ideological identity[11] and actual operations[12] of the security agencies. Here it is important to consider not only the official discourse of the security agencies, which can be distilled from official statements made by their chiefs and from their broadcasts, bulletins, and websites, but also the way things work "on the ground" and the way in which different communities in the state perceive specific messages of and actions taken by the security agencies.

Importantly, the legitimacy of the security sector and, ultimately, its ability to enforce stability, security, and rule of law do not stem solely from its effectiveness; that is, its power to achieve results that correspond to its professional ethos. Equally important, if not more so, is the extent to which the various communities in the state have a sense of ownership toward the security agencies. Only then will the security sector—and the state—be perceived as exercising a monopoly on legitimate physical force within the country's territory (Weber, 2003).

In divided societies, there is often a trade-off between the sense of ownership toward, and the effectiveness of, the security sector. Security agencies such as the military and the police can be well armed and trained, and they may be capable of carrying out the security tasks assigned them very efficiently. But if these tasks are seen as targeting one particular community while serving the interests of another, such behavior can produce feelings of alienation from the security sector within the targeted community. Persistent behavior and alienations of this sort can fuel defection from the security agencies and, in the worst-case scenario, bring about the security apparatus's disintegration. In addition, this bias can reflect negatively on the state's other institutions, especially on its political institutions. Law-and-order operations (i.e., policing) are particularly sensitive in terms of their potential to target particular communities at the expense of others and thus beget institution-wrecking disaffection.[13]

The Security Sector and Intercommunal Relations: Models and Examples

In this section I present four models of security sector organization that correspond with the major patterns of intercommunal relations in divided societies presented earlier (i.e., control, stalemate and repression, and power sharing). I then ground each of these models in a particular period in the history of Lebanon. In each period I discuss the security sector's recruitment strategy, the character of its command and civilian controlling bodies, its identity, and its actual operations, as well as the trade-off in effectiveness and legitimacy observed in each.

Before discussing these models and illustrating them, let me provide some necessary background on the Lebanese case. Before the outbreak of civil war in 1975, Lebanon was considered a successful example of a democracy governed by a power-sharing agreement (Lehmbruch, 1974; Lijphart, 1977; Smock and Smock, 1975). In 1943, on the eve of its independence from France, leaders from Lebanon's two most powerful communities, the Maronite Christians and the Sunni Muslims, reached a political settlement known as the National Pact, which meticulously divided up all of the state's political and administrative posts between its varied communities and gave all major groups a voice in and a stake in the political system.

However, by the mid-1970s, opposition groups in Lebanon, and especially Muslim-dominated Pan-Arab and leftist movements, openly challenged the power-sharing settlement. Some argued that the pact had become a tool for domination, or control, by the country's traditional elite. Others posited that the Christian communities, which were no longer the majority in Lebanon, benefited from it more than the Muslim communities, namely, that the pact no longer reflected reality. Mounting tensions in the region, mostly related to the Israeli-Palestinian conflict, further exacerbated communal and socioeconomic divisions within Lebanon. The intercommunal conflict in Lebanon came to a head in 1975 with the outbreak of civil war, leading to the failure of the Lebanese state and the intervention of numerous foreign players—most notably the Palestine Liberation Organization, Syria, and Israel—in the conflict (Barak, 2003; Hanf, 1993).

In the course of the civil war in Lebanon, several attempts were made to reform the country's political institutions and security sector, but these were, on the whole, unsuccessful (Barak 2009: 111–149). Only in November 1989, after the conflict had raged on for fourteen years, following intensive all-Arab mediation, did leaders of Lebanon's communities reach a political settlement known as the Ta'if Agreement. About a year later, a joint Syrian-Lebanese military operation terminated the conflict, and reconstruction of the state began (Hanf, 1993; Picard, 1996).

Precedence was given to the reform of two spheres during Lebanon's reconstruction: the political system and the security sector. Most scholarly attention has, thus far, been given to the reform of the political system. To recap the reform of the former, the distribution of power among the major actors in Lebanon's political system (i.e., the president, government, and Parliament) was made more balanced. As in the past, each of these institutions was to be headed by a member of a different community (the president is a Maronite Christian, the prime minister is a Sunni Muslim, and the speaker of Parliament is a Shiite Muslim). But since the positions of prime minister and speaker of Parliament were considerably strengthened at the president's expense, the redistribution of power guaranteed a multicommunal troika responsible for managing the state's affairs. In addition, Lebanon's six largest communities were assured representation in the cabinet, and the proportion of Christians to Muslims in Parliament, heretofore fixed by the 1943 pact at a 6:5 ratio, was changed to increase the proportion of Muslims to an even parity with Christian members of Parliament (Di Mauro, 2008).

The Lebanese security sector was also overhauled, the details of which will be described below. But to set up a baseline for discussion of the evolving role of the security agencies in Lebanon, I should present some historical background. Lebanon's security sector is composed of several agencies, but the largest and most important among them is the Lebanese Armed Forces (LAF). Established in 1945, the LAF was construed as an enlarged police force and was primarily entrusted with maintaining law and order throughout the country. The LAF was a small and weak army compared to most of its Middle Eastern counterparts at the time, the consequence of the aversion of Lebanon's socioeconomic elite to the creation of a powerful military that might be in a position to suppress them. The LAF's weakness was also a consequence of this elite's antipathy to introducing a compulsory draft, which was liable to change the ethnic balance within the LAF to their detriment. Despite these limitations, the LAF proved pivotal in managing several crucial political crises that occurred in Lebanon in its early decades, such as the forced resignation of President Bechara el-Khoury in 1952 and the first civil war of 1958 (see below). Following the latter episode, the LAF commander, General Fouad Chehab, was elected president, attesting to the LAF's persistent legitimacy. In the period 1958–1970, the LAF, through its intelligence branch, assumed a dominant position in Lebanon's political system, but in the early 1970s, it was removed from power by the country's traditional leaders (Barak, 2009).

Lebanon's first civil war in 1958 brought to the fore a variety of grievances that preoccupied some of its Muslim communities (especially Sunnis and Druze),[14] including the complaint that they enjoyed insufficient representation in the armed forces. Thus, in the wake of the 1958 war, limited reforms were introduced in the LAF, including the appointment of a Druze officer as its chief of staff (a post formerly held by a Catholic). Notably the position of army commander continued to be reserved for a Maronite. In addition, the officer corps of the LAF became more communally balanced: the ratio of Christians to Muslims was raised to 55 percent to 45 percent (virtually identical to the Christian-Muslim ratio of 6:5 fixed by the National Pact of 1943 for political appointment). In addition, the number of Maronite officers dropped to 34.8 percent (Barak, 2006: 89). Still, the Christians, and particularly the Maronites, dominated this institution.

As far as the ideological identity and operations of the LAF were concerned, the decade and a half following the 1958 civil war can be divided into two parts. Until the mid-1960s, Lebanon's foreign policy conformed to that of other Arab states (especially Gamal Abdul Nasser's Egypt), and as such the LAF enjoyed a broad domestic consensus. However, in the latter half of the 1960s, and especially following the Israeli-Arab War of 1967, the identity and operations of the LAF became increasingly subject to contestation. The LAF's efforts to dominate the Lebanese political system, quash the Palestinian factions in Lebanon (at which it proved unsuccessful, mainly on account of a combined domestic-external veto), and repel Israel's military raids on the country (also unsuccessful) exacerbated Christian-Muslim tensions and increasingly identified the LAF, at least in the eyes of the Muslim community, as communally biased. The result was growing Muslim criticism of the predominance of Christians, and especially Maronites, in the LAF's officer corps and high command. This criticism became apparent during political crises in 1968–1969 and again in 1973, but it reached its apex in 1975 amidst events that led to the outbreak of the civil war. By that point the legitimacy of the LAF was called into question, and many Muslims (and some Christians) regarded it primarily as a tool of the Christians' hegemony in Lebanon (Barak, 2009).

The remainder of this section is divided into three parts. In each part, I explore the role and position of the security sector associated with the different patterns of intercommunal relations discussed earlier (i.e., control, repression and stalemate, and power sharing), providing illustrative examples from the Lebanese case to clarify the essential trade-off between legitimacy and effectiveness present in each.

Control

The main task of a security sector that corresponds to the control model is to reinforce the dominant position of a particular community in the state. This goal is accomplished by partial or total exclusion of the subaltern communities from the security agencies (Peled, 1998; Quinlivan, 1999), along with staffing these agencies' command structures, as well as the civilian bodies that control them, with members of the dominant community. A security sector that corresponds to the control model sometimes attempts to project a national as opposed to communal identity to its own members and to society in general. But to members of the subaltern community in the country, as well as to outside observers, the security sector's identity has an unmistakable communal character to it. The same is true with regard to the security sector's actual operations, which are seen as serving the dominant sector.

Notably, this type of security sector can, sometimes, be very effective in terms of delivering order and stability. But since all or most of its agencies do not elicit a sense of ownership from all communities in the state, even when the security sector performs in an exemplary manner, it is not (and perhaps cannot be) legitimate in the eyes of members of the subaltern communities.[15]

As far as the Lebanese case is concerned, the period that corresponds to the control model began in 1968–1969,[16] when the first major crisis erupted between the Palestinian-armed factions in Lebanon and their local supporters (mostly Muslims), on the one hand, and the LAF and its supporters (Christians, especially Maronites), on the other hand. This period came to an end in 1975, with the outbreak of the Lebanese civil war (Khalidi, 1979; Rabinovich, 1985; Salibi, 1976).

As with other state institutions in Lebanon, the LAF was supposed to reflect the country's intrinsic pluralism. However, evidence that I collected on the LAF shows that until the late 1970s, the country's Christian communities, especially the Maronites, which constituted the largest and most powerful community in Lebanon, dominated its officer corps as well as most senior posts in the LAF, including that of the army commander (Barak, 2006: 89). This factor, coupled with the deteriorating consensus with regard to the identity and operations of the LAF, particularly since the late 1960s, when it attempted to suppress the Palestinian factions in Lebanon, compromised the legitimacy of the LAF, especially among Lebanon's Muslims (most notably Sunnis and Druze) but also among those Christians who supported the Palestinian national struggle. Indeed, toward the mid-1970s, opposition groups in Lebanon began to refer to the LAF as a "Christian army" referring both to its composition and to its political agenda.

What about the effectiveness of the LAF in this period? Although the LAF leadership was dominated by Christians (especially Maronites) throughout this period, their control did not necessarily mean that the LAF was ineffective. First, until the presidential elections of 1970, which put an end to the LAF's role in Lebanese politics, military leaders presided over the parliamentary elections and intimidated or co-opted their rivals. Second, the LAF effectively mobilized its forces against the Palestinian factions during the crises of 1968–1969 and 1973, and domestic and external political pressures, and not its own military capacities, clearly constrained its actions in these periods.

Repression/Stalemate

Similar to the control model, the main task of the security apparatus in the repression model is to serve and advance the domination of society by one particular group. In contrast to the control model, under the repression model the security apparatus proves willing to use massive violence against other communities to defend the position of the dominant group. However, repression (as in Syria since 2011) sometimes gives way to a stalemate, where the main challenge of the security sector is to prevent its fragmentation according to communal lines. Under these circumstances, security agencies composed of members of diverse communities are particularly vulnerable, and the same is true with regard to diverse command and control bodies and structures. In both the repression and stalemate models, security personnel from the subaltern communities face immense pressures to defect from the security agencies, which are seen as illegitimate, and to fight shoulder to shoulder with their community members. However, only in a stalemate does this result in the partial or full fissure of the security agencies into rival parts, impairing their effectiveness. As divisions within the security sector deepen, the shared identity that these institutions foster becomes contested, and their operations are carried out only with great difficulties, not least because of the constant threat of delegitimization by communal leaders and other entrepreneurs.

In Lebanon evidence can be seen of this slide into repression and stalemate with the outbreak of the civil war of 1975. In the initial phase of the conflict (1975–1976), both the civilian and military bodies controlling the LAF were predominately Christian, and the LAF's officer corps was under Christian (primarily Maronite) hegemony. In addition, the identity and operations of the LAF were clearly identified with the defense of the Christian community, as evidenced by the extension of active support by some LAF units to the militias of the major Maronite-led parties (Camille Chamoun's National Liberal Party and Amine Gemayel's Phalanges Party). Such partisanship on the part of the LAF elicited significant criticism from Muslim-dominated leftist and Pan-Arab factions. It led to the first revolt in the history of the LAF and the first coup attempt by one of its senior officers. Still, large-scale defection from the LAF did not yet occur. Most of the LAF's personnel did not join the opposing militias, which occasionally targeted the LAF, but instead went home to defend their towns and villages or waited for the crisis to end. Some of these soldiers, who continued to receive their salaries from the LAF, rejoined it later when efforts were made to reconstruct it (Barak, 2009: 104).

In order to forestall the threat of institutional disintegration and redress the blow to its society-wide legitimacy, the LAF undertook major reforms to reconstruct it as a multicommunal institution. Thus, several power-sharing mechanisms were introduced into the army's high command and in the civilian bodies controlling it. In addition, Christian-Muslim parity was engineered in the LAF's officer corps through induced retirements of Christian officers and enlistment of Muslim cadets. Despite these reforms, however, the identity and actual operations of the LAF remained contested and lopsided in favor the Christian community. This lopsidedness was in large part due to the lack of parallel reforms in Lebanon's political system, so that the Christians still exercised executive control (Barak, 2009: 116–122). Thus, the decline in the LAF's society-wide legitimacy continued.

The gap between the sense of social ownership and effectiveness of the LAF reached its apex in the period 1982–1984, when the LAF used massive violence against non-Christian communities in Lebanon. Despite (or perhaps because of) its effectiveness, the legitimacy of the LAF began to seriously break down. The result was increasing defection from the LAF by non-Christian members. By 1988, this embrace of discriminatory violence split the armed forces into two. The illegitimacy of the security sector compromised its institutional integrity and ended the LAF's monopoly on the means of coercion.

Encouraged by the support he received from the Reagan administration, Lebanon's president Amine Gemayel (Maronite), elected in 1982, set out to dominate the Lebanese political system and sought to use the LAF to achieve this end. As part of Gemayel's efforts, he suspended the intercommunal power sharing in the LAF command installed in the period 1977–1982, though in terms of its composition, the LAF remained communally balanced (McLaurin, 1991: 546). In addition, the identity and operations of the LAF expressly favored the Maronites and their allies, who included some Sunni leaders. This favoritism was mostly evident in the attempts made by the LAF to deploy its forces in several (non-Sunni) Muslim-dominated regions, which alienated members of the Druze and the Shiite communities (McLaurin, 1991: 560–561). The Muslim alienation from President Gemayel and the LAF reached its apex in 1983–1984, when army units were ordered to deploy in the Druze-controlled Chouf Mountains and in Shiite-controlled South Beirut to carry out law and order operations. The two major Druze and Shiite militias, Walid Jumblatt's Progressive Socialist Party and Nabih Berri's Amal Movement, opposed these moves, which they saw as attempts to undermine their power, and called upon the LAF's Druze and Shiite soldiers to defect and join their brothers. Berri's open call to the LAF's soldiers on February 4, 1984, is, in this respect, very telling:

> My brother soldier[s] . . . I not only call upon the Shi'is among you, and not only upon the Muslims. . . . Have you forgotten who defended you and protected you, and who shed his blood for this institution [the LAF]? We fought our coreligionists, our brothers, our Arab brethren, and our family members . . . for the sake of preserving the existence of the LAF. . . . Why, then, does the government want you to shoot your brother . . . ? They are not preparing you for the liberation of the South. They are preparing you to be a tool in the hands of the [Christian] hegemony. We want you to be everyone's army, and they want you to be their army. (quoted in Barak, 2009: 128)

As a result, some units of the LAF, such as its Fourth Brigade, disintegrated, and others, such as its Sixth Brigade, joined the militias.

A similar scenario of increasingly violent partisanship on the part of the LAF, spelling illegitimacy and disintegration of the security sector, came in 1988–1990. During this period, the army commander, General Michel Aoun (a Maronite), was appointed as prime minister by outgoing president Gemayel (also a Maronite). Aoun sought to "liberate" Lebanon from Syria's "occupation," despite the opposition of the latter and of Lebanon's Muslim communities, and unleashed the LAF units under his command against the Syrian forces in Lebanon and their local clients. Aoun's initiative put a final nail in the coffin of the LAF's legitimacy and fueled its rupture. Subsequently, the LAF split into two parts: the Christian-dominated units under Aoun's command and the Muslim-dominated units controlled by the Muslim cabinet led by a Sunni politician, Salim el-Hoss (McLaurin, 1991: 550).

Once a security agency embraces violent intercommunal repression, it is often seen as no more than a communal militia in military garb.[17] Unlike a security sector that operates under intercommunal control, this security sector does not only seek to manipulate the identities of members of the subaltern communities who serve in its agencies in order to maintain their loyalty but also turns them into accomplices to its violent campaign against the subaltern communities, thus leading these individuals to be branded as collaborators with the regime (Quinlivan, 1999). One should note that this type of security sector can be effective at achieving its objectives particularly when the regime faces a fragmented opposition that does not enjoy firm outside support. Syria since 2011 is a case in point. But the use of massive force by the security agencies against the opposition, effective as it might be in the short run, is liable to tarnish the security sector's image and lead to defection and institutional rupture over the long haul. Such rupture, of course, eliminates the security sector's monopoly over the legitimate means of coercion within the state.

Power Sharing

The identity and composition of the security sector in the context of a power-sharing system is very different from that observed in the other models described above. Under a power-sharing system, the security sector recruits members from all communities in society, is commanded and controlled by security and civilian officials representing all of these communities, and, through its identity and actual performance, seeks to reflect (and foster) intercommunal accommodation. When successful, this security sector can reinforce the power-sharing settlement between the country's political leaders. But a security sector that operates under an intercommunal power-sharing arrangement also has several drawbacks. Since it is owned by all communities, it is expected to operate on the basis of intercommunal consensus, and its ability to enforce the rule of law vis-à-vis some or all of these communities is sometimes constrained. Specifically, the security sector may not be a very effective instrument of coercion when the political system has not delivered intercommunal consensus on policy and when some communities enjoy veto power over policy choices. Nevertheless, the security agencies may still prove effective in delivering order in terms of their capacity to coerce and contain various "others" such as foreign armed groups and actors that are not part of the domestic consensus. Such effective containment suggests that the role of the security sector as provider of order and stability in divided societies ought to be reconceived. In this context, the security sector ought to be seen not only as a law enforcement institution but also as an institution that, via its very multicommunal constitution, mitigates intercommunal tensions.

Lebanon's post–civil war era fits this model of intercommunal relations. After the end of the conflict in 1990 and as part of the subsequent reconstruction of the state and its institutions, the LAF was rebuilt on the basis of a new intercommunal consensus. Its units were restructured on a multicommunal basis, eliminating excessive links and affiliations between specific units, communities, and regions in Lebanon. Considerable efforts were made to maintain a communal balance in its officer corps (Muslims now had a slight majority of 52.9 percent; see Barak, 2006: 89) and to restore power sharing in its command and in the controlling civilian bodies. These goals were achieved, at least in part, by reducing the prerogatives of the Lebanese president (Maronite) and increasing those of the prime minister (Sunni) and the speaker of Parliament (Shiite). At the same time, efforts were made to accord the LAF a unifying, multicommunal identity (Barak, 2009: 162–165). Reforms were also introduced in Lebanon's other security services, which were headed by members of different communities.[18] Notably, in the first years after the end of the conflict in Lebanon, Syria played a critical role in the reconstruction of the state and its security sector. Later, however, the Syrians overplayed their hand in Lebanon and had to withdraw their forces from its territory in 2005.

The reforms introduced in the LAF in the postwar era made it more representative of Lebanon's divided society and thus enhanced its legitimacy. These reforms enabled the LAF to curb all attempts by local and external actors (including the Palestinian factions, which still maintain an armed presence in Lebanon) to challenge stability in the postwar era. Moreover, the fact that the reforms introduced in this period focused on the political system and the security services all at once had a positive impact on Lebanon's Muslim leaders, who had been reluctant to join the political system so long as the security sector remained in Christian (especially Maronite) hands. It also had a positive impact on Muslim officers, who had difficulty serving in the LAF in the absence of a political settlement that was acceptable to their communities. The enhanced legitimacy of the LAF has been demonstrated not only in public support for this institution, which cuts across the lines of community, region, and clan, but also in the election of two army commanders—Émile Lahoud and Michel Suleiman—as presidents of the republic in 2004 and 2008, respectively (Barak, 2009: 171–196; see also Gaub, 2010; Nerguizian, 2009).

This gain in legitimacy, however, has come at the expense of some of the security sector's effectiveness. Particularly when conflicts emerge between Lebanese communities over issues that have not been resolved at the political level, the security agencies, and especially the LAF, often find themselves powerless to intervene and force a solution. The best example of this dilemma in recent years is the continuing conflict between Lebanon's two rival political factions, the March 8 and March 14 blocs, which were formed in 2005 in the wake of the assassination of Lebanon's former prime minister, Rafic Hariri. Indeed, during the violent clashes between these factions in Beirut in 2007, as well as on other occasions, LAF personnel inserted themselves between supporters of the two factions, without using their force against either of them, in order to avoid politicizing the army (Barak, 2009: 202). Later, in the wake of the revolt against President Bashar al-Assad and his Alawite-dominated regime in Syria, when tensions within Lebanon mounted, particularly in Tripoli, where members of the Sunni and Alawite communities live side by side, the LAF deployed in the city and attempted to reduce the tensions but without using massive force against the rival parties.

In short, in the postwar era the LAF is constrained in its ability to exercise its coercive power in contexts that will undermine its image as a communally neutral institution. This attempt to maintain neutrality, in some ways, compromises its effectiveness as an instrument of law and order. However, the fact that the LAF continues to be perceived as a multicommunal security agency owned by all of Lebanon's communities and favoring none in itself contributes to the durability of civil peace and amity in the country, and the security sector's enduring legitimacy also prevents defection and fragmentation of its agencies. This cohesion preserves the security sector's monopoly on the means of coercion. The relative success of the LAF in Lebanon suggests that the goals of effectiveness and legitimacy can be reconciled even in divided societies, albeit at some cost.

Conclusion

Many studies on, as well as actual policies of, postconflict reconstruction of divided societies outside the West (most notably the US-led "nation-building" project in Iraq since 2003) claim that robust and effective civilian and military institutions can be built in these countries in the same way they were built in the established democracies in the West. However, the above discussion suggests that in divided societies, which constitute the majority of Arab states, the communal element cannot be put aside (Cf. Wong, 2006), even in a professional institution such as the security sector. Indeed, in these settings the state can successfully claim the monopoly of legitimate physical force and sustain civil peace only if its security sector is owned by members of all of the state's communities. If the security sector is under the exclusive control of one community, then it is liable to elicit fears of domination among the subaltern communities. Such exclusive control may in turn exacerbate intercommunal tensions in the state, and even if the security sector itself is effective at delivering order in the short-term, the long-term prospects for its institutional cohesion, and for the capacity to sustain a monopoly on the means of coercion, are very dim indeed.

Let us now return to the four patterns of intercommunal relations presented earlier and focus on the trade-off between legitimacy and effectiveness of the security sector in each of them. This trade-off is summarized in Table 8.2.

As demonstrated by the table, the security sector in divided societies can be effective, but effectiveness unfortunately usually occurs where the pattern of intercommunal relations is control or coercion. In these circumstances, moreover, the security sector is not seen as legitimate in the eyes of the subaltern communities. When intercommunal relations are characterized by power sharing, the security sector is legitimate in the eyes of all communities but is not always very effective since it operates on the basis of a broad consensus. When such consensus is absent and when the various communities have veto power over its actions, the security sector is incapable of imposing order through force. This limitation on its capacity to adjudicate between communities does not mean, of course, that the security sector cannot operate effectively against various "others," who are incapable of exercising such a veto power, such as foreign, armed groups, ter-

Table 8.2 Effectiveness and Legitimacy of the Security Sector in Divided Societies

	Effective	Not Effective
Legitimate	—	Power sharing
Not legitimate	Control/coercion	Civil war

rorist networks, and spy networks. And it does not mean the security sector is ineffective in fostering civil peace and comity through its very existence as a multicommunal institution. But short of reconceiving "effectiveness" in this way, the tension between legitimacy and effectiveness stands.

The relationship between the state's pattern of intercommunal relations, on the one hand, and the security sector, on the other hand, which I have sought to elucidate in this chapter, is relevant not only when trying to comprehend the past and present roles of the security sector in Arab states that are also divided societies but also when thinking about a political future for these states. If these states aim to transition toward democracy, their security sector, too, will need to undergo comprehensive reforms. This process is especially fraught in divided societies such as Yemen, Libya, and Syria, which witnessed the Arab Spring, but also in post-2003 Iraq. For these countries, the communal factor will need to be addressed, and as in the Lebanese case, the inherent tension between the security apparatus's effectiveness and legitimacy will have to be balanced carefully.

Notes

1. The security sector includes the military but also other law enforcement agencies, such as the police, the paramilitary forces, the border guards, and, if relevant, the coast guard and the intelligence and internal security services, as well as the military industries and the nuclear authority. The professional, that is, the nonpolitical, components of the country's ministry of defense can also be considered part of the security sector. Although in the current chapter, I focus mainly on the military, I do provide examples of other security agencies.

2. Ted Gurr quoted in Hudson (1977: 1–2). See also Eckstein (1971: 50).

3. As far as the military is concerned, effectiveness refers to its ability to engage in successful armed combat (Huntington, 1957: 11), sustain order, and maintain a monopoly on the means of coercion. As for other security agencies, effective-

ness refers to their ability to successfully carry out tasks such as policing and intelligence gathering.

4. According to Heller (2000: 488), "formal democracies" are states where "functionally and geographically, the degree of public legality . . . remains severely constrained" and "the component of democratic legality and, hence, of publicness and citizenship, fades away at the frontiers of various regions and class, gender and ethnic relations."

5. On the relative neglect of this topic before the Arab Spring, see Barak and David (2010). On the Arab security sector during the Arab Spring, see Bellin (2012) and Lutterbeck (2013).

6. See, e.g., Rabbani (2011).

7. See Lustick (1979: 325). These social divisions can, however, ameliorate over time. Lijphart (1968) argues that divisions in the Netherlands, which necessitated a power-sharing settlement between the country's "pillars" in the period 1917–1967, later declined.

8. Hartzell and Hoddie (2007: 33) suggest that territorial power sharing can be allocated through territorial autonomy, and that "by creating forms of decentralized government that are territorially based (e.g., federalism and regional autonomy), autonomy effectively divides political influence among levels of government."

9. Such political disarray is also the case in post–civil war settings. See Hartzell and Hoddie (2007).

10. In Iraq, the result was that Sunni Arab hegemony over the military was replaced by Shiite hegemony over the Iraqi Security Forces with the Kurds forming their own security sector, the Kurdish Security Forces.

11. The ideological identity of the security sector refers to the general values, or ideologies, that its agencies attempt to project to their members but also to society at large, which in divided societies can be communal or multicommunal.

12. This refers to what the security agencies actually do, or claim to be doing, in the area of security (e.g., defending the state or preserving law and order in its territory).

13. On the dilemmas of policing in divided societies, see Guelke (2012: 55–76). O'Leary (2013: 4) argues that "security bodies must be organized so that power sharing within the political bodies is meaningful."

14. The Druze in Lebanon are not Muslims in the religious sense but are considered a Muslim community for political purposes.

15. A telling example is Israel's security sector, particularly the Israel Security Agency, known by its Hebrew acronym Shabak (or Shin Bet). In the 2012 film *The Gatekeepers* by Dror Moreh, six former Shabak directors narrate their efforts to suppress the Palestinians' resistance to Israel's rule in the Occupied Territories since 1967. But despite the fact that all of these officials put their best efforts into achieving this goal, Palestinian resistance to Israel's occupation continued, and each official had to cope with essentially the same problem as his predecessor.

16. One can argue that the control model was evident already in 1958, when Lebanon's Muslim communities and Christian communities were at loggerheads over President Camille Chamoun's pro-Western tendencies and his opposition's identification with Egyptian president Gamal Abdul Nasser and Arab nationalism. However, the fact that in this period the Christians (especially Maronites) dominated the LAF, whereas the opposition was mostly composed of Muslims, prompted the LAF command, and especially General Chehab, from employing it against the opposition, and in the aftermath of the crisis, the LAF underwent reforms that increased the Muslims' sense of ownership toward it. See Barak (2009: 53–62).

17. Examples include the Serbian Army after the breakup of Yugoslavia and the Iraqi army in the wake of the Gulf War of 1991.

18. These are the Internal Security Forces, which include the police and gendarmerie and are currently headed by a Sunni Muslim; the General Directorate of General Security, which is currently headed by a Shiite Muslim; and the General Directorate of State Security, which is currently headed by a Catholic.

9

The Politics of Police Reform in New Democracies

Diane E. Davis

A special dilemma confronts postrevolutionary regimes attempting to transcend prior dictatorships and transition to democracy. These regimes must procure their own security, routing whatever counterrevolutionary remnant survives in society, at the same time that they lay the institutional foundations for democracy. These two objectives are often in tension with each other, especially when it comes to constructing the police. To secure public order as well as regime authority, the regime needs a strong, centralized, and politically steadfast police force, willing and capable of asserting coercive power against the regime's political enemies. However, the procurement of these very qualities—centralized control and staunch loyalty—is liable to undermine the foundation of democratic practice and impartial rule of law by politicizing the police force and immunizing it from popular accountability.

In the wake of the uprisings of 2011, this was (and remains) a dilemma faced by a number of Arab countries. But the problem is not unique to the Arab world. Postrevolutionary Mexico faced precisely the same conundrum in the early twentieth century and exploring its case offers a historical perspective on as well as analytic insight into the dynamics of this quandary. Unfortunately the Mexican case constitutes something of a cautionary tale since the decision by the postrevolutionary regime in Mexico to prioritize protection from counterrevolutionary forces led to the compromise of democratic institutions and forged a long legacy of police corruption and abuse of power. By reflecting on the dynamics of the Mexican experience, one can examine the relationship between police practice and democratic transition as well as shed light on the essential paradox faced by postrevolutionary regimes: even those committed to democratic ideals often must rely on nondemocratic practices in the service of democratic transition. These practices, especially deployment of undue coercion and overly centralized power, may, in the long run, undermine the democratic character of the regimes they are intended to secure.

The Arab Spring in Comparative-Historical Light: Reflections on the Case of Mexico

Historical evidence suggests that postrevolutionary regimes have an extraordinarily difficult time toeing the fine line between establishing postregime security, enabling state accountability to citizens, and transitioning toward democracy. Or at least this appears to be the case if one takes a closer look at Mexico following the 1910 revolution that ousted longtime dictator General Porfirio Díaz and ushered in a new regime committed to democracy and a fundamental change in governance. An examination of the evolution of policing in postrevolutionary Mexico, with a view to its impact on longer-term political developments in that country, gives ample evidence that prioritizing the requisites of policing and security over those of creating democratic institutions can set a country on a downwardly spiraling slippery slope of armed conflict and deteriorating rule of law. In the Mexican case, policing dynamics clashed with constitution-making dynamics, undermining rather than strengthening the rule of law in ways that limited longer-term efforts to establish robust democratic institutions and practices. The immediate challenges faced by the postrevolutionary leadership with respect to carving out room for maneuver vis-à-vis their political enemies led to the creation of a highly centralized state connected to an expansive and powerful police apparatus that proved to be too difficult to reform once regime transition was complete and political stability eventually returned to Mexico.

In what follows, I describe how and why the challenges of policing during regime change in postrevolutionary Mexico laid the foundation for that country's descent into despotism, why the trade-offs made between democracy and security established neither, and why the changes enacted in policing institutions to protect the citizenry from the old dictatorship's counterrevolutionary challenges ultimately led to the development of a new, perhaps more insidious, form of nondemocracy built around a rotting edifice of police corruption and abuse of power. My hope is that such knowledge will generate policy insights to help administrators and police practitioners learn from history, so that Egypt, Tunisia, and other contemporary Arab countries experiencing democracy-inspired regime change and growing tensions over police power can avoid the pitfalls that befell Mexico.

Clearly, the comparison with Mexico has its limits. The Mexican Revolution of 1910 was much more violent and protracted than the "velvet revolutions" experienced in countries like Egypt and Tunisia in 2011. In Mexico, the main point of contestation among regime-change protagonists was class and provincial power within a single nation-state, with ethnic and cultural differences within the population subordinated to these general aims.[1] In the Arab world, by contrast, contestation over cultural issues such as secularism and the role of Islam in governance has divided the population in ways that have complicated the new regime's security aims and political priorities. Finally, the Mexican Revolution was primarily an internal affair undertaken by a deeply divided nation (even if the shadow of the United States hung over the conflict). By contrast, the fate of postrevolutionary regimes in the contemporary Arab world cannot be understood without an eye to the instability of the larger regional environment and the ways that the United States, Europe, Israel, and the Arab League all have a stake in the fate of the postrevolutionary regimes.

Despite these differences, in all these cases the mere fact of regime change produced a set of common dilemmas: How would the new administration secure its hold on power in the face of opposition? To what degree would the police versus the military be the primary forces for achieving this aim? And what institutional, legal, and political obstacles would new governing authorities face in the process? By reflecting on these general dynamics in Mexico's transition from authoritarian rule to democracy, one can generate some comparative insights that can be applied to the post–Arab Spring countries as they turn to the task of promoting democratic regime change in today's world.

Before beginning, a few words about sources and methodology are in order. The research on Mexico is based on primary and secondary sources, including historical archives visited in Mexico City.[2] Several key published works on the history of policing and the history of local government also served as primary reference materials, some of which also relied on the same archival resources.[3] Finally, it bears repeating that the goal of this chapter is to use the case of Mexico and its experience with regime change to unpack the policing dilemmas and challenges facing countries undergoing democratic transition, using this material to offer these insights as a basis for considering the fate and future of policing, regime change, and democracy in these other contexts.

Policing and Democratic Transition: What the Literature Says

The contemporary literature on policing has been slow to examine the relationship between police practice and democratic regime change. Indeed, much of research on professionalized policing starts from the assumption that police forces have not played an important role in fostering democratic transition because democratic state building is usually seen as preceding rather than following the advent of modern and centrally controlled police forces (Emsely, 1991). If scholars do look for the relationship between democracy and policing, they usually only wish to identify the impact that democracy has on policing (Bayley, 1976, 1985), rather than vice-versa.[4]

Additionally, most scholars work under the premise that policing is a particularistic, nation-specific matter that reflects emergent cultural values and unique local histories in the given country or within its policing subcultures. This premise explains why most scholars suggest that police systems have considerable permanence over time (Bayley, 1985: 81; Shelley, 1995: 105; Waller, 1994: 276). To be sure, the literature has identified a variety of variables that are important in comprehending differences and similarities in policing and police institutions over time: criminal and prosecution systems (McEldowney, 1991: 15), the civilian versus military nature of policing (Bayley, 1975: 330; Emsely, 1991), the timing of the inception of the first national police system (Bayley, 1975; Kalmanowiecki, 1995: 13), role behavior and professional image (Bayley, 1975, 1976), internal organization (Bayley, 1975: 330), the nature of accountability (Bayley, 1975, 1985), and the balance of class relations and the ideological context of state power (Bayley, 1975; J. Davis 1991: 14; Shelley, 1995). But most of these studies have looked at cross-national differences, rather than changes within the same country over time, thereby reinforcing the sense that culture and history set police patterns through police organizational structures and subcultures, independent of political regime type. Such assumptions are further reinforced by the large body of literature claiming that police organizations show a natural tendency toward autonomy, especially in democratic societies (Berliere, 1991: 49; Shelley, 1995: 42).

The main exception to this rule can be found in the literature on authoritarian or colonial policing, which suggests that in times of radical regime change, the function and character of police institutions may also drastically change. This observation is explored in Edward Crankshaw's (1956) work on the Gestapo in Nazi Germany and by J. Michael Waller's (1994) work on the Soviet Union, as well as by Richard Hill's (1991) work on New Zealand. But in these cases, the observed regime change involved the transition from democracy to either authoritarianism or some form of caretaker colonialism (the latter of which abrogated the democratic rights of the colonized), not the other way around. Furthermore, the primary focus of this work was to explore the impact of regime change on the capacity of the police to repress enemies of the state or establish social control (see also Anderson and Killingray, 1991; Brewer et al., 1996; Huggins, 1998).

Consequently, surprisingly few scholars have explored the larger theoretical questions about the role of police in democratic regime change, be it positive or negative. And very little research has been done on the role of the police when political transition is born through violence.[5] Perhaps this lack of research is due to too few historical examples in which large-scale violence internal to a nation actually ousted dictatorship sufficiently to enable a more durable democratic regime change. But if one were to look more carefully at cases of violent national conflicts in which transcending dictatorship and institutionalizing democracy were the stated goals, and in which police were called upon to establish security in the wake of continued violence and conflict over the transition, as in the Mexican Revolution, one might be able to assess the policing and security conditions that help or hinder a country's democratic transition.

In doing so, one should focus on four areas of inquiry that have developed within the general police literature but that have not necessarily been applied to studies of democratic transition. The first concerns the establishment of a clear legal order and the writing of a constitution and whether this process comes before or after the development of police institutions (Anderson and Killingray, 1991: 5). This question, in short, is one about timing and sequencing. A second concern involves the relationship between the military and police and the impact of this relationship on police action and regime consolidation. Do significant divisions exist within the coercive apparatus, and will they problematize the transition? A third concern relates to the degree of centralization necessary for regime consolidation and for establishing an effective public security apparatus. Will centralization of control over the security sector enable or constrain democratic transition? And the last concerns the conditions under which police will become overtly or covertly involved in political activities, and whether the politicization of security services will strengthen or weaken a democratic regime.

Overall the literature suggests that police work most effectively and least abusively when a state's legal and administrative systems are well established prior to the development of policing institutions (McEldowney, 1991). Further, these conditions are most likely to be met at later stages of state formation after the military's key role in regime consolidation is established, and police replace the military as the key source of social order and public security (Brewer et al., 1996). The literature also suggests that the more centralized the state regime, the more likely police are to respond to the state and not to citizens (Bayley, 1976; Huggins, 1998; Shelley, 1995). And finally, the more the current political order is threatened by violence, or the more the initial and principal mandate of the police is to defend the political regime, the more likely the police are to become involved in political processes in ways that hold the potential to circumvent the democratic order (Bayley, 1985; Waller, 1994).

The task in the upcoming pages is to see if any or all of these conditions were reproduced in postrevolutionary Mexico, why or why not, and with what effect on the character of policing as well as on the success of the country's democratic transition. I will focus on four key dimensions of the police-regime change nexus: (1) the timing and sequencing of police reforms with respect to changes in democratic institutions, including constitutional reforms, (2) the level of centralization involved in the construction of the postrevolutionary policing apparatus, (3) the degree of politicization of police institutions, including the extent to which their primary role was to create social order versus root out political enemies, and (4) the degree of division within the state's coercive apparatus, understood both institutionally (i.e., between police, military, and the courts) and ideologically.

Regime Change in the Context of a Divided Citizenry

As with most political transitions associated with revolutionary regime change, a mass of citizens that unite to forcibly oust a dictator will not always share a common vision of the future, as was certainly the case in the Mexican Revolution of 1910 (Hart, 1978). Prior to the revolution, the presidential administration of General Porfirio Díaz found popular support among the upper classes and commercial elite, who benefited greatly from the economic model the administration pursued in partnership with foreign and domestic capital. As a career military officer himself, Díaz was also very popular within the upper ranks of the professional military, many of whom were his allies if not his personal friends. The main source of opposition to Díaz's rule consisted of a national coalition of labor, peasants, and the rural middle classes. Among other things, these citizens resented the fact that General Díaz had betrayed the democratic principles of the nation, imposing himself as president for close to three decades by sheer military and political force and in blatant disregard of the country's constitution (Hart, 1987; Krauze, 1976).

Given the strong support Díaz enjoyed among the military and the country's economic elite, the ousting of Díaz from the presidency proved highly contentious. His removal divided the citizenry along class and regional lines and provoked considerable violence. Even after Díaz fled in 1911, Mexico faced a protracted period of violent political conflict, much of it centered in or around the capital city. The country spent nearly a decade embroiled in open contention over who would gain sufficient state power to consolidate the country's political transition after decades-long military dictatorship. In this battle, he who controlled the streets and coercive institutions of the capital city would ultimately control the regime.

In Mexico City the new revolutionary regime that replaced Díaz's rule faced an uphill battle precisely because forces allied with the prior dictatorship still dominated the military and police. Félix Díaz, also a general in the Mexican army (as well as the nephew of the ousted president and the former police chief of Mexico City) led the counterrevolutionary movement and facilitated its draw on military allies, local police officers, and the city's commercial elite to undermine the revolutionary government's efforts to change the nature of governance. Further complicating matters, the new regime faced significant security challenges posed by intense conflict within its own political ranks and civilian base about the direction the country should take after the revolution.

In contrast to the revolutions of the Arab Spring, where one of the fundamental fissures concerned the secular-religious divide and where divisions between moderate and conservative Islamic forces also complicated matters, in Mexico the primary cleavage focused on matters of class and the merits of embracing a radical economic model. The revolution's middle-class loyalists were integral players in this conflict. Unsure about what form of governance they preferred, the middle-class supporters were distinguished by one common denominator: a desire to insure that urban life would continue as before. The middle class, working class, and peasantry were all represented in the revolution, but they disagreed about which leader should take the nation forward. Consequently, internal conflict lasted for almost two decades after Díaz was deposed. The first ten years after the revolution were extremely violent and politically contested (Knight, 1986), and the country witnessed a range of assassinations and betrayals within the so-called revolutionary family.

The ongoing protests and violent skirmishes between pro- and anti-regime protagonists were significant not only because they showed the degree of disunity within civil society about the future of the revolutionary transition but also because they underscored the precariousness of the new regime's hold on power and its tenuous capacity to impose order. The continued unrest helps explain why the police soon become one of the most important forces in postrevolutionary political consolidation, and why the capital city police emerged as a particularly key political player.

In the context of regime transition, the legitimacy and efficacy of policing functions become extremely important. And as the history of Mexico's revolutionary consolidation shows, the new regime's capacity to effectively manage its security functions, and to separate policing security from military objectives in an accountable fashion, proves to be the Achilles' heel of any successful democratic transition.

Establishing Order: First Step Toward Regime Consolidation?

In Mexico, the problem of establishing security in the capital city was particularly difficult in the face of a partially armed citizenry, a still unconsolidated regime change, and the persistence of loyalists linked to the old regime in both the military and the police, all elements that a counterrevolutionary movement could exploit. Under such conditions, the political leaders of the revolutionary regime felt they had little recourse but to develop an entirely new set of police institutions that they could control and mobilize in the service of consolidating a new democratic system (Picatto, 2001). This was easier said than done, primarily because the revolutionary elite faced the double challenge of mounting a new police force while rendering the old police inoperative. The policy choice they embraced was to patch together a rough and tumble police force comprising poorly trained personnel who could be politically trusted to keep the local peace as the new leaders sought to consolidate their still tenuous hold on power (Iñigo, 1994).

Many of the new police recruits were provincial peasants whose loyalties to the revolution had been established by their willingness to join the armed struggle against the old regime in the revolution's early phases. In other words, many of the new police recruits were rural folk with little understanding of city life or policing and with little understanding of the law or how to guarantee it. They had few social, personal, or even political connections to the urban middle-class citizens they were charged with safeguarding, many of whom had remained politically uncommitted to the revolutionary struggle to oust the old regime.[6] These factors exacerbated an environment of mistrust between citizens and the police.

In the face of these constraints, the postrevolutionary government experimented with a series of police reforms. Each was intended to strengthen the government's hold on the state while also restoring order. But each led to a series of political challenges that drove the institutional evolution of policing in unexpected and increasing problematic ways. Mexico's postrevolutionary leaders learned the hard way the importance of establishing a local police force they could count upon to protect their hold on the state. For example, Gustavo Madero, the immediate successor to Porfirio Díaz, was assassinated in an attempted military coup only a year after taking office in 1912. This was in no small part due to Madero's inability to count on the local police in Mexico City to protect him from counterrevolutionary military forces operating in the city.[7]

Some have gone so far as to say that Madero's biggest mistake was his failure to completely disband the Mexican Army after taking office. The army retained Porfirian loyalists in its leadership even after Díaz had fled the country, and it remained headquartered in military barracks within striking distance of the presidential residence (Hart, 1987; Knight, 1986). As a civilian ruler, Madero knew very little about the military mentality and had few connections to the military elite, either social or political, particularly as he sought to consolidate his new democratic regime. Although his civilian status was a welcome change from the military control that had characterized the prior Díaz administration, it probably spelled his undoing.

The threat posed by a coercive apparatus riddled with counterrevolutionaries (and the need to court and contain it) was lost on Madero, who was committed to writing a new constitution and hoped to build democratic institutions at the national level. But the threat was not lost on Madero's political successors, whose efforts to weaken—if not undercut— both Porfirian-era police institutions and independent citizen militias pushed them down a slippery slope of institutional reforms. These changes steadily empowered police vis-à-vis civil society and connected police and military institutions in ways that strengthened the authoritarian features of the new state. The foundations for this slow but steady transformation started with Madero's original decision to arm citizen militias and continued with his revolutionary successors as they sought to weaken the counterrevolutionaries in the military and political elite.[8]

In the political chaos that followed Madero's death, revolutionary forces had little recourse but to turn to citizens to help them wage battle against counterrevolutionary elements, especially in the capital city, given the presence of the Porfirian-dominated police force. Emboldened by support from urban citizens who had taken up arms on their behalf in 1911, revolutionary forces again formalized a role for local citizen militias to help secure the city after Madero's assassination (Rodríguez Kuri, 1996a). Initially, such militias in Mexico City were used primarily for the purposes of subduing contending peasant factions of the revolutionary coalition. The military was left to fight the counterrevolutionary forces in the provincial battlefields.[9]

In Mexico, the arming of urban citizens during a period of intense confrontation further contributed to everyday street violence, especially in the capital city, further creating an urgent need for the state to step in and establish public order. The problem was that although many of the original citizen militias had been strong supporters of Madero, by 1913 and 1914 many of the newly armed Mexico City citizens did not feel the same passion for the political vision advanced by the new revolutionary leaders— Generals Venustiano Carranza and Álvaro Obregón.[10] Thus, as soon became obvious to the regime leadership, some type of independent police force—and hopefully a disciplined and politically loyal one—had to be established in order to meet the twin aims of establishing social order and public security.

Municipal Police, Citizen Militias, or the Military: Who Should Secure the Transition?

As the first step toward this aim, General Carranza ordered the armed forces directly under his command to take on policing functions in 1915, replacing civilian police with military personnel.[11] The revolutionary army by then comprised personnel that Carranza and his allies felt they could both organizationally control and trust to root out political enemies. But such moves were very unpopular. Many Mexico City citizens abhorred the uncivilized, drunken, and uneducated recruits who formed the core of the military rank and file, and as a result they put very little confidence in the regime-led army's policing capacities. They also felt that the new recruits abused their power and created an environment of fear by wielding guns and other firearms that were now only available to the military.[12] For this reason, revolutionary leaders also allowed some of the previous municipal police officers to carry on their duties but limited their domain to nonsecurity activities such as regulating commerce and approving building permits.[13] The new militarily-constituted police force was given control over the security situation.

Soon, however, it became clear that the imposition of military personnel into the policing domain as the main guarantors of public security created its own problems. First, organizational competition arose between the municipal police (a locally oriented city police force) and the military police (answering to national defense authorities). Both struggled to monopolize coercive capacity. Such tensions often led to fistfights between military and police personnel, actions that in turn delegitimized the security services as a whole and limited effectiveness.

Second, ambiguity developed over which of these forces should be calling the shots with respect to providing security at the level of the city, and with which clients in mind, citizens or the state. This ambiguity, too, reinforced organizational tensions in ways that reduced the state's capacities to guarantee security. Logic has it that centralizing security services in the hands of the militarily-coordinated police force would have delivered greater regime control over security services. But because of tensions and conflicts between different police organizations, the regime could not always impose its aims at the street level, where municipal police and military police battled each other to carve out and protect their own turf.

Third, and most important, perhaps, the regime's heavy-handed efforts to centralize control over security forces suggested authoritarian and militaristic tendencies among regime elites. Furthermore, those involved in local policing functions were increasingly perceived as political actors working on behalf of the regime rather than security forces seeking to protect the citizenry.

Police Reform and Democratic Legitimacy: Is There a Relationship?

In Mexico, regime authorities responded to the instability and contestation that surfaced after the revolution by mixing police with military personnel and using the army for everyday policing purposes. But soon they turned their attention to the creation of a new police force institutionally separated from the military. In June 1916 President Carranza issued a decree to overhaul and reform municipal-level "policing and vigilance, which he considered necessary to the task of purging the country of armed partisans left over from the intense revolutionary movements" (Pacheco Miranda, 1998: 134). He was partly motivated by the fact that even within the military, whose personnel had been empowered to police the city in order to purge counterrevolutionaries, certain factions remained loyal to Emiliano Zapata and Pancho Villa. Zapata and Villa were peasant-oriented revolutionaries who were pushing for a more radical vision than Carranza sought to pursue. Thus, even within the so-called revolutionary family and its military loyalists, ideological divisions surfaced, creating problems for regime stability. To reduce the threat of an internally led military coup d'état, Carranza sought a new security structure that would counterbalance full military control over local police, giving the latter more power in the capital city. This new police was to answer directly to the president, not the military.

Significantly, this decree also emerged in the context of a call for a move from a "military to a constitutional regime" and in tandem with Carranza's vocal support for a restoration of democratic elections at the level of the municipality. The motto of "Municipio Libre" (free municipality) had been one of the rallying cries of the revolution, and postrevolutionary leaders often resuscitated such claims to generate goodwill among the citizenry. This move from military to constitutional rule in which municipalities were to be afforded powers of self-governance could be interpreted as an effort to respond to citizen dissatisfaction with lack of accountability at the local level, to limit the political power of the military, and to slowly move Mexico toward a constitutional democracy.

Although these reforms were intended to buttress the regime's political legitimacy vis-à-vis the citizenry and open a pathway toward democracy, security concerns were also primary. The Carranza regime still faced opposition from radical forces within the revolutionary ranks, each of whom had allies within the military. This fact, combined with the fallout generated by citizen fears that the new presidentially appointed police force was motivated more by political than security concerns, motivated Carranza to further limit the political muscle of the national military apparatus by denying electoral rights to "active members of the military" as well as "those individuals who had aided the governments or factions hostile to the constitutionalist cause, either through armed struggle or *public service*" (Pacheco Miranda, 1998: 134; emphasis added). The latter category applied to holdover municipal police from the prerevolutionary period as well as newer military recruits whose loyalties lay with Zapata or Villa rather than Carranza.

Carranza and others supporting the introduction of a constitutional regime hoped that by both reforming the city's police and electorally disenfranchising armed opponents in one fell swoop, he could solve the problem of public insecurity, outmaneuver regime enemies at the local level, diminish political infighting among the armed forces, and perhaps deliver elusive political legitimacy to his nascent democratic constitutional order, at least in the capital city. Yet none of his objectives were realized, in part because of the timing and sequencing of these reforms. In particular, the fact that a new democratic constitution outlining the legal rights of citizens had not yet been approved by a constitutional assembly (a constitution would not be approved until 1917), combined with the fact that municipal elections were still pending, meant that the newly created municipal police would continue to work largely on behalf of the centralized revolutionary leadership. Faced with a disconnect between the longer-term democratic aims of the initial 1916 reform and a transitional situation in which the revolutionary leadership still kept tight control over municipal-level security, the people's dissatisfaction accelerated.

Both the municipalities and a growing cadre of local opposition political parties actively questioned the new regime's efforts to meddle in local affairs with respect to security. With municipal elections promised for the future, political activity at the local level began to accelerate dramatically. The municipality was the only place where competing political forces could make a claim for representation in the new postrevolutionary context. Hence, both revolutionary and counterrevolutionary enemies of the regime soon began to mobilize at the level of the community, at times using local militia, police, or military loyalists in their campaigns or to disrupt political meetings of opponents. These developments often resulted in violence and led the Carranza regime to backtrack on the idea of restructuring police services so as to function only at the municipal level.[14] In 1917, scarcely a year after the initial call for separating police from the military, the revolutionary government introduced yet another security sector reform that ended up centralizing policing power once again, albeit not solely in the hands of the military.

The reform called for the creation of yet another police force that would operate in the densest and most economically significant areas of the city, a conglomeration of previously distinct municipalities that would now be known as the Distrito Federal (DF), or Federal District. This district, which held the most important governing offices and economic activities of the capital city became in effect a separate political jurisdiction within Mexico City, and one that was to be constitutionally subject to national government control.[15] The chief of the new police force for the DF now would answer to the president, and in order to foster better coordination of the police and the military, a military man was named chief of the capital city police.[16] In addition, the DF police force was instructed to work with other locally appointed police in the municipalities surrounding the DF, thus introducing the possibility of DF police meddling in the affairs of surrounding localities whose police were more connected to the locality.

In many ways, this reform was a compromise move intended to lessen tensions between the police, military, citizens, and the revolutionary regime. Carranza hoped this change would reduce opposition and stabilize the political situation so as to speed up democratic transition. But one consequence of this reform was a strengthening of the authoritarian character of the state, mainly through the imposition of military discipline in the capital city's police organization. Military mentalities were adopted in daily police practices, reflected in the use of military protocols in daily drills and in the development of a policing mind-set in which local citizens who pushed the limits of the law were considered potential enemies of the state. The fusion of military and state objectives in the local policing apparatus also shifted police practice away from quotidian monitoring of petty crime and urban service provision and toward clandestine surveillance of citizens who criticized the regime.[17] In this environment, coercion and fear became the modus operandi of local governance in the DF, security related or otherwise. Such objectives not only limited the possibilities for democratic deliberation among civil society actors but, in the long run, also led to the development of unparalleled police power, reflected in greater individual and institutional discretion on the part of police officers to act with total impunity in the capital city.

Police Power and the Justice System: Conflict over Regulatory Capacity

In Mexico, the growing powers and capacity of police to monitor security in the capital city after 1917 led to major tensions within the larger administration of the justice system. The centralization of the DF police and its sharing of power with the military may have enabled it to deliver on the regime's articulated security aims of rooting out political enemies in the capital, but it also put the new police force in conflict with both more radical prodemocracy advocates and more liberal judges and lawyers in the justice system. These ideologically diverse forces joined together to call for limits on the new regime's centralizing tendencies, particularly with respect to who had the authority to establish the rule of law and guarantee democratic procedures.

The growing concern over the regime's centralizing and authoritarian tendencies was further intensified by ongoing social conflict over repeated efforts by the regime to exempt the central areas of the city (i.e., the DF, where the main economic and social infrastructure and almost all national offices of government were located) from the constitutional guarantees of the *municipio libre* built on direct electoral democracy. Much of this tension came to a head in 1928, when the government completely eliminated democratic elections in all municipalities in Mexico City, although this move was only the last of a series of centralizing acts set in motion by the transformations of policing in the decade after the revolution.

Perhaps the most consequential of these moves came in 1917, a year after the creation of the special DF police force, which now answered directly to the president. It came in the form of a new law reforming the legal status and juridical sway of police, a shift that became enshrined in the 1917 constitution, the document that Carranza and his revolutionary coalition used to establish the ideological and legal blueprint for the new democratic regime. This 1917 reform separated Mexico City police into two types of coercive forces, labeled the "preventative" and the "judicial" police. The category of preventative police was meant to encompass all those traditional activities of urban regulation that contributed to the social, commercial, and aesthetic order of the city, a set of tasks considered to constitute good governance (*buen gobierno*) and related to conventional views of public security as articulated by citizens who worried about street crime. The preventative police functioned like beat cops who kept an eye out for social disorder and violations of urban regulations.[18] The category of judicial police, in contrast, encompassed those forces legally charged with determining whether a crime had occurred and arresting these violators of the law. Put differently, judicial police were given the power to legally sanction (i.e., arrest), investigate, and try or jail citizens for infractions of the law.[19]

This division of labor between the preventative and the judicial police was intended to link a special cadre of loyal and thus "political" police with judicial power directly to the state, while leaving more "normal" police forces who interacted with citizens on a daily basis without such powers.[20] Part of Carranza's rationale for introducing this reform was his contention that many of the existent preventative police—meaning those long-standing municipal police employed by the "free" municipalities who worked as beat cops—held counterrevolutionary or nonrevolutionary sentiments. That is, they were ideologically unsympathetic to his administration's efforts to consolidate a new regime. Hence, he sought to limit their power in ways that ultimately strengthened the state's authoritarian capacities.

Before Carranza's reform of the constitution, the preventative police had the authority to detain and fine almost anyone under the pretext of his or her having violated the law. Carranza worried that this practice would give them undue power to thwart the new regime's political aims (if only by giving them the legal power to harass or persecute revolutionary loyalists). One way to undermine the punitive and prosecutorial power of the regime's enemies was to limit their powers and concentrate them in a new police corps, the judicial police. The latter would be subject directly to state oversight (i.e., bound to the Public Ministry [Ministerio Público]) rather than to citizens organized at the level of the municipality. By contrast, the preventative police, or beat cops, remained under the oversight of the municipalities. Yet this reform also gave Carranza a way of seizing hold of the administration of the justice system. The judges and the larger court system were known to be laced with counterrevolutionary loyalists to the Porfirian regime, and thus by empowering the judicial police to serve as intermediaries between the judges and lawyers of the court system on the one hand and street police on the other, the Carranza regime was positioned to counter what they saw as the antirevolutionary biases in the legal and police system.[21]

Thus, starting in 1917, the powers of the courts and street police were reduced and the newly formed judicial police force was given the authority to investigate, arrest, and bring citizens to trial. In this way, the postrevolutionary government could minimize the counterrevolutionary tendencies of police and judges who sought to undermine its larger revolutionary aims. Because the judicial police were organizationally located in the Public Ministry staffed by national cabinet appointment, they were formally considered part of the executive branch and not the judicial branch. Hence they were even more likely to act in accordance with the interests of the new regime. And needless to say, after the reform was enacted, the regime was most likely to offer positions in the judicial police to revolutionary loyalists, reinforcing the political loyalties of this newly empowered police force. The loyalty of the new force was in stark contrast to the beat police and the judges, many of whom owed their appointments to the prerevolutionary Díaz government and hence could not be trusted.

Politicization of Police: The Fallout

Carranza's 1917 constitutional reform of the police ultimately proved successful at undermining the political challenges posed by liberal democratic forces within the court system. The reforms strengthened the connection between the security apparatus and the new regime sufficiently so as to allow Carranza to carry out the rest of the 1917 constitutional mandate, which included land reform, labor rights, and other democratic ideals. This alliance effectively fostered the consolidation of the Mexican Revolution, but it also ushered in more than seven decades of one-party rule in which police had inordinate power within the regime. To explain how the democratic mobilization and constitutional principles of the Mexican Revolution failed to counterbalance these undemocratic tendencies, one must return, ironically, to the policing reforms that made regime consolidation possible.

The answer rests in a closer look at the centralization of the DF police in 1916 followed by legislative changes introduced in the 1917 constitution. The imposition of a military-led special police force answering to the president in the DF, and the new laws separating judicial from preventative police and giving the former power to influence the justice system, led to an ever more politicized security apparatus, with both police and the military working on behalf of the state. The use of security forces for eminently political purposes was of course a trend that dated to the early postrevolutionary period. But it was reinforced by the appointment of military generals as police chiefs and administrators after 1916 and then by the creation of the judicial police tied directly to the Public Ministry the next year. By the late 1910s and early 1920s, with tensions over the democratic versus authoritarian nature of the regime still continuing, Mexico City police (both judicial and preventative) were routinely ordered by their superiors in the regime to harass and arrest protesting laborers, renegade social movements, and opposition party activists.[22]

Complicating matters, the politicization of policing reinforced a high degree of disunity, division, and competition among different types of police forces, thus establishing a nearly irresolvable power struggle between local and national authorities who competed for control of the general policing of the city and particular police forces within it. The balance of power within the police forces (not to mention the legal system as a whole) shifted dramatically given the strong personal and political connections the judicial police forces enjoyed with the national revolutionary leadership. (Appointment to the judicial police came via the executive branch.) With such privileged access to the regime elite and endowed with enhanced legal capacity to investigate and try criminals, the power of the judicial police rapidly began to that of both the preventative police and the court system. The privileged position bestowed on the judicial police led to everincreased competition and conflict with the preventative and judicial police, as well as a delegitimization of the rule of law. At minimum, rule of law was subordinated to purely political concerns.[23]

Even so, the preventative police did not sit by quietly as the judicial police came to wield ever greater authority over citizens. To advance their own interests and fill their pockets, the preventative police developed new forms of rent seeking, primarily related to the regulation of urban commercial and social activities, contributing to a growing culture of impunity in the exercise of police authority in Mexico City over the subsequent decades.[24] The incidence of bribery and opportunities for extortion arose at every stage of the criminal prosecution process, owing to the regime's continuous efforts to establish and centralize control over a cadre of loyal police steadfast in their support of the regime. Not only did the separation of arrest from prosecutorial powers make rent seeking and corruption possible at both levels, but also the preventative police and the citizens themselves had great incentive to engage in small-scale bribery right at the level of the street, since this exchange could prevent a case from even getting to court (where bribery "costs" were much greater, given what was at stake in the judicial proceedings).

Making matters worse, the judicial police were quite aware of this development. Consequently, they often crossed beyond the established legal bounds of their jobs, usurping preventative police duties. With citizens facing distinct yet competing authorities at a variety of discrete points in the journey, from suspicion to arrest to prosecution to conviction, a vicious cycle of greater rent seeking (i.e., corruption) evolved. Since many of the police agents implicated in these corrupt processes were political appointees, answering to the executive branch or the municipality, governing authorities themselves became party to the corruption.

As early as the late 1920s, a pecking order of bribery and corruption became well established in the police, such that the beat cop on the ground could not acquire or keep a job without direct payments to superiors. This situation further fueled police shakedown of citizens (especially small retailers), thereby estranging the police from citizens even more. And the greater the rent seeking, the more the law was flouted, since regulation or enforcement of the law became merely another commodity to be bought and sold within the police forces. By the early 1930s, postrevolutionary Mexico's political profile was firmly set: a highly centralized political system, built on the use of the police to protect the fragile state and undermine political opponents, and a justice system that itself became ever more corrupted. By the 1940s and 1950s, the police had become one of the most corrupted forces in the country, working in tandem with the military to grease the wheels of impunity and becoming involved in illegal activities that further undermined their legitimacy as a force of social order (Alcocer, 1997; Alvarado and Arzt, 2001; Andreas, 1998).

By the late 1960s and early 1970s, the abusive behavior of the police on behalf of an increasingly centralized, nondemocratic state led them to flaunt their impunity in a variety of ways, ranging from stopping motorist for bribes to shooting student protesters who clamored for democracy in the famous 1968 massacres at Tlatelolco (Aguayo, 1998). By the 1980s and 1990s, police and military involvement in drugs, guns, and money laundering put them even beyond the control of the state. They became the tail that wagged the regime dog, rather than vice versa (Bailey and Godson, 2000; Zepeda, 1994).

Mexico's descent into this unenviable quagmire occurred for a variety of reasons, but some of the most important can be traced to the requisites of postregime change policing and public security, the amalgamation of police and military organizations in the service of this aim, and the undermining of municipal-level democratic institutions in order to establish politically loyal police forces capable of insuring "public order." By privileging police functions over all else, and by prioritizing political reliability over all else, Mexico laid the seeds for its own troubled path.

Over the last fifteen years, Mexico has shaken off its authoritarian heritage, after decades of citizen struggle for democracy. Even so, the country has not yet disposed of its rotten internal core. It continues to be plagued by one of the most corrupt police forces in the world. The complicity of the police and military in international drug and gun-running operations have catapulted Mexico to the top of global crime nexus and have made the country a home to mafias, money launderers, and numerous other "illiberal" forces.[25]

Security vs. Democracy:
Final Remarks on the Challenge of Regime Change

One would be foolish to assume that as they seek democratic regime change, countries like Egypt and Tunisia will necessarily follow the path taken by Mexico and end up saddled with the same tremendous burdens of a highly corrupt police force and an illegal economy burgeoning out of control. Even so, it is worth noting that in both countries, citizens complain about police corruption and human rights abuses and call for security sector reform. The problem of institutionalized impunity must be addressed without crossing the fine line that separates it from political policing, because both can limit true democratic transition. Successful democratic revolution requires transforming the police from an institution that protects the regime to an institution that protects the people. Mexico faced this challenge with limited resources and in the midst of widespread domestic upheaval. In this respect, its experience resembles Egypt and Tunisia, which are two primary cases in this volume. One might thus argue that the central challenge for Arab regimes is to undertake police reform, which will almost certainly entail some disruptive changes that reduce its effectiveness in the near term, while still ensuring that the police remain strong enough to maintain order. Mexico has confronted this challenge for close to a century, and as such, its struggles provide some useful insights.

In particular, an important lesson to be drawn from the Mexican experience is the question of timing and sequencing of police reforms. In Mexico, the initial 1917 changes in police organization preceded the finalization of Mexico's new revolutionary constitution. And, as noted earlier, the new legislative clauses that redrew police powers strengthened police-state connections in ways that were intended to consolidate the regime's hold on power. Stated differently, changes to postrevolutionary police functions were conceived of conceptually prior to constitutional reform, insuring that the police would act, first and foremost, on behalf of the state to secure the constitution rather than vice versa. Although this sequence seemed necessary in the Mexican case in order to reduce anarchy and disorder and consolidate regime change, it also laid the foundation for corruption, impunity, and decades of authoritarian rule.

In Tunisia and Egypt, new constitutions have been enacted prior to the enactment of significant police and security sector reform. In Tunisia, at least, the debate over police reform remains subject to parliamentary legislation, thereby insuring that whatever police reform eventually materializes will be democratically vetted through parliamentary deliberation from all sides (Najjar and Ghanmi, 2013). Such oversight in turn means that reform will have to be agreeable to all contesting parties, not merely the regime currently in power, and, consequently, the country may avoid the trend toward authoritarianism fueled by politically driven police reform as was seen in the Mexican case. In Egypt, as well, police reform will come after the enactment of a new constitution. But the questionable democratic character of political life after the presidency of Mohamed Morsi suggests that police reform may indeed be tainted by the prioritization of regime survival, not democratic transition. And in this regard, too, the Mexican case may provide an important cautionary lesson.

The creation of an effective police system must be a top priority for all the countries in the Arab world aiming to break free from decades of authoritarian rule. With police reform, the legacy of true regime change—that is, the creation of a stable and democratic state—will be much more likely.

Notes

The author wishes to thank both the Carnegie Corporation of New York and the John D. and Catherine T. MacArthur Foundation for research support on the role of policing in the context of political transition (originally focused on Russia, South Africa, and Mexico) that led to this essay.

1. For one of the best overall accounts of the Mexican Revolution, see Knight (1986).

2. Mexico City Historical Archives (Archivo Histórico del Ayuntamiento de la Ciudad de Mexico) and the Mexican National Archives (Archivo General de la

Nación). The catalogue for the Mexican National Archives is available on the web (http://www.agn.gob.mx/) and more information on the Mexico City archive can be obtained at http://lanic.utexas.edu/project/tavera/mexico/ayuntamiento.html. For more academic discussion of both archives and other historical materials on policing and criminality in Mexico City, see Picatto (2001: 220–223) and Bliss (2001: 217).

3. These studies, available in Spanish for the most part, include works by Picatto (2001), Illades and Rodríguez Kuri (1996), Rodríguez Kuri (1996a), Iñigo (1994), and official government documents (Procuraduría General de la República, 1994).

4. Among the newer historical instances where such a focus is clearly evident, see the literature on South Africa's democratization and its impact on policing (Brogden and Shearing, 1993; Levin, Ngubeni, and Simpson, 1994).

5. Although Waller (1994: 278) does see changes in internal police practices of the KGB as laying the foundation for the emergence of a new Soviet political leadership committed to perestroika, this event clearly occurred within a nonviolent context, and whether it really constituted a democratic regime change, as opposed to partial democratic reform, is entirely up for debate.

6. Because the old regime of Porfirio Díaz had privileged Mexico City's economic growth at the expense of many rural areas, by pouring investments and building modern amenities in the capital (one of the many gripes of the revolutionaries in the first place), and because many of the fruits of the Porfirian economic model's largesse were concentrated in the public and private sector employment opportunities in Mexico City, many residents were quite unsympathetic to the revolution, which was likely to be seen as a rural-based scramble for national political power. Among capital city residents, industrial laborers mainly led the ranks of revolutionary protagonists. For more on political dynamics in Mexico's capital in the decades following the revolution, see D. E. Davis (1994).

7. Equally important to Madero's political defeat, albeit much less analyzed in the historical scholarship, was the fact that Mexico City's police forces were themselves still riddled with counterrevolutionary loyalists. The assassination of Madero on the streets of the capital city in broad daylight would not have happened if police had been vigilant. That they were not should have been no surprise given the fact that in the immediate prerevolutionary period, as noted before, the chief of police in Mexico City was the dictator's nephew. Under his guidance, the city's police force had worked on behalf of the private sector, repressing street vendors, keeping labor and other undesirable social forces under control, and making it possible for President Díaz to carry out his desired infrastructural projects and commercial or industrial policies in the capital city. For precisely this reason, in fact, the new presidential administration of Gustavo Madero should have questioned the local police's loyalty to him as well as to the city's business leaders.

8. For a serious discussion of the difficult process of state consolidation and the ten years of infighting among leaders of the revolution, see Knight (1986).

9. This division of labor was most evident when the more moderate forces in the revolutionary coalition, Generals Venustiano Carranza and Álvaro Obregón, rose to the position of the country's supreme leaders and then the presidency and used citizen militias from Mexico City to help keep their considerably more radical rural counterparts, Emiliano Zapata and Pancho Villa, from capturing the capital city and seizing control over the postrevolutionary state. At this early point, conditions were still too unstable to call national elections for president, so the use of force was the most direct route to higher seats of government.

10. For further information on these key revolutionary leaders, especially the relationship between Villa and Madero, see Katz (1998) and Krauze (1976).

11. For full discussion of the invasion of the city by peasant revolutionaries, and the urban response, see Rodríguez Kuri (1996b).

12. After the problems associated with arming citizen militias, under Carranza neither citizens nor the existent police were allowed to be armed, except through petition in exceptional circumstances.

13. Before the war, policing in Mexico involved mainly community-level vigilance directed toward health, sanitation, and public servicing concerns (street maintenance, traffic flows, and so on) built on the Spanish colonial tradition of *"buen gobierno,"* or good governance. This model was very much the one Georg Wilhelm Friedrich Hegel had in mind when he identified policing as central to the integration of society and the establishment of connections between citizens and rulers. For more on policing in Mexico and how it changed in the period surrounding the revolution, see Picatto (2001).

14. For a good discussion of the conflict over democratic rights afforded to *municipios* (i.e., municipalities) in Mexico City, and how these rights were eventually undermined throughout the 1920s, see Pacheco Miranda (1998) and Lear (2001).

15. Clearly, Carranza's desires in this regard were not unrelated to his concerns that with a democratically constituted municipal system still in place, police would answer to local (and elected) not national (and militarily-imposed) authority. An independent police force could be disastrous in downtown Mexico City, the most economically vibrant and bourgeois section of the city, filled with Porfirian loyalists and other revolutionary skeptics of Carranza's regime.

16. Noteworthy is that the first two police chiefs after 1912 were civilians, but starting in 1913 (at the point of Madero's assassination), primarily military personnel, usually colonels or generals, dominated. With the exception of a short-lived period during 1915 when two civilians headed the force (and a year in which the chief of police in Mexico City actually changed five times), all subsequent police chiefs from 1916 to 1929 were military personnel. After 1929 this pattern continued, with a civilian police chief appointed only twice thereafter (in 1930 and 1931–1932) between then and 1988. For names and terms of office see *El Nacional* (1996).

17. Worth remembering is that this new structure of policing emerged in a still-contested and unstable social, political, and economic situation, in which police were expected to restore local order and regulate the urban economy while also being called upon to secure the fragile regime. Given the high levels of suspicion and mistrust between citizens and the police as well as citizens and the new regime, sometimes distinguishing the "political" from the "normal" policing functions was hard, especially if one was a policeman. Everyone who violated the law was in some ways thwarting the power of the new state although many of the city's commercial classes—those most likely to be at the receiving end of urban regulation—were generally assumed to have questionable revolutionary credentials.

18. In the debate over the reform the then-existent (preventative) police forces opposed the shift, as did many judges and lawyers. Unable to outvote the revolutionary forces in the Congress of the Union and in the Constitutional Convention, they could not fully avoid the reform. But their influence was seen in several compromises that worked themselves into the text after much extended debate, including reserving the capacities for preventative police to impose fines, detain suspects for up to thirty-six hours, and work with judicial police in the gathering of evidence. See *Diario de los Debates*, January 12, 1917, no. 52.

19. In theory, the 1857 constitution also provided for the establishment of a so-called judicial police. But they were considered only "decorative"; and during both congressional and constitutional debates on the reform all sides agreed that Carranza's proposal to separate the tasks and legal responsibilities of preventative and judicial police was an entirely "novel" innovation. See *Diario de los Debates,* December 1916 (no. 12, 19, 29, 30) and January 1917 (no. 43, 44, 52).

20. In practice, however, this distinction was somewhat problematic, since even after the constitutional reforms were enacted, preventative police still retained the authority to detain citizens on potential violations of the law, but only for a certain number of hours (no more than thirty-six) if they did not pay an initial minimum fine, and because they were expected to actively help judicial police with the criminal end of the investigation by gathering evidence for subsequent arrest and prosecution. Nonetheless, the judicial police were more empowered in the criminal prosecution process, such that with this constitutional reform, judicial police were granted the greatest authority to prosecute and legally uphold the law.

21. During the initial period of postrevolutionary instability, and before, the courts had been no friend of the revolutionary government. Most of the nation's judges and trial lawyers were social and economic elites who supported the Porfirian government and frequently used their authority to quell revolutionary reforms. Up until the time of the Carranza police reform, moreover, judges and lawyers had the singular authority to seek, try, and convict "criminals," or those citizens charged with serious offenses or violations of the law as laid out in the 1857 constitution.

22. The 1920s was a particularly contentious period in Mexico City, and ongoing social movement rallies and organized labor actions against the state marked everyday life. Partly for this reason, the postrevolutionary government deviated widely from its commitment to democracy and abrogated the rights of citizens to elect representatives and a mayor in Mexico City. For more on this, see Lear (2001) and D. E. Davis (1994).

23. The first link in this treacherous chain of developments was established and then reinforced by the development of a variety of different police forces in the postrevolutionary period, some overlapping in function but each answering to a different set of authorities (local vs. national, city vs. municipality, politicians/parties vs. elected or civilian officials, different agencies of the local or national state). Not only did this institutional fragmentation of Mexico City police make controlling the police forces more difficult for party or governing officials, but it also established competition among them for access to rent-seeking capacities, a situation that was especially clear with respect to the relations between preventative and judicial police, since after 1917, preventative police no longer monopolized the power to arrest or investigate criminals. With judicial police holding this monopoly, they had access to much larger sources of bribery and corruption because they were the last stop before a suspected criminal was sent to the courts and jail. They wielded their rent-seeking power accordingly.

24. Preventative police also used the minimal powers they retained even in the 1917 juridical reform to strengthen their rent-seeking position vis-à-vis both citizens and the judicial police themselves. After all, to the extent that they could still impose minimal fines and hold citizens for up to thirty-six hours, even as they were expected to work with the judicial police to collect data that would be channeled to the Public Ministry for investigation and possible prosecution, they still held considerable power to extract bribes or kickback payments.

25. For more on the problems of contemporary police corruption and impunity, see Davis and Alvarado (1999) and D. E. Davis (2003, 2006).

10

Between Collapse and Professionalism: Police Reform in Egypt

Tewfiq Aclimandos

Reform of the security services in Egypt is a pressing matter. The enduring and extensive misconduct of the police was a major impetus driving the revolution of 2011, and since the fall of Hosni Mubarak, little substantive progress has been made in correcting this problem. In this chapter, I reflect on the lineage and contours of security sector misconduct in Egypt and suggest some measures for reform. At the same time, I reflect on the political obstacles that hinder the achievement of reform. The persistence of these obstacles makes clear that restructuring the security apparatus will remain a long-term objective rather than a short-term accomplishment.

Historical Overview of the Security Services

The internal security force and its institutional home, the Ministry of Interior, is a large apparatus—both imposing and opaque to outsiders. Over the years it has grown in size dramatically. In 1951, as reported by Abd al Khaliq Faruq (2012: 18–20, 27), the ministry employed 123,000 persons for 18 million Egyptians (one ministry employee for every 143 Egyptians). After Gamal Abdul Nasser's death, the number of employees rose to 214,000. By the eve of the 2011 revolution, the Ministry of Interior employed more than 1.5 million people (one for every fifty-three Egyptians). This number included 40,000 police officers (half of whom worked in the criminal police), 3,000 officers who worked in the State Security Investigations Service (abbreviated SSI, the agency responsible for tracking and controlling internal "threats," such as the Muslim Brotherhood, human rights activists, and student groups), more than half a million noncommissioned officers and policemen, and 300,000 to 400,000 conscripts who served in Central Security Forces (al-Amn al-Markazi, which serves as an antiriot police force and is responsible for suppressing protests and sustaining public order), as well as 300,000 informers.

The Ministry of Interior is opaque in its organization, methods, and even its financing. No outsider really knows how things are done and what goes on inside. And the law is very harsh against policemen who "unveil" professional secrets about internal operations (al-Batran, 2013: 173, 259).[1] As for its budget and funding, these too are quite obscure. For example, a significant portion of the ministry's funding is widely assumed to come directly from oil and Suez Canal revenues, channeled to the police (and armed forces) through the presidency.

The narrative arc of the security apparatus's history reveals significant changes in its mission, reputation, and morale over time. According to General 'Abd Al Hadi Badawi (2012), during the 1950s, 1960s, and a good part of the 1970s, the Ministry of Interior was a stable and efficient institution. The police officers corps was reliable and honest. Its members were drawn from "good families" (read: the middle class). Despite this caveat (or perhaps because of it), recruitment was meritocratic. The rules organizing hiring, promotion, transfers, and professional trajectories were transparent (Badawi, 2012: 27). However, throughout the Nasser period, the suppression of violent political dissent was basically the army's business so the Ministry of Interior was relieved of this responsibility.

During the 1970s, however, things began to change in ways that expanded the Interior Ministry's repressive role, fostered corruption, and undermined its efficiency. First, the regime reassigned the suppression of political dissent from the army to the Ministry of Interior, thereby considerably expanding the latter's domain. Second, the regime proved increasingly incapable of "delivering" social and symbolic goods to the Egyptian population, leading it to rely on ever higher levels of repression to secure control. Increasing reliance on repression led to significant expansion of the antiriot police and the state security department (Badawi, 2012: 30).[2] Third, a culture of nepotism and corruption developed that undermined the meritocracy and effectiveness of the institution. Increasingly, admission to the police academy became a matter of systematic cronyism as the president, the ministers, and members of the Parliament and the ruling party were each allotted a quota of unconditional admissions for their clients or their clients' sons. Within the ranks, meritocratic norms governing transfers, professional trajectories, and retirements were increasingly flouted. For example, more and more exceptions were made for well-connected young officers at the start of their careers, relieving them of the traditional obligation to serve several years on the beat ("the indispensable school") before they could serve in the "investigative services" (*ajhizat al bahth*) or the main headquarters. The consequences of this special treatment were huge and incalculable. Officers without the necessary knowledge or experience had increasing clout, and officers who were directly appointed to the antiriot forces without prior service in police centers on the ground easily became combatants, behaving like military men in hostile territory.[3]

In addition to these failings, the security services were increasingly plagued by corruption due to access to a host of secret funds (Badawi, 2012: 33–35).[4] These problems metastasized in a general political context that discouraged any top-down accountability. In an increasingly centralized presidential system, the interior minister was totally dependent on the goodwill of the head of the state and almost never dared to say "no" to his superior. At the same time, the minister had considerable latitude to define concrete policies (Badawi, 2012: 30), without feeling compelled to take into account the opinion of the rank and file or the ministry's research centers' recommendations.[5]

By the 1980s, conditions had gotten so bad that Hamdi al-Batran (2013) refers to this period as the "lost decade." The police apparatus was characterized by complacency, underdevelopment,[6] and "low morale,"[7] as well as excessive centralization. The fact that Egypt was placed under martial law from the start of Mubarak's presidency in 1981 (in the wake of Sadat's assassination) meant that very few police officers from that point on became acquainted with the notion of service under the rule of law. Furthermore, inconsistent leadership at the top of the Ministry of Interior did not help matters. As the analyst Badawi (2012: 36–37) argues, some like Hassan Abu Basha (minister of interior from 1982 to 1984) had a "soft spot for torture" and was exceedingly generous to his clients.[8] Others like Zaki Badr (minister of interior from 1986 to 1990) lacked political experience (Badawi, 2012).[9] Some of the ministers were praiseworthy, notably Ahmad Rushdi (minister of interior from 1984 to 1986), who fought against internal corruption and drug trafficking and did much to improve the ministry's image and public relations (Badawi, 2012). But overall, by the early 1990s, the security apparatus fell short, most importantly in ways that allowed radical Islamic fundamentalists to consolidate their networks, take hold on the ground, especially in Upper Egypt, and strongly challenge the state.

The regime did not develop a strategy to deal with the Islamist challenge until 1993 when the danger became "clear and present." Prior to that crucial moment, the security apparatus did not try to improve its performance. But once the mortal threat became apparent, the hurried response of the underdeveloped security system took the form of great expansion in the number of police, acquisition of better weapons, brutality, abrogation of the rule of law, and a variety of bad practices that had terrible costs.[10] SSI was charged with leading the repression of Islamists and that agency's power and prerogatives grew. The antiriot police forces were also strengthened: the number of officers and conscripts in this corps was increased, and they were armed with better weapons. The Ministry of Interior used this "opportunity" to maximize its gains and acquire more secret funds, more weapons, more privileges, and more impunity.[11] The police allied itself with organized crime to quell insurrection (Badawi, 2012: 45–46; al-Batran, 2013).[12] In crucial zones, the police commanders more often than not behaved like thugs.

Leadership at the top of the Ministry of Interior did not curb the misconduct of the security forces during the 1990s (and after), nor did it serve the regime well. As Badawi (2012: 40–44) argues, Abd al Halim Musa (minister of interior from 1990 to 1993) was incompetent, corrupted and corrupting, bitter, addicted to cronyism and nepotism, weak, and inefficient against Islamist radicals. During his time in office, the police officers' corps increasingly exploited its position and extracted ever more resources from society. The police corps' quest for money, lands, and material and symbolic advantages became frantic. Hassan al-Alfi, who succeeded Musa as minister of interior from 1993 to 1997, was no better a leader. His primary achievement was the appointment of a brilliant officer, Habib al Adly, as head of SSI (al-Diwwi, 2012: 11).

In 1997 Habib el-Adly was named minister of interior, and he went on to serve the longest term in this post (lasting until the end of the Mubarak regime in 2011). El-Adly's legacy is mixed (Badawi, 2012: 49; al-Batran, 2013: 173). In some ways he read the security situation in Egypt well and worked to improve the discipline and coherence of the security apparatus. But in other ways, he damaged the institution by persisting in abusive practices and sustaining a culture of corruption and nepotism.

Upon coming to office, el-Adly made one of his primary objectives tightening control (and discipline) within the Ministry of Interior as well as fortifying its resources. El-Adly quickly obtained a modification of the law governing the Ministry of Interior, enabling him to decide the fate of the generals, brigadiers, and colonels serving within it (al-Diwwi, 2012: 18).[13] El-Adly could now end their careers at the end of any year, without having to provide any justification. He also made the sanctions against leaks harsher. In this way el-Adly was able to guarantee discipline in the ranks and concentrate power in his hands.

El-Adly also expanded his empire by collaborating with the United States and regional powers and by getting his budget increased. But he was a sly political player who recognized the challenges posed to his operations by a variety of forces (pressures posed by an increasingly autonomous middle class, international NGOs committed to advocating a human rights agenda, Bush's advocacy of democratization, and exposure of his force's tactics thanks to the rise of the Internet and new independent media). To navigate these challenges, el-Adly embraced a multipronged strategy. For example, he improved prison conditions (especially for political prisoners), and he also privatized repression so as to prevent the media from capturing pictures of police forces beating political opponents or strikers. (To that end, el-Adly created private militias under police and ruling-party control in order to lend credence to a counternarrative that cast his sponsored repression as a fight between supporters and opponents of the regime.) Furthermore, el-Adly introduced intensive "human rights courses" at the police academy (taught by prominent human rights activists and liberal journalists) in order to appease the human rights community. At the same time he changed nothing essential in the training or procedures of the corps.

El-Adly gradually built his empire in the Ministry of Interior, including a small economic empire that included a shoe industry, hotels, and firms specialized in the import of goods needed by policemen. The top jobs in these economic ventures were distributed as spoils to his allies. He did nothing to fight cronyism and nepotism, as was the general pattern of Mubarak's ministers, and as a result, the highest posts often remained in the same hands for too long. El-Adly was also complacent about corruption and did nothing to counter the increasing "racketeering" and other misdeeds by the small and petty policemen. Under his rule, corrupt practices were no longer monopolized by the officers corps.[14] Consequently, everyone in society, poor, middle class, and rich, was a potential victim. No one could feel secure.

Some defend el-Adly's legacy arguing that he worked to improve the readiness and mobility of the antiriot police and that he strengthened SSI and the criminal police, especially in Greater Cairo and Alexandria. They argue that he had the common touch (he was polite with "poor people") and very accurately read the "security situation." Many policemen defend el-Adly's tolerance for corruption and nepotism arguing that this was a good way to secure allegiances. And they argue that under his watch the ministry and the police saw an increase in resources.

But overall, there is no question that el-Adly did not restore the meritocratic culture and prestige that the security apparatus had enjoyed in its earliest days. And most importantly, he was not successful in contending with the challenge posed by the Muslim Brotherhood. In 2005, a top officer reported in an interview, "Previously we never had such close knowledge of the Brotherhood. We never had so many informants. We never had so much detailed data. Despite this, the situation is out of control and the Brotherhood is spreading."[15] The officer reported that the Brotherhood had learned (the hard way) how to protect its secrets and how to safeguard the names of the new members. The security services reacted by trying to disrupt the organization by perpetual harassment and frequent arrests. But this approach had terrible consequences for many people (in addition to being illegal), and such tactics only increased the public's sympathy for the Muslim Brotherhood. The latter could rightly claim that the security apparatus was imposing pure tyranny on society.

The security apparatus was tainted in another way as well. The Interior Ministry was widely (and rightly) seen as the main supporter of the "succession plan," grooming Gamal Mubarak for the presidency. The symbolic damage to the ministry's reputation was great, and many officers expressed uneasiness with this plan. During the 1950s and the 1960s, the Ministry of Interior served a regime with considerable legitimacy. During the 1970s, it contributed to "calming the waters" in ways that freed President Anwar Sadat to liberate occupied Sinai. During the 1980s and until 1997, it was fighting terrorism, which seriously threatened the Egyptian economy and specifically the tourism industry. In other words, the security apparatus was doing a "dirty job" that was serving noble causes. Or at least its actions could be construed as such. But by the late 1990s the interventions of the security apparatus were increasingly seen as linked to sustaining a particular political dynasty. The legitimizing rationale for its "dirty work" was increasingly nullified as was the reputation of the institution as a whole.

Training and Culture of the Security Services

Contributing to the security services' deeply compromised performance was a training system that was also deeply flawed. The infection of Egypt's police academy with nepotism, social discrimination, poor standards, and an inappropriate curriculum gave rise to a security force that was ineffective as well imbued with a culture that was dismissive of citizen's rights and inattentive to the rule of law.

Egypt's first police "school" was created in 1896. In 1925, it became an "institute," and a royal decree stipulated that only those who had earned a baccalaureate could be admitted to it. The period of studies lasted three years. In 1941, the institute became an academy producing police officers after four years of study. The academy underwent further restructuring in 1975 and again in 1998. Today the police academy includes three faculties (police faculty, higher studies faculty, and a training and development faculty) as well as a research center. The police faculty is divided into two sections: one devoted to training general police officers and one for more "specialized officers." The latter faculty admits candidates who have already earned a degree (e.g., medicine, engineering, pharmacy, sports) and who then study police sciences for a single year. Since 1984, this "specialized section" has also accepted women, according to the ministry's needs (Miliha, 2010: 20). Competition for acceptance into the academy is tight. In recent years, about 13,000 applicants have applied for admission with space for only 2,000.

Between Collapse and Professionalism: Police Reform in Egypt 179

Admission to the police academy is a twice-biased process. First of all, the academy is a "club" of wealthy or middle-class well-connected families. It is almost impossible for a candidate from a modest social background to be admitted to the academy. Most candidates are the sons of well-connected families of rural notables who consolidate their local hegemony by placing their sons in key branches of the state apparatus. Second, during the last thirty to thirty-five years, the "objective criteria" (fair or unfair) have not been enforced,[16] and cronyism and connections have played a key role in governing admission.

The social bias present in the admission process at the police academy was exposed in an important article published by the newspaper *Sawt al-Umma* on August 8, 2009. The article made clear that several segments of the Egyptian population are denied access to the academy. (The article fails to mention that the requirements for fitness and health are also likely to play against the admission of candidates from the most disadvantaged backgrounds.) According to the newspaper, four unstated criteria are used to exclude candidates. Two are "social" and two are "political." With regard to the "social" criteria, the academy rules out candidates who live in what are considered "inappropriate" areas and those who have "external" loyalties. As for "political" criteria, the recruiters rule out those who have parents, brothers, or cousins affiliated with Islamist groups and those who have attended schools with a religious curriculum (particularly those that attend Azhari Islamic schools), as well as potential "traitors" (whatever that means). In its ninety-two-year history, the police academy has never admitted a single graduate of the religious institution al-Azhar. Coptic Christians are also subject to an unspoken quota: the authorities do not recruit more than 2 percent in any class. This limit does not reflect Muslim ethnocentrism but rather the rejection of any religious affiliation that might have political implications or contribute to even a hint of "double allegiance." (Along the same lines, Copts are denied access to sensitive security functions.) The authorities also exclude candidates whose parents have "marginalized" professions, which means professions "not identifiable by the State" or "without a clearly identifiable workplace." Interviewed by the newspaper, General Fuad 'Allam, one of the prestigious "elders" of the SSI police, defended this state of affairs, recalling a minister whose father was a gravedigger and who was the greatest thief in the institution's history, though I have reason to believe this claim was not true.

Another article in *Sawt al-Umma* from August 8, 2009, provides further evidence of the social bias inherent in the constitution of the security apparatus. It lists a number of wealthy families that have founded dynasties of policemen in Egypt. These include the Saqr family, which has twenty-seven members who are police officers at the Ministry of Interior; the al-Dab' family, which has thirty-eight members, including five generals: the Kilani, Qurashi, 'Abd al-Jawwad, and al-Jahir families, who together provide a total of twenty-five officers; the Abu Sihli family, with twenty-three members who are police officers, the Tanihi family, with fourteen officers in its ranks, including some in the SSI. One village, Tawabiyya, in the governorate of Assiut, provided forty-five police officers although it has only 40,000 inhabitants.

The consequences of relying on such criteria to govern admission to the academy are obvious. First of all, many police officers come from families that have ties to the "old regime." Second, the Muslim Brothers have been historically underrepresented in the police officers' corps. (The regime's aim was to deny them complete access to the academy, but the "screening" was never as rigorous as that practiced in the military academy.)[17] Third, the cronyism has had a devastating effect on the professional level of the police officers with less-than-meritorious candidates rising in the ranks. Consequently, the quality of candidates admitted to the academy has declined over the years. During the 1980s, for example, the standards for admission to the police academy were as exacting as that of any law faculty, and the cadets were often better than the law faculties' students, something that is no longer the case.

Besides a flawed admission process, the police academy is blighted by an ill-designed curriculum. Basically the cadets at the police academy study law. They typically attend six hour-long sessions of lectures on Egyptian law and sharia on a daily basis. Although future police officers need to know criminal and procedural law, the utility of familiarity with the laws governing retirement, agricultural activities, health insurance, succession, and so on, is less clear, especially when such training comes at the expense of courses on investigative techniques. The cadets are also exposed to courses with particular political biases such as a course on the Muslim Brotherhood. This course depicted the Muslim Brotherhood as a sect, dangerous for national security, and documented their past crimes (notably assassination and terrorism) as well as their international networks and their practices. This course was eliminated during Morsi's rule.

The training at the academy is flawed also in its inculcation of a militaristic culture that discourages independent thinking and establishes a social gulf between the officers and the general population. Cadets bitterly complain about the roughness and the daily violence in the academy and the training that often resembles drilling. An anonymous cadet wrote that "we are just learning to obey" (Faruq, 2012: 158), and he complained about the militarization of the police academy. Since the police "mission" is different from that of the military academy, he argued, the training should not be similar. The same cadet complained about "the psychological message" conveyed by the police academy authorities: "People hate you. We are tough on you to prepare you for the people's hostility" (Faruq, 2012: 158). The cadet's observations are confirmed by al-Batran (2013: 157), who provides some striking accounts of the absolute brutality of the drilling in the academy, the strongly corporatist discourse employed, and the identity cultivation that inculcates the young cadets in a culture of cynicism, amorality, and haughty attitudes toward the people.

A culture of disrespect for the rule of law and for the people is also reinforced by "on-the-job" training as well as by the general political conditions in Egypt. Shadin Nusayr, a professor at the police academy, expressed this situation starkly in a 2013 speech:

> [In the academy] the cadet learns law. Then he starts professional life. And he learns from elders the "know-how," the "job's secrets," which have nothing to do with the rule of law. These are quite simple: If you want to fight drug dealers, you have to ally yourself with some drug dealers to arrest the others. If you want to fight terrorists, you must torture them; you must build an alliance with thugs. If you want to arrest a suspect in the Sinai, arrest all his family until he surrenders. The police officer simply does not know how to enforce the law without violating it.[18]

Mubarak's long reign also inflicted considerable damage to the concept of "rule of law." As mentioned above, Egypt was governed by martial law from the start of Mubarak's presidency. The former president's impulse was to forbid everything by promulgating odious laws (which served as a sword of Damocles over the citizenry) and then apply them almost never or inconsistently and arbitrarily. Training and working in such an arbitrary environment meant that very few police officers have had any experience with "service under the rule of law."

Overall, the instinct of the police is to be hostile to the concept of rule of law. Without their traditional techniques, which often violate conventional legal norms, the policemen feel powerless. For example, most believe that soft interrogation is sheer nonsense. Furthermore, most of the police have yet to accept the fact that the average citizen has a right to dignity and should be treated accordingly.[19] They tend to construe *the* problem in Egypt today as a need to restore the "ability to be feared" (*hayba*).

The fact that the police have been at odds with the general population is evident from the course of the uprising of 2011. Police abuses and bad practices (torture, racketeering, collective punishment, collusion with criminals, widespread phone tapping, etc.) were major causes of the Egyptian revolution. During the course of the uprising, popular outrage at the police became apparent when furious demonstrators attacked and destroyed 100 police centers, destroying nearly 3,000 police vehicles and stealing thousands of weapons.[20]

In the wake of this clash, antipathy and distrust characterize the attitude of the police toward the general population. Many officers say, "January 2011 was our June 1967," in other words, a moment of catastrophic defeat. Observers and analysts concur that the police saw the revolution as a humiliating defeat of one tribe—the police—in a fight against other tribes—the Muslim Brothers (assisted, in the eyes of the police, by Hamas militants) as well as young activists (supported by the Egyptian people generally). The police see themselves as a convenient scapegoat for all the ancien regime's sins and crimes. But the police's hatred has been primarily focused on the Muslim Brothers, against whom they had been at war since 1948. For many months after the revolution, the police were furious with the military hierarchy. For the police, the military's endorsement of democratic transition was tantamount to "delivering the keys of power" to their mortal foe. And their distrust was only confirmed during the first months after the revolution when the Supreme Command of the Armed Forces (SCAF) accepted the Brotherhood's demand to fire or transfer hundreds of SSI officers.

Clearly reform of the security sector is necessary, and the recipe for such reform is well known.

Reforming the Security Sector

Loosen the Grip of the Ministry of Interior on Citizens' Lives

As it stands, the Interior Ministry oversees every sort of citizen documentation: driver's licenses, civil status, registration of birth, death, and marriage, IDs, and passports. It has the power to monitor closely almost every kind of social, political, and religious activity. To that end, phone tapping has been a common practice. The Ministry of Interior has effective "right of veto" on the nomination of citizens to positions in the state apparatus, the universities, the official media, and beyond. Its intervention in student and labor elections has been blatant and heavy handed. This practice must end.

Along the same lines, Badawi (2012: 56) argues that the Interior Ministry has too many missions. It should redefine its purpose to focus on the most essential ones. For example, fighting corruption should be a top goal for the ministry, and the "financial police" should be strengthened. The mission of SSI (now renamed Homeland Security) should be defined more narrowly (the same goes for antiterrorist activities) and its practices (torture, phone tapping, etc.) modified. The antiriot police (al-Amn al-Markazi) should be purged and downsized. (This particular branch of the police protects too many "public buildings"; too many places and squares are deemed "strategic.") Its mission should be limited and stricter rules of engagement enforced.

Foster More Professionalism Within the Security Apparatus

More professionalism can be achieved through a variety of means: better training at the police academy, a more meritocratic process governing admission to the police academy as well as promotion in the ranks, and purging "bad apples" as necessary. I have already pointed out the strong criticism of the police's "militarization," which begins with the training received at the academy, something that must be changed. Similarly, the academy's biased admission process, which favors candidates from influential families from the countryside often with ties to the old regime, must end. A fairer system for promotion of noncommissioned officers to officer status must be embraced.[21] Overall, the criteria that govern promotion to higher ranks must be rethought and modified. Without more professionalism among officers, changing the deeply entrenched "police culture" will be impossible.

Reduce the Temptation for Corruption by Paying the Police a Decent Wage

In order for the police to be rule abiding and reliable, they must be paid decently. Otherwise, the officers will be tempted to extract revenues from the population, through bribes and racketeering, and to sell their weapons to criminals and terrorists. Notably, the level of wages paid to graduates of the police academy (excluding bonuses) is low. Lieutenants are paid a salary of 500 Egyptian pounds (EGP; US$64) per month, captains are paid around 600 EGP (US$77), and commanders are paid around 700 EGP (US$90). The promotion from captain to commander is quite slow, but even at that, a lieutenant colonel is not paid more than 1,100 EGP (US$141).[22] These low salaries have long created a sense of "malaise" within the police force that preceded the revolution. For example, between 2008 and 2009, more than 2,000 officers resigned from the force. To rejuvenate the police and forestall corruption, wages must be increased.[23]

Foster Accountability and Eliminate the Fear That Governs Police-Citizen Relations

Accountability and better police-citizen relations can be achieved through the introduction of means for better civilian monitoring of the police, as Badawi (2012) recommends. And they can be fostered through reforms as simple as having the names of policemen visible on their shirts and trousers.

How to Bring About Reform

These reforms are just a few of those that are necessary to revamp the security services. As to how to actually do this, Hosam Bahgat, from Egypt's Personal Rights Initiative, makes a cogent political point, arguing that these reforms should be presented as a "package deal," bundling together a rise in wages and new benefits with new norms, more transparency, sanctions against those responsible for misdeeds, and processes for transitional justice.[24]

Reformers would also be well served to heed the insight of French scholars who have argued that defining and implementing reform are easier when the actor who oversees them is admired or at least respected within the institution to be reformed, and he or she can build up credible internal coalitions. The best solution, therefore, would be to find one or more high-ranking officers who are respected by the rank and file, who thus can secure some crucial support, and who are really committed to restructuring and will lead the process. Judging from past experience, such a respected champion (and referee) would be a huge asset to the process.

Obstacles

Although the steps necessary to reform the security services are clear, the obstacles to carrying out such reform are many. First, and most importantly, there has been no political will to carry out serious substantive reform. Or more accurately, many of the political actors who would be central to this process have shown no interest in forcing through such reform. Such has been the case ever since Mubarak fell. The army, led by SCAF, was dead set against a project to radically restructure the police during their rule. The army was first and foremost interested in reducing its own presence on the streets since casting the army in the role of domestic policemen was eroding the army's capacities and prestige. Given the disastrous security situation, however, the army recognized the need for a strong police presence. Consequently, the SCAF as well as Interior Minister Mansur al-Issawi focused on strengthening the police, not restructuring it. Reform, they thought, could wait.

As for the Muslim Brotherhood, they too had little interest in loosening the police's tight grip on citizens' lives. At most they sought to change the composition of the police force—purge some of the officers who were corrupt and loyal to the old regime and replace them with their own clients.

Finally, even many liberal and secular parties were reticent about taking on the project of police reform. They did not want to antagonize this damaged yet still powerful institution, especially in a context of deep insecurity and deep conflict with the Muslim Brotherhood. (The police hated the Muslim Brotherhood and could be counted on to oppose them.)

Given the lack of political will to undertake police reform, no reform of any significance has been carried out. A small number of officers have been removed or reassigned. But the modus vivendi of the police has not changed. The figures and statistics are telling. According to Hosam Bahgat, the numbers of citizens killed by police bullets or tortured in the years since Mubarak fell are as high if not higher than those under the Mubarak regime.[25]

The second major obstacle to reform of the security services is the fact that many of the police themselves are deeply opposed to reform. They are hostile to the notion of civilian control and consider those who lobby for police reform as enemies, be they civilian activists or other police officers. Police force insiders committed to reform are a minority and are considered by the majority to be traitors.[26] Without inside support, however, reform of the police is very difficult given the opacity of the police apparatus and its networks. Reformers need to find insiders who will serve as allies and advisers. Yet the law remains very harsh against policemen who unveil professional secrets, making the mobilization of momentum for reform all the more difficult (al-Batran, 2013: 173).

A third major obstacle is financial. Recommendations such as improved training and better wages are all well and good, but these recommendations require huge investments. Given Egypt's precarious financial situation, such an investment is highly problematic.

A fourth major obstacle derives from the fact that the security situation in Egypt is so fraught. Never in Egypt's history have so many people had access to so many weapons. The weapons market is flourishing. Weapons come from Libya, Sudan, Gaza, and Israel. Some areas, in Upper Egypt, have long had a tradition of armed notable families. But now the ownership of guns, automatic guns, and Kalashnikovs has been democratized, and some families even buy missiles. Even many middle-class citizens buy weapons to protect their families. In this context the people call out for the police to protect them. And so tension has developed between the demand to restore security and the demand to reform the police. In this disastrous security situation a delicate balance must be found between public liberties and police reform on the one hand and the fight against crime and terrorism on the other.

A fifth obstacle derives from the politically and morally complex question of how to assign responsibility for human rights abuses committed by the police. For example, with regard to opening fire on demonstrators, the police defend themselves saying they were simply "obeying orders." Politically speaking, any government must provide political cover for policemen who follow its orders if it wants to be sure its orders will be obeyed in the future. The political solution thus far seems to be to impose heavy sentences on the top leaders (the president, the interior minister) but to find most police officers and even top generals "not guilty." Although this approach may be politically sage, it does nothing to correct a culture of impunity that prevails among the police.

Conclusion

So far little progress has been achieved in the area of security sector reform. Many analysts and activists say that a golden opportunity was squandered: the first months after Mubarak's fall were the proper time for police sector reform. At that time the police were too weak and too humiliated to oppose serious resistance. By failing to tackle this issue at the start, the SCAF mishandled the issue.

But the truth is, the terrible security situation faced by Egypt provided powerful arguments to those who said reform should be delayed. When the waters are turbulent, the police should be tough; democratic niceties can wait. Moreover, political leaders are afraid to destroy an engine that serves them well. When they feel threatened by revolutionary processes, they tend to concentrate power in their hands, not relinquish it.

The modern Egyptian state is 200 years old, and it has always been centralized, authoritarian, and patrimonial. A strong state with a vigorous security apparatus is a powerful weapon in the hands of any ruling party, and even those with a liberal leaning would face the strong temptation not to destroy it but to use it. The state has developed considerable know-how as well as a large repertoire of effective practices to handle serious political and social challenges. The state apparatus cannot be changed suddenly, even with the best of intentions. Trying too brutally to force things could provoke a total collapse, with disastrous consequences. The battle for police reform may not have been lost, but, without question, it will be long.

Notes

1. Al-Batran (2013) rightly says these laws prevent public debate. He also adds that the Defense Ministry, which imposes similar restrictions (nothing should be published by an officer without authorization) has in fact a more relaxed attitude, as it is well aware that the publication of autobiographies and testimonies is both a good public relations operation and a significant contribution to the "correction of mistakes." It seems, I should add, that a kind of reciprocity is observed between the Interior Ministry and its officers: the Interior Ministry delays providing information on officers' misdeeds to the media for as long as it possibly can.

2. Later on an antiterrorist section was created under the supervision of the SSI. Many of its officers were trained in the United States (Badawi, 2012: 30).

3. This militarization included the tendency to resort to live fire when faced with the challenge of civilian protesters.

4. Badawi (2012: 33–35) goes to great lengths to make his point, and the details are indeed shocking.

5. The last point stems from al-Batran (2013).

6. Al-Batran (2013: 68) quotes a leaked memo written by Interior Minister Hassan al-Alfi in 1993. The regime was facing a kind of insurrection in Upper Egypt. The Interior Ministry badly needed more officers, more weapons, more installations, more armored cars, better professional formation, better communication skills, and better transmission and telecommunications. It also needed to reconsider its structural organization chart and internal and external coordination, along with creating or improving a database of security threats and coming up with a clear and well-thought-out strategy to combat insurrection. It also needed to deal with the fact that identifications (IDs) and official papers were easily falsified. The low morale of the rank and file was also another problem (see next note). Rules concerning transfers and nominations were too unclear and wages were too low. Last but not least, the relations between the citizens and the police were quickly deteriorating.

7. After Anwar Sadat's assassination, the regime adopted a twofold strategy: it tried to suppress the groups that were responsible for the president's death while opening a "new page" with the main fundamentalist and radical forces. Some forty-four police officers suspected of torturing radical militants were tried during the first half of the 1980s. The impact of this trial on the troops was tremendously negative: they felt that they had rescued the regime, had agreed to do a terribly nasty job, and were not given political coverage. See al-Batran (2013: 55–56). I may add, from my personal fieldwork, that police forces were dismayed about the court ruling in the trial of the activists of al-Jihad who had been implicated in the assassination of Sadat and in the unrest that followed. The court did not sentence anyone to death despite the fact that some eighty-five (or more) policemen had been murdered by militants during the sudden attack on Asyut police centers a few days after Sadat's death.

8. Badawi (2012) ignores the fact that Abu Basha is widely credited for the first deradicalization program, which aimed to fight fundamentalist ideas with more moderate religious ideas.

9. However, he did have considerable know-how in general (criminal) security, strengthened the internal affairs section, fought internal corruption (or at least his foes' wrongdoings), and tried to devise ways to prevent the development of ties between officers and local businessmen and notables.

10. For instance, the police adopted the practice of collective punishment (massive arrests of suspects' relatives). Reliance on this practice greatly explains the loss of control in Sinai today.

11. Not all departments in the Ministry of Interior benefited from this turn of events.Those who lost out included the criminal police, the financial police, and the internal affairs department.

12. Al-Batran (2013), who provides great details, says the collaboration with some thugs, who act as informants, is a long-standing procedure and hence more or less "normal." Certain norms, however, do govern this collaboration. This time, all red lines were crossed on an almost permanent basis. In other words, the war against radicals perverted a relatively "normal" practice.

13. El-Adly felt insecure during his first two years as a minister, as he had to report to the government's strongman, Talaat Hammad. But he slowly gained Mubarak's trust. See al-Diwwi (2012): 18.

14. The journalist Khalid al-Sirgany (2008) did a brilliant job describing the rackets. A typical racket might go as follows: The policeman (most often in civilian clothes, sometimes in uniform) asks to see a citizen's ID. If the citizen is not carry-

ing one, he is arrested. The poor guy is jailed. The police wait for his family to come to negotiate (i.e., to buy) his freedom. See Anhri.net, the Arabic netword for human rights information, http://www.anhri.net/hotcase/2008/1109.shtml.

15. Interview with Interior Ministry officer, Cairo, 2005.

16. Miliha (2010: 26–27) provides details of this bias. A committee checks the candidates' applications and the accuracy of data provided, which includes information on the candidates' families. A second committee oversees written exams. These evaluate, among other things, the "general culture" of the candidate. A third committee checks the physical fitness of the candidate. A fourth committee checks the candidate's health, a fifth his physical abilities, and a sixth his psychological condition.

17. During the reign of the Morsi regime, in a new and significant development, candidates belonging to the Brotherhood were admitted to the academy. The Morsi regime also seemed to have ended the old practice of "political investigation," that is, checking the ideological affiliations of the candidates' families.

18. Intervention at the workshop Security in Times of Transition, organized by the Arab Reform Initiative and the Arab Forum for Alternatives, June 10, 2013, Cairo.

19. Professor Nusayr acknowledged this attitude during the 2013 workshop. I heard many security officers, military officers, and policemen say the "average citizen" in Egypt was a "very bad one."

20. Antiriot forces had tried to contain the demonstrations of January 25–28 without success. Exhausted after three days and without reservists, the police force collapsed and by and large fled.

21. During his year of rule, Morsi moved in this direction, giving noncommissioned officers quasi-automatic access to the officers corps after a certain number of years of service. Clearly, the Brotherhood embraced this idea since noncommissioned officers were, by and large, much more sympathetic to their ideas then were the veteran officers.

22. Bonuses, however, can exponentially multiply officers' wages. Officers in certain positions have been known to earn bonuses that raise their salaries to more than 150,000 EGP (US$19,200) per month.

23. Even if an increase in the total amount of wages paid is impossible, then at the least a more egalitarian wage structure should be introduced. This point was made by former member of Parliament Amr al Shubaki (2013).

24. Interview with the author, June 13, 2013

25. Ibid.

26. Many activists made this point during the workshop organized by the Arab Reform Initiative and the Arab Forum for Alternatives.

11

Dismantling the Security Apparatus: Challenges of Police Reform in Tunisia

Querine Hanlon

Tunisian president Moncef Marzouki took a calculated risk. It was September 14, 2012, and the US Embassy compound in Tunis was under attack. Three days earlier in neighboring Libya, the US consulate had been attacked, and the US ambassador and several other US citizens were killed. US secretary of state Hillary Clinton had placed an urgent call to Marzouki, requesting the immediate dispatch of forces to protect the US compound.[1] Under the regime of Zine El Abidine Ben Ali, the likely response would have been to dispatch loyal internal security forces, armed not with rubber bullets but with real ones, to round up and arrest protesters as they did in the wake of the demonstrations that followed Mohamed Bouazizi's immolation on December 17, 2010.

But this was the new democratic Tunisia, and the demonstrations that prompted the collapse of the Ben Ali government had been motivated in part by the impunity of the internal security forces. One can imagine Marzouki's quandary: If he ordered elite security forces to protect the compound, bypassing the minister of interior, would he undermine Tunisia's nascent security sector reform and its democratic transition? If he failed to protect the embassy, would he lose critical US and Western support for Tunisia's democratic transition and its economic recovery? And if he intervened forcibly against conservative Islamist, or Salafist, attackers, would his actions rupture the already tense ruling coalition of the moderate Islamist Ennahda party and its two secular partners while the critical constitution-drafting process had not yet been completed?

Marzouki took the unprecedented step of ordering his well-armed, elite Presidential Guard forces to protect the compound. But they arrived after the attack had already been halted. The army then deployed to protect the embassy in the wake of the violence.[2] The delayed response by the Tunisian government did not come without cost (Ben Bouazza, 2012). Four attackers were killed, and forty police and protestors were injured (CNN.com, 2012). Salafists imprisoned during the demonstrations began a fifty-four-day hunger strike that ended only after two inmates died (*France24*, 2012). A member of the National Constituent Assembly, Azad Bady, entrusted with drafting Tunisia's new constitution, captured the growing frustration with the new government's stewardship of the transition process: "It is unacceptable to have Tunisians die in prison . . . after the revolution" (quoted in Trablesi, 2012). The police were themselves equally dissatisfied with the government's response to the protests and their aftermath. After the incident, the police demonstrated, demanding new training, new instructions for riot and crowd control, and better protection in the field (Agence France Presse, 2012a; Trablesi, 2012). Opposition parties faulted the government for failing to reform the security apparatus and protect Tunisia from the growing threat of extremist violence.

The attacks on the US Embassy were a watershed event for the Tunisian government and particularly for the leadership of Tunisia's security institutions. The failure to respond quickly and effectively exposed serious gaps in institutional capacity—particularly in situational awareness, command and control, and coordination among the security forces and among senior government leaders. Amazingly, while the attacks were under way, many senior leaders and commanders were completely in the dark about the severity of the attacks or about actions being taken to respond. A senior military officer was moved to tears that the attacks had been allowed to escalate and that the army had not been notified to deploy in time to prevent the destruction of the school and the damage to the embassy compound.[3] Experienced police were embarrassed and demoralized by the very public failure of their institution to do its job and protect such a high-profile location as the US Embassy.[4] "As the protestors marched by, we just stood there," related one police officer, "waiting for instructions."[5]

The attacks, and the escalation of violent incidents throughout Tunisia in the months following, also exposed, publicly and dramatically, that little if any reform had been accomplished in the year and a half since Tunisia's democratic government was elected. In the aftermath of the attacks, there appeared to be signs that the new government recognized the grave risks of failing to implement reform. But this recognition was not enough to stem the tide of criticism against the Ennahda-led government. Opposition parties renewed their demands for a government reshuffle to place technocrats in charge of the key interior and justice ministries to manage the reform process and the provision of security. When one of its most outspoken critics, Chokri Belaid, was assassinated months later in February 2013,

Ennahda was forced to bow to opposition demands and relinquish the interior, justice, and foreign affairs ministries (Fahim, 2013). Minister of Defense Abdelkarim Zbidi, the only member of the cabinet appointed by Tunisia's first transition government in 2011, resigned his post in frustration over the lack of progress implementing Tunisia's democratic transition, noting that "Tunisia is not on the right path" (quoted in Ghribi, 2013).

The security apparatus that had been created to protect the old Tunisia of Ben Ali is ill designed to secure the new democratic Tunisia. Before the collapse of Ben Ali's regime, the biggest threat a police officer was likely to face "was fists."[6] Two years later, weapons replaced the fists, and derision replaced the fear that Tunisia's police used to instill among ordinary Tunisians. Fear was a powerful weapon. Fear of torture prompted Tunisian detainees to confess to crimes, and these confessions became the sole evidence upon which they were convicted. Fear that family members would be targeted kept prison populations docile. Fear of Ben Ali's police state prevented ordinary citizens from seeking justice through the criminal justice system. But the collapse of the Ben Ali regime overturned the relationship between police and citizen. Now the police where the ones who were afraid.

Existing rules of engagement and standard operating procedures, designed when violent public incidents were rare and the primary mission of the security services was regime protection and not necessarily public order, are not suited to the new mission of Tunisia's internal security forces. The instruments of government—the Ministry of Interior, as well as the Ministry of Justice, the judiciary, and Tunisia's prisons—were tools to impose "regime allegiance."[7] Public service was an alien concept. The organs of government existed for the purpose of protecting the regime and enriching the elite few. Corruption was so prevalent that it was elevated to "a system of government" under Ben Ali.[8] Thus not surprisingly, the overthrow of Ben Ali's regime was triggered by a disillusioned young man in Tunisia's neglected interior who chose to immolate himself when his entire means of livelihood were confiscated because he could not get a license to sell fruit from a street cart.

Despite the government's commitment to reform, Tunisia's complex security apparatus remains, with few exceptions, largely intact.[9] And as Tunisia's security challenges continue to mount, the risk of undertaking comprehensive reform is that it weakens the ability of existing security forces to provide security at a moment when the challenges are growing. These concerns weigh heavily against popular demands for reform even among government and security officials most committed to transforming Tunisia's security apparatus into a democratically accountable institution of public service. Yet serious comprehensive reform of the security sector is essential if Tunisia's transition to democratic rule is to succeed in the long term. Only through these reforms can Tunisia's security apparatus transition successfully from an authoritarian control structure designed to protect the regime to a democratic security service focused on protecting and serving the people of Tunisia. Security sector reform (SSR) will be critical for building trust in the government and its security institutions and central to the construct of a national narrative that undergirds a new social contract between the people of Tunisia and their government.

An Early Arab Spring Favorite

Until the attacks on the US Embassy in Tunis, Tunisia appeared to be the hope of the Arab Spring—the one country that was most likely to transition successfully from authoritarian to democratic rule (Lutterback, 2012; Sedra, 2011). There was great cause to be optimistic about Tunisia's prospects for implementing reform. The military embraced civilian control of the armed forces, and Tunisia's armed forces did not have a stake in Tunisia's economy as did their counterparts in Egypt. Nor was the military involved in the massive corruption that had become "a deliberate system of government" under Ben Ali.[10] The armed forces were also lauded as heroes for their refusal to follow Ben Ali's orders to forcibly suppress the demonstrations in December 2010 and January 2011 that led to the collapse of his regime (Hanlon, 2012b).

After the initial demonstrations, and for most of the early transition period, violent incidents were rare. The explosions Tunisia experienced were of public discourse and debate. Another positive metric of change was the number of political parties and civil society groups that emerged during the first year of transition. Under Ben Ali, Tunisia had five official political parties. During the October 2011 election, 111 competed. Civil society also burgeoned. Some 2,000 new civil society groups emerged in Tunisia after the revolution.

Even in the most visibly lingering vestige of the old regime, the widely reviled Ministry of Interior, people saw cause for hope. The early transition government produced a white paper detailing a plan to reform the security sector. It correctly identified the police and the intelligence capabilities as being most in need of reform. It gave particular attention to the opacity of the ministry and its labyrinth security structures and actors.[11] An entire chapter was devoted to the public image of the security services. The report noted that no communication plan alone can change a "bad image." The Ministry of Interior's image will only transform "when the professional practices of all its agents are transformed" (Republic of Tunisia Ministry of Interior, 2011: 12). Mechanisms to accomplish this transformation included not only new uniforms and open reception areas in police stations and guard bureaus, but also new codes of conduct and greater police transparency (Republic of Tunisia Ministry of Interior, 2011). Notable were the calls for reforms of police custody practices, police intelligence, and techniques for video surveillance and electronic monitoring, and the banning of imprisonment for religious or political ideas.

Remarkably, Tunisia also experienced three peaceful transitions in government in the first year after the collapse of the Ben Ali regime. Although the first transition government ruled for just over a month, it created three critical national commissions: the National Commission to Investigate Violence During the Riots, headed by Tawfik Bouderbala; the National Commission to Investigate Corruption, headed by Abdelfattah Amor; and the High Commission for the Fulfillment of Revolutionary Goals, Political Reform, and Democratic Transition, headed by Iyadh Ben Achour. In creating the commissions, the first transition government sought to address the demands of the millions of Tunisians who had successfully protested to end the Ben Ali regime. The commissions also established the critical ground rules for Tunisia's transition to democratic rule.

By mid-April 2011, the Ben Achour commission had mapped a transition process that included creating the National Constituent Assembly to draft Tunisia's new constitution, holding elections using a proportional representation electoral system for seats in the assembly, and granting the assembly the authority to appoint a caretaker government for Tunisia during the constitution-drafting process. Ben Achour's commission also invited international observers to monitor the elections and created an independent electoral commission by moving the Independent High Authority for Elections out of the Ministry of Interior. Finally, the commission recommended the dissolution of Ben Ali's ruling party, the Democratic Constitutional Rally (Stepan, 2011). According to Albert Stepan (2011), "this Commission is one of the most successful and consensual organizations in the history of crafting a democratic transition."

The third transition government (December 2011–late 2014) was a caretaker government,[12] elected in Tunisia's first truly competitive election since it declared independence from France in 1956. More than 90 percent of registered Tunisian citizens participated in the election. The previously banned Islamist Ennahda party won a plurality of 89 of the 217 seats in the National Constituent Assembly (Ajmi, 2011). Ennahda combined with the secular Congress for the Republic party and the left Ettakatol party to form a caretaker government, the so-called Troika, to run the country during the yearlong period in which the assembly was charged with drafting a new constitution (Amara, 2011b). Ennahda's secretary-general, Hamadi Jebali, became the new prime minister, and Moncef Marzouki, head of the Congress for the Republic, became Tunisia's president. At its first meeting, the assembly confirmed the selection of Mustapha Ben Jafar, leader of Ettakatol, as speaker of the new assembly. This carefully constructed "unity government" reflected Ennahda's commitment "from day one" to secure "the full participation of everyone across the spectrum" in an inclusive and representative transition government.[13]

Even after the elections, as the realities of dismantling the Ben Ali state became apparent, citizens still had cause for optimism. The National Constituent Assembly quickly began work drafting a new constitution for Tunisia. Its members adopted a "miniconstitution" in December 2011 that defined government and parliamentary authority until the new constitution was adopted. In mid-January 2012, members also approved internal bylaws to govern the constitution-drafting process.[14]

Despite these significant accomplishments, the attacks on the US Embassy, the assassination of Chokri Belaid, and the escalation of violent incidents between police and protestors and between Salafists and secularists that appeared to occur with alarming frequency changed the perception that Tunisia's transition was progressing successfully. They have exposed serious institutional and capacity gaps in Tunisia's security sector. Nearly two years after the demonstrations that sparked the collapse of the Ben Ali regime, Tunisia's security services appeared less capable of providing security.

A Critical Tool for Democratic Transition

SSR is a comprehensive tool for fixing the dysfunctional security sectors in fragile states that are emerging from conflict, for developing capacities to meet the human security needs of their populations, or for transitioning from authoritarian rule (Hänggi, 2004; McFate, 2008). SSR is also an important tool for the prevention of conflict. In many fragile states, the security institutions are themselves a major source of *insecurity*. Transforming the security sector into one that is democratically accountable and functions in accordance with the rule of law is an important step toward averting the recurrence of insecurity and conflict and preventing newly democratic or transitioning regimes from reverting to authoritarian rule.

The SSR agenda is an ambitious one. SSR aims to strengthen the professionalism and effectiveness of the security sector. The SSR concept adopts a broad definition of the security sector, one that encompasses six components:

1. Statutory forces with a formal mandate to ensure the safety of the state and its citizens (e.g., armed forces, police, gendarmerie, paramilitary forces, intelligence, secret services, and border and customs guards).

2. Nonstatutory forces and security providers (e.g., armed groups, nonstate paramilitary organizations, militias, and private security companies).
3. Governance functions that exercise the state monopoly over coercive power (e.g., executive government, ministries of defense and interior, and parliament and its specialized committees).
4. Justice institutions (e.g., ministries of justice, the judiciary, criminal investigation and prosecution services, and prison regimes) (Hänggi, 2004).
5. Informal justice or community dispute resolution structures that function alongside or in place of formal state institutions (e.g., tribal *shuras*, or councils).
6. Civil society groups (e.g., the media, academia, NGOs, and human rights advocacy institutions) that monitor and report on the activities of the security services and their oversight institutions and hold them accountable for their actions.

Not all security sectors will include all of these components. Each state's SSR challenges will also vary depending on whether there are dysfunctionalities across the entire security sector or whether these dysfunctionalities are limited to one or more subsectors. How these challenges present in a particular state will also vary according to legacies of conflict; tribal, ethnic, or religious patterns; systems of government; colonial legacies; the level of economic development; environmental conditions; the vibrancy of civil society; and transnational influences, to name but a few. In other words, no one formula for SSR will be applicable to all states.

SSR is the "complex task of transforming the institutions and operational forces that safeguard the state and its citizens into *professional, effective,* [and] *legitimate* actors that are accountable to those they serve" (Perito, 2012b; emphasis added). Successful SSR can be measured by the capacity of the security forces and the degree of their oversight, transparency, and accountability by parliamentary and executive authorities (Sedra, 2010: 16). Ultimately, successful SSR changes the institutional culture of the entire security apparatus so that the security providers, such as the police, and the oversight institutions, such as the ministry of interior, embrace a mission of service to the population and its elected government.

Tunisia's security sector challenges widened and deepened in the two years following the collapse of the Ben Ali regime. Today Tunisia's security sector does not feature informal or traditional justice providers. And until recently, Tunisia's security sector challenges did not include the presence of nonstatutory forces, as is the case in neighboring Libya. But the troubling emergence of armed groups in 2012 suggests that Tunisia's SSR challenges have increased by an order of magnitude. Armed citizens were unheard of under Ben Ali. In the post–Ben Ali period, weapons, drugs, and terrorists transit Tunisia's borders with Algeria and Libya, and Tunisia's security forces have captured weapons caches and battled armed groups not only in the remote Chaambi Mountains but also in Tunis suburbs.[15] The existence of nonstatutory armed groups, with or without the consent of the government, indicates that the security apparatus no longer has a monopoly on the use of force.

With justice reforms addressed elsewhere in this volume, the most critical security sector challenge in post–Ben Ali Tunisia is the reform of the security apparatus. Tunisia's security apparatus is a complex labyrinth of government ministries and security providers, some of which have their own intelligence capabilities, and all of which intersect and overlap in complex ways that were designed to "coup-proof" the Ben Ali regime. Their mission under Ben Ali was regime protection, not public security. Despite their vaunted size and network of informants, the security forces have struggled to provide security in a post–Ben Ali environment that features a host of new security threats and a distrusting population. Transforming Tunisia's security apparatus into a democratically accountable security *service* that operates in accordance with the rule of law will require two categories of reform initiatives: (1) reform of Tunisia's internal security forces and (2) reform of Tunisia's Ministry of Interior. Each will be examined in turn below.

Reforming the Internal Security Forces

Tunisia's security forces are controlled by the presidency and the ministries of interior and defense. Tunisia's internal security forces are controlled by the Ministry of Interior. They include the police and the National Guard. The police operate principally in urban areas and the National Guard in rural areas. Under both the police and the National Guard are a number of specialized units. Under the police, these specialized units include the Judicial Police, which operates under the Ministry of Justice and the courts but is controlled by the Ministry of Interior, and the Intervention Forces (specialized tactical units), which include crowd control, antiterrorism, explosives, very-important-person (VIP) protection, canine, cavalry, and other specialized capabilities. The political police, which also reported to the Ministry of Interior, were disbanded by the first transition government in April 2011. Under the National Guard, specialized units mirror those of the police, including a Judicial Affairs department and Intervention Forces.

When the regime fell, estimates that numbered the internal security forces at 200,000 were quickly revealed to be hollow. According to Lazhar Akremi (2013), the minister delegate to the minister of interior in charge of reforms under the second transitional government, the internal security forces under the Ministry of Interior (police, National Guard, and civil defense forces) numbered 49,000 before the overthrow of the Ben Ali regime.[16] The police subsequently recruited an additional 12,000 forces, bringing the total to 61,000.[17] Estimates place the National Guard at 26,000, including all specialized units. Under the police, the Intervention Forces are estimated to number 12,000. The total number of Ministry of Interior personnel, including administrative support functions, municipal and regional administrations (mayors, governors), and civil support units (emergency services), as well as security units, is reportedly 110,000.

The Presidential Guard is under the authority of the president. It provides security to the president and the head of the National Constituent Assembly, protects presidential installations and other key government facilities, and protects visiting heads of state. After some 400 Presidential Guard forces were dismissed after the revolution, the total number of Presidential Guard forces is estimated to number 2,300.[18]

Although the army provided internal security after the collapse of the Ben Ali regime, the armed forces report to the Ministry of Defense and do not normally have an internal security function. The Tunisian Armed Forces include the army, navy, and air force. Both Presidents Bourguiba and Ben Ali kept the armed forces deliberately out of the center of power. Conscript-filled military ranks were deployed to less populated regions of the country to do public works projects. Deployments were chiefly for peacekeeping missions in Africa, which kept the armed forces engaged elsewhere. And the military was kept small, between 40,000 and 43,000 individuals. At the time of Ben Ali's fall, the army numbered only 27,000 forces (Knickmeyer, 2011). Yet the army's experience participating in UN peacekeeping missions gave it the essential experience to fill the void left by the security forces as Ben Ali's government collapsed. The armed forces quickly moved to protect key infrastructure, restore law and order, and maintain security and stability.

During the first transition year, the armed forces gradually returned back to the barracks, particularly in urban centers. In some rural areas, however, the army continued to provide an internal security function. The army also remained engaged in a variety of internal missions, such as the military campaign in Jebel Chaambi near the Algerian border where the army was fighting armed groups like Ansar al-Sharia and other extremists who had been linked to the US Embassy attack and the assassination of Chokri Belaid (Yasm, 2013).

Although the army seeks to return to its traditional role, the escalation of extremist violence has prompted the repeated renewal of the state of emergency, first declared in 2011, that authorizes the army's internal security function. The army's ability to resume its traditional role, however, will in large part be determined by the pace of reform of the internal security services. Until these reforms enhance the capacity of the internal security forces to provide security, the army will likely remain an important guarantor of internal security, a role the army fulfilled to great popular acclaim in the aftermath of the fall of the Ben Ali regime.

For a number of complex reasons, the internal security forces in Tunisia are struggling to provide security. Even though these security forces remain largely unchanged from the Ben Ali period, the environment in which they are operating has been transformed by the collapse of Ben Ali's police state and the transformative impact of the Arab Spring across the region. Weapons, explosives, and drugs cross porous borders, and extremist violence is escalating. Protests are nearly a daily occurrence. Police and National Guard officers have been seriously injured and killed in clashes with extremists.

Reforming Tunisia's internal security providers will require addressing both the capacity and capability of Tunisia's internal security forces. Key reform initiatives will need to focus on (1) training and recruitment; (2) practices, procedures, and operations; (3) pay, benefits, and equipment; and (4) legal reform.

Training and Recruitment

Although new police have been recruited to fill the ranks of Tunisia's internal security forces, training programs, with the exception of some new modules on human rights, have not been reformed since the transition to democratic rule. The inadequate police response to the US Embassy demonstrations can be explained in part by a lack of training: many of the police initially deployed to deal with the attack on the US Embassy were not experienced officers but new recruits brought on after the collapse of the Ben Ali regime.[19]

Under the second transition government, some 12,000 new recruits were brought in to inject new untainted officers into the force, to manage the rise in crime and drug and weapons trafficking, and to replace the forces that disappeared after the fall of the regime.[20] To bring these forces online quickly, entry standards were reduced and new recruits were given an expedited three-month training program in place of the nine-month standard program, which included classroom training and an internship in the field.[21] Senior police officers themselves acknowledge that the admission standards and training for these new recruits were inadequate.[22]

Tunisia's police, from new recruitments to senior officers and civilian police officials, are trained at five, and possibly more, different police academies. The National Guard similarly maintains its own training institutions. Some important changes and additions have been made in their training curricula, particularly for new recruits and junior officers. Various international organizations, including the United Nations and the International Committee of the Red Cross, have partnered with Tunisian police institutions to develop and deliver new curricula, including a program to train the trainers in some police institutions (Mechiche, 2013). The content of human rights training, which existed before the revolution, has been updated, and the number of hours devoted to human rights training has also increased. Additionally, human rights experts have been hired to teach the new curriculum.[23] International donors have also offered specialized training programs focused on police investigation, interrogation, and detention practices.[24] Although these are positive indications that the curriculum of Tunisia's police training institutions is being changed, and that some police units have received new training, much remains to be done.

Each of the police and National Guard schools has specialized curricula that will need to be redesigned to address the new role of the police in a democratic Tunisia. Curricular reform will need to focus on updating the content of courses that deal with general policing skills as well as specialized skills, such as crowd and riot control, border management, counterterrorism, and negotiation. And in the future, as new policies and procedures are designed and implemented to transform the police into an accountable, service-oriented institution, continued training will be essential for ensuring that Tunisia's police understand the new policies and procedures and know how to implement them in the field.

Across police and National Guard training programs, new curricula will need to be developed that focus on educating and training police throughout the ranks on the roles and responsibilities of a police *service*.[25] This process is as much about training for a new skill set as it is about inculcating a new mind-set and fostering an institutional culture focused on serving and protecting the population. A principal feature of the Ben Ali security apparatus was the tight control of police operations, and the security services were accustomed to acting only upon direct orders from "the palace." A critical component of reforming Tunisia's recruitment and training programs will need to focus on changing mind-sets and an institutional culture that eschewed discretion and initiative and favored following direct orders even for routine and seemingly mundane initiatives, such as the day-to-day operations of a local police station.

Whether or not new training will have an impact on actual police operations, however, is dependent on the commitment of the uniformed commanders and their civilian leadership. New practices, procedures, and modes of operation will need to be implemented to ensure that the new training content, with its focus on preparing police for a new mission of service and inculcating a new mind-set and institutional culture, are also reflected in how the police actually operate in the field. When these practices reflect a new commitment to service, they are also critical to building a relationship between the police and the population.

Reform of the content and capacity of training programs for Tunisia's internal security providers is only one, albeit critical, component of reforming the internal security apparatus. The entire police infrastructure—training and recruitment, as well as promotion, pay, and benefits, rules of engagement, standard operating procedures, appropriate equipment, and the laws governing the internal security forces—must all be reformed if Tunisia's authoritarian security apparatus is to become a democratic police service. And none of these reforms will be possible if the senior police leadership, ministry officials, and political leadership do not also embrace a new mission for the police, commit to implementing reform, and engage themselves with the population in ways that reflect a new commitment to service. If senior leaders do not embrace these new practices and methods, including the devolution of command and control, then improved training and recruitment will not prevent disillusionment among police officers and heightened distrust among Tunisia's citizens.

Practices, Procedures, and Operations

After the collapse of the Ben Ali regime, the ingrained reflex to "wait for instructions" rather than to take initiative has continued to shape, even in extremis, how police conduct operations and react to events on the ground. The lack of police capacity evident in front of the US Embassy can in part be explained by the need to wait for orders from central command.[26] As the protestors marched from the center of Tunis to the elegant Berges du Lac neighborhood where the US Embassy sits, their large entourage was clearly visible and resulted in more than a few traffic snarls.[27] Along the way, police at various checkpoints noted the large group of demonstrators and radioed for instructions. "It was a very dangerous situation," one officer explained, and "[we had] no equipment and no instructions."[28] The police response to the embassy demonstrations suggests that rules of engagement and standard operating procedures, designed when violent public incidents were rare and the primary mission of the security services was regime protection and not public order, are not suited to the new mission of Tunisia's police.

Civil society observers who have tracked police operations since the revolution note that, even two years after the revolution, the police are "still using old methods."[29] This tendency can be explained in part by the "ingrained reflexes" of some of Tunisia's seasoned police officers, "dinosaurs" in the system who don't want to change, and leaders who hesitate to adapt procedures when the security environment is fluid and threats to police officers in the field are escalating.[30] Despite new training programs and an apparent commitment to reform, police officers continue to use "old methods" because their leadership believes these are necessary to "save the state and protect the population."[31]

Tunisians widely believe that torture continues in prisons and particularly in pretrial detention,[32] although government officials claim that torture has ceased since the revolution (Mechiche, 2013). Whether torture has in fact ceased or not, the fear of torture—and of police violence more generally—remains a tool for the police in post–Ben Ali Tunisia. In discussions with civil society members about the challenges police face in post–Ben Ali Tunisia, a police officer expressed the frustration shared by many of his fellow officers: "How am I to secure the evidence?" he asked. "If torture is no longer allowed, how will I get [a suspect] to admit to the crime?"[33] The police are struggling with how to conduct investigations and collect evidence in a confession-based legal system while protecting citizen rights. Until police practices and procedures are changed, police are trained in the new approaches, the ministry leadership embraces these changes, and the institutional culture is reoriented, such practices will likely remain, and the police will continue to rely on fear as an enforcement tool. Reform of Tunisia's confession-based legal system and its reliance on pretrial detention are beyond the scope of this chapter, but the frustration police feel with the lack of new procedures for doing their jobs suggests that new alternatives to "old methods" must be a reform priority.

Before the revolution, demonstrations and riots, with the exception of an occasional clash during a sporting event, were rare. However, in the first year after the collapse of the Ben Ali regime, there were 13,000 demonstrations.[34] The police and the National Guard, and even the specialized Intervention Forces, are unprepared for this new challenge, which lies not only in the large number of demonstrations but also in finding ways to appropriately respond to demonstrations and prevent such events from escalating while protecting the lives of demonstrators, bystanders, and even the police themselves.

The response to the demonstrations in Siliana in November 2012 dramatically illustrates the urgent need for reform of police procedures and rules of engagement. As demonstrators threw rocks at the security forces, erected barricades, and set tires on fire, internal security forces in armored personnel carriers fired tear gas and chased fleeing protestors down the streets. On the second day of the protests, they reportedly fired bird shot at demonstrators. The violent response to the demonstrators garnered international attention. That same day, both Amnesty International and the UN high commissioner for human rights urged the government to cease using "excessive force" against the protestors in Siliana (Amnesty International, 2012; UN News Centre, 2012). International organizations documented cases of shotgun wounds to the head, back, and face, as well as eye injuries and broken bones. Some 300 protestors were injured, including seventeen who were blinded by bird shot (UN News Centre, 2012).

The use of bird shot was actually an attempt to improve on the "old methods." Internal security forces decided to use "less lethal" ammunition in dealing with the demonstrators even though the 1969 police law, which remains in effect, authorizes the use of lethal force against demonstrators.[35] In the absence of new laws and new rules of engagement and operating procedures, the police have taken to improvising new ways of responding to challenges like demonstrations. The decision to use "less lethal" bird shot was likely predicated on the assumption that Tunisia's citizens would interpret the use of less lethal means as a positive change—an example of voluntary restraint that would ultimately contribute to improving the relationship between citizens and the police. Instead, it produced an international backlash that stunned the already battered police and Interior Ministry leaderships.

The police have responded to the surge in large demonstrations by attempting to intervene earlier to prevent large crowds from forming. But keeping sufficient forces at hand in the eventuality of another large demonstration forming has reduced police presence elsewhere.[36] In some instances, these gaps have been filled by local "militia"—armed neighborhood watch associations organized to protect lives and livelihoods where the police are either not present or not trusted to do the job (Masrour, 2013).

As the police and National Guard have struggled to provide security, various armed actors have also begun to operate. Particularly worrisome is the emergence of Leagues for the Protection of the Revolution, associations that have been linked to the Ennahda party, although both Ennahda and the leagues deny any formal relationship (Seghaier, 2013). These groups emerged at the time of the revolution and were given the official status of associations a year and a half later (Samti, 2013b). Some of the leagues reportedly employ violence to intimidate Ennahda's political opponents (*Business News (Tunisia)*, 2013; Marks, 2013; Wolf, 2013). They have also been linked to attacks on meetings of various parties, including Nidaa Tounes meetings in Djerba and in Gafsa.[37] One of the most outspoken opponents of the leagues, and a critic of Ennahda, was Chokri Belaid, who was assassinated in February 2013. Belaid's death sparked mass demonstrations and the emergence of neighborhood militia and other citizen security patrols not just in Tunis but also in Sousse, Hammamet, Sfax, and Bizerte. Some of these groups were reportedly linked to Ansar al-Sharia in Tunisia and the Leagues for the Protection of the Revolution (Masrour, 2013).

The police recognize the serious risks of allowing "parallel police institutions" to operate in Tunisia.[38] According to a deputy police chief, "if such behavior is repeated, people will think that Salafist groups will take the place of policemen, which is harmful to the public image of security institutions as well as to the image of the state's institutions."[39] The police are also aware that "old methods" are not only failing to provide security but also intensifying public hatred of the police.[40] But they are struggling with how to change and improve their operations in ways that will provide security, protect the police themselves, and build trust among the population. "Our global objective," a police union member noted, "is to end the practices of pre–14 January [2011]."[41]

Pay, Benefits, and Equipment

Although the internal security forces were at the apex of the security apparatus under the Ben Ali regime, it appears that these forces were poorly paid and that working conditions were quite dismal. Furthermore, these conditions appear to be unchanged after the transition to democratic rule. Combined with the derision with which police are generally treated by ordinary Tunisian citizens, morale among police officers is understandably low.

For police and National Guard in post–Ben Ali Tunisia, working conditions in the field have become far more dangerous. One significant change in post–Ben Ali Tunisia is that armed groups have crossed porous regional borders to establish bases of operations and sanctuaries from which to train and recruit. Weapons are available, and some citizens are now armed. Police and National Guard officers themselves have been attacked and even killed in the line of duty. According to Ministry of Interior officials, a principal way to address the lack of police capacity is to improve their pay and working conditions. For example, in 2012 police received only a monthly stipend of 20 dinars (US$11) for danger pay, an amount that ministry officials believe grossly undercompensates the police for the dangers they encounter in their daily jobs. At an international conference on police reform in January 2013, Said Mechiche, the Ministry of Interior secretary of state for reform, noted that the "current situation . . . is not satisfactory." He went on to conclude that "we cannot ask the police to reform without addressing their basic needs. . . . The priority is making more means available for the police" and ensuring that they have the appropriate equipment so that they are "not afraid to act."[42]

The police do lack basic equipment. For example, the force has an insufficient number of helmets with functioning shields and too few gas masks to protect the police themselves from tear gas. Vehicles are another key gap, particularly when limited transportation is available to move internal security forces to respond to security needs around the country.[43] But new equipment is not a panacea. New equipment alone will not guarantee that police adhere to human rights standards or follow procedures for dealing with riots and demonstrations according to international standards.

Although new equipment, such as shields, may make police officers less afraid to act, their reticence to fulfill basic police functions is more likely driven by the absence of new operating procedures and of a legal framework that clearly defines the role of the police in the new Tunisia.

Legal Reform

A final element of the reform agenda for the internal security forces is the revision of the 1969 Police Law and other legal statutes governing the police and the National Guard. This legal framework, which dates back to the Bourguiba and Ben Ali regimes, continues to define the role of the police and police operations in Tunisia (Ben Mahfoudh, Loetscher, and Luethold, 2012).[44] Not only do the laws need to be revised, but also some of what is currently in the law, such as the detailed "use-of-force pyramid,"[45] may more appropriately belong in Interior Ministry policy than in legal statute. Ministry officials have been working to draft a new law for submission to the National Constituent Assembly,[46] but neither the police unions nor civil society organizations focused on police reform or on human rights in Tunisia appear to be aware of its contents or how the process is being conducted (Samti, 2013a).[47] Some police and National Guard officers were involved in early discussions to revise the law but are unaware of the outcome of the process.[48]

The lack of legal reform seriously impinges police capacity and keeps the Ben Ali security apparatus intact. Under Ben Ali, the police were under the direct political authority of the president.[49] According to police and National Guard officers, the law defined their role as "enforcement of the political, social and economic policies of the government."[50] Both in practice and in law, Tunisia's security apparatus was designed as an instrument of government control that extended beyond police and gendarmerie functions.

Existing laws will need to be revised to reflect Tunisia's transition to democratic rule. The law governing demonstrations (Law 69-4) is a clear example of a legal framework that authorizes Tunisia's police and National Guard to act in ways that are antithetical to a democratic police force.[51] These laws are also complex and ambiguous, and absent clear instructions from police leadership and the Ministry of Interior, Tunisia's police and National Guard are struggling to interpret them.

Under the existing law, significant constraints have been placed on the right to assembly. Although Chapter 1 of the law, which defines public meetings, notes that "public meetings shall be free" (Article 1), subsequent articles suggest otherwise. The law requires a declaration of the time and date, with two signatures of people "in possession of their civil rights," filed with the local government "no less than 3 days and no more than 15 days before the meeting" (Article 2). Additionally, there must be a stated purpose (Article 3), and meetings cannot continue after midnight (Article 4). Furthermore, Article 5 requires a chairing committee of three members who "shall be responsible for maintaining order, preventing violation of the law, ensuring that the meeting adheres to its original purpose as stated in the declaration, and prohibit any speech that is inimical to public safety or morals or incites conduct defined as a crime or offense." Article 6 requires "an official tasked by the national security authority" to attend the meeting. Finally, the official has the authority to terminate the meeting, and "persons . . . [are] required to disperse upon the first order" and prohibited from taking the meeting to "public streets" (Article 8).[52]

Outside gatherings, or demonstrations, are covered in the remaining chapters. "Armed gatherings" and "large gatherings likely to disrupt the peace" are prohibited (Article 13). A gathering is considered "armed" when one or more participants are carrying a concealed or nonconcealed weapon or if participants pick up a weapon on-site (Article 14). Thus, if protestors pick up a rock or other object, or if even one protestor is carrying a concealed weapon, police have grounds to disperse the gathering.[53]

How a gathering is dispersed is then dealt with in the remaining chapters that focus on use of arms and criminal penalties. Articles 15–18 specify that the order to disperse must be given by an official in uniform (or wearing an insignia). The official must announce his presence, order the gathering to disperse using a megaphone or an audible or illuminated signal, and then order dispersal a second time if the first order goes unheeded. The second order also carries a warning that force will be used. Although the law notes two warnings, four, in effect, are to be given if force is to be used—a requirement determined by the very failure to disperse after the second warning even though other measures—water cannon and tear gas—have yet to be employed (Article 19).[54]

These articles are confusing even for experienced police officers.[55] The discretion suggested in the law for police to escalate the series of warnings before using force to disperse large crowds did not exist in practice because the police "always operated under the instructions of the government."[56] In post–Ben Ali Tunisia, police are thus left to interpret these laws on the ground in highly tense situations for which they have had limited real-world experience and training.

Even more problematic is the use of force detailed in Articles 20, 21, and 22. Police officers cite these as "very complex" and particularly difficult to interpret.[57] According to these articles, if the demonstrators refuse to heed the warnings as detailed above, the "security authorities" are authorized to use "the following means in the following order": (1) spray water or use billy clubs, (2) spray tear gas, (3) fire a shot vertically in the air to frighten demonstrators, (4) fire a shot over their heads, (5) fire a shot at protestors' legs, and (6) if the last fails to disperse the protesters, shoot directly at them, per Article 22.[58] Listed separately, Article 20 also authorizes police to shoot when a "suspect refuses to comply and attempts to flee."[59]

Articles 20–22 constitute Tunisia's use-of-force pyramid for demonstrations. The law authorizes warning shots, a practice eschewed in democratic police structures where the tendency is to authorize only to "shoot to kill" as a way of controlling police use of lethal force.[60] Not only is a warning shot authorized by the 1969 law, but police are authorized to fire a three-shot warning (in the air, over the head, and at the feet) before they can shoot to kill. Effectively, the law authorizes police to shoot in multiple directions to disperse protestors, a situation that is fraught with peril and likely to produce large numbers of injuries and casualties from stray shots alone. And when a protestor flees the scene, once the warnings have been issued to disperse, police are authorized to shoot "to compel him to stop" (Article 20).[61]

It is thus not surprising that protestors have sustained the numbers and types of injuries reported in the press and documented by human rights organizations or that police officers insist that their use of force is in accordance with the Police Law. These laws do authorize police to use lethal force in ways that are likely to injure large numbers of civilians—not just protestors but bystanders as well. Unless and until these practices are changed and codified in a new legal framework, or perhaps more appropriately in ministry policy, Tunisia's police will not transition to a democratic service-oriented institution even if they have received excellent training, better pay, benefits, and equipment, and new practices, procedures, and operations. None of these reforms will have a lasting impact if they are not grounded in a new legal framework and in new policies that define how the police serve the population of Tunisia in accordance with democratic principles and the rule of law.

Reforming the Ministry of Interior

Reforming the internal security forces addresses only one, albeit important, piece of Tunisia's SSR agenda. "The most critical—and most often neglected—focus of SSR is the bureaucratic agency responsible for the police and other internal security forces" (Perito, 2009: 3). The Interior Ministry is responsible for recruiting, training, equipping, managing, supervising, and supporting the internal security forces. Within a democratic system of government, the Interior Ministry is also answerable to oversight institutions, such as parliamentary committees, and to the executive for how it manages those internal security functions, allocates and oversees the internal security budget, implements government programs and policies, including reform, and fulfills its core functions. It should have an appropriate legal foundation and mission, function according to clearly defined policies, and be administered and supervised by appropriately trained and supervised personnel (Perito, 2009).

In Tunisia, the Ministry of Interior is the proverbial black box of the security sector. The organizational chart of the ministry is closely guarded information that is not publicly available, which complicates the task of mapping the internal security structures controlled by it as well as the oversight mechanisms within the ministry.

The Byzantine-like organizational structure of the Ministry of Interior and the internal security forces reflects classic "coup-proofing" features. The ministry is complexly organized, divided into directorates and subdirectorates that do little to promote efficiency, resource allocation, or strategic decisionmaking and planning but that work extremely well to keep suborganizations siloed and isolated. There is also a great deal of duplication and overlap—many of the Ministry of Interior directorates have their own "common services" subdirectorates that manage pay, resources, and logistics. Equipment management is similarly decentralized, resulting in uneven and often ineffective allocation.

Under Ben Ali, little to no basic intradepartmental coordination took place. Outsiders who attended meetings in the ministry after the revolution were shocked to discover that senior officials who had had offices in relative close physical proximity or who had worked on similar issues had, over the course of their careers, never met each other before these meetings.[62] Officers who attended the military academy together but subsequently entered different institutions in the security sector reported having no contact after graduation. "This is only beginning to change now, slowly, two years after the revolution," remarked one officer.[63] Another agreed: "It is beginning to be possible to speak with former classmates."[64]

The organizational complexity is also reflected in the structure of the security services overseen by the Ministry of Interior. Directorates exist to oversee the police and the National Guard. The police are further divided into uniformed and civilian police. Additionally, both the police and the National Guard are divided into officers and enlisted police, or agents. Interestingly, the local police, or "beat cops," are civilian police who wear civilian clothes with no visible police insignia, whereas uniformed police are kept at central or district headquarters and dispatched to areas when local police require assistance. The National Guard members are all uniformed; they operate like a gendarmerie outside of urban centers although their functions (and subdirectorates) mirror those of the police. Prison officers were part of the Ministry of Interior until Ben Ali moved them to the Ministry of Justice in 2001; however, with regard to some ministerial functions, such as interministerial transfer policies and uniforms, the separation from the Interior Ministry appears to not have been completed. The Judicial Police, who work in the Ministry of Justice, are also part of the Ministry of Interior. In addition to controlling internal security forces, the Interior Ministry oversees internal governance at the local, district, and governorate level.

A clear priority for reform of the ministry is its reorganization to break the siloed structure and remove duplicative functions. This reform would also need to address divesting the Ministry of Interior of control and intelligence functions that do not belong in a democratic polity or in a ministry of interior. Additional reform priorities would need to focus on enhancing ministerial level functions like strategic planning, policy implementation and execution, and change management—skills that were neither valued nor promoted in Ben Ali's security apparatus. Much like the police who have been conditioned to wait for instructions, ministry officials too need to overcome reflexes to wait for orders from the palace. Taking initiative, proposing creative solutions, and working collaboratively with specialists and experts in and outside the ministry will be essential skills that interior personnel will need to design, implement, and manage reform of the ministry.

Although reform of the Ministry of Interior has been a stated priority of Tunisia's transition governments, little meaningful reform has been achieved in the two years since the revolution. One reason for the apparent inaction is the sheer size and complexity of the reform task. The challenge in Tunisia is not to rebuild the ministry from the ground up, as is often the case in postconflict SSR projects, but to reform an existing, highly bureaucratized ministry. This endeavor is not an easy or quick one, even under perfect conditions. As security conditions in Tunisia worsen, internal security officials and their political leadership will likely hesitate to undertake structural or procedural reforms that could, in the near term, have a negative impact on police capacity to respond.

Second, SSR is a highly political process that will create both winners and losers, particularly when it involves the reform of a ministry that was at the center of the old regime's power structure. Reforming and restructuring the Ministry of Interior will threaten the power and prerogatives of individuals and constituencies in the ministries who risk losing their position and influence. There is also a fear that reforms will open the door to score settling and restructuring of once powerful directorates within the ministry (Brumberg, 2012). A successful reform project will need to contend with potential spoilers and create buy-in for reform. As long as uncertainty surrounds the reform process, key power brokers in the ministry may refrain from supporting change or actively oppose it.

The standoff between the minister of interior and the director of one of the ministry's subordinate security forces in January 2012 dramatically underscores this point. Then minister of interior Ali Laarayedh sought to remove Monsef Al Ajimi, the director of the Intervention Forces, from his post. Ajimi had been formally accused of firing on crowds in Thala during the revolution. But Ajimi had the loyalty of his forces, who physically blocked access to the accused director and then organized a strike in protest of his attempted removal. One of the police unions intervened, persuading the strikers that their interests were not being served supporting a senior member of the Ben Ali security apparatus—one who had fired on the people. Ultimately, the minister of interior was forced to move the accused director to a position elsewhere in the ministry.

Tunisian human rights activists characterized the relationship between the former minister of interior Laarayedh and his ministry as "a war."[65] Whether or not this relationship will improve with Lotfi Ben Jeddou as the new interior minister is unclear. According to a legal activist engaged in promoting security sector reform before the 2013 cabinet reshuffle, "some senior officers are not collaborating with the new government. They are resisting any reform and are seeking to protect their interests, their positions, and themselves."[66] Opposition parties believe little reform will take place even under new leadership since the new interior minister reports directly to the new prime minister, who happens to be the former minister of interior (Akremi, 2013).

Finally, SSR is a slow process and success is likely measured in decades. Mechiche (2013) notes this constraint in early 2013 when addressing civil society charges that the government had failed to undertake reform of the Ministry of Interior and the internal security forces:

> The great structural aspects cannot be tackled today. Today we cannot tackle the issue of separating the ministry into two or three departments or of the substitution of the intelligence department and replacement with an intelligence agency, or of the amendment of the [security] statutes. Our agenda is very important and we don't have enough time to carry these out. This will wait for the next government.

Efforts to reform were thus postponed until after the elections of late 2014.

A Final Task: Reorienting the Institutional Culture of the Security Sector

Serious comprehensive reform of the security sector is essential if Tunisia's transition to democratic rule is to succeed in the long term. The raison d'être of the Ben Ali security apparatus was to protect the regime. That this apparatus is ill designed to secure the new democratic Tunisia is amply demonstrated by the escalating incidents of violence and the apparent lack of police capacity to provide security.

Two categories of reform initiatives will be essential if Tunisia's security apparatus is to transition successfully from an authoritarian control structure designed to protect the regime to a democratic security service focused on protecting and serving the people of Tunisia. These include the reforms focused on the internal security providers—the various forces and specialized units that provide security on the ground in Tunisia—and on the internal security oversight institutions—the Interior Ministry, which manages all aspects of the security forces and the provision of security in Tunisia. In the future, this category will likely also include parliamentary oversight committees. Both categories of reforms are essential. Focusing on only one at the exclusion of the other will, at best, address short-term problems but will likely further complicate the long-term transition to democratic rule.

A third overarching reform task, however, is equally applicable to the operational and ministerial levels but is frequently overlooked. Dismantling Ben Ali's security apparatus will also require reorienting the institutional culture of the internal security forces and the Ministry of Interior to a service-oriented mission delivered in accordance with the rule of law, to transparent communication with both the public and government oversight bodies, and to real accountability for the provision of security, management of public resources, and implementation of reform. This reorientation is the most difficult SSR challenge because it requires changing the mind-sets of individuals and transforming the culture of an entire organization whose *raison d'état* was regime protection, not serving and protecting the population. In other words, the population was a potential threat to monitor against and not a customer to be served and protected.

Effecting this change is a larger endeavor than merely reforming processes and procedures, conducting new training, developing a new legal framework, or restructuring the Ministry of Interior. Reorienting an institutional culture requires transformative measures across the internal security sector at all levels—from the most junior police recruit to the most senior operational and civilian leaders. At all levels of the security sector, personnel must embrace a new culture of service, transparency, and accountability both to the democratically elected government that oversees them and to the population whom they serve. Effecting this change will require time. It will also require addressing key obstacles to that reform.

One place to begin is the lack of transparency. The existing institutional culture views the disclosure of ministry information to the public with distrust. Tunisia's government and any future parliamentary oversight committees, as well as the population itself, should have access to basic information about the ministry and its internal security capabilities. For example, a published organizational chart of the Interior Ministry would be a good place to start. They should also have information about the ministry's plan for reform as well as the process by which the ministry's leaders intend to design and implement reform. Will this process involve closed-door meetings with select individuals? Or will the process be a transparent one? Will civil society organizations be allowed to influence the process? Will rank-and-file police officers be allowed to participate in designing a reform agenda?

Another obstacle to reorienting the institutional culture is the deep distrust of outsiders—particularly the public and civil society organizations but also other parts of the Tunisian government. A deep distrust reportedly also exists between the ministries of interior and defense and between the internal security forces and the army. The president of the Tunisian League for Human Rights, Abdessatar Moussa, was confronted by security officials at the Siliana demonstrations in late November 2012. "Why are you here?" they demanded. Although he was present to monitor the police response to the demonstrations, the police assumed that his presence was meant to incite violence (Moussa, 2013). A clear perception can be found, among civil society and members of the government, that civil society organizations are viewed by the government as untrustworthy, subversive, or even outright threats. The government does not recognize that civil society can be an ally in the reform process, particularly in helping the government communicate with the population and build trust. The Ministry of Interior needs to open its doors literally and figuratively.

A third obstacle to reform is fear. In short order, the internal security forces and the Ministry of Interior went from being at the apex of Ben Ali's authoritarian regime to being the most reviled institution of the old order. The sudden reversal from a position of power and respect to one of weakness and derision has generated frustration, fear, and anger. A strong current in Tunisian society seeks justice, if not revenge. Many police fled as the government collapsed, fearing retribution for their roles both before and during the revolution. The police all know colleagues who are serving time in jail for the actions they took during the revolution. They are fearful that they will be targeted for revenge or prosecuted for their roles in Ben Ali's security apparatus. This fear has limited their ability to perform their normal police functions at a time when security conditions are worsening. Tunisia's police and National Guard cannot provide security effectively—even with the best new training and equipment, increased danger pay, and clear legal guidelines—unless this fear is addressed and overcome.

The attack on the US Embassy appears to have been a watershed moment—it shocked the ministry leadership, the police, and Tunisia's population and dramatically underscored the serious risks of delaying reform. The assassination of Chokri Belaid months later only added to the urgency. In very public and tangible ways, Tunisia has become less secure, and with the passage of time, the risks of further delay are clearly only increasing.

212 *Querine Hanlon*

Although a renewed commitment appears to have been made by the government to deploy security forces to better protect the population and even to prevent smaller-scale events from escalating out of control, these changes were only employed after the Belaid assassination. Whether these changes will measurably improve the security situation remains to be seen. And improved security does not obviate the need for reform. Reforming the internal security sector is absolutely essential if Tunisia's slide toward insecurity is to be halted in the near term and its transition to democracy is to be successful in the long term.

Notes

1. Author interviews with US government officials, October 5 and November 5, 2012. See also Walt (2012).
2. Author interview with US government officials, Washington, DC, May 27, 2013.
3. Ibid.
4. Author interviews with Tunisian police officers, Tunis, Tunisia, January 2013.
5. Ibid.
6. Ibid.
7. Interview with Tunisian Magistrate, Tunisia Association of Judges, Tunis, Tunisia, January 2013.
8. Author interview with Samir Annabi, president, Tunisian Corruption Authority, March 15, 2014.
9. One notable change was the disbandment of the political police, a specialized unit in the Directorate of Special Services in 2011.
10. Only 2 of the 11,000 cases of corruption submitted to the ad hoc National Commission to Investigate Corruption, created by the first transition government, involved members of the armed forces. Both cases involved petty corruption (arranging free medical care for members of Ben Ali's family in the military hospital) (Annabi, 2012).
11. The most comprehensive plan for reform of Tunisia's security sector is the Ministry of Interior white paper *Security and Development: A White Paper for Democratic Security in Tunisia*. The report was released by Tunisia's interim president, Foued Mebazaa and the minister delegate to the minister of interior in charge of reforms, Lazhar Akremi, in November 2011. Akremi was nominated to the ministry in July 2011 to lead the reform effort and charged by the minister of interior, Habib El Essid, to draft a white paper with proposals for reform specifically targeted to the needs of Tunisia. Akremi called on experts throughout the ministry and from France, Spain, and Switzerland to participate in drafting the proposal, and the white paper was submitted for review to a seminar in September 2011. The final document contains their critiques. Author interview with Lazhar Akremi, Tunis, Tunisia, January 25, 2012. See Republic of Tunisia Ministry of Interior (2011).
12. Tunisia's Ennahda-led "caretaker government" was replaced January 29, 2014, by a "technocrat government" that governed Tunisia until new elections were held in late 2014. The parliamentary elections were held in October 2014, and the presidential election and runoff election took place on November 23 and December 21, 2014.

13. Author interview with Ennahda political bureau members in Tunis, Tunisia, January 25, 2012.
14. Rules of Procedure of the National Constituent Assembly, adopted January 20, 2012.
15. Author interviews with Tunisian and Algerian border security officials, Algiers, Algeria, and Tunis, Tunisia, March 11–20, 2014.
16. Author interview with Mohammad Lazhar Akremi, Tunis, Tunisia, January 25, 2012.
17. Ibid.
18. Author interview with Tunisian security forces, Tunis, Tunisia, January 2013.
19. Author interviews with police officers and with representatives of an international humanitarian organization, Tunisia, January 2013.
20. Author interview with Mohammad Lazhar Akremi, Tunis, Tunisia, January 25, 2012.
21. Author interview with senior police officers, Tunis, Tunisia, January 2013.
22. Author interview with representatives of an international humanitarian organization, Tunis, Tunisia, January 2013.
23. Author interview with senior police officials, Tunis, Tunisia, January 2013; author interview with representatives of an international humanitarian organization, Tunis, Tunisia, January 2013.
24. For an overview of donor assistance in Tunisia, see Institute for Integrated Transitions (2003).
25. I am grateful to Nadia Gerspacher of the US Institute of Peace for her comments regarding appropriating training for a police service.
26. Author interviews with police officers and civil society activists, Tunisia, January 2013
27. Author interviews with Tunisian witnesses to the procession, Tunis, Tunisia, January 2013.
28. Ibid.
29. Author interview with representatives of an international humanitarian organization, Tunis, Tunisia, January 2013.
30. Author interviews with police officers and with civil society activists, Tunisia, January 2013.
31. Author interviews with police officers, Tunisia, January 14–25, 2013, and with representatives of an international humanitarian organization, Tunis, Tunisia, January 2013.
32. According to Human Rights Watch, several accounts were given of people who died under torture in 2013. Author interview, Tunisia, January 2013.
33. Author interview with Bassem Bouguerra, President, Tunisia Institutional Reform, Tunis, Tunisia, January 25, 2013.
34. Author interview with Ministry of Interior official, Tunis, Tunisia, January 2013.
35. Author interview with police officials, Tunis, Tunisia, January 2013.
36. Author interview with representatives of an international humanitarian organization, Tunis, Tunisia, January 2013.
37. Author interview with Mohammad Lazhar Akremi, Tunis, Tunisia, January 2013.
38. Salah Edhaoui, Deputy Chief of Police in Omrane Supérieure, quoted in author interview with Mohammad Lazhar Akremi, Tunis, Tunisia, January 2013.
39. Salah Edhaoui, Deputy Chief of Police in Omrane Supérieure, quoted in Masrour (2013).

40. Author interview with police officers in Tunisia, January 2013.
41. Author interview with police union members, Tunis, Tunisia, January 2013.
42. Tunisian Institutional Reform Regional Conference on Police Reform, Tunis, Tunisia, January 25, 2013.
43. Author interview with police officers, Tunis, Tunisia, January 2013.
44. For a listing of legal statutes governing the security sector, see Ben Mahfoudh, Loetscher, and Luethold (2012).
45. A use-of-force pyramid, or force continuum, establishes the level of force used in response to an incident or situation. It provides police officers with scale-of-force alternatives to mediate the level of response. Responses range from officer presence, verbal commands, and use of less lethal alternatives to the use of deadly force.
46. Author interview with senior Tunisian Ministry of Interior official, Washington, DC, March 2013.
47. Comments by civil society activists at the Tunisian Institutional Reform Regional Conference on Police Reform, "Post-Revolution Police Reform: Current State and Challenges," Tunis, Tunisia, January 25, 2013. See Samti (2013a).
48. Author interview with police and National Guard officers, Tunisia, January 2013.
49. Author interview with police officer, Tunis, Tunisia, January 2013. Law cited is Law 17, Article 2 from 1982.
50. Ibid.
51. Government of Tunisia, Law 69-4 of January 24, 1969, Regulating Public Meetings, Processions, Parades, Demonstrations, and Large Gatherings.
52. Ibid.
53. Ibid.
54. Ibid.
55. Author interview with police and National Guard officers, Tunis, Tunisia, January 2013.
56. Ibid.
57. Ibid.
58. Government of Tunisia, Law 69-4 of January 24, 1969.
59. Ibid.
60. The author is grateful to Robert Perito and Nadia Gerspacher of the US Institute of Peace for the discussion of democratic police practices.
61. Government of Tunisia, Law 69-4 of January 24, 1969.
62. Author interview with international NGO focused on security and justice sector reform, Tunis, Tunisia, January 2013.
63. Author interview with Tunisian military officers, Tunis, Tunisia, January 2013.
64. Author interview with Tunisian police officer, Tunis, Tunisia, January 2013.
65. Author interview with human rights activists, Tunisia, January 23, 2012.
66. Author interview, Tunis, Tunisia, January 24, 2012.

12
From Contention to Reform: Deep Democratization and Rule of Law
Michael Johnston

Tunisia is well rid of the Ben Ali regime, and Egypt will not miss Hosni Mubarak. Far less certain, however, is what comes next. Whether or not a flowering of liberal democracy is desirable—a question for the people of the region to decide—such is not likely at this juncture. But can the societies of the region establish the rule of law? If the old style of rule by top factions and families is not to give way to new varieties of personal domination, no one can be above the law. Can the countries of the region make that a reality, and can they do so without a backlash from remnants of the old order?

This chapter is about building the rule of law through political contention among self-interested groups and citizens. Its immediate focus is corruption and its control; although corruption is scarcely the only problem faced by the new regimes, it is a key factor undermining laws and institutions. Specific varieties of corruption, correctly understood, can indicate systemic weaknesses and opportunities for reform. The ultimate challenge is to build open, accountable institutions that respond to public needs and demands and that implement fair and legitimate policies under the law. Understanding the politics of such a process, as well as its institutional and economic dimensions, and the role of citizen self-interest in driving such changes is essential. So is recognizing the potential value of "halfway" changes and situations. These ideas are part of what I call "deep democratization"—not building democracy Western-style, necessarily, but rather enabling citizens to advocate and defend their interests by political means, and building a society that is governed, not exploited, by those in power.

The Indifferent Track Record of Reform

A generation and more of renewed efforts to fight corruption, backed by an unprecedented coalition of public and private sector interests and aided by impressive new scholarship, has had only middling success at best. Reform campaigns abound, drawing upon a consensus that corruption impedes democratization and development while harming the many and benefiting the few. But although successes do occur at the level of specific agencies and programs, and in small jurisdictions such as Singapore and Hong Kong, demonstrable, sustained reductions in corruption in full-scale states are few (Birdsall, 2007; Mungiu-Pippidi, 2006; UN Department of Economic and Social Affairs, 2010).

Corruption is tenacious, often sustained by powerful incentives and at times protected by violence. No one ever knows just how much any particular society experiences, and tracing trends is even more difficult. But many reform efforts suffer from a crime prevention approach that views reform in terms of punishing and preventing specific behaviors and from a tendency to portray reform as a public good ("better government for everyone"). These approaches invite a range of collective action problems. Most problematical of all is the tendency to treat corruption as though it were the same thing everywhere, using one-dimensional corruption indices and thinking mostly in terms of more versus less. Deep systemic influences, contrasts from one society to another, and the need to enhance anticorruption strength in whole societies do not receive the attention they deserve.

At the same time, some countries have managed to check corruption over time. A corruption ranking in the seventeenth century, for example, might well have given England poor scores; 200 years later the United States might have been seen as extensively corrupt. The fact that successes can be found suggests a fresh look at some basic ideas.

Corruption will persist, and may in fact be the norm, until those with a stake in ending it can oppose it in ways that cannot be ignored. That argument is straightforward: checking corruption is not primarily a matter of moral redemption, good intentions, or process-oriented institutional reforms. It is, instead, a matter of checking power with power through political processes that will usually be quite contentious—for after all, the core issue is often who governs society, by what means, and within what limits (Johnston, 2013).

Historically, a number of societies have brought corruption under control in the course of contention over other issues. Corruption often provides some of the "vocabulary" of such contention, but key grievances are typically driven by self-interest.

Instead of devising grand reform strategies and then appealing to citizens for support, reforms must help them advocate for their own needs and interests. Reform efforts too often fall victim to collective action problems, particularly when the goal is defined in terms of distant public goods that lack credibility. After all, fighting corruption is difficult and often risky: reform campaigns may amount to mobilizing the weak against the strong in a climate of poverty, insecurity, and distrust. Citizens may not see clear connections between reform and the problems of everyday life, and often they have heard it all before. Some, in fact, may have a stake in the status quo if they receive petty gifts and patronage crumbs from corrupt leaders or think they will get them in the future. Those willing to give up such benefits may not trust their neighbors to do likewise and refuse to be the only altruist on the block. Particularly in postconflict societies, others may see any significant change of any sort as likely to make matters worse. Thus it is tempting to let others do the heavy lifting: after all, if reform really is a public good, those who stay on the sidelines will still benefit from any successes. If most respond that way, however, little will be accomplished. A better way to sustain citizen backing for reform may be to emphasize quality-of-life issues. The list will vary from one situation to the next, but concerns such as jobs, housing, basic services, and ending police brutality may be more effective appeals than "good government" for its own sake.

Citizen engagement based on self-interest is the heart of "deep democratization." Deep democratization, in turn, entails four key tasks: (1) enhancing pluralism, or bringing more voices into the political arena; (2) opening up safe political and economic space or providing an environment where citizens can associate, advocate, and defend their interests without repression; (3) encouraging reform activism, or channeling grievances over specific issues into pressure for changes in politics and government; and (4) maintaining accountability, or ensuring that citizen voices and competing political and economic interests continue to be effective. Those tasks point to a broad sequence of deep democratization tasks created by various syndromes of corruption. They do not generate an anticorruption checklist that says, "Do X, then Y, and Z will happen." We can, however, help citizens demand a place at the political table and build accountability and meaningful limits on official power in the process.

Political settlements emerging out of self-interested contention can be the foundations of the rule of law. The key here is not the triumph of civic virtue but rather pragmatic arrangements—often ad hoc, compromised, and emerging out of political stalemate—that acquire legitimacy because they help people protect their interests—that is, because they work. Such settlements can become institutionalized, over time, as ways to ensure fairness and a measure of accountability.

Even the best anticorruption ideas require political and social foundations. Supporters with lasting reason and the ability to defend themselves politically against abuses by others are necessary for change to take place. That process may well be contentious—after all, any agreement strong enough to protect one group is likely to restrain someone else—but over time such local empowerment is a form of democratization (a similar argument appears in Acemoglu and Robinson, 2012). Corruption control and better government, in such scenarios, are by-products of democratizing contention, not the fruits of master plans for reform, but they draw their strength from the demands and aspirations of real people and groups.

Drawing the Lines: Historical Examples

One should consider, for example, the case of the Magna Carta (Drew, 2004). Far from heralding the dawn of democracy, the Magna Carta was a list of grievances enumerated by a few barons who were fed up with King John's demands for money and soldiers to fight in France. The king signed, motivated no doubt by his quest for land, but still he agreed to limits regarding property, taxation, trials and the treatment of prisoners, and other concerns. "Good government" had little to do with the deal; the barons spoke primarily for themselves but had the resources and political "space" to exercise some influence. The Magna Carta's restrictions had to be reasserted many times but eventually took hold because people with a stake in the political order, including monarchs themselves after a time, had good reasons to see that both limits and authority be honored.

Stuart England: Crown, Parliament, and Power

Sometimes the key parties to contention are other officeholders. In Stuart England, Parliament took the lead in resisting what it saw as abusive uses of royal power (Peck, 1990; Roberts, 1980). Both houses spoke for segments of society, but Parliament was primarily defending itself in a struggle over religion, royal influence, and its own autonomy.

By the 1620s, Parliament's influence had been significantly undercut by generations of royal patronage. Tudor and Stuart monarchs, although far more powerful than those of the modern era, still had to go to Parliament to request tax levies, backing for wars, and the like. That was of particular urgency for Stuart monarchs such as James I, who was chronically short of cash and who, as a newcomer from Scotland, could not take political backing for granted. To circumvent uncooperative Parliaments, monarchs bought support with patronage and the sale of a range of offices and titles.

Parliament debated several antibribery bills and measures to curtail the trade in offices during the 1620s (Peck, 1990: 196). Such initiatives were proposed as checks on corruption but were also attempts by Parliament to protect itself. Proposals to extend the franchise similarly were backed by "surprisingly radical arguments . . . about the need to involve as many men as possible in elections to withstand the threat from the great opposition to parliament's existence" (Hirst, 1986: 136). Legislating limits on the sovereign was out of the question, but Parliament could move against the counselors through whom he acted. Thus during the years before the civil wars of the 1640s, Parliament revived its old thirteenth-century powers of impeachment. As in impeachments today, charges were drawn up against the accused, who was then summoned to Parliament for trial. Unlike today's procedures, however, conviction could lead not just to loss of office but to execution (Peck, 1990). A series of sensational trials of royal protégés ensued (Doig, 1984; Hirst, 1986; Peck, 1990); not only were evidence and the applicable laws hotly contested, but new ideas about accountability also emerged from the struggle. In 1640–1641, for example, Parliament tried the earl of Strafford on charges of influence dealing (Roberts, 1980). Accusers, looking to strengthen their hand against this royal protégé, claimed that despite his role as counselor to the sovereign, Strafford was accountable to Parliament and could thus be tried despite royal objections. He responded with an idea of his own: Parliament could not impeach him on its own, because both Parliament and royal counselors were accountable to the electors. Important notions of accountability were arising not as plans for good government but as clubs to swing in a political fight. Those ideas survived three civil wars, a regicide, a restoration, and an "abdication" by James II. The principles of a constitutional monarchy emerged as part of the political settlement of 1688–1689. That "Glorious Revolution," Daron Acemoglu and James A. Robinson (2012: 306) contend,

> was not the overthrow of one elite by another, but a revolution against absolutism by a broad coalition made up of the gentry, merchants, and manufacturers as well as groupings of Whigs and Tories. . . . The rule of law also emerged as a by-product of this process. With many parties at the table sharing power, it was natural to have laws and constraints apply to all of them, lest one party start amassing too much power and ultimately undermine the very foundations of pluralism. Thus the notion that there were limits and restraints on rulers, the essence of the rule of law, was part of the logic of pluralism engendered by the broad coalition that made up the opposition to Stuart absolutism.

Given the elite standing of the contending groups in these cases, was England really witnessing "deep" democratization? The answer is "yes," in the sense that self-interested contention engaged political interests, some of them newly energized, with grievances against the sovereign—grievances that provided sustained motivation to take up the risks of challenging the royal power. Neither the barons nor Parliament resulted in any movement of the have-nots; indeed, they would likely have fought any such mobilization. But both episodes brought new voices and interests to the table and eventually culminated in new concessions by and limits upon the Crown.

The interests and coalitions involved in such processes need not be civic minded. Indeed, their component groups may not greatly trust each other—hence, the necessity of the rationality of laws binding upon all—or they may agree far more about what they oppose than about what they seek. But they must have something at stake in order to sustain the considerable long-term effort involved in working out new ways of governing.

Fighting the Bosses in US Cities

The struggle against political-machine bosses in US cities during the nineteenth and early twentieth centuries was a more self-conscious campaign for reform and gave rise to numerous schemes for better government. Reformers tapped into moralistic impulses; one stream of the movement flowed directly out of Civil War–era abolitionism, for example (Anechiarico and Jacobs, 1996), and the Anti-Saloon League and early stirrings of the women's rights movement were engaged too (Kerr, 1980; Okrent, 2010). Social reformers, urban planners, and antislum activists swelled the ranks of those campaigning for good governance, whereas anti-immigrant and anti-Catholic groups joined for reasons of their own.

So blatant were the abuses by many city bosses that it is tempting to view the reform movement through its own images of good versus evil. But the reform movement and its targets were energized by self-interest, too (Hofstadter, 1955). Once-powerful "native" or "Yankee" elites resented the bosses who pushed them out of their "natural" positions of privilege using votes from immigrant and poor neighborhoods. Later-arriving immigrants who might have welcomed machine patronage saw it monopolized by earlier arrivals. High taxes, the waste and theft of public funds, poor services and facilities, demands for kickbacks, and favoritism drove many businesspeople into the camp of reform. Arguments that city government should be "run like a business" were not just an objection to corruption but also a complaint by once-dominant elites who could no longer win. Meanwhile the "spoils system" rewarded the machine's friends and sustained its street-corner army (Arnold, 2003). Small benefits—food, help with the police and landlords, and occasional bits of cash—flowed to voters who had nowhere else to turn (Merton, 1957). Still, the boss was no friend of the poor, and his help came at a price: the point was not social uplift but control.

The reform movement did not end corruption, and many of its innovations have come to be seen as less than helpful in terms of accountable, responsive local government. Some of its backers acted on motives one might find distasteful today. But here again a moralizing anticorruption movement was sustained by self-interest and energized new voices in its fight with the bosses. Many changes benefited reformers themselves: bureaucratization catered to well-funded organized interests, at-large elections raised the costs of campaigning, and civil service codes favored the educated. But in many places it did uproot political machines and helped end the worst municipal excesses. Some victories happened at the polls; others took place in state legislatures rife with antiurban sentiment. By the mid-twentieth century, full-blown machine politics was but a memory in many US cities.

From Contention to Convergence to the Rule of Law

How can contention and clashing interests lead to the emergence of legitimate institutions? On what basis can one hope interests will converge? The simplest answer is that there is nothing inevitable about such outcomes. More often than not, contention leads to more contention, often with the initial issue and participants getting lost in a larger process. "Steering" contention, in the sense of keeping it contained and focused, is even less likely, if only because the essence of deep democratization is people acting for themselves. Institution building can be costly and uncertain, particularly in fragile or low-trust situations. Still, some key values can emerge. One is impartiality—for Bo Rothstein (2011), a far more important criterion of the quality of government than democracy as such. In a strict sense impartiality means that government and officials' decisions and actions "shall not take into consideration anything about the citizen/case that is not stipulated beforehand in the policy or the law" (Rothstein, 2011: 13, citing Strömberg, 2000). As a practical matter, impartiality makes a useful point of convergence among people who might not trust each other any more than they trust those in power. Robert E. Goodin (2004) makes a similar point, arguing that the "antithesis of justice is favouritism" (100; see also Barry, 1995; Dworkin, 1977; Kurer, 2005). Impartiality does not impose any particular policy or institutional framework upon a society (Rothstein, 2011: 24–30), but it does emphasize fairness and predictability and set standards for dealing with all comers. It is a useful idea for people seeking to negotiate a new system of order in the aftermath of contention against old ones. Our historical examples suggest that sometimes contention can lead to political settlements and new institutions that originate in real concerns and, if they work tolerably well, can acquire legitimacy and credibility. That they may be far less than ideal is in some respects a secondary concern, at least initially; what is essential is that they serve a broader range of views and interests than did those they replaced.

Another factor that can make for convergence and political settlements is that contention usually has significant costs for all sides: in addition to the direct costs of taking action, there are also more general risks and uncertainties. The disruption of lives and economies and the opportunity costs of forgoing other activities are real. Sheer fatigue and exhaustion also play a role, particularly where contention has been protracted. Although those being challenged have much to lose, they may find continuing uncertainty and repression even more costly: the stress of facing enemies, rather than competitors playing by certain rules, can be considerable.

For all sides, then, a point can be reached at which settlements seem desirable. Such agreements are usually flawed from everyone's perspective but can be a way to get, or protect, some benefits. Top figures may accede to agreements with little intention of honoring them—or may honor them mostly to avoid an even more uncertain future. During the agitation that led to the first Reform Acts in Britain, Prime Minister Charles Grey had little affection for the idea of broadening the franchise, but nonetheless acquiesced: "There is no-one more decided against annual Parliaments, universal suffrage and the ballot, than I am. My object is not to favour but to put an end to such hopes and projects. . . . The principle of my reform is, to prevent the necessity of revolution . . . reforming to preserve and not to overthrow" (quoted in Acemoglu and Robinson, 2012: 311).

Most political settlements contain no magic; they may fall apart or simply shift contention to other grievances. In other cases, however, regularized taxation may yield more predictable revenues, stronger property rights can contribute to overall prosperity and reduced violence, and the sovereign's gangs may evolve into more of a police force. It is less important that emerging institutions embody "best practices" than that, in the eyes of diverse groups, they work.

At times the best one can hope for are useful stalemates: situations in which struggle proves inconclusive, yet going back to the old ways is unacceptable. Participants might just be looking for some way out of a deadlock. Such stalemates might look like failures of reform at the time but can yield pragmatic agreements that will be closely monitored by numerous parties. Stalemates can put Rothstein's (2011) values of impartiality on the table, to the extent that participants insist that new ways of doing things, although unsatisfying in some ways, will at least not leave them worse off than anyone else.

Contrasting Syndromes of Corruption

As if matters were not complicated enough, corruption is not the same thing everywhere it occurs. It reflects contrasting opportunities, incentives, and costs, and affects societies in quite different ways, depending upon both deep-rooted and contemporary influences. Differing sorts of corruption problems require reforms and strategies for deep democratization appropriate to their histories, realities, and prospects.

Some time ago I explored contrasting corruption problems in a book, arguing that four major syndromes of corruption can be observed in countries around the world (Johnston, 2005):

1. Influence markets. In a climate of active, well-institutionalized markets and democratic politics, private wealth interests seek influence over specific processes and decisions within strong public institutions, not only bribing officials directly but channeling funds to and through political figures who put their access and connections out for rent. In the book, the United States, Japan, and Germany were discussed as case studies.

2. Elite cartels. In a setting of only moderately strong state institutions, colluding elites—political, bureaucratic, business, military, and so forth—build high-level networks by sharing corrupt benefits and thus stave off rising political and economic competition. Examples presented in the book were Italy, South Korea, and Botswana.

3. Oligarchs and clans. A small number of contentious elites backed by personal or family followings pursue wealth and power in a climate of very weak institutions, rapidly expanding opportunities, and pervasive insecurity, using bribes and connections where they can and violence where they must. Opponents of corruption and of dominant parties and politicians face major risks and uncertainties. Distinctions between public and private sectors, and between personal and official loyalties and agendas, are very weak in this syndrome. Case studies included Russia, the Philippines, and Mexico.

4. Official moguls. Powerful individuals and small groups, either dominating undemocratic regimes or enjoying the protection of those who do, use state and personal power—at times, a distinction of little importance—to enrich themselves with impunity. The primary loyalties and sources of power are personal or political, rather than official in nature; anticorruption forces, like opposition to the regime generally, are very weak. In this final group, China, Kenya, and Suharto's Indonesia were examined in detail.

These four syndromes are "ideal types" (Coser, 1977: 223–224) highlighting important similarities and contrasts and do not necessarily describe any one country's corruption problems exactly. Moreover, some generic problems such as police corruption occur everywhere. The syndromes are not "system types": countries that differ in important ways may be found within each group, a given society can move from one to another over time, and although they are meant to highlight a society's dominant corruption problems, more than one syndrome might be at work in various regions, economic sectors, or levels of government. They do not embody a developmental sequence (e.g., from official mogul corruption through intermediate stages toward influence markets); a variety of trajectories are possible. Nor can they be ranked as "high" versus "low," or "bad" versus "good," corruption by other names.

Instead, the four syndromes reflect underlying trends in, and balances or imbalances between, participation and institutions: how people pursue, use, and exchange wealth and power, and the institutional frameworks within which they do so. Participation involves not only liberalization of markets and politics, but also a society's balance between political and economic opportunities. Institutions can both protect and restrain participation and may be of several types: social institutions (e.g., reciprocity or the values and strength of civil society); political institutions (parties, electoral systems, and patterns of leadership and followership); and public institutions including not only laws, courts, police, and bureaucracies, but also banking systems, regulatory bodies, and so forth. Strong and legitimate institutions can build predictability and trust, serve as guarantors for commitments, cut transaction costs, and improve government performance. Weak and illegitimate institutions not only are likely to fail at such tasks but can also be used to pursue and protect a variety of corrupt and unjust activities. Those factors were examined in my 2005 book through both quantitative indicators and a series of case studies to explore corrupt processes in contrasting settings.

Corruption, Impunity, and Change

No two societies' corruption problems are alike, but most in the Middle East and North Africa contend with the official moguls syndrome in various manifestations. That sort of corruption tends to be found in undemocratic settings where economic opportunities are growing, at least to a degree, and where institutions are very weak. There might be great confusion in oligarch-and-clan cases as to who—if anyone—is in charge, but official moguls cases are dominated from the top. Powerful figures plunder the economy, often with impunity; business opportunities, corrupt or otherwise, may be distributed to family or personal favorites as patronage in an economy that is highly centralized and poorly institutionalized. Opposition forces and civil society, if they exist, are weak, intimidated, compromised, or divided. In smaller or more unified societies the key figures may be a dictator, family, or ruling circle, and power is personal in its sources and use. In larger or more fragmented settings, multiple people or groups exploiting fragments of state authority may operate more independently. Of the four syndromes this one is least focused upon influence within official processes: state institutions and offices may be merely useful tools for those in power. Many societies dealing with official moguls are poor (although corruption is in no way the only cause of their poverty); still, a political monopoly can be the source of great wealth, if only from tapping into aid, loans, and any investment flowing in from outside.

Mature market democracies resemble each other in many ways, but in official mogul societies, much depends upon the personalities and agendas of those in power. Some may seek reform or at least refrain from the worst corruption, and where that is the case, considerable growth may occur. Others ruthlessly exploit both state and economy with devastating results. Official mogul societies are not necessarily stable, however, and insecurity may drive "hand-over-fist" corruption as leaders take as much as they can, as fast as they can (Scott, 1972). Corruption-and-development trends within this group of countries will thus vary widely. In official mogul cases institutional reforms accomplish little without the backing of top figures, for there are few independent political forces to demand accountability. Privatizations, anticorruption commissions, and intensified bureaucratic oversight may make things worse, becoming tools for political discipline or revenge against critics or smoke screens for self-enrichment.

Tunisia: Small Country, Large Stakes

In 1987 the ailing Habib Bourguiba, founder of modern Tunisia, was forced from power by Zine El Abidine Ben Ali. An interlude of political decompression followed: parliamentary elections held in 1989 were more free than any under the old regime, and Tunisia for a time had the air of a modernizing secular Arab state. By the early 1990s, however, the power of Ben Ali's political and economic machine, and the corrupt tactics it employed, were becoming clear. Ben Ali, his wife, Leila Trabelsi, and members of the extended family had moved into real estate, tourism, and exports in a big way.

A commission established in the weeks after Ben Ali's overthrow in January 2011 examined some 5,000 complaints of corruption. Its report eventually exposed a vast system by which Ben Ali relatives and cronies helped themselves to the best of everything: stakes in the most lucrative businesses, exemption from customs dues, choice public land. Tax authorities, the judiciary, and private banks became instruments of coercion: business rivals or critics often suffered bureaucratic harassment and saw their loans revoked (Chayes, 2012). For those still not intimidated, there was always a risk of torture, administered by both police and national security forces. In 2008 police forces reportedly fired on protesters, killing several; during the 2010–2011 uprising, the police were more widely feared by many Tunisians than was the army (Code, 2012).

The new regime has worked hard to identify and reclaim stolen assets, but the sheer complexity of the Ben Ali business empire has made for slow progress:

> When it comes to dealing with internal assets, the Tunisian government has managed to confiscate hundreds of businesses, banks, insurance companies and several pieces of real estate that were controlled by the previous regime. Many of these are in the form of conglomerates, such as Princesse Holding—controlled by Ben Ali's son-in-law—that encompasses businesses in all major sectors of the Tunisian economy, ranging from car importers to publishing companies and banks. . . . Nearly all major businesses were either owned outright by the former ruling family or had arrangements with them. Government ministries were often used as tools for furthering the same interests. (Aliriza, 2012)

The family had a lavish existence, appropriating valuable antiquities for their various homes. When one of the family's seaside villas was thrown open to the public after the old regime fell, visitors reportedly were stunned by the level of opulence (Raghavan, 2011). Belhassen Trabelsi, Ben Ali's forty-nine-year-old brother-in-law, found the family business very profitable indeed:

> According to U.S. Embassy cables leaked by the whistleblowing website WikiLeaks, Belhassen Trabelsi is "the most notorious family member" in Ben Ali's extended family. The cables refer to the entire family as a "quasi-mafia," noting that "the Trabelsis' strong-arm tactics and flagrant abuse of the system make them easy to hate." Described in the French press as a "hoodlum," Trabelsi profited from his sister's 1992 marriage, using public institutions and resources to create a Tunisian business empire that included luxury hotels, an airline, a radio station, a newspaper and two banks. (Aliriza, 2012)

Many family assets held abroad proved difficult to trace and repatriate; police sources suggest that Ben Ali family members had at one time held between C$10 million and C$20 million in assets in Canada alone (Tu, 2012). A 2008 US diplomatic cable released by WikiLeaks in 2010 observed that "seemingly half of the Tunisian business community can claim a Ben Ali connection through marriage, and many of these relations are reported to have made the most of their lineage" (Thorne, 2012). Whether or not that 50 percent claim is an exaggeration, extensive and powerful networks of Ben Ali beneficiaries continue to be powerful. Samir Annabi, the chief of the National Commission Against Corruption and the Misappropriation of Funds claimed, "Our main difficulty lies with those people who profited in the old system. . . . They will try to defend themselves. It's a continuation of the old system" (quoted in Chayes, 2012).

"Corruption" in Tunisia thus does not refer only to elite actions, or to day-to-day harassment and demands for bribes, but rather to a nationwide, top-to-bottom system of "extractive" governance backed up by violence, torture, and human rights violations (Acemoglu and Robinson, 2012). The real test of reform will be the openness and fairness of society as a whole, the extent to which citizens can advocate and defend their interests within a safe and fair political process, and ultimately, whether they will have a chance at a better life.

Egypt: Three Decades of Hosni Mubarak

Egypt is both one of the world's oldest societies and one of its youngest. Half of its estimated 85 million citizens are under twenty-five years old (UN Central Intelligence Agency, 2012). Over four in ten Egyptians are urbanites, with more than 10 million living in and around Cairo. Many, particularly among the young, are educated, for universities are nearly free, yet unemployment is endemic. By one account 87 percent of the unemployed are between fifteen and twenty-nine years old, and university graduates are far more likely to be unemployed than are those who did not attend (Camplin, 2011). Growth centers in the economy—oil and mineral extraction, large-scale agriculture, real estate—are effectively closed to most young Egyptians, and since the 2011 uprisings, some sectors have been in decline. That the demonstrations in early 2011 were heavily populated by unemployed young people surprised no one.

Official mogul corruption has long been both cause and effect of such inequalities. As in Tunisia, being born into the ruling family was an excellent career move: sons Alaa and Gamal Mubarak prospered in both legitimate business and more dubious pursuits (Agence France Presse, 2012b; *Telegraph*, 2012). Their financial empire, variously estimated at between $2 billion and $70 billion at the time Hosni Mubarak left office, included military cronies, government ministers, and what one observer termed "a thuggish clique of businessmen and politicians" in the National Democratic Party (Hansen, 2012). Some were involved in Mubarak family dealings; many more carried out their own schemes under the dictator's protective gaze. In the wake of the uprising, Zakaria Azmi, Mubarak's onetime chief of staff, was convicted of corrupt activities netting an estimated $7 million (Associated Press, 2012a, 2012b). The former oil minister, security chief, and tourism minister have all been convicted of major corruption; so were former trade minister Rachid Mohamed Rachid and a prominent steel executive who was a Rachid crony (Associated Press, 2012a, 2012b).

Military leaders' economic clout in "The Egyptian Republic of Retired Generals" was extensive (Abul-Magd, 2012b). Businesses owned by military organizations or top officers made up an estimated 10 to 45 percent of the economy (Hansen, 2012); more accurate figures are not known. At one point in 2011 the military lent the Egyptian Central Bank the equivalent of US$1 billion, apparently without great difficulty (Hansen, 2012). A *Sydney Morning Herald* report underlined the generals' stake in defending the corrupt old ways of doing business: "Major-General Mahmoud Nasr warned that . . . there would be no civilian encroachment on the military's sprawling business empire. 'We'll fight for our projects,' he harangued local reporters. 'We have sweated for 30 years and we won't leave them for anyone to destroy'" (McGeough, 2012).

Land, be it in sprawling Cairo or in fertile and seaside areas, was a major focus of wheeling and dealing. One case involved the large and, after thirty years, still-unfinished Gezira Tower and Hotel. Developer Khaled Aly Fouda, a former government statistician, acquired the hotel site in 1968 and by the early 1980s began excavations for the tallest building in Egypt. He was plagued, however, by bureaucratic hassles and political obstructions that seemingly had no purpose other than allowing better-connected businessmen to intervene and officials to demand payments. After several years' frustration, he received an offer from Hussein Salem, a politically connected businessman, to break through the bottlenecks; all Salem wanted in return was full ownership—for which he would have paid only $500,000. Fouda refused the deal and was left with title to an empty high-rise shell. Another of his projects, a beachfront resort in the Sinai, was about to open in 1996 when the Ministry of Defense seized the land, citing "strategic interests." The wrangling lasted fifteen years until Fouda, on the eve of the Cairo uprisings, agreed to sell to the ministry for just a fraction of his overall investment. By contrast, businesspeople who agreed to share part of their revenue with officials could often buy land at low prices and see projects through to conclusion (Hope, 2012).

Arable farmland is particularly strategic. As Abu Dhabi's *The National* reports:

> [Yussef Wali, the former Egyptian agriculture minister,] was convicted earlier [in 2012] and sentenced to 10 years in prison for a deal that saw thousands of hectares of public land near Luxor transfer into the hands of Hussein Salem, a businessman close to Mubarak. Under the terms of the deal, the land—valued at over 208 million Egyptian pounds [around US$34.3 million] . . . was sold to Salem for just 8 million Egyptian pounds [about US$1.3 million]. (Collard, 2012)

Salem, familiar from the Cairo case above, used his political connections well. But another factor was 1990s-era development aid intended to irrigate new regions and encourage efficient farming. A significant portion of such funds ended up benefiting top officials and military officers:

> Instead of seeding the desert with the wheat and affordable produce required to feed Egyptians, most of this reclaimed land was given to connected businessmen who cultivated high-profit strawberries, guavas and mangos bound for European supermarkets. . . . In theory, the money earned from these cash crops would be used to buy cheaper goods (like wheat) on the international market, while at the same time being invested in projects to create jobs for Egypt's unemployed. Instead, investors built heavily mechanised mega-farms, providing few jobs and little food for the domestic market. At the same time, many allege that large international loans were used to fill coffers, rather than implement development projects. (Collard, 2012)

Poorer farmers—saddled with government cuts in subsidies, unfavorable lending policies, and bans on agricultural unions (Collard, 2012)—had little choice but to leave the land for the city. Meanwhile Egypt, once roughly self-sufficient in terms of food production, became one of the world's largest importers of wheat.

As in Tunisia, officials' sense of impunity extended to the everyday treatment of citizens. Police demands for bribes from drivers, shopkeepers, and others continued after the uprisings (Husain, 2012). Mubarak's regime abounded with contrived regulations that had little purpose other than to put pressure on citizens and small-business operators. Too often, abuses were more direct: under the infamous Emergency Law as many as 100,000 Egyptians were imprisoned as political prisoners, some for as long as twenty years. Legal recourse via Mubarak's politicized judiciary was out of the question. Al-Nadim, a human rights group, reported in 2007 that "torture is the official state policy and not only the responsibility of an officer here or there" (Al Nadeem, 2007). Another parallel to Tunisia has been the difficulty of locating and recovering stolen assets (Evripidou, 2012; McGrath, 2012). The wide variation in estimates of Mubarak's wealth gives some indication of the uncertainties of that task, although there is little doubt that the former president, his family, and his cronies took great wealth out of a society in which two of five citizens subsist on less than two dollars a day (Hansen, 2012).

What Can Be Done?

Official moguls corruption in Tunisia and Egypt is no simple story of official misconduct, but rather symptomatic of the fundamental absence of the rule of law. No society is corruption-free, but where such corruption has been checked by nonauthoritarian means, citizens expect, and officials generally accept, that those in power must be accountable. As has been seen, such limits often are forged through political contention. But in situations as uncertain as those of Tunisia and Egypt, where might those checks on corruption begin?

As noted earlier, four long-term tasks are essential if citizens are to hold leaders accountable and institute the rule of law: increasing pluralism, opening up safe and secure political "space," implementing reform activism, and maintaining accountability. Each is a transformative process, not an item on a reform checklist; indeed, many established democracies fall short on these criteria, and in some undemocratic regimes at least some of these tasks may already have been undertaken. A society's performance on one or more tasks may also deteriorate, sometimes very rapidly. In addition, one should not expect to see one task "completed," followed by the beginning of the next; instead, substantial progress on one task may set the stage for others. Each is a contentious proposition—in some respects, must be so—and accountability is not a destination but rather another process needing continuing energy. The emphasis on the various tasks, and therefore the anticorruption agenda, will vary considerably depending upon the syndrome of corruption in question.

Official moguls corruption is dominated by a dictator, tight ruling circle, or other sort of undemocratic regime; top figures engage in corruption with little real opposition. Corruption in general is often described in the language and symbolism of a dread disease, spreading relentlessly through a society and threatening it with general collapse. But dramatic as such depictions may be, when applied to official moguls corruption, they can be misleading. The syndrome of corruption found in Tunisia and Egypt was (and is) not something undermining the system of governance; rather, it *was* the system, or at the very least it provided powerful incentives sustaining political hegemony. As such it underwrote a political synergy that is as tenacious and long lived as it is unjust and devastating to social development. Whereas the endgame in several societies during the uprisings of 2010–2012 was surprisingly quick, the regimes that eventually fell had been in place for twenty-four (Ben Ali), twenty-nine (Mubarak), and forty-two years (Libya's Muammar Qaddafi). To be sure, official state institutions were very weak—a factor that hastened the fall once it had gathered momentum—but the fundamental loyalties of the old regimes were personal, underwritten by very large incentives for cronies. The military, large segments of the bureaucracy, the courts, and a predatory political-business class remain in the frame, and they will not give up their advantages easily. Building pluralism, and doing so gradually, is thus no simple task: in Tunisia and Egypt, opposition groups and interests exist, but many are weak and divided. Direct challenges to such regimes could result in repression or might induce the hand-over-fist corruption noted earlier. The worst outcome might be the abrupt collapse of the regime, with the society—still lacking credible institutions—lapsing into the disorder of oligarchs and clans.

What sorts of participation and contention, among what sorts of groups and outlooks, are necessary for change to take place? Contention among just a few large factions over relatively few issues, and particularly over issues that cannot be compromised, is more likely to become a series of feuds than a fluid political process, particularly where material need is great and trust is scarce. By contrast, large numbers of groups offering individuals multiple simultaneous identifications (political groups, yes, but also social, recreational, and cultural groups, mutual-aid societies, and so forth); groups of differing sizes and scopes (neighborhood groups, but also political parties; economic interests, but also groups of people sharing various regional or cultural affinities); and those offering diverse rewards and incentives, not only dealing with shared problems but also offering sociability and a degree of prestige, all of these are a more promising alternatives. Similarly, contention over non-zero-sum issues that are open to compromise would seem a useful counterbalance to debates over religious doctrine and could diffuse antagonisms rather than reinforcing them. Groups that can cooperate in pushing for better public utility services in several districts at once might well differ over other issues without having the latter divide them permanently.

Although such ideals echo Western pluralist thinking in some of its essentials, they fall well short of a calling for liberal democracy. Rather, they are tentative steps toward changing habits and expectations deeply engrained during generations under the old regimes. Enticing farmers, entrepreneurs, teachers, women, and other citizens to speak for themselves, in a setting where official impunity has been a long-term fact of life, is a challenge. Citizens, individually and in groups, will need to come forward, and observers need to realize that just because they seem to share a common interest does not mean they will do so. The expectation that political participation is pointless and the understandable apprehension that participation might still be dangerous will not be dispelled overnight. The idea of trusting one's neighbors may be slow to take hold. Today's established liberal democracies often seem less than vibrant; how dare anyone hope for anything better in the wake of official moguls?

The inevitable temptation is to attempt to organize purposive, reform-oriented groups—organizations seeking government reform for the public as a whole. But as noted, such groups will likely encounter collective action problems, and taking issue with the status quo (or the recent past) can be dangerous. But citizen groups need not have explicit anticorruption agendas nor, indeed, even be overtly political. Those offering more diverse incentives and appeals, such as social activities, awards and recognition, and mutual-assistance schemes, can be of great value, building trust and networks that can be put to a wide variety of uses (Johnston and Kpundeh, 2002). Over time their growth and autonomy can open up political space and highlight its existence.

A more general aspect of the citizen's role is as the beneficiary of public services—ideally, as part of the constituency whose needs guide and justify the whole governing process. Judicious deregulation of many routine activities, so that citizens need not waste endless hours at government offices; performance indicators on the functions that must remain (how long it takes, and how many steps are involved, to get a license, and how much of the time public utilities are functional); and rewards, even if intangible, for officials who serve citizens well can help build both the appearance and reality of greater accountability. Citizen groups of many sorts can help assess the quality of services—one aspect, in turn, of encouraging participation focused upon issues that are open to cooperation and compromise, rather than upon conflicts over identity and religion. Better government performance can, in turn, help change expectations.

New economic opportunities and growth will be essential both to improving the quality of life and to encourage new interests and viewpoints to come into politics. Long-standing difficulties in the region's economies, the wider global situation, and corruption itself make such economic changes difficult to produce. Still, aiding economic development in ways that are particularly useful for encouraging grassroots initiatives might be possible. Creating or expanding microcredit schemes and similar initiatives, as well as well-monitored aid for small and medium enterprises, could have great promise. As has already been shown by the experience in Egypt, some previous aid schemes were hijacked by well-connected military figures, bureaucrats, and political cronies, pushing small-scale farmers and many other citizens aside. Schemes to channel start-up resources to the grassroots—perhaps, overseen by international or other third-party guarantors—might be a valuable initiative.

Safe political space is a longer-term challenge, if only because to create it numerous groups must occupy and use it. Here, guaranteeing civil liberties for citizens, NGOs, and journalists, securing property rights, and providing free and fair elections is of the essence and is a major challenges in its own right.

To this end, as well as for its own sake, deep democratization strategies will still require some focused anticorruption and institution-building efforts. This can advance both the pluralism and safe political space agendas. The police and security forces, which have long practiced repression and intimidation rather than enforcing the law, and politicized judiciaries would seem to be prime early targets. Training, recognition, and higher status for ethical and effective officials, and (where possible) higher pay, can be powerful incentives. Military corruption could be an equally urgent, but even more difficult, priority; depending upon the strength of civilian regimes, second- and third-best options might be most prudent. Opportunities for partial financial amnesties in exchange for resignation from the armed forces or, for former-generals-turned-businessmen, conflict-of-interest restrictions on dealing with military bodies could be a step forward. Unsatisfying as amnesties with new rules will be, they might over time begin to fragment the economic interests of the military. Moves against police and military corruption will of course require a more independent, professional, and credible judiciary, which is, again, no small challenge in its own right.

A second anticorruption priority—one particularly important for opening up safe political and economic space—will be underwriting and demonstrating the "stateness" of the state and, thus, credible prospects for the rule of law. That means building a state that does the basic things states should do—maintaining order, defending society, policing its borders, and raising and spending revenue in effective ways—and that governs via public roles, institutions, and loyalties rather than personal power. Again, the police and security forces will be critical, as may others such as the customs authorities; reorienting them through changed incentives, training, and new leadership away from domestic repression toward service and protection is both challenging and essential. Taxation that is simple, predictable, perceived as equitable, and linked to results will be a priority. Clichéd as signs reading, "Your tax dollars at work," may be, they reflect an important aspect of accountability. The military, once again, is a prime target—in this instance, showing that it too is subject to the law. For example, the Spanish government that followed the death of Francisco Franco succeeded in changing its own inward-looking and repressive military into a more modern, professional defense force via new resources, technology, and the status flowing from Spain's NATO connections (Heywood, 1995).

A lamentable synergy may be identified between official mogul corruption and international flows of aid, investment, and capital. To the extent that that is true, the uses of such funds, from the time basic agreements are reached until the resources are actually put to use, should be an early priority for corruption controls. Societies struggling to shake off the official moguls cannot carry that burden alone: donating and investing countries and international organizations will have to look to their own monitoring and control procedures, and Western societies must pay particularly close attention to money laundering and flows of illicit funds into and through their financial institutions, as well as actively help to locate and repatriate stolen assets. But those challenges also offer opportunities: in a closer-to-ideal world, one might imagine agreements under which expedited repatriation, within the bounds of due process and common sense, is linked to detailed conditionality regarding the uses of those funds, and perhaps of other capital flows into and out of reforming societies as well. In that event the quality of accounting and audit standards would need to be targets for reform.

A variety of domestic measures might make concealing, or exporting, capital and other assets more difficult. Although it is unlikely that financial manipulations could be ended completely, banking, finance, and important economic sectors could be made more "tamper-evident." Requiring real names on bank accounts; creating credible and more transparent rules for registering businesses and trading in securities; developing domestic "know your customer" programs for banking and finance sectors, along with other anti-money-laundering initiatives; and enhancing conflict-of-interest rules coupled with financial disclosure requirements (a change that well-placed political businesspeople will resent, but one that might be linked to various amnesties) can make some corruption more difficult to carry out or conceal. Over time those sorts of controls could also increase the sense that the economic arena, too, is safe and more open.

Notes of Caution

Official moguls corruption is not an abstraction; rather, as Egyptians and Tunisians know all too well, it is the extension of the power and interests of specific figures and their allies. Although the goal is to develop a social and political counterbalance for such dominant interests, reformers must avoid putting citizens at risk in struggles they have no hope of winning. Another hazard is that new anticorruption powers, and such credibility as may flow from them, may be taken over by one elite faction to be used against others. Corruption has been a pretext for many coups and political crackdowns around the world; if reforms merely become a pretext for arresting leaders of opposition parties or emerging civil society groups, they will have done much more harm than good.

Reform plans that are overly simple or set up on too-short timelines are also to be avoided. A frequent suggestion is to set up an independent commission against corruption, but that idea requires genuine independence and major resources. If such a commission is deemed essential, a country might be well advised to bring it into being as a part, or as an outcome, of a credible, impartial, truth-and-reconciliation process and to define its mandate carefully: better to do a few things well than to proclaim an across-the-board offensive that fails. Even then, any such commission will require continuing support, particularly as its activities begin to address the actions of entrenched interests. Two of the so-called prongs of the classic independent commission strategy—public education and advice and training aimed at corruption prevention—should not be overlooked as early priorities. An independent commission against corruption or any other direct attack on corruption may take many years to bear fruit and, indeed, may seem to cause more bad news and controversy than public virtue in its early stages.

An additional dilemma is that many reform efforts intended to raise the risks of corruption do far more to create uncertainty. Risks can often be estimated, whereas uncertainties cannot; indeed, the latter often make way for more corruption, as various middlemen and sharp operators go into business offering to reduce uncertainties, for a price (Khanna and Johnston, 2007; Oldenburg, 1987). Reforms that are poorly structured, uncertain in their backing, or erratically enforced tend to undermine better measures by making the whole enterprise less credible and by reducing demonstration effects in the eyes of both potential wrongdoers and law-abiding citizens and investors. A few laws and controls that demonstrably attain even relatively modest and focused goals are far preferable to a wave of ill-conceived and poorly implemented reforms.

The final hazard is the biggest of all. Too much pressure upon official moguls corruption, without building sound institutions in areas such as law enforcement, banking, and the courts and fostering independent political forces capable of stepping into a power vacuum, might well tip it over into the far more disruptive oligarchs-and-clans syndrome. This transition may take place in several ways: A combination of high political stakes, combined with few rules or institutional limits to restrain prominent contenders, marks the oligarchs-and-clans syndrome and makes it devastating to economic and democratic development. Too much institutional change too soon, too much liberalization in the absence of sound institutions, and too much insecurity for elites and citizens alike can all produce a disastrous change of corruption syndromes. Similarly, overly rapid or poorly monitored influxes of aid and investment may encourage oligarch-and-clan corruption by putting new opportunities out on the table for the powerful and well placed to wrestle over.

Conclusion

If this discussion has any validity, what are its implications for reformers? Clearly, one is to stay with the task of reform, remembering that in a number of societies now seen as generally well governed, checking corruption took generations and more. Remember too that reform may well have to be an indirect process—not so much mounting a dramatic assault against the ramparts of entrenched privilege but rather opening up the political arena, engaging more interests, and helping them chip away at centralized power and its abuses for their own reasons, and in pursuit of their own agendas. That sort of change is aimed not at corrupt practices alone, but at the deeper factors that make them possible, profitable, and difficult to challenge. Deep democratization will not only be lengthy but also messy, controversial, and subject to numerous reversals. Distinguishing between the good news and the bad news may well be difficult at times, although such is often the case with reform, whose earliest results often tend to come in the form of painful revelations. But over time, citizens in the Middle East and elsewhere, like their earlier counterparts in England, the United States, and elsewhere, may gradually tighten the boundaries around abuses of wealth and power, taking major steps toward the sustainable rule of law by contending over issues that matter in their daily lives.

A related lesson is to be aware of the value of "halfway" situations. Many would-be reformers, once they win a share of power, announce a "zero-tolerance" policy with respect to corruption—an approach that has never succeeded anywhere and that, given the controversial nature of the basic idea of corruption itself, is likely a logical impossibility. Such proclamations are rarely taken seriously and do not deserve to be, but when they inevitably collapse, they do considerable harm to the political and social foundations for corruption control. Measures that, instead, make for (and demonstrate) better government performance might well be possible and might have a far more useful impact upon citizen expectations. Similarly, a country that shifts over time from the abuses of official moguls corruption, or the disruptions and insecurities of oligarchs and clans, toward elite cartel varieties will still have a significant corruption problem (only a handful of countries today do not have such problems), but they may also sustain economic growth and move toward more genuinely democratic politics in measured steps (for a discussion of several cases in such terms, see Johnston, 2005, especially Chapter 5). Instead of Tunisia trying to become Denmark over the span of a decade or so, perhaps Tunisia should spend some time emulating South Korea.

Finally, and perhaps most paradoxical of all, reformers in many situations should aim to be unexciting. Postdictatorial and postconflict societies exist in various states of fragility: institutions are weak and lack credibility, government performs its functions poorly (if at all), trust among people and in their leaders is weak, and the memory of violence may be all too fresh in many minds. Reform in such situations, however well intended, is yet another form of stress for such societies. Whipping up mass sentiments against corruption, or attempting to launch national redemption campaigns, will at best raise expectations that cannot be met—thus hardening sentiment and cynicism against the next group of reformers to emerge. At worst those strategies will lead not to political contention but to renewed fighting and efforts at revenge. Neither scenario corresponds to deep democratization or the rule of law. Far better, perhaps, to show that government can govern—that it can deliver even one or two basic services in a fair and effective way, and that it can both demonstrate such performance and be open to further debate over it (Johnston, 2011). That sort of effectiveness—utility services that are restored and delivered on a reliable basis, roads actually built where leaders say they are supposed to be built and to usable standards, courts that protect property rights, and police who not only come when called but actually protect citizens—can build government credibility and, perhaps, persuade suspicious citizens that politics is not a zero-sum game. Such steps can, in short, show that reform is real, not an abstract public good, and that citizens can take their needs and grievances to officials and expect a response. That sort of unexciting response may, in many societies, be the most attention-getting reform message of all.

13

Strengthening Governance and Fighting Corruption in the Arab World

Günter Heidenhof and Lida Bteddini

The discourse on development since the mid-2000s has focused on the determinants of sustainable economic growth. Corruption is at the heart of this debate given its significant impact on undermining state institutions and weakening development prospects. An economic perspective provides one with a better understanding of the incentives for corruption, which arise in every country context to varying degrees. At the same time, such analysis leads beyond corruption to confront the deeper and more structural governance breakdowns that create an environment more susceptible to government failure. Recognition of the important role governance plays in fostering sustainable economic growth has transformed the way the international community engages in developing countries. Since the mid-2000s, the World Bank has evolved toward a more explicit acknowledgment that inefficiencies and weaknesses in the institutional environment have a direct impact on the achievement and the quality of development results. Today, governance reform is articulated as a key pillar in the World Bank's engagement strategy for the Middle East and North Africa (MENA) region.

Measuring the quantitative "costs" of poor governance is difficult, though international development practitioners generally agree that corruption bears a significant toll on the effectiveness of public policies that aim to foster development outcomes and improve the lives of the most vulnerable. Development practitioners understand corruption as a consequence of governance breakdowns or, in other words, a symptom that fundamental weaknesses exist in the functioning of state institutions, the underlying formal and informal rules and regulations, and the capacity of these institutions to ensure tangible development outcomes. Governance breakdowns in institutional quality, the rule of law, poorly designed policies, or misaligned performance incentives have a negative impact on economic and social development, including slower growth, weak delivery of government services, and limited mechanisms for citizens to hold government to account. Sometimes, poor governance can result from relatively minor problems such as capacity constraints. More problematic forms of poor governance are manifested through financial mismanagement and corrupt procurement practices, or, in more extreme circumstances, through grand corruption and state capture.

Ultimately, development is about improving the lives of people—improving their quality of living and providing equal opportunities for prosperity and well-being, with wider choices and opportunities for people to realize their potential, and opportunities to participate in decisionmaking that has an impact on their lives. Lessons learned from international experience illustrate that there is no "one size fits all" to deliver on these goals. In fact, governance reform may be a difficult, uncertain, long, and risky process, but better governance leads to improved development outcomes—outcomes that make the efforts worth the risk. This chapter is not meant to be a comprehensive overview of the many dimensions of development but rather a brief overview of the governance considerations that can have an impact on sustainable economic growth. In the first section, we provide a general framework illustrating the principal dimensions of good governance and potential governance breakdowns. In the second section, we contextualize this framework for MENA and draw on some key considerations in light of ongoing transitions in the region. In the third section, we present some lessons learned on what has worked in the field of governance reform based on World Bank engagement in this domain.

Good Governance Dimensions and Breakdowns

The World Bank's revised governance and anticorruption strategy and implementation plan recognizes that poor, weak, and ineffective governance, as well as corrupt practices, can have negative implications for the prospects for sustainable growth and poverty reduction (World Bank, 2012). Governance is difficult to define, as practitioners and institutions have a different understanding of its scope. Broadly speaking, the World Bank frames governance as the processes by which authority is exercised in the management of a country's economic and social resources and as the capacity of governments to design, formulate, and implement policy and deliver goods and services. Building capable, transparent, and accountable country institutions is considered fundamental to ensuring sustainable development. The quality of governance (and thus the nature and extent of corruption) depends fundamentally on the strength of relevant institutions, on the soundness of government policies and procedures, and on the capacity of the administrative machinery to implement government policies. In other words, good governance boils down to questions of how accountable the state is in its use of power and the effectiveness of oversight institutions. Good governance touches on whether citizens' rights, needs, and aspirations are responded to and whether citizens are well represented.

The principles of transparency, accountability, and participation are crosscutting themes and make up the foundation of good governance. Transparency is an indispensable ingredient to better accountability, especially with regard to external accountability. In addition, increased transparency will provide a platform for increased public participation in government decisions, thus reinforcing accountability and government efficiency. In this sense, the principles of transparency, accountability, and participation can be envisioned as complementary components to a good governance strategy and are mutually reinforcing. To be accountable, the governance process must hold a commitment to respond to and balance the needs of diverse stakeholders in decisionmaking processes and activities and deliver on this commitment, whether in the area of economic governance, private sector governance, or service delivery. Thus, the principles of transparency, accountability, and participation help to provide a framework by which such commitment can be measured and assessed.

Good governance is thus understood as the management of economic and social resources according to principles of inclusiveness, transparency, and accountability. Generally speaking, good governance constitutes six essential dimensions that, together, foster viable institutional arrangements that facilitate a constructive engagement between the state and nonstate actors. These six dimensions include (1) political accountability (i.e., political competition, transparency and regulation of party financing, and the disclosure of parliamentary votes), (2) effective public sector management (e.g., strong systems of procurement and financial management, meritocracy in human resource recruitment, and efficient delivery of public services), (3) the rule of law, including an independent and effective judiciary, legislative oversight, and effective supreme audit institutions, (4) decentralization and local participation, including beneficiary participation and oversight mechanisms by local user groups, (5) private sector interface (i.e., streamlined regulations, public-private dialogue, corporate governance, and collective business associations), and (6) civil society and media, including elements of freedom of the press, the right to access information, and public engagement mechanisms. Governance breakdowns negatively affect the functioning of this system. They exist in the form of political corruption and state capture, secrecy and information asymmetry, low capacity and public spending inefficiency, patronage and nepotism, lack of performance and quality, excessive administrative discretion, and little involvement of civil society and stakeholders in the decisionmaking process.

In support of governance reform, the World Bank focuses on addressing these governance breakdowns, in particular in the following areas: strengthening of core public sector systems, including the management of public finances and the efficiency of public procurement processes; and improving the broader governance environment within which the public sector operates (i.e., supporting institutions for public accountability, such as parliaments and offices of the ombudsman, strengthening the rule of law, and fostering greater access to information and public engagement). Within this framework, corruption is addressed through preventative measures that aim to limit incentives for corrupt behavior and strengthen mechanisms to hold government to account.

The impact of governance on economic growth remains highly debated among development experts worldwide. In *The Cost of Failing States and the Limits to Sovereignty*, Lisa Chauvet, Paul Collier, and Anke Hoeffler (2007) assert that countries suffering from poor governance experience 2.3 percent less GDP growth on average per year, relative to other developing countries. Other development studies argue that one cannot make a direct positive link between governance and economic development in aggregate terms. More in-depth analyses point to direct positive linkages between individual components of governance (such as security of property rights, government credibility, or efficiency of bureaucracy) and economic development and growth (Acemoglu and Johnson, 2005; Acemoglu, Johnson, and Robinson, 2001; Knack and Keefer, 1995; Rodrik, Subramanian, and Trebbi, 2004). But what do these findings mean for the daily lives of citizens? The World Bank's 2004 Development Report, *Making Services Work for Poor People*, made a convincing case that poor governance impacts the institutional arrangements and accountability relationships that ultimately weaken public service provision. According to the report, a direct correlation can be found between governance and selected human development outcomes (see Figure 13.1). In countries with higher literacy rates the rule of law tends to be better, and in countries with elevated corruption levels, infant mortality is higher.

The strength of a country's governance system also has implications on the business environment, particularly in regard to foreign investment. A good investment climate has a significant impact on economic growth. Numerous World Bank studies document the relationship between governance and private sector activity. The 2009 World Bank Flagship Report titled *From Privilege to Competition* recognizes the important role government policies play in ensuring a business environment conducive to private-led growth. The report also asserts the important role of the state and

Figure 13.1 Dividends of Good Governance

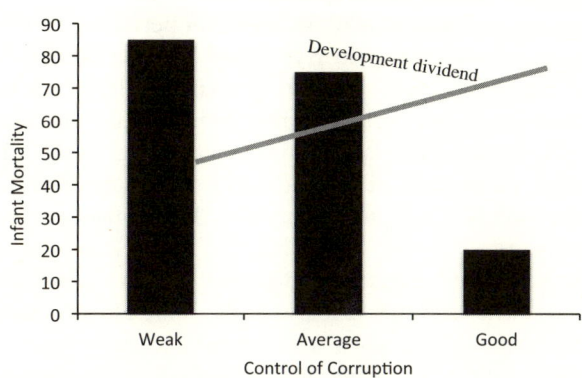

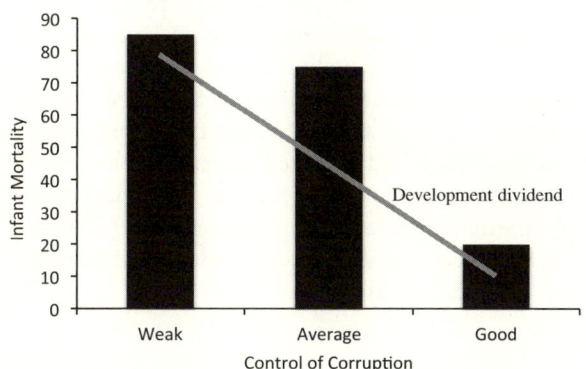

Source: Data from World Bank (2004). Reprinted from "The Challenges of Governability in the Arab World," © International Bank for Reconstruction and Development/World Bank.

regulatory institutions on ensuring proper functioning of private markets. Businesses react to incentives, costs, and constraints that form their business environment. In turn, the shaping and the implementation of public policies influence their capacity and willingness to invest.

The Ongoing Transitions in MENA

With its demographics and rich natural resources, the MENA region holds promising development potential. In the past few decades, this potential has not been realized; the context across the MENA region is characterized by numerous challenges, including political instability, policy uncertainty, and weakened macroeconomic fundamentals. At the time of writing, slow growth in Europe poses additional problems for Maghreb countries, and in Egypt and Tunisia, unemployment is up by around 4 percentage points from before the Arab Spring. Violence in Syria has escalated, compounding broader regional challenges and implicating countries like Lebanon and Jordan. In Yemen, security is fragile, although the National Dialogue Conference is under way with the aim of constitutional reform. In the aftermath of the Arab Spring, a range of economic factors have deteriorated as a result of political instability and uncertainty and their impact on economic activity and investment.

Although the Arab Spring has presented the MENA region with new challenges, most countries are still faced with the same old structural challenges that led up to the revolutions, with governance weaknesses at the core. Even though a lack of or weak access to data in this region compounds the difficulty of measuring governance empirically, numerous indexes provide an indicative overview on the strength of governance systems in a range of countries within the region on issues such as public sector accountability, transparency, public engagement, and the rule of law.

The existence of a "governance deficit" is widely known: actionable governance indexes, such as Global Integrity, indicate that MENA lags behind other parts of the world on many governance dimensions. The gaps are particularly pronounced in areas such as transparency, civil liberties, media freedom, participation, and social accountability. As a consequence, overall government accountability is weak, and public sector service delivery does not meet the expectations of citizens.

Public Sector Employment

A common theme across the MENA region is that most countries, to varying degrees and in different forms, are characterized by a large, expensive, and underperforming public sector. In resource-rich countries in the Gulf, the public sector is considered as a means to "redistribute the wealth." In the wake of the Arab Spring, many countries in the region responded to popular unrest by increasing jobs or pay within the public sector. For example, various countries in the Gulf announced increases in public sector salaries of up to 100 percent in September 2011 (Al-Atiqi, 2013). During the last days of Hosni Mubarak's regime, Egypt raised civil service salaries by 15 percent. And in August 2011, Jordan provided a onetime cash transfer to public sector employees totaling $112 million. As a reaction to the political unrest and to economic constraints, many countries in the region increased subsidies on energy and food and expanded unemployment benefits.

But the Arab Spring is not the beginning of this phenomenon. The MENA region was already characterized by bloated and unsustainable public sectors. A general overview of the public sector in MENA shows that the region has the highest central government wage bill in the world (as a percentage of GDP)—9.8 percent of GDP compared to a global average of 5.4 percent. The high wage bill partly reflects the comparatively high ratio of public to private sector workers in MENA and the fact that public sector wages in MENA are on average 30 percent higher than private sector wages, compared to 20 percent lower in other parts of the world (Ahmed, 2012). As a result, government hiring practices have typically inflated wage expectations and placed a premium on diplomas over actual skills as many new labor market entrants do not have the skills to meet private sector demands.

Recent efforts by governments throughout the region to appease social discontent through short-term policies of increased public sector jobs and pay only compound fiscal pressures and continue to reduce the attractiveness of private sector employment and development. The dominant role of the public sector as employer throughout MENA has distorted labor market outcomes and over the long run may cause lower total factor productivity growth. This situation further undermines efforts to improve government efficiency. International experience indicates that large governments are harder to reform, particularly when the public sector accounts for a large share of jobs in the modern sector (Ackerman, 1999). Any major reform would require hard political decisions such as privatization and layoffs, two issues that would have explosive consequences in the current context of many countries in the region.

Public Sector Accountability and the Rule of Law

Public sector accountability is particularly weak in most MENA countries, as many accountability institutions, such as supreme audit agencies, ombudsmen, or anticorruption agencies, are not fully independent. The region is characterized by a considerable gap between legal frameworks and actual implementation of laws. The enforcement of the law is unequal and inconsistent, which has had a detrimental impact on public trust in government. Global Integrity ratings for the strength of the rule of law in MENA highlights enforcement of judicial decisions as an area of particular weakness (see Figure 13.2). Before the Arab Spring (2008, 2009), with the exception of Jordan, all MENA countries assessed received a Global Integrity score of less than 50 percent on implementation of legal frameworks.

Independent judiciaries are an integral part of the overall system of checks and balances, and many MENA judiciaries suffer from a lack of

Figure 13.2 Strength of the Rule of Law in MENA

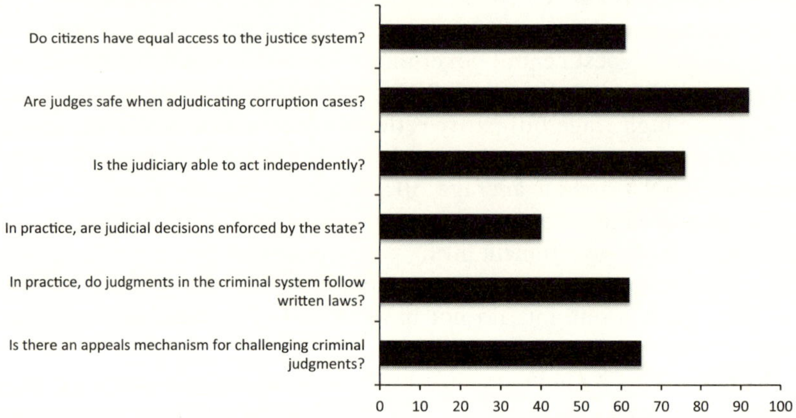

Question	Score
Do citizens have equal access to the justice system?	~62
Are judges safe when adjudicating corruption cases?	~92
Is the judiciary able to act independently?	~75
In practice, are judicial decisions enforced by the state?	~40
In practice, do judgments in the criminal system follow written laws?	~62
Is there an appeals mechanism for challenging criminal judgments?	~65

Source: Data from Global Integrity Report (2012). Reprinted from "The Challenges of Governability in the Arab World," © International Bank for Reconstruction and Development/World Bank.

independence. The *Arab Human Development Report* by the UN Development Programme (2009) states clearly that threats to judicial independence in Arab states do not come from respective constitutions, which generally support the principle of independence, but from the executive branch that dominates both the judicial and legislative branches. Of the two countries that score considerably higher on enforcement of decisions on the Global Integrity Scorecard, decisions in Lebanon are the product of a particularly weak legal framework to begin with, and decisions in Egypt are based on a system with very low judicial accountability. In Egypt, 75 percent of respondents to a survey conducted by the Information and Decisions Support Center on the justice sector report nonenforcement of judicial decisions as a problem (al-Gharini, Al-Rashidi, and Al-Gamal, 2009). Even in Jordan, which has arguably made the most recent advances in judicial reform, enforcement of judicial decisions remains problematic. Judicial independence is further undermined by parallel systems of security or military courts, by which politically sensitive cases, often including corruption cases, are removed from the regular criminal courts and transferred to military or security tribunals. In these courts, general safeguards related to fairness and independence may fall further below minimally acceptable standards.

As a result, judiciaries throughout the region are often not in a position to provide adequate checks and balances in regard to the executive and legislative branches, providing an ample environment for poor governance and corruption. Numerous constitutional reform efforts in the region have tried to address the issue of judicial independence directly, most notably

Morocco where judicial reform has been a topic of the national debate since the onset of constitutional reform in 2011. Similarly, the judiciary branch in Tunisia has been the object of significant criticism over its independence, neutrality, and relationship to the executive branch. Legally, the independence of the judges was guaranteed by the constitution, and in principle, the Higher Judicial Council was meant to protect the judiciary. In reality, the executive frequently interfered, particularly on judicial appointments. Furthermore, courts did not ensure due process in politically motivated cases and regularly issued convictions, including postprison terms of "administrative control" or internal exile.

Poor Governance and the Business Environment

In the MENA region, misaligned incentives and poorly designed public policies have weakened the environment for productive investments and have led to a general lack of a level playing field, creating a sense of unfairness and mounting social tensions—the source of much of the uprisings in MENA today. As mentioned previously, many countries in the region have problems of weak, unpredictable, or discretionary implementation of policies and regulations. Enterprise surveys conducted by the World Bank over a period of several years in ten countries in the region show that issues related to the rule of law and how it is applied—including informal and anticompetitive practices, collateral issues, and property rights—are among the main concerns (World Bank, 2009).[1] Corruption is cited as one of the top-five constraints in seven of these countries. Regulatory constraints (labor, licensing, tax administration, regulatory policy) are the key issues in six countries. In Lebanon, for example, entrepreneurs complained about unfair competition—from privileged firms with special subsidies or protection, to informal firms operating in clear disregard of the law. Private sector development in MENA is often hampered by political interference. State capture of politically well-connected individuals means coercive practices are targeted at prosperous private sector firms, driving some out of investments and preventing others from investing.

Access to Information and Public Engagement

Governments throughout the MENA region do not fare particularly well on international indexes measuring transparency and openness. Although transparency, access to information, and media freedom are crucial elements to ensure and strengthen government accountability, the access-to-information deficit in the MENA region is probably the most pronounced governance deficit if compared to other parts of the world (see Figure 13.3 with data from Global Integrity).[2] Challenges stem in part from legal and

Figure 13.3 Open Budget and Access to Information in Selected Regions Compared to MENA

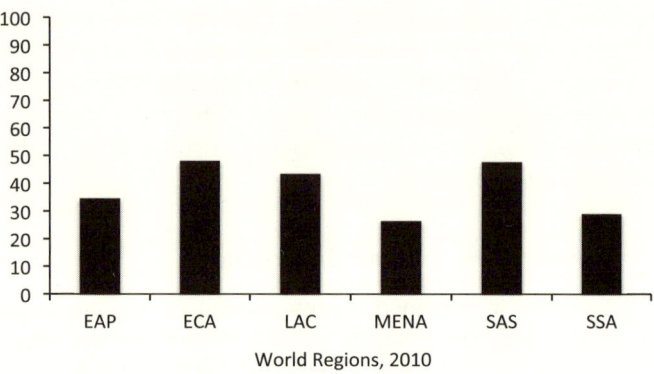

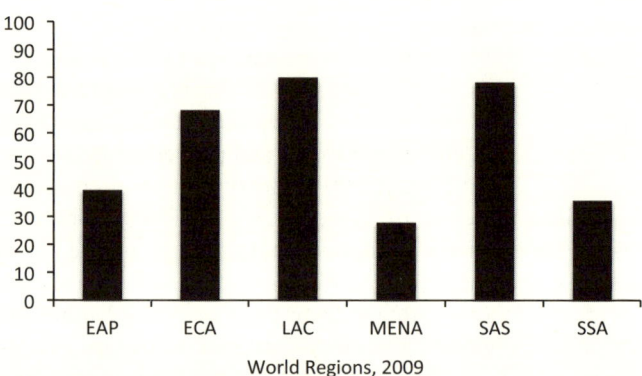

Source: Data from Global Integrity Report (2012). Reprinted from "The Challenges of Governability in the Arab World," © International Bank for Reconstruction and Development/World Bank.

Notes: EAP = East Asia and Pacific Islands; ECA = Europe and Central Asia; LAC = Latin America and the Caribbean; SAS = South Asia; SSA = sub-Saharan Africa.

political restrictions that stifle the media and impose limitations on public involvement in government affairs. The lack of proactive information disclosure by governments and the restrictions on the media have had a negative impact on informed public debate about the role of government, accountability, and service delivery. With a few exceptions, civil society is relatively weak and underdeveloped throughout the region, and civil society engagement in government decisionmaking processes has been limited. Legal and procedural restrictions concerning the registration of civil society

Strengthening Governance and Fighting Corruption 249

organizations continue to hamper the development of effective civil society organizations. Furthermore, in the absence of conflict-of-interest frameworks, including systematic implementation of income and asset disclosure regimes, holding the members of the executive and legislature accountable remains difficult. In addition, higher-level officials are often exempt, either de jure or practically, from investigation by oversight and anticorruption agencies.

Budget transparency is another important element of a functioning governance system since it can help the public to review, discuss, and influence decisions on the allocation of resources to specific policy priorities and programs. The Open Budget Index's 2012 survey indicates that virtually no country in MENA provides extensive budget information to the general public; most countries provide only limited access to selected budget documents. Taking a closer look at the most recent country-level data from Global Integrity, Jordan fares better than other countries in the region on de jure and de facto measures of the strength of the overall budget process (see Figure 13.4).

The lack of information in MENA combined with limited recourse mechanisms weaken opportunities to contest government decisions and to hold government to account. Before the Arab Spring, Jordan was the only country in the MENA region with a specialized freedom-of-information

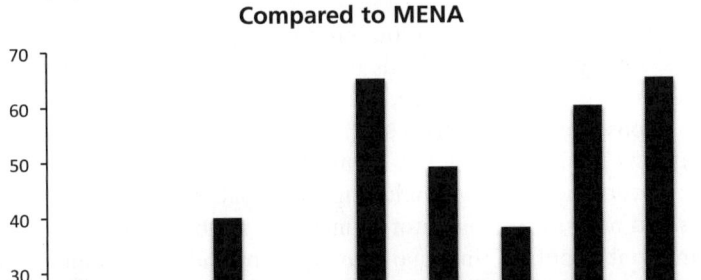

Figure 13.4 Strength of the Budget Process in Eastern Europe and Central Asia and Latin America and the Caribbean Compared to MENA

Source: Data from Global Integrity Report (2011). Reprinted from "The Challenges of Governability in the Arab World," © International Bank for Reconstruction and Development/World Bank.
Notes: WBG = West Bank and Gaza; ECA = Eastern Europe and Central Asia; LAC = Latin America and the Caribbean.

law, though it does not meet international good practice standards. Since the Arab Spring, efforts to address the information gap can be seen in many parts of the region: Yemen has recently adopted a freedom-of-information law, and as this book goes to print, Tunisia, Egypt, and Morocco are in the process of adopting dedicated legislation on access to information.

Selected Governance Issues and Priorities

As a result of the Arab Spring, the emphasis on governance has been more pronounced, particularly in areas that saw little previous traction such as access to information and public engagement reforms. Countries across the region face a wide range of complex governance challenges that have a direct impact on prospects for social and economic growth. The World Bank's governance strategy aims to respond to demands for social justice and equality, better public services, and more accountable governments. Relevant governance reforms focus prominently on greater transparency, accountability, and participation, while at the same time supporting important systemic economic and social policy reforms. In this section, we provide a brief overview about selected key issues and priorities that are geared toward fostering governance and addressing corruption in the region.

State and Institution Building

In many ways, state and institution building is prerequisite of a good governance system with a strong focus on government accountability and service delivery. As a consequence, the World Bank has supported relevant reforms in postconflict countries such as Iraq, Yemen, and Libya. Many of these reforms focus on a few key elements that make up the foundation of a viable governance system, including the capacity of the state to deliver services and perform its regulatory functions, the building of core systems including viable public financial management and procurement, and the development of accountability frameworks that help build state legitimacy and ensure the rule of law. Although state- and institution-building efforts generally take place in fragile or conflict-prone contexts, the Arab Spring, however, has triggered more demand from nonconflict states for support in reshaping core government functions to better reflect popular demands and ensure conformity with international good practice. Such support is needed in virtually all countries in the region, in particular in transition countries that seek to build a new system of governance.

Reforms to core systems and institutions are often more difficult to implement than sector-specific reforms. This type of reform is often confronted with challenges in coordination across different government agencies, upon which its success relies. Sector-specific reforms are generally more targeted, and the scope of implication is narrower, which makes implementation easier to ensure. In countries where World Bank efforts have been largely focused on core functions, numerous systemic constraints have negatively affected the outcomes of the intended reforms. For example, over the past few years, World Bank engagement in Iraq has aimed to support the strengthening of government functions and institutions, but the impact of this engagement has been stifled by various impediments relating to the administrative environment, political constraints, capacity weaknesses, and security considerations. More recently, the World Bank has been involved in state-building efforts in Libya, where the establishment of legitimate and credible government institutions is considered essential to avoiding the threat of relapse into conflict and encouraging public confidence in the functioning of the state. World Bank efforts in Libya to date have been focused on building or strengthening core government functions, primarily with regard to public spending and the delivery of public services.

Government Accountability

Overall, the MENA region does not fare well in global rankings of government accountability, and many citizens consider corruption and conflict-of-interest issues to be at the heart of the governance problems in the region. According to Global Integrity's most recent rankings (see Figure 13.5), Yemen fared particularly low on government accountability measures at the onset of 2011. Since the Arab Spring, efforts to increase accountability of public and elected officials have often been at the center of public debate across the region. Many ongoing reforms are currently geared toward ensuring the results focus of the public administration and the value for money of public spending (see Figure 13.6). Reforms in this area focus on strengthening local governments, which are believed to be more accountable to citizens than central bureaucracies. Such reforms can be observed in several countries in the region, including Morocco, Tunisia, and Yemen.

Supporting expenditure management reforms, including public procurement, is another core aspect of ongoing efforts to strengthen accountability systems. In close collaboration with countries such as Morocco, Yemen, Iraq, Lebanon, Tunisia, and the West Bank and Gaza, the World Bank's main focus has been on improving outcome-based budgeting and supporting reforms aiming to increase budget transparency and comprehensiveness. Support includes the strengthening of key accountability institutions such as the supreme audit bureaus, anticorruption agencies, and the judiciary. Many of these initiatives are complemented by significant train-

Figure 13.5 Government Conflict-of-Interest Safeguards and Checks and Balances in South Asia and Latin America Compared to MENA

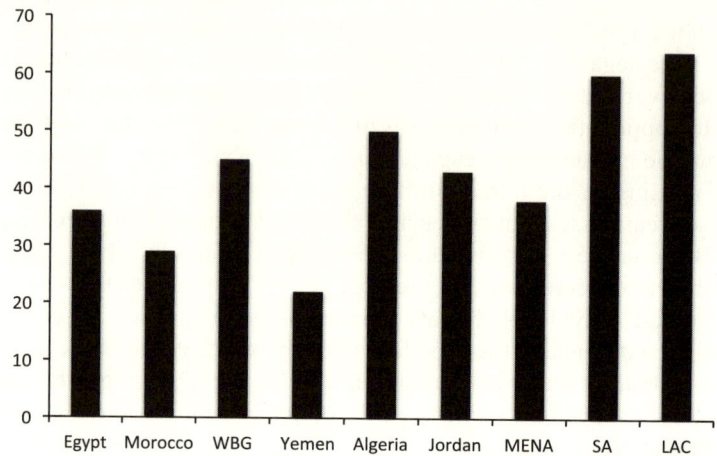

Source: Data from Global Integrity Report (2012). Reprinted from "The Challenges of Governability in the Arab World," © International Bank for Reconstruction and Development/World Bank.

Notes: WBG = West Bank and Gaza; SA = South Asia; LAC = Latin America and the Caribbean.

Figure 13.6 Strength of Legislative Oversight of Budget Processes

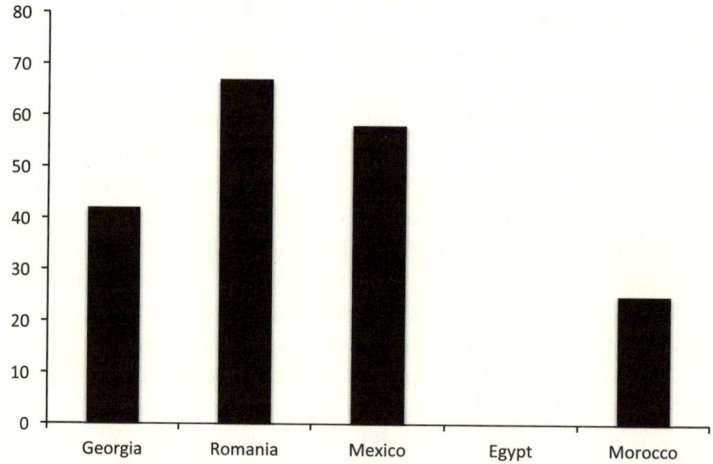

Source: Data from Global Integrity Report (2011). Reprinted from "The Challenges of Governability in the Arab World," © International Bank for Reconstruction and Development/World Bank.

ing and capacity-building efforts to ensure implementation of the intended reforms and policy changes.

To strengthen the private sector, the World Bank is also promoting corporate governance reforms that focus on increased disclosure, on business ethics, and on the use of international reporting and compliance standards, with a particular focus on financial sector reforms such as those in Egypt, Morocco, and Tunisia. The key objective of these reforms is to overcome a prevalent culture that sees privilege and preferential treatment as ways of promoting private sector development.

Open-Government Reforms and Civil Society Engagement

In many MENA countries key enabling factors such as citizen access to information, freedom of the press, and transparency of government operations are restricted. Economic and social data, which are fundamental for informed policymaking and for informed citizen choices and feedback, are not shared with citizens. According to the World Justice Project's Rule of Law Index, Egypt and Tunisia's rankings on open government between 2012 and 2014 illustrate a marked discrepancy and a reflection of contextual developments. Whereas Tunisia's score on open government improved during this period, Egypt experienced a notable decline in open government according to the World Justice Project's Rule of Law Index (see Figure 13.7). A prevailing culture of secrecy and a general lack of transparency of all relevant state actors were two of the main complaints during the Arab Spring uprisings. As a consequence, many governments in the region have focused on promoting open-government reforms to respond to relevant demands from civil society and the private sector. In collaboration with other development partners, the World Bank is supporting government-led initiatives in the region that aim at developing freedom-of-information legislation and at liberalizing access to socioeconomic information. For example, in 2011 Tunisia passed freedom-of-information legislation in an effort to promote open and transparent policy debate. Yemen passed similar legislation in 2012 granting citizens the legal right to request government information. For the first time in Morocco, the new constitution recognizes the citizens' right to information, and a draft law on access to information— written in collaboration with the World Bank—is currently undergoing public consultation.

The World Bank is also working with governments in the region to find ways to improve the quality and client focus of public services, for example through the introduction of measurable service standards, the simplification of procedures to reduce transaction costs and discretion, or through e-government reforms such as in Morocco, Tunisia, and Jordan. The World Bank also supports governments to promote systematic involve-

Figure 13.7 Strength of Open Government in Egypt and Tunisia

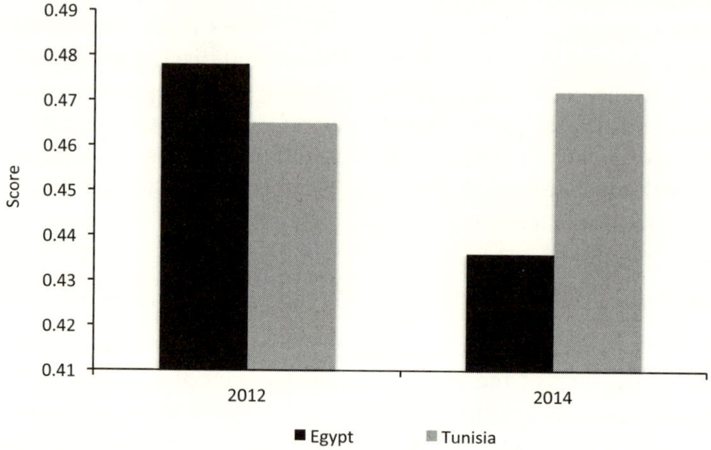

Source: Data from World Justice Project, www.worldjusticeproject.org. Reprinted from "The Challenges of Governability in the Arab World," © International Bank for Reconstruction and Development/World Bank.

ment of users of public services and of civil society organizations in the design, the implementation, and the monitoring of government programs (e.g., in Morocco, Egypt, Jordan). New civil society laws have been adopted in Iraq and the Kurdistan Regional Government; Tunisia, Egypt, and Jordan have initiated revisions of their respective legislations. In Morocco, civil society has gained new constitutional rights, and the framework for public engagement is being redefined. The country is now undergoing a participative consultation process with civil society to translate these new principles in a legal and policy framework, and the World Bank is supporting the development of an organic petitions law and right to submit legislative propositions.

Rule of Law

Ensuring a level playing field with equal treatment of all citizens and firms has been at the heart of governance reforms since the Arab Spring. Relevant reforms are typically summarized under efforts to improve the rule of law. World Bank engagement on the rule of law is focused on two main areas, including anticorruption and legal and judicial reform.

Even before the Arab Spring, the region saw an expansion in efforts to combat corruption. These efforts were mainly driven by the ratification of the UN Convention Against Corruption (UNCAC) Treaty. During the period from December 2003 through December 2005, virtually all countries of the region became signatories to the UNCAC Treaty, and ten countries subsequently ratified it. Within the context of the UNCAC Treaty, new institutions specifically dedicated to combating corruption were established in Morocco, Jordan, Iraq, and Yemen. A number of countries in the region initiated reform to prevent corruption, mainly by improving accountability mechanisms, such as internal and external audit systems (e.g., Tunisia, Morocco, Jordan), by making procurement practices more open and transparent (e.g., Morocco, Yemen, Jordan), and by streamlining and reengineering business processes within the public sector to reduce opportunities for corruption (e.g., Morocco, Egypt, Jordan). And yet corruption remains a serious problem throughout the region, as evidenced by available survey data from organizations such as Transparency International and Global Integrity.

The World Bank's anticorruption engagement in the region focused for a long time on assisting governments to strengthen the regulatory and institutional framework to fight corruption and thus to improve the business environment, as well as on public financial management reforms to reduce the embezzlement and fiduciary risks. Although these reforms had some positive impact on the reduction of petty corruption and leakages and the improvement of the business environment for large and international firms, they fell short of expectations. A flagship report outlining key governance challenges (including corruption and conflict-of-interest issues) was intended to stimulate dialogue with our clients, but the overall impact of these activities has been limited (World Bank, 2003).

Although most countries in the region have ratified the UNCAC Treaty, a considerable gap often can be found between the legal framework that exists for addressing corruption and its actual implementation. This implementation gap exists not only with regard to anticorruption legislation: throughout the MENA region the enforcement of laws and regulations are unequal and inconsistent. This inconsistency in enforcement has had a detrimental impact on public trust in government. To address this issue, the World Bank is working to support governments to strengthen the rule of law, for example through a better enforcement of judicial decisions (e.g., Morocco, Jordan, Iraq). In several countries in the region, the World Bank is also advising governments how to strengthen the application of existing anticorruption legislation (e.g., Tunisia, Jordan) and to develop conflict-of-interest regulations (e.g., Iraq, Kuwait).

Conclusion

The current transitions in the MENA region are volatile and uncertain. Fulfilling the aspirations and demands of the Arab Spring is a significant challenge for governments in transition (and even those that are not). Recognition of these challenges necessitates a fundamental rethinking of the way in which economic and social development is approached and of the importance governance plays in shaping development outcomes. Many of the core governance reform priorities we have illustrated in this chapter have been on the agenda of governments in the region for decades, clearly suggesting that the task is not an easy one, and often contentious efforts to reshape core government functions will be met with significant resistance. At the same time, people throughout the region have strong expectations of concrete and tangible results of governance reform in the short term.

The Arab Spring has strengthened the emphasis on key governance issues such as access to information and civil society engagement in decisionmaking. We see more promising opportunities in these areas and believe that considerable potential exists to involve civil society more systemically in the design, the implementation, and the monitoring of government activities. The demand for governance support remains high in the MENA region, in particular with regard to strengthening public sector efficiency and improving expenditure accountability. The World Bank supports local NGOs through the Affiliated Network for Social Accountability in MENA, which brings together civil society practitioners from the whole region.

So far, progress on governance reforms in the region has been uneven; some countries appear to respond more effectively to demands to strengthen economic governance and transparency than others. And it is still too early to assess whether or not the reforms that have been initiated contribute to the development of a new social contract between the governments and citizens in the region. In the immediate future, continued pressure will be placed on the governments in MENA (and on the development community) to launch deeper reforms in these important areas.

Notes

This chapter summarizes the views and perspectives of the authors; it does not represent the official view of the World Bank.
1. World Bank enterprise surveys 2003 and 2005–2008.
2. Global Integrity, www.globalintegrity.org.

14

Lessons, Challenges, and Puzzles for Building Rule of Law in the Arab World

Eva Bellin

Building rule of law in the Arab world requires both institutional reform and political savvy. Comparative analysis drawn from the experience of other regions suggests a menu of measures to build accountability, impartiality, and reliability into state institutions. It also helps identify political obstacles to implementing such reform as well as certain remedies to overcome these obstacles. Nevertheless, the political scene in the Arab world presents some distinctive challenges for building rule of law. In this chapter, I distill several of the general lessons suggested by comparative analysis as well as some of the contemporary realities found on the ground in Egypt, Tunisia, and other parts of the Arab world. I highlight a number of the distinctive challenges faced by the region, put forward some observations about the larger questions such as the relationship between rule of law and democratization, and suggest issues worthy of future research in the field.

Toolkit for Building Rule of Law: Comparative Lessons

Building Rule of Law in the Arab World has drawn on extraregional experience to assemble a "toolkit" for building four of the institutional pillars of the rule of law: the judiciary, the police, the army, and anticorruption/regulatory agencies.

The judiciary, as Lisa Hilbink explains, contributes to the delivery of rule of law through the provision of impartial and consistent arbitration of conflict as well as impartial and consistent application of the law. To achieve this objective, the judiciary must be independent from the control of government officials as well as other powerful actors in society. The latter is crucial to guarantee that the law will be respected "by rulers and ruled alike."

To achieve judicial independence a number of conditions must be met. First and foremost, the judicial corps must not be beholden to the state for its professional well-being. More specifically, issues such as judicial appointment, promotion, tenure, salary, and budget must be beyond the discretion of the executive branch. Ideally, such terms will be anchored in constitutional guarantees and implemented by judicial councils that are separate from the executive. In addition, Hilbink recommends that a variety of measures designed to enhance the "professionalism" of the judicial corps be adopted. These measures include enhanced professional training (through the creation of judicial academies) as well as the provision of respectable judicial salaries. Both will raise the intellectual and professional caliber of individuals entering the judiciary as well as make the judges "less vulnerable to 'improper influences.'" Although Hilbink argues that a variety of political factors beyond the scope of mere institutional reform are also crucial to ensuring judicial independence (see below), the aforementioned institutional modifications are indispensable conditions for the creation of an independent judiciary. These are lessons drawn from extensive study of a host of late-developing countries and most extensively illustrated by the Chilean case, and they are, no doubt, valid for the Arab world as well.

The police, Querine Hanlon and Diane Davis explain, contributes to the provision of the rule of law through the maintenance of public order—delivered consistently, fairly, predictably, and in accordance with the law. The primary mission of the police must be focused on guaranteeing popular safety, not regime protection. The police must embrace a mission of service to society and abandon fear as a tool of enforcement.

To achieve this objective, the police must embrace "oversight, transparency, and accountability." Reaching this goal calls for the creation of various auxiliary institutions (e.g., oversight commissions located in parliament as well as in society) in addition to the incentivization of transparent communication between the police and these oversight bodies. New training regimens and recruitment criteria must be embraced to inculcate a new "culture of service," enhance professionalism, and reinforce respect for human rights. Adequate salaries must be paid to reduce the temptation of corruption. Finally, legal reform is necessary in order to specify limits on the use of force, clarify the public's right to assembly and free speech, and delineate the regime's commitment to human rights.

The military, as Zoltan Barany explains, contributes to the delivery of rule of law through the provision of order and public defense in a manner that is depoliticized, accountable before the law, and subject to civilian control. To achieve the provision of order and public defense the government must establish clear subordination of the military to civilians through a number of institutional measures. As Barany suggests, a clear chain of command must be spelled out with the civilian president designated as commander in chief, and the top-ranking member of the military subordinated to a civilian defense minister. The budget as well as the conduct of the military must be subject to parliamentary (as well as executive) oversight. Members of the military must be depoliticized, meaning that they must relinquish any political role "other than exercising their civic right to vote." In addition, drawing on the experience of a broad array of countries from across the world, Barany recommends a number of auxiliary measures including contraction of the military's role on the domestic front (e.g., it should not be used for crowd control, containing domestic unrest, or developing the national economy), identification of new missions (international peace keeping, humanitarian assistance, and disaster relief abroad), and provision of adequate resources (decent salaries, up-to-date materiel), as well as markers of prestige and respect.

Finally, anticorruption/regulatory agencies, as Michael Johnston, Günter Heidenhof, and Lida Bteddini explain, contribute to building rule of law by ensuring that governments define and implement their policies and regulations in an impartial, rule-bound, and predictable fashion. In addition, these agencies are tasked with preventing government officials from misusing public funds for private ends. To achieve this objective, regulatory agencies such as audit agencies, ombudsmen, and anticorruption commissions must be empowered to monitor government behavior and sanction wrongdoing (O'Donnell, 1999: 28). These powers are the essence of exercising oversight. Measures such as recruiting highly professionalized auditors, providing the agencies with resources "independent and insulated from the executive," and placing opposition party members in leading positions in the regulatory agencies, are just some of the reforms advocated by leading analysts (O'Donnell, 1999: 48). However, Johnston, especially, is skeptical about the effectiveness of institutional reform in rooting out official malfeasance and delivering rule-bound governance. His insistence on a host of auxiliary measures makes salient the need to address the question of the timing and sequencing of different political reforms.

Politics

Given the extensive experience of so many countries with building the rule of law, identifying a menu of advisable institutional reforms turns out to be a relatively straightforward task. However, the process of implementing these reforms proves most challenging. Aside from the high cost of such reform (which, as Tewfiq Aclimandos points out, is a substantial deterrent for many late-developing countries), the process of implementation is intensely political. Building autonomous judiciaries, accountable and transparent police, militaries subject to civilian control, and regulatory agencies with substantive power to monitor and sanction government officials is a process that "threatens the power and prerogatives" of important individuals and constituencies who have significant incentives to act as spoilers of the reform process, as suggested by Querine Hanlon, but something noted by many of the authors. The challenge is not simply to delineate the technical measures essential to building rule of law but to muster the political will and wherewithal to carry them out. To successfully build the institutional foundations of rule of law, reformers are advised to keep three things in mind.

First and foremost, reformers must pay conscious attention to fostering "buy-in" by potential spoilers within the state institutions. Querine Hanlon, Zoltan Barany, and Tewfiq Aclimandos, among others, suggest a host of strategies. Aclimandos proposes bundling institutional reform together with improvements in salary and working conditions and then presenting the ensemble as a "package deal," to lure potential spoilers. Barany recommends "diversionary" tactics: for example, providing the military with new missions and professional opportunities (international peacekeeping or disaster relief abroad) to compensate for the elimination of some of its prior prerogatives. Still others focus on a "divide and rule" approach, cultivating insiders who may be more receptive to reform (due to generational differences, training differences, ethnic/sectarian differences) while maneuvering the ouster of others less receptive to change. No matter the diversity of these strategies, the underlying imperative is the same. To build rule of law, the sustained and concerted commitment of crucial stakeholders within these institutions must be cultivated. As Hilbink warns, technical reform of state institutions alone will not deliver rule of law.

Second, and related to the first, harnessing the interest of stakeholders outside the state institutions is also essential to fostering rule of law. This is why so many champions of rule of law stress the importance of civil society's development—the cultivation and empowerment of locally grounded collectivities in society that will monitor the state's behavior, expose wrongdoing, and hold the state accountable (Peruzzotti and Smulovitz, 2006; Schedler, 1999: 25). This logic also drives the analysis put forward by Michael Johnston, who argues that harnessing self-interested contention is necessary to build the rule of law. The study of countless cases of anti-corruption campaigns around the world has persuaded him that institutional fixes and formal legal changes alone are ineffective at delivering good governance. More important is what he calls "deep democratization," that is, the opening up of political space in a safe and secure way so that citizens may advocate for, and defend, their own interests. The only way to truly ensure the rule of law, Johnston argues, is to give those with a stake in ending official abuse the means to oppose it that cannot be ignored. Or, in other words, to check power with power through political processes of contention. Without such empowerment, he argues, institutional and legal reform packages not only may be ineffective at delivering rule of law but may actually make matters worse.[1] This conclusion raises the question of the logical linkage between democratization and building rule of law; the matter of proper sequencing will be explored below.

Third, the evidence from countless cases around the world suggests the importance of appropriate time horizons. Building rule of law is a long and arduous process that may take many years to bear fruit. Institutional reform that is overly accelerated and comprehensive is likely to antagonize and unify opponents and thereby sabotage the process. Barany's exploration of successful reform of the military in Chile and Indonesia, where subordination to civilian control came in stages (Chile) and where a full frontal attack on the military's economic privileges was postponed (Indonesia), provides compelling support for the wisdom of a gradational approach to reform. The lesson seems to be accept a long time frame, embrace gradualism, and recognize that persistence is the key to success. As Johnston points out, to this day, many advanced industrialized democracies still experience lapses in good governance and rule of law. We must recognize that realization of this objective is a slow and never-completed process.

Timing and Sequencing

The last two observations raise the issue of the optimal timing and sequencing of reforms to the political system. Should activists pursue democratization before they attempt to build rule of law? Or is establishing the institutional foundations of rule of law necessary to, and hence logically prior to, the effective pursuit of democratization? There are at least two good reasons to believe that building the institutional foundations of rule of law ought to come first. First, democracy without rule of law is robbed of much of its meaning. Second, order is to some degree prior to freedom.

With regard to the first, the distinctive quality that defines democracy is its vaunted capacity to make government accountable to the people, the essence of what Guillermo O'Donnell (1999: 29) calls "vertical accountability."[2] The classic institutional mechanism that delivers vertical accountability is free and fair elections, which empower citizens to reward or punish politicians by voting the latter in or out of office. The problem is that elections are insufficient to guarantee accountability that is closely attuned to popular preferences because elections are intermittent, the behavior of officials is often opaque, and voting is a blunt instrument that cannot target too many specific issues. To compensate for these gaps, O'Donnell calls for the development of institutions of "horizontal accountability," that is, agencies within the state empowered to investigate, expose, and sanction governmental wrongdoing (O'Donnell, 1999).[3] These institutions include many of those that constitute the foundational core of rule of law: independent judiciaries, effective regulatory agencies, and the like.

In the absence of mechanisms of horizontal accountability, governmental malfeasance can skyrocket and accountability to popular preference is robbed of its meaning, no matter how free and fair the elections held. In fact, the failure to develop adequate "horizontal" checks on state power explains the widespread popular disappointment with many of the democracies created in Africa, Asia, and Latin America during the third wave. Although these transitions ushered in free and fair elections, governmental corruption remained rampant, and executives were often heedless. This made a mockery of governmental accountability to popular preferences and emptied democracy of much of its valued content. The experience of these countries suggests a certain priority for the development of rule of law if democracy is to be meaningful and effectively deliver on its distinctive promise of accountability.

The second reason one might argue that building rule of law should precede the pursuit of democracy is that, psychologically, order is to some degree prior to freedom. Without some modicum of safety and stability, it is impossible to exercise (and enjoy) freedom and choice in any meaningful way. This truism is reflected in the classics of human psychology, notably, Aaron Maslow's (1943) hierarchy of needs, through which he suggests that the desire for self-actualization is pursued only after one's need for security and safety is guaranteed. Although this conclusion does not mean that all the institutions associated with rule of law must be established prior to the pursuit of democracy, it does suggest that at least some of its foundational elements (a military with a monopoly on the means of coercion, a police force that is effective and reliable) are logically necessary prior to democratization.

But before sequential precedence is given to building rule of law, two contrary observations should be made. First, establishing the institutional foundations of rule of law without democratic "backup" is likely to leave those institutions impotent. Second, building rule of law in the absence of democracy is politically improbable.

With regard to the first, experience around the world suggests that many of the conditions that are associated with democracy are indispensable to making the institutional foundations of rule of law effective. Freedom of speech, freedom of information, a robust media, and engaged and autonomous associations in civil society are all necessary to facilitate exposure and oversight of official behavior. Fragmentation of power (as in rule by alternating parties) has proven essential to encouraging officials in oversight agencies to challenge powerful state officials.[4] And as Johnston so eloquently argues, "deep democratization," that is, empowering citizens so that they may advocate for their own interests and harness their interests to "check power with power," is crucial to giving backbone to institutions of oversight and to preventing them from being abused or misdirected for official ends.

With regard to the second, building rule of law in the absence of democracy is politically improbable, the cardinal insight of Thomas Carothers (2007) in his pioneering reflection on the question of sequencing. As Carothers (2007: 14–15) shows, nondemocratic regimes are unlikely to set their sights on building rule of law because an inherent contradiction lies between the logic of the rule of law and the logic of autocratic rule. Impartial application of the law, an independent judiciary, and guaranteed rights for all citizens "restrict or remove the tools that autocrats typically employ to control political life and stay in power." Rule of law contradicts the typical autocrat's raison d'être as well as his modus vivendi (respectively, self-advantage and the elimination of political challengers). Autocrats, like Singapore's Lee Kuan Yew, who embrace the rule of law because they prioritize their country's overall betterment (especially its economic development) are few and far between. Those intent on building rule of law must realize that the hope of achieving this goal in a nondemocratic setting is seriously far fetched.[5]

What this question suggests is a chicken-egg conundrum: Which comes first, rule of law or democracy? But in fact, as Carothers (2007) argues, abandoning a sequential approach and instead recognizing that the two processes are mutually reinforcing is best. Neither one is complete without the other. Consequently, both rule of law and democratization should be pursued simultaneously. This may be why, as Günter Heidenhof and Lida Bteddini show, the World Bank has embraced aspects of both processes in its prescription for the pursuit of good governance.

Recognizing the mutuality of the two processes, however, does not mean that both will be achieved simultaneously or that we should expect linear progress on both. A better analogy might be taken from sailing. Countries intent on achieving both democracy and rule of law can expect to tack back and forth between the two in the hope that, over time, the ship of state will advance on both fronts. But there is no reason to be paralyzed by failure in any one of these areas. As Johnston implies, we can't wait until all the tectonic plates are perfectly aligned to get started. Regression and failures are part of the process. As Sheri Berman (2007) wisely observes with regard to the experience of Western Europe, achieving political reform "is difficult. But it cannot be completed if it never starts."[6]

Stocktaking in the Arab World

Building the institutional foundations of the rule of law is an ambition embraced by many in the Arab world. But progress thus far has been limited. The empirical evidence collected by our authors suggests that the obstacles faced in other regions of the world carry over to the Arab context as well. At the same time, certain challenges distinguish the Arab world and present special obstacles to building the rule of law. The following distills some of the major empirical findings of the book.

With regard to the judiciary, Mohamed Salah Ben Aissa confirms that in Tunisia one of the key obstacles to the development of judicial independence during the first years after the revolution was the failure to shield judges' appointment, compensation, advancement, and discipline from executive discretion. Historically, the Tunisian Constitution (ratified in 1959) had adopted a conception of the justice system that designated the judiciary as merely a "tool" in the service of the state. More specifically, the regime had created the High Judicial Council (responsible for supervising the professional lives of the judges), which was entirely dominated by the executive branch. In the first years following Ben Ali's fall, a reform-minded group in parliament attempted to, but did not succeed at, getting a majority to vote for the creation of an independent judicial council. This initial failing, Ben Aissa argues, was due to the opposition of the Islamist party, Ennahda, which controlled a significant share of the seats in the Constituent Assembly as well as the leadership of the Ministry of Justice. The failure to reconfigure the judicial council led to high-handed and irregular management of the judiciary in those first post–Ben Ali years. Ben Aissa argues that without substantial reform of judicial council, establishing judicial independence was impossible.

By 2014, however, some progress was evident. A new constitution, hammered out through an inspiring if exhausting political process of dialogue and compromise between the major parties in Tunisia, provided both rhetorical support for the principle of judicial independence as well as the legal foundation for shielding the supreme judicial council (to some degree) from domination by the executive branch. Political compromise and emphasis on national unity by the major political parties made this reform possible. But the process of reforming the judiciary is still incomplete, and different forces in civil society (judges, lawyers, etc.) continue to jockey over the content of these reforms. The future, Ben Aissa argues, lies in the political will of the public and most importantly the political will of the legal professionals themselves.

With regard to the judiciary in Egypt, Nathalie Bernard-Maugiron finds that, as in Tunisia, the outsize role played by the executive branch in the process of judicial appointment constituted a major obstacle to the development of a fully independent judiciary. Prior to the enactment of the constitution of 2014, the president of the republic enjoyed full discretion in the appointment of many leading judicial figures, including the chief of the Supreme Constitutional Court and the chief of the Court of Cassation. The executive branch also controlled the staffing of the key institutions that oversaw judicial nominations, promotions, salaries, and discipline such as the Supreme Judicial Council and the Judicial Inspection Department. In addition, the executive branch maintained a special court system to try cases it deemed "sensitive." It also selectively enforced the judiciary's rulings. All of these practices compromised the judiciary's autonomy and its capacity to deliver rule of law. (Nevertheless, Bernard-Maugiron documents the surprising fact that the Egyptian judiciary occasionally managed to carry out some bracing acts of independence that challenged the executive during the Hosni Mubarak era despite these constraints.)

The constitution enacted in 2014 promised to correct some of this executive overreach. Certain key judicial appointments (such as the general prosecutor and the chief justice of the Supreme Constitutional Court) have now been taken out of the hands of the executive. And the budget allotted to the judiciary is also more insulated from executive manipulation. But many of the institutional mechanisms for executive domination of the judiciary remain unchanged.

Beyond these institutional constraints on the judiciary's autonomy, Bernard-Maugiron identifies an equally troubling development that has compromised the judiciary's capacity to contribute to building rule of law in Egypt, that is, the extraordinary politicization of the judiciary since the fall of Mubarak. Bernard-Maugiron recounts the battle that raged between the judiciary and the executive branch prior to and during the rule of the Muslim Brotherhood president Mohamad Morsi (i.e., 2012–2013) and then, after July 2013, the judiciary's collusion with the regime of Abdel Fattah el-Sisi. She recounts the political overreach that characterized many of the judiciary's rulings during 2011–2013, rulings that included the dissolution of Parliament as well as political exclusion laws. This political assertiveness was met with retaliatory measures taken by the Morsi regime, aimed at "unpacking" the Supreme Constitutional Court, purging the judiciary, and declaring itself (temporarily) beyond judicial review. Following the removal of Morsi in 2013, the courts began to deliver selective justice, meting out lenient treatment to culpable members of the old regime (accused of misusing public funds and killing political protestors) at the same time that they delivered extremely harsh punishment to opponents of the Sisi regime (whether secular or Muslim Brotherhood affiliated). Such behavior has tainted the reputation of the judiciary and compromised its reputation as a politically dispassionate locus of power.

Most interestingly, Bernard-Maugiron does not link these two problems causally. That is, she does not attribute the political partiality evidenced by the judiciary directly to its lack of institutional autonomy from the executive branch. Bernard-Maugiron argues that there is no evidence that the judiciary's problematic rulings, such as failure to deliver impartial treatment of regime opponents under Sisi or the judiciary's general hostility to Morsi, have been due to direct interference from the executive (or the army). Rather she traces this behavior to the judiciary's cultural mind-set as well as to the demographic profile that characterizes the "guild" of Egyptian judges. Bernard-Maugiron argues that most judges in Egypt hail from the middle or upper middle class. Consequently, she argues, most judges have a "patriarchal and conservative" mind-set, they prioritize the stability of the country above all else, and they are suspicious of the Muslim Brotherhood, which they perceive as an "alien force" that has brought the state (including state institutions like the judiciary) under attack. Building more institutional autonomy for the judiciary, then, is not likely to deliver the politically dispassionate institution necessary to guarantee rule of law, at least not in the short-term.[7] The Egyptian case shows just how difficult it is to create the conditions for an impartial judiciary in a time of enormous political flux and polarization.

With regard to the police, Querine Hanlon explores the Tunisian case and the difficulty of transforming an institution that had historically been committed, first and foremost, to regime protection into an institution devoted primarily to public service and the provision of public safety in accordance with the law. Hanlon shows that in Tunisia, the Ministry of Interior's opaque and complex organizational structure undermines police accountability, poor training and low pay discourage professionalism, and ambiguity in the laws governing the use of force and citizens' rights undermines the protection of basic human rights. She recommends more transparency, better training, better pay, clearer laws, and parliamentary and citizen oversight to correct these problems.

But even if the institutional recipe for reform is straightforward, the process to implement it is politically fraught, partly as a result of internal resistance mobilized from within the police force itself. (Hanlon describes the physical resistance and the strike organized by security sector insiders in 2012 to stave off the punishment of one of their "own.") Part of the delay in police reform stems from a lack of political will on the part of the Tunisian politicians to prioritize police reform amidst a host of other competing political goals. The larger security context, the challenges Tunisia faces from extremists both within the country and from neighboring Libya, and the porous borders that facilitate access to weapons, explosives, and drugs, all make Tunisian leaders (and citizens) wary about dismantling and restructuring the police apparatus, even in the name of reform. Consequently, Tunisia has largely avoided police reform in the first post–Ben Ali years.

Tewfiq Aclimandos traces a similar dynamic with regard to reforming the police in Egypt. As in Tunisia, the police in Egypt, Aclimandos argues, need to embrace a major shift in culture: espouse a mission of service in the name of the rule of law and abandon a long history of corruption, nepotism, and human rights abuse. As in Tunisia, the heinous behavior of the police in Egypt was motivated by the definition of their mission as primarily one of regime protection, and its efforts were focused, first and foremost, on eradicating the Islamic threat. And as in Tunisia, the primary question in the post-Mubarak era has been whether sufficient political will and wherewithal can be cultivated to carry out police reform. Police insiders, of course, resist reform. The process is expensive, and as Aclimandos points out, Egypt's financial situation is precarious. But the most important obstacle to police reform is the fraught security situation. The "disastrous security situation," Aclimandos argues, makes even many "liberals and secular parties . . . reticent about taking on the project of police reform." Again, the political will necessary to carry out police reform seems destined to make this a reform postponed.

Subordinating the military to civilian control and eliminating its political autonomy is the defining marker of a military performing in service to the rule of law. But as Robert Springborg shows in the Egyptian case, this ambition has proven elusive in the years following the ouster of Mubarak. During the first three years, the military and the Muslim Brotherhood engaged in constant jabs and counterjabs to determine who would prevail. An early alliance of convenience soon gave way to confrontation. Two months after his election to the presidency, Muslim Brotherhood leader Mohamed Morsi took advantage of a moment of military failure in the Sinai to exploit generational discontent in the military, retire some of its leadership, and promote more amicable insiders. But despite the removal of some senior generals, the military quickly reasserted its autonomy, parrying precisely the sorts of reforms that Barany argues are necessary to subordinate it to civilian control. Specifically, the military forced through constitutional provisions that assigned control of the Ministry of Defense to an active duty officer (not a civilian) and denied Parliament any oversight regarding its operations or budget. In addition, the military retained its hold on an enormous array of economic ventures providing it with substantial financial independence. These provisions created the institutional foundation for the army to reassert itself as supreme ruler less than three years after Mubarak had been deposed.

Springborg describes the elaborate cat-and-mouse game played by the Muslim Brotherhood and the military in the years following Mubarak's ouster. Cultural, strategic, and institutional interests put the two at odds from the beginning. But Springborg argues that the military in Egypt would have resisted democratic oversight no matter the ideological color of the elected government (Islamist or not) because such oversight would have been likely to reveal the military's bloat and inefficiency as well as erode its economic privilege. The popular uprising of early 2011 presented a unique moment in Egyptian history when the military might have been tamed politically. But, Springborg argues, that moment quickly passed. The economic disarray, the crime spike, and the general insecurity that assailed Egypt in 2012–2013 made the populace receptive to a return to the "strong hand" of the military. The unprecedented public demonstrations calling for Morsi's removal in the summer of 2013 provided the military with the political cover to unseat him and take charge. The consequence: Egypt has returned to a military-led regime unconstrained in its ability to rule in fully repressive fashion.

The situation of the military in Tunisia could not be more different. In the post–Ben Ali era the Tunisian military proved altogether prepared to submit to democratic control. Risa Brooks attributes this acquiescence to the prior strategy of "marginalization and exclusion" adopted by both Zine El Abidine Ben Ali and Habib Bourguiba vis-à-vis the military. The adoption of this strategy was facilitated by historical contingencies (the negligible role played by the military in the independence struggle) as well as geographic accident (Tunisia's distance from any serious enemy or external security challenges). Both factors spelled political weakness for the military from independence on. The military's weakness was then compounded by the ruling autocrats' strategy to consign it to the periphery of the regime and starve it of resources. This strategy, however, had unanticipated consequences for the authoritarian regime's survival. The strategy worked to depoliticize the military. It cultivated a strong corporate ethos within the institution as well as a self-understanding that saw intervention in domestic politics as beyond its mandate. Instead, a sense of mission evolved that focused on defense of the country from external enemies and radical threats rather than protection of the state from its own citizens. The autocrats' strategy also prevented the military from developing any material stake in sustaining the authoritarian status quo or any vestige of the old regime. In short, the autocratic regime's treatment of the military in Tunisia prepared the military to embrace democratic transition and civilian oversight in a way quite atypical for the region.

For a military to contribute to building rule of law, it need not only meet the challenge of subordinating the coercive apparatus to civilian control. To contribute to rule of law, the institution must also live up to the Weberian ideal; that is, it must exercise a legitimate monopoly on the means of coercion. Establishing a legitimate monopoly on the means of coercion is especially challenging in countries that are deeply divided ethnically (e.g., Iraq, Syria, and Yemen). These countries face the dilemma of how to build a military that is perceived as committed to the defense of the entire society rather than partial to specific communities within it. The challenge is to cultivate a sense of ownership for the military among all the communities found in society. Oren Barak explores this challenge, drawing on extensive experience with the Lebanese case to address this issue. He argues that in divided societies an inevitable trade-off must be made between the military's legitimacy and its effectiveness. In order to cultivate legitimacy, the military must prioritize inclusiveness in its recruitment as well as modesty in its missions. The latter means that at times it may have to duck some of its role of providing order through the use of force. The best evidence of such modesty, Barak argues, may be found in the Lebanese military's unwillingness to arbitrate the conflict between the March 14 and March 8 alliances in 2007. The military made this decision in order to sustain its image as a nonpartisan institution and to avoid dividing the military along ethnic lines. Barak argues that the tension between the military's dual goals of effectiveness and legitimacy can be reduced by reframing the role of the military. Observers must recognize that the military contributes to national security not only by being the provider of order through force of arms but also by its inherent multicommunal inclusivity. Through its all-inclusive constitution, the military by its very existence mitigates intercommunal tension and contributes to civil peace.

Finally, Günter Heidenhof and Lida Bteddini confirm the complexity of fighting corruption and building good governance in the region. Collecting evidence on the region as a whole, they show that the Arab world lags behind most other regions on a variety of governance measures, and they attest to the significance of the political obstacles to correcting this lag. The problem lies less in deficiencies in the legal framework necessary to address corruption and poor governance and more in the political will to implement these rules. The World Bank advocates "transparency, accountability, and participation" as the foundation of successful governance reform, but in the absence of civil liberties, freedom of information, and political freedom, achieving any of these is difficult. The legacy of pervasive authoritarianism in the region that persists even in the wake of the uprisings of 2011 throws a wrench in the "deep democratization" that analysts like Michael Johnston argue are essential to anchoring good governance. They make this aspect of rule of law the most distant prospect of all four facets explored here.

Exceptional Challenges in the Arab World to Building the Rule of Law

Comparative analysis suggests a fair degree of parallelism in the factors that subvert the establishment of rule of law around the world as well as parallelism in the likely remedies. Nevertheless, a number of conditions make building rule of law exceptionally difficult in the Arab world and merit special attention and brainstorming.

First, the Arab world is renown for its exceptionally long and deep experience with authoritarian rule. This legacy has created a number of especially formidable obstacles to building rule of law. For example, many of the authoritarian regimes in the region embraced elaborate "coup-proofing" strategies to survive (Quinlivan, 1999). These strategies led to significant replication, fragmentation, and opaqueness of the coercive apparatus. Consequently, building a rule-governed, professionalized, transparent, and service-oriented police and military is especially challenging. It requires a thorough overhaul of the coercive apparatus, which is extremely costly politically.

An additional legacy of long-standing authoritarianism is the relative underdevelopment of civil society, the inexperience of the media in investigative work, and the lack of experience with (or cultural expectation of) freedom of information. These are all crucial assets for bolstering the rule of law, and without them, the struggle to establish it is more challenging. In short, countries that are faced with the dual challenge of transitioning to democracy and building rule of law simultaneously face much more serious challenges than is the case of even imperfect democratic countries whose ambition is more single minded, with a focus on building better governance alone.

Second, many countries in the Arab world are deeply divided on the basis of identity, whether this cleavage is drawn along ethnic lines (as in Syria, Yemen, Iraq, Lebanon, Bahrain, and Libya) or along ideological lines (notably, Islamist vs. secular as witnessed in Egypt and Tunisia). In many cases this division has been drenched in blood and violence—sometimes even full-fledged civil war—and this experience has scarred society and undermined trust across the divides. In this deeply polarized context, it is especially difficult to build institutions that can be perceived as "impartial" (which is central to building rule of law). Every appointment, every institutional innovation is closely scrutinized for "capture" by one group or another. Close attention to balanced inclusion and representation of all groups may alleviate some of this distrust, though as Barak shows in the case of Lebanon, such inclusion may compromise the effectiveness of some of these institutions.

Third, many Arab countries faced with the challenge of building rule of law today are situated in extremely challenging security conditions. The proximity of failed states (in Libya and Syria) and the reality of porous borders shared with those states lead to the dangerous proliferation of weapons and extensive drug running and crime. This situation makes building rule of law more challenging, not least because in this context, society and state tend to prioritize the establishment of order, even if that order comes at the expense of law. This trade-off has certainly been an obstacle to reform of the coercive apparatus in Egypt and Tunisia as Aclimandos and Hanlon have shown. In addition, extrastate forces, be it international franchises, like al-Qaeda, or conventional states with regional ambitions, such as Iran, Qatar, and Saudi Arabia, often intervene in domestic power struggles and tip the balance in ways that do not serve the domestic adjudication of rule of law.

General Lessons, Further Research, and Conclusion

Comparing the experiences of several Arab countries with those of other regions of the world suggests a number of important lessons for building rule of law in the Arab world and beyond.

First, we should not underestimate the role of unintended consequences in building the rule of law. The importance of this factor was first made clear in the venerable experience of medieval and early modern Europe, where competing ambitions between rulers and rivals inadvertently led to the creation of the institutional foundation of the rule of law. The same is true today as evidenced by the case of Tunisia. The strategy of military "marginalization and exclusion," embraced by Bourguiba and Ben Ali to safeguard the survival of their autocratic regimes, inadvertently gave rise to a military with just the sort of corporate ethos and sense of mission that facilitated the jettisoning of authoritarianism and the construction of rule of law. Of course, recognizing the impact of "unintended consequences" does not mean negating the importance of conscious intent and purposeful political mobilization to building rule of law (see lessons three and four below). But it does call attention to the fact that political trajectories are complex, and this complexity can lead to unpredictable outcomes, both desirable and not.

Second, institutions create a social legacy that may long outlive the institutions themselves. Hence, we should not expect institutional reform to deliver immediate results in terms of creating rule of law. This is one of the lessons of the Egyptian case. Simply building more autonomy into the institution of the judiciary will not immediately deliver a politically dispassionate legal institution. The demographic constitution of the judicial "guild" confers a distinctive political bias to the court system. In time, reduced interference by the executive in the screening of judicial hopefuls may change the social profile of the judiciary in Egypt and reduce this bias. But this change will not come overnight.

Third, as has been emphasized by "second-generation" analysts of the rule of law, cultivating local stakeholders is crucial to the long-term entrenchment of rule of law. This view is confirmed by incidents of both success and failure at building rule of law observed in the cases presented in this book. In Tunisia the partially successful reform of the High Judicial Council was the product of persistent lobbying carried out by engaged associations of lawyers and judges. In Egypt the failure to reform the judiciary substantially was, in part, the consequence of the decision of the formerly activist Judges' Club to refrain from activism at this time. As second-generation analysts have elaborated, without the engagement of local forces with long-term horizons and on-the-ground knowledge, building rule of law is impossible since perseverance and vigilance are the essential bedrock of this process.

Why do we see this variable engagement by local forces in the drive for rule of law? This question leads to the fourth lesson, the importance of political will to building rule of law. The failure of both Tunisia and Egypt to make any progress in carrying out police reform, for example, is first and foremost attributable to a lack of political will and the refusal to prioritize such reform by both political leaders and the citizenry.[8] Countries that have proven successful at building rule of law in the last thirty years have generally been distinguished by the presence of leaders or forces in civil society expressly committed to carrying out such reform (Mungiu-Pippidi, 2006). Building rule of law is a battle, and without the will to wage it, this ambition is unlikely to be realized.

The lack of political will evidenced in our cases links into a fifth lesson: when it comes to building rule of law, Maslow's hierarchy of needs prevails. The reluctance to prioritize reform by many in the region derives from the preoccupation with (and prioritization of) concern for safety and security. The precarious security situation in the Arab world, itself the consequence of the proliferation of failed states, the easy access to weapons, and the rise of extremism, has persuaded many citizens that a focus on accountable governance is a luxury that must be postponed. Building rule of law is a challenging process no matter the context. In an apt metaphor, Colgate political scientist Bruce Rutherford compares it to "reconstructing a ship while it is at sea."[9] In the Arab world today the challenge has been compounded by the fact that the sea is exceptionally stormy. The pervasive sense of crisis has sapped the will to reform.

The sixth lesson, also related to the problem of will, concerns the problem of polarization. As mentioned above, it is especially difficult to build "impartial" institutions in a society that is deeply divided along ethnic, sectarian, or ideological lines. Every institutional innovation is closely scrutinized for "capture" by one group or another. The will to introduce "impartiality" into state institutions is compromised by profound skepticism about the possibility (or even the desirability) of such a goal. Such polarization characterizes much of the Arab world today, inhibiting the drive for rule of law. The exception is Tunisia, where a constellation of broad-minded leadership, timing, and luck led to a collaborative stance across the country's ideological divide (Bellin, 2013), thus permitting the rule of law to progress. But without explicit strategies to build bridges across these divides (e.g., through inclusiveness or explicit quotas that guarantee representation of all groups), progress elsewhere is stymied.

Many of the challenges facing the Arab world are not unique to the region. Research focused on comparable cases from beyond the region could shed needed light on how to address these issues. How has ethnic and ideological division been "de-charged" elsewhere to overcome the distrust necessary to build effective judiciaries and police? How have other countries with deeply authoritarian legacies managed to dismantle their coercive apparatuses? Could other clever ways be found to incentivize "buy-in" by potential spoilers? These are just a few of the outstanding questions.

But perhaps the most pressing issue comes back to the question of sequencing and whether building rule of law is possible in the absence of democracy.

This book project was conceived during a moment of great optimism in the Arab world, when authoritarian regimes were collapsing, masses of ordinary people were mobilizing in the streets, seizing self-empowerment, and democratic transition seemed a possibility for the first time in a number of countries. Several years on, the mood in the Arab world is much more somber. The chances for near-term democratization are dim in most Arab countries, with the exception of Tunisia. And so the question arises as to whether this grim political reality should spell despair about the possibility of building rule of law in the Arab world, at least for the near term. Does the absence of democracy make building rule of law impossible?

Our prior discussion of democratization and rule law rejected the notion of any unequivocal sequencing of these two processes. It found instead that rule of law and democratization were interdependent and mutually reinforcing, that linear progress in any one without the other was unlikely, and that the metaphor of "tacking" (taken from sailing) probably best captured the likely advance of the "ship of state" on both fronts. Nevertheless, Carothers (2007) makes a compelling argument for why progress on building rule of law was improbable in the context of thoroughgoing authoritarianism. The logic of rule of law contradicts both the raison d'être and the modus vivendi of the typical autocrat.

At the same time there is reason for hope. This should be drawn from Johnston's keen observation that to achieve meaningful rule of law one must mobilize power against power and interest against interest. As Johnston argues, institutional reform is merely an empty shell unless the structure of power in society is reconfigured in ways that make the state assailable. And in fact, structural and technological changes are afoot in the Arab world and are changing the balance of power. The spread of literacy, the growth of the middle class, the organizational and informational capabilities made possible by the Internet, all point to an inexorable shift in the distribution of power that favors society over the state in ways not anticipated a generation ago.

This conclusion is not meant to be a naïve or mechanistic regurgitation of modernization theory. Building the rule of law is in no way structurally inevitable, no matter the level of a country's development. Building rule of law requires focused political will and tireless political mobilization. Moreover other structural factors—identity cleavages and conflict and international rivalries and interventions—may work to undermine the process. Nevertheless, new sources of power are evolving in the Arab world that will progressively challenge the state's invulnerability. The Wael Ghonims of the world are not going to disappear; they are only going to grow in number. And with their growing power, they will have the possibility of setting sail, one issue at a time. Fully realized democratization need not be a prerequisite.

The goal of this book is to provide an empirical and theoretical foundation to launch creative thinking about cultivating rule of law in the Middle East and North Africa. Analysts and activists alike are committed to ending arbitrary rule in the region. Joining this effort are the scholars who have authored this book.

Notes

1. For example, he argues that the creation of anticorruption commissions, without the proper social foundation, may become the regime's tools of factional conflict, means for political reprisal, and smoke screens for self-enrichment.

2. He uses the term *vertical* because of the hierarchical relationship implied, with government (above) held accountable to the people (below).

3. O'Donnell (1999) uses the term *horizontal* because the institutions involved are on an equal footing as fraternal components of the state.

4. Lisa Hilbink (2012) explores the importance of alternating party rule for cultivating political autonomy in the judciary. She argues that when one party dominates the political system, the party's ability to punish judges unilaterally discourages judicial independence. See also Helmke and Rosenbluth (2009).

5. Carothers (2007) goes further and shows how democracy, although not without its own problems of governance, is philosophically in line with rule of law given the fact that both are committed to subordinating government officials to the law and both respect political and civil rights.

6. The question of timing also raises the question of the proper sequencing of reform of the different institutional anchors of rule of law. Should police reform logically precede judicial reform? Or military reform precede all others? Again, there is a degree of mutuality between these different facets of rule of law. There can't be an effective judiciary without a reliable police force to enforce its rulings. There can't be an effective anticorruption agency without an effective judiciary to enforce its sanctions. And of course there can't be any rule of law without an effective army monopolizing coercion and maintaining order (although perhaps it need

not be subordinated to civilian control to achieve this end). Although some rough logical priority might be drawn (army first, police and judiciary next, regulatory agencies last), in fact the four are inextricably linked and mutually reinforcing. How this sequencing actually plays out comparatively would be worthy of future research.

7. Of course Bernard-Maugiron recognizes that the demographic profile of the Egyptian judiciary has been shaped by explicit interference from the arms of the executive branch. State security services long screened all applicants for positions in the judiciary, and they eliminated candidates of lower-class origin as well as those with Islamist associations. Such executive interference, however, is quite different from "telephone justice" (where the executive phones in rulings to pliant judges). Standard reforms to improve the judiciary's autonomy from the executive (such as permitting the judges' "guild" to elect leading posts in the court system) would not eliminate the political bias that currently characterizes the judiciary in Egypt.

8. See Sayigh (2015) for a very rich account of the failure of police reform in Egypt and Tunisia that echoes the observations put forward by Hanlon and Aclimandos.

9. Personal communication with the author, January 25, 2015.

Bibliography

Abdel-Baky, Mohamed. 2012a. "Change of Allegiance?" *Al-Ahram Weekly*, September 27–October 3.
———. 2012b. "Choice of a Clean Slate," *Al-Ahram Weekly*, November 11–17.
———. 2013. "Just Another Report?" *Al-Ahram Weekly*, January 9–16.
Abdel-Malek, Anouar. 1968. *Egypt: Military Society*. New York: Random House.
Abu Seada, Hafez. 2008. "Exceptional Courts and the Natural Judge," in Nathalie Bernard-Maugiron, ed., *Judges and Political Reform in Egypt*. Cairo: American University in Cairo Press.
Abul-Magd, Zeinab. 2011. "The Army and the Economy in Egypt." *Jadaliyya*, December 23.
———. 2012a. "The Generals' Secret: Egypt's Ambivalent Market," *Carnegie Endowment for International Peace: Sada*, February 9.
———. 2012b. "The Egyptian Republic of Retired Generals," *Foreign Policy*, May 8.
———. 2012c. "The Army and the Economy in Egypt," *Jadaliyya*, December 23.
Acemoglu, Daron, and S. Johnson. 2005. "Unbundling Institutions," *Journal of Political Economy* vol. 113, no. 5 (October): 949–995.
Acemoglu, Daron, S. Johnson, and J. A. Robinson. 2001. "The Colonial Origins of Comparative Development: An Empirical Investigation," *American Economic Review* vol. 91, no. 5 (December): 1369–1401.
Acemoglu, Daron, and James A. Robinson. 2012. *Why Nations Fail*. New York: Random House/Crown Business.
Aclimandos, Tewfiq. 2012. "Healing Without Amputating: Security Reform in Egypt," *Arab Reform Initiative*, September 12.
Ackerman, Susan Rose. 1999. *Corruption and Government: Causes, Consequences, and Reform*. New York: Cambridge University Press.
Africa News. 2011. "Unrest Spreads As Protests Hit Capital," January 12.
Agence France Presse. 2012a. "Tunisia Security Officers Protest Against Salafist Attacks," November 1.
———. 2012b. "Mubarak Sons on Trial for Corruption." Dawn.com, July 9.

Aguayo, Sergio. 1998. *1968: Los Archivos de Violencia*. Mexico City: Reforma-Grijalbo.
Agüero, Felipe. 1995. *Soldiers, Civilians, and Democracy: Post-Franco Spain in Comparative Perspective*. Baltimore: Johns Hopkins University Press.
Ahmed, Masood. 2012. "Youth Unemployment in the MENA Region: Determinants and Challenges." Washington, DC: International Monetary Fund.
Ahram Online. 2012a. "Sacking of Egypt's Top Administrative Watchdog Comes as 'Surprise,'" October 7.
———. 2012b. "Constitutional Court Head Slams Morsi's Statement to Foreign Media," December 17.
———. 2013a. "Families of Lost Egyptian Fishermen Storm Alexandria Naval Base," January 8.
———. 2013b. Egypt's Islamist MPs Prepare for Battle Against Judiciary," April 21.
Al-Ahram Weekly. 2013a. "Newsreel," January 17. http://weekly.ahram.org.eg/News/1054/17/Newsreel.aspx.
———. 2013b. "Release of 8 April Officers," January 17–23.
Ajmi, Sana. 2011. "Tunisia's Populist Surprise Headed for Marginalization in Constituent Assembly," *Tunisia Live*, November 10.
Akremi, Mohammad Lazhar. 2013. Nidaa Tounes Spokesman, speech at the US Institute of Peace, Washington, DC, June 12.
Alcocer V., Jose. 1997. "Inseguridad Pública," *Proceso*, September 28.
Alexa, Peter C., and Michael Metzsch. 2003. "The Democratic Warrior: The Future for the Bosnian Military," *Baltic Defense Review* vol. 9, no.1 (January): 143–162.
Alexander, Christopher. 1997. "Authoritarianism and Civil Society in Tunisia: Back from the Democratic Brink," *Middle East Research and Information Project*, no. 205 (October–December): 34–38.
———. 2011. "Anatomy of an Autocracy," *Foreign Policy*, January 14.
al-Ali, Zaid. 2013. "Egypt's Missed Constitutional Moment," *Foreign Policy*, December 17.
Aliriza, Fadil. 2012. "The Godfathers of Tunis," *Foreign Policy*, May 25.
Al Jazeera. 2011a. "Tunisia Gripped by Uncertainty," January 16.
———. 2011b. "Tunisia Disbands State Security," March 8.
———. 2015. "Tunisian Blogger Sentenced for Defaming Army," January 20.
Al Nadeem. 2007. "Torture in Egypt—Facts and Tesimonies." alnadeem.org/en/note/399.
Alvarado, Arturo, and Sigrid Arzt, eds. 2001. *El desafío democrático en Mèxico: Seguridad y estado de derecho*. Mexico City: El Colegio de Mèxico.
Amara, Tarek. 2011a. "Tunisian Police Protest Ban on Joining Unions," *Reuters*, September 6.
———. 2011b. "Tunisia's Constitutional Assembly, Elected After a Revolution That Inspired the 'Arab Spring' Uprisings, Held Its Opening Session on Tuesday, Described by Officials as an Historic Step Toward Democracy," *Reuters*, November 22.
Amnesty International. 2009. "Tunisia: Behind Tunisia's Economic Miracle: Inequality and Criminalization of Protest," June 18.
———. 2011. "Tunisia in Revolt: State Violence During Anti-Government Protests," February 2.
———. 2012. "Tunisia: End Excessive Force Against Protesters in Siliana, Open Immediate Investigation," November 30.
———. 2014. "Egypt: Roadmap to Repression: No End in Sight to Human Rights Violations," January 23.

———. 2015. "Tunisian Blogger Should Be Released," January 6.
el-Amrani, Issandr. 2011. "Tunisia's Diary: Ammar's Move? (2)," *The Arabist*, January 24.
Anderson, David, and David Killingray, eds. 1991. *Policing the Empire: Government Authority and Control, 1830–1940*. New York: St. Martin's Press.
Andreas, Peter. 1998. "The Political Economy of Narco-Corruption in Mexico," *Current History* vol. 97 (April): 160–165.
Anechiarico, Frank, and James B. Jacobs. 1996. *The Pursuit of Absolute Integrity*. Chicago: University of Chicago Press.
Annabi, Samir. 2012. Rule of Law in the Arab World-in-Transition Workshop presentation, Naval War College, Newport, RI, November 15.
Al Arabiya. 2012. "Al Arabiya Inquiry Reveals How Tunisia's Ben Ali Escaped to Saudi Arabia," *Al Arabiya News*, January 13.
Arieff, Alexis. 2011. "Political Transition in Tunisia," *Congressional Research Service*, December 16.
Arnold, Peri E. 2003. "Democracy and Corruption in the 19th Century United States: Parties, 'Spoils' and Political Participation," in Seppo Tiihonen, ed., *The History of Corruption in Central Government/L'histoire de la corruption au niveau du pouvoir central*. Amsterdam: IOS Press.
Asharq Al-Awsat. 2013. "Tunisian Army Chief of Staff Announces Resignation," June 26.
———. 2014. "Tunisian Defense Minister: War on Terror Requires Patience," August 20.
Ashour, Omar. 2012. "Egypt's Draft Constitution: How Democratic Is It?" *Al Monitor*, December 21.
Associated Press. 2012a. "Close Mubarak Aide Jailed for Corruption," *Guardian*, May 27.
———. 2012b. "Egypt Mubarak-Era Minister Jailed for Corruption," *Seattle Times*, July 13.
Atallah, Lina. 2014. "A State in Shackles," *Mada Masr*, January 1.
Al Atiqi, Sulaiman. 2013. "Laboring Against Themselves," *Carnegie Endowment for International Peace: Sada*, February 13.
Auf, Yussef. 2014. "Prospects for Judicial Reform in Egypt," *Atlantic Council*, October 21.
Aviles, Luis. 2008. Interviewed by Lisa Hilbink. Santiago, Chile, October 6.
Aydinli, Ersel. 2009. "A Paradigmatic Shift for the Turkish Generals and an End to the Coup Era in Turkey," *Middle East Journal* vol. 63, no. 4 (Autumn): 581–596.
Aziz, Sahar. 2014. "Egypt's Judiciary, Coopted," *Carnegie Endowment for International Peace: Sada*, August 20.
Badawi, 'Abd al Hadi. 2012. "Asbâb inhiyâr al jihâz al amnî wa marâhilihi wa wasâ'il al mu'âlaja," in 'Abd al Khaliq Faruq, ed., *Kayfa nu'îd binâ' jihâz al amn*. Cairo: Markaz al Nil li-l dirâsât al iqtisâdiyya wa-l strâtijiyya.
Bailey, John, and Roy Godson, eds. 2000. *Organized Crime and Democratic Governability: Mexico and the U.S.-Mexican Borderlands*. Pittsburgh: University of Pittsburgh Press.
Barak, Oren. 2002. "Intra-Communal and Inter-Communal Dimensions of Conflict and Peace in Lebanon," *International Journal of Middle East Studies* vol. 34, no. 4 (November): 619–644.
———. 2003. "Lebanon: Failure, Collapse, and Resuscitation," in Robert I. Rotberg ed., *State Failure and State Weakness in a Time of Terror*. Washington, DC: Brookings Institution Press.

———. 2006. "Towards a Representative Military? The Transformation of the Lebanese Officer Corps Since 1945," *Middle East Journal* vol. 60, no. 1 (Winter): 75–93.
———. 2007. "Dilemmas of Security in Iraq," *Security Dialogue* vol. 38, no. 4 (December): 455–475.
———. 2009. *The Lebanese Army: A National Institution in a Divided Society*. Albany, NY: SUNY Press.
Barak, Oren, and Assaf David. 2010. "The Arab Security Sector: A New Research Agenda for a Neglected Topic," *Armed Forces and Society* vol. 36, no. 5 (October): 804–824.
Barany, Zoltan. 1997. "Democratic Consolidation and the Military: The East European Experience," *Comparative Politics* vol. 30, no. 1 (October): 21–44.
———. 2003. *The Future of NATO Expansion*. New York: Cambridge University Press.
———. 2011. "Comparing the Arab Revolts: The Role of the Military," *Journal of Democracy* vol. 22, no. 4 (October): 27–39.
———. 2012. *The Soldier and the Changing State: Building Democratic Armies in Africa, Asia, Europe, and the Americas*. Princeton, NJ: Princeton University Press.
———. 2015. "Exits from Military Rule: Lessons for Burma," *Journal of Democracy* vol. 26, no. 2 (April): 86–100.
Barros, Robert. 2002. *Constitutionalism and Dictatorship*. New York: Cambridge University Press.
Barry, Brian. 1995. *Justice as Impartiality*. Oxford: Oxford University Press.
al-Batran, Hamdi. 2013. *Al amn min al manassa ila al maydân*. Cairo: Dar al Ayn.
Bayley, David. 1975. "The Police and Political Development in Europe," in C. Tilly, ed., *The Formation of National States in Europe*, 328–379. Princeton, NJ: Princeton University Press.
———. 1976. *Forces of Order: Police Behavior in Japan and the United States*. Los Angeles: University of California Press.
———. 1985. *Patterns of Policing: A Comparative International Analysis*. New Brunswick, NJ: Rutgers University Press.
BBC Monitoring (Middle East). 2008. "Al Jazeera TV Maghreb Harvest Programme 2130 GMT 6 June 08," June 7.
———. 2011. "Tunisian Interim President Asks Al-Jazeera to 'Contribute to Encouraging Calm,'" January 16.
BBC News. 2002. "Tunisian Army Chief Dies in Air Crash," May 1.
———. 2012. "Egypt Court Halts All Work Amid Islamist 'Pressure,'" December 2.
Beatty, David. 1994. "Human Rights and the Rules of Law," in David Beatty, ed., *Human Rights and Judicial Review: A Comparative Perspective*, 1–56. Boston: Martinus Nijhoff.
Belaid, Sadok. 1974. *Essai sur le pouvoir créateur et normatif du juge [Essay on the creative and normative authority of judges]*. Paris: Librairie Genérale de Droit et de Jurisprudence.
Belkin, Aaron. 2005. *United We Stand: Divide and Conquer Politics and the Logic of International Hostility*. New York: SUNY Press.
Bellin, Eva. 2004. "The Robustness of Authoritarianism in the Middle East," *Comparative Politics* vol. 36, no. 2 (January): 139–157.
———. 2012. "Reconsidering the Robustness of Authoritarianism in the Middle East: Lessons from the Arab Spring," *Comparative Politics* vol. 44, no. 2 (January): 127–149.
———. 2013. "Drivers of Democracy: Lessons from Tunisia." Middle East Brief 75,

Crown Center for Middle East Studies. http://www.brandeis.edu/crown/publica tions/meb/meb75.html.
Ben Aissa, Mohammed. 2012. "La compétence exclusive du conseil supérieur de la magistrature en matière disciplinaire 'ou'. . . . : quand le conseil constitutionnel brise la jurisprudence du tribunal administratif," *En hommage à Dali Jazi*: 151–181
Ben Bouazza, Bouazza. 2012. "2 Dead, 40 Injured at US Embassy Protest in Tunis," *Boston.com*, September 14.
Ben Mahfoudh, Haykel, Jonas Loetscher, and Arnold Luethold. 2012. *La Législation du Secteur de la Sécurité en Tunisie: Index 1956–2011*. Geneva: Center for the Democratic Control of the Armed Forces.
Bergman, Marcelo. 2009. *Tax Evasion and the Rule of Law in Latin America*. University Park: Pennsylvania State University Press.
Berliere, Jean-Marc. 1991. "The Professionalisation of the Police Under the Third Republic in France, 1875–1914," in Clive Emsley and Barbara Weinberger, eds., *Policing Western Europe: Politics, Professionalism, and Public Order, 1850–1940*. New York: Greenwood.
Berman, Sheri. 2007. "The Vain Hope for Correct Timing," *Journal of Democracy* vol. 18, no. 3: 14–17.
el-Bey, Doaa. 2013. "Policies, Not Persons," *Al-Ahram Weekly*, January 9–15.
Biddle, Stephen, and Robert Zirkle. 1996. "Technology, Civil-Military Relations, and Warfare in the Developing World," *Journal of Strategic Studies* vol. 19, no. 2: 171–212.
Birdsall, Nancy. 2007. "Do No Harm: Aid, Weak Institutions and the Missing Middle in Africa," *Development Policy Review* vol. 25, no. 5 (September): 575–598.
Bliss, Katherine. 2001. *Compromised Positions: Prostitution, Public Health, and Gender Politics in Revolutionary Mexico City*. University Park: Pennsylvania State University Press.
el-Borai, Negad Mohamed. 2008. "The Government's Non-Execution of Judicial Decisions," in Nathalie Bernard-Maugiron, ed., *Judges and Political Reform in Egypt*, 199–212. Cairo: American University in Cairo Press.
Borowiec, Andrew. 1998. *Modern Tunisia: A Democratic Apprenticeship*. Westport, CT: Praeger.
Boston Globe. 2003. "Policing Iraq's Police: US Tried to Train Force to Maintain Local Security," May 24.
Bou Nassif, Hicham. 2013. "Wedded to Mubarak: The Second Careers and Financial Rewards of Egypt's Military Elite, 1981–2011," *Middle East Journal* vol. 67, no. 4 (Autumn): 509–530.
———. 2015. "A Military Besieged: The Armed Forces, the Police and the Party in Bin 'Ali's Tunisia, 1987–2011," *International Journal of Middle East Studies* vol. 47, no. 1 (February): 65–87.
Brewer, John, Adrian Guelke, Ian Humem, Edward Moxon-Browne, and Rick Wilford. 1996. *The Police, Public Order and the State: Policing in Great Britain, Northern Ireland, the Irish Republic, the USA, Israel, South Africa and China*. New York: St. Martin's.
Brinks, Daniel. 2005. "Judicial Reform and Independence in Brazil and Argentina: The Beginning of a New Millennium?" *Texas International Law Journal* vol. 40, no. 3 (Spring): 595–622.
———. 2010. "Institutional Design and Judicial Effectiveness: Lessons from the Prosecution of Rights Violations for Democratic Governance and the Rule of Law," in Scott Mainwaring and Timothy Scully, eds., *Democratic Governance in Latin America*. Stanford, CA: Stanford University Press.

Brogden, Michael, and Clifford Shearing. 1993. *Policing for a New South Africa.* New York: Routledge.

Brooks, Risa. 1998. "Political-Military Relations and the Stability of Arab Regimes," *Adelphi Paper* 324, New York: Oxford University Press.

———. 2004. "Civil-Military Relations," in Nora Bensahel and Daniel Byman, eds., *The Future Security Environment in the Middle East,* 129–162. Santa Monica, CA: RAND Corporation.

Brown, Nathan J. 1997. *The Rule of Law in the Arab World: Courts in Egypt and the Gulf.* Cambridge: Cambridge University Press.

———. 2012a. "A Guide Through the Egyptian Maze of Justice," *Carnegie Endowment for International Peace: Sada,* June 6.

———. 2012b. "Still Fighting the Last War? Egypt's Judges After the Revolution," *Carnegie Endowment for International Peace: Sada,* October 16.

———. 2013a. "Great Sanhuri's Ghost!" *Foreign Policy,* January 25.

———. 2013b. "The Supreme Constitutional Court in Post-Revolution Egypt," *Tahrir Squared,* January 25.

———. 2014. "Why Do Egyptian Courts Say the Darndest Things?" *Washington Post,* March 25.

Brumberg, Daniel. 2012. "Sustaining Mechanics of Arab Autocracies," *Foreign Policy,* December 19.

Buscaglia, Edgardo. 1998. "Obstacles to Judicial Reform in Latin America," in Edmundo Jarquín and Fernando Carrillo, eds., *Justice Delayed: Judicial Reform in Latin America.* Washington, DC: Inter-American Development Bank.

Business News (Tunisia). 2013. "Tunisie–Lazhar Akremi et Mehrez Zouari chez le juge d'instruction," February 14.

Camplin, Troy. 2011. "Egypt's Revolution and Higher Education," *Pope Center for Higher Education Policy, Commentary,* February 6.

Carothers, Thomas, ed. 2006. *Promoting the Rule of Law Abroad: In Search of Knowledge.* Washington, DC: Carnegie Endowment for International Peace.

———. 2007. "How Democracies Emerge: The Sequencing Fallacy," *Journal of Democracy* vol. 18, no. 1: 12–27.

Chauvet, Lisa, Paul Collier, and Anke Hoeffler. 2007. "The Cost of Failing States and the Limits to Sovereignty," WIDER Research Paper No. 2007/30. Japan: United Nations University.

Chayes, Sarah. 2012. "Corruption Is Still Tunisia's Challenge," *Los Angeles Times,* June 10.

Chomiak, Laryssa, and John P. Entellis. 2011. "The Making of North Africa's Intifadas," *Middle East Report* no. 259 (Summer): 13–15.

CNN.com. 2012. "As Protests Calm, Tensions Remain as U.S. Seeks to Protect Embassies," September 16.

Cockburn, Patrick. 2011. "Troubles like These Are Brewing All Over the Middle East," *Independent,* January 15.

Code, Bill. 2012. "Tunisia's Jobless Demand Action," *SBS World News,* April 26.

Cody, Edward. 1987. "Tunisian President 'Senile' Is Removed by His Deputy, Habib Bourguiba's 30 Year Rule Ends," *Washington Post,* November 8.

Cohen, Stephen P. 2001. *The Indian Army: Its Contribution to the Development of a Nation.* New Delhi: Oxford University Press.

Collard, Rebecca. 2012. "'Crony Capitalism' Undermines Egyptian Food Security," *National,* April 28.

Correa, Jorge. 1999. "Cenicienta se queda en la fiesta: El poder judicial Chileno en la década de los 90," in Paul Drake and Iván Jaksic, eds., *El modelo chileno,* 155–177. Santiago: LOM.

Coser, Lewis A. 1977. *Masters of Sociological Thought: Ideas in Historical and Social Context*, 2nd ed. New York: Harcourt Brace Jovanovich College.

Couso, Javier, 2007. "The Seduction of Judicially Triggered Social Transformation: The Impact of the Warren Court in Latin America," in Harry Scheiber, ed., *Earl Warren and the Warren Court*, 237–263. Lanham, MD: Lexington.

———. 2010. "The Transformation of Constitutional Discourse and the Judicialization of Politics in Latin America," in Javier Couso, Alexandra Huneeus, and Rachel Sieder, eds., *Cultures of Legality: Judicialization and Political Activism in Latin America*, 141–160. New York: Cambridge University Press.

Couso, Javier, and Lisa Hilbink. 2011. "From Quietism to Incipient Activism: The Ideological and Institutional Roots of Rights Adjudication in Chile," in Gretchen Helmke and Julio Ríos-Figueroa, eds., *Courts in Latin America*, 99–127. New York: Cambridge University Press.

Crankshaw, Edward. 1956. *Gestapo: Instrument of Tyranny.* California: Presidio.

Crouch, Harold. 2010. *Political Reform in Indonesia After Soeharto*. Singapore: Institute of Southeast Asian Studies.

Dahl, Robert A. 1989. *Democracy and Its Critics*. New Haven, CT: Yale University Press.

Daily News Egypt. 2012. "SCC Accuses Presidency of Lying," December 17.

Damaska, Mirjan R. 1986. *The Faces of Justice and State Authority*. New Haven, CT: Yale University Press.

Daragahi, Borzou. 2011. "A Tunisian State Police Officer Shares Harrowing Inside View," *Los Angeles Times*, February 3.

Davis, Diane E. 1994. *Urban Leviathan: Mexico City in the Twentieth Century.* Philadelphia: Temple University Press.

———. 2001. "Detective Story: Tracking the Capital City Police in Mexico's Political Historiography," Paper presented at the International Symposium on History, Culture, and Identity in Mexico City: The Last and Next 100 Years. Mexico City, UAM-Atzcapotzalco, May.

———. 2002. "From Democracy to Rule of Law? Police Impunity in Contemporary Latin America," *ReVista: The Harvard Review of Latin America* (Fall): 21–25.

———. 2003. "Law Enforcement in Mexico City: Not Yet Under Control," *NACLA* vol. 37, no. 2 (September–October): 3–14.

———. 2004. *Discipline and Development: Middle Classes and Prosperity in East Asia and Latin America*. Cambridge: Cambridge University Press.

———. 2006. "Undermining the Rule of Law: Democratization and the Dark Side of Police Reforms in Mexico," *Latin American Politics and Society* vol. 48, no. 1 (Spring): 55–86.

Davis, Diane, and Arturo Alvarado. 1999. "Descent into Chaos? Liberalization, Public Insecurity, and Deteriorating Rule of Law in Mexico City," *Working Papers in Local Governance and Democracy* vol. 1, no. 99: 95–197.

Davis, Jennifer. 1991. "Urban Policing and Its Objects: Comparative Themes in England and France in the Second Half of the Nineteenth Century," in Clive Emsley and Barbara Weinberger, eds., *Policing Western Europe: Politics, Professionalism, and Public Order, 1850–1940*. New York: Greenwood.

De Atkine, Norvell. 1999. "Why Arabs Lose Wars," *Middle East Quarterly* vol. 6, no. 4 (December).

Di Mauro, Danilo. 2008. "The Consociational Democracy at Stake: Four Approaches to Explain Lebanon Past and Present," *Acta Politica* vol. 43: 453–471.

Diario de los Debates. 1916–1917. UNAM Biblioteca Juridica Virtual. https://archive.org.

El-Din, Gamal Essam. 2013. "Islamist MPs to Rubber Stamp a New Election Law Thursday," *Ahram Online*, January 16.
El-Din, Mai Shams. 2013. "Under New Constitution, the Battle Continues Against Military Trials of Civilians," *Al Masry al Youm*, January 17.
al-Diwwi, Bilal. 2012. *Al 'Adly wa-l mushir.* Cairo: Maktabat jazirat al wurûd.
Doig, Alan. 1984. *Corruption and Misconduct in Contemporary British Politics.* Harmondsworth, UK: Penguin.
Domingo, Pilar. 1999. "Judicial Independence and Judicial Reform in Latin America," in Andreas Schedler, Larry Diamond, and Marc F. Plattner, eds., *The Self-Restraining State: Power and Accountability in New Democracies*, 151–175. Boulder, CO: Lynne Rienner.
Domingo, Pilar, and Rachel Sieder. 2001. *Rule of Law in Latin America: The International Promotion of Judicial Reform.* London: ILAS.
Drew, Katherine Fischer. 2004. *Magna Carta.* Westport, CT: Greenwood.
Duce, Mauricio, and Cristian Riego. 2007. *Proceso Penal.* Santiago: Editorial Jurídica de Chile.
Dunn, Christopher. 2007. "Democracy in the 21st Century: Canada Needs a War Powers Act," *Canadian Parliamentary Review* vol. 30, no. 3 (September): 2–3.
Dworkin, Ronald. 1977. *Taking Rights Seriously.* London: Duckworth.
Dyzenhaus, David. 1998. *Judging the Judges, Judging Ourselves: Truth, Reconciliation and the Apartheid Legal Order.* Portland, OR: Hart.
Eckstein, Harry. 1971. *The Evaluation of Political Performance: Problems and Dimensions.* Beverly Hills, CA: Sage.
Eco Journal. 2012. "Interview with Samir Annabi," May 25–31.
Egyptian Initiative for Personal Rights. 2014. "Egypt: Where Impunity Is Entrenched and Accountability Is Absent," December 31.
Eleiba, Ahmad. 2012a. "Military Messages on Sinai," *Al-Ahram Weekly*, October 18–24.
———. 2012b. "The Rise and Fall of the SCAF," *Al-Ahram Weekly*, December 19.
———. 2012c. "The Brotherhood and the Army," *Al-Ahram Weekly*, December 29.
———. 2013a. "Point to Point," *Al-Ahram Weekly*, January 2.
———. 2013b. "F-16 Deal Redefines US Relationship with Egypt's Morsi Administration," *Ahram Online*, January 14.
Emsely, Clive. 1991. "Police Forces and Public Order in England and France During the Interwar Years," in Clive Emsley and Barbara Weinberger, eds., *Policing Western Europe: Politics, Professionalism, and Public Order, 1850–1940*, 241–267. New York: Greenwood.
Enloe, Cynthia. 1980. *Ethnic Soldiers.* Athens: University of Georgia Press.
Erdle, Steffen. 2004. "Tunisia: Economic Transformation and Political Restoration," in Volker Perthes, ed., *Arab Elites, Negotiating the Politics of Change*, 207–238. Boulder, CO: Lynne Rienner.
———. 2010. *Ben Ali's "New Tunisia" (1987–2009): A Case Study of Authoritarian Modernization in the Arab World.* Berlin: Klaus Schwartz.
Ertman, Thomas. 1997. *Birth of the Leviathan: Building States and Regimes in Medieval and Early Modern Europe.* New York: Cambridge University Press.
Esman, Milton, and Itamar Rabinovich, eds. 1988. *Ethnicity, Pluralism and the State in the Middle East.* Ithaca, NY: Cornell University Press.
Evripidou, Stefanos. 2012. "Searching for Mubarak's Millions in Cyprus," *Cyprus Mail,* June 10.
Ezzat, Dina. 2012. "Egypt: The President, the Army and the Police," *Ahram Online*, December 27.
———. 2013. "New Year Blues," *Al-Ahram Weekly*, January 2.

Fahim, Kareem. 2013. "Tunisia Includes Independents in New Cabinet," *New York Times*, March 8.
Fair, C. Christine. 2012. "Increasing Social Conservatism in the Pakistan Army: What the Data Say," *Armed Forces and Society* vol. 38, no. 3 (June): 438–462.
Farrell, Theo. 2005. "World Culture and Military Power," *Security Studies* vol. 14, no. 3: 448–488.
Faruq, 'Abd al Khaliq. 2012. *Kayfa nu'îd binâ' jihâz al amn*. Cairo: Markaz al Nil li-l dirâsât al iqtisâdiyya wa-l strâtijiyya.
Feaver, Peter. 1999. "Civil-Military Relations," *Annual Review of Political Science* vol. 2, no. 1: 211–241.
The Federalist. 1964 [1787]. New York: Modern Library (Random House).
Filkins, Dexter. 2004. "Failing to Disband Militias, U.S. Moves to Accept Them," *New York Times*, May 25.
———. 2011. "After the Uprising," *New Yorker*, April 11.
Finer, Samuel. 1962. *Man on Horseback: The Role of the Military in Politics*. London: Pall Mall.
Finkel, Jodi. 2008. *Judicial Reform as Political Insurance: Argentina, Peru, and Mexico in the 1990s*. Notre Dame, IN: Notre Dame University Press.
First Study Commission of the International Association of Judges. 2003. General report on meeting in Vienna, November 9–13, general report. http://www.iaj-uim.org/iuw/wp-content/uploads/2013/02/I-SC-2003-conclusions-E.pdf.
Fitch, Samuel J. 1998. *The Armed Forces and Democracy in Latin America*. Baltimore: Johns Hopkins University Press.
Fomby, Matthew Robert. 2006. *Military Development: Twenty-Five Years of U.S. Military Aid to Egypt, 1980–2005*. MA Thesis submitted to the Department of Political Science, American University in Cairo.
France24. 2012. "Second Salafist Dies After Two-Month Hunger Strike," November 17.
Fukuyama, Francis. 2011. *The Origins of Political Order*. New York: Farrar, Straus, and Giroux.
Gaaloul, Badra. 2011. "Back to the Barracks: The Tunisian Army Post Revolution," *Carnegie Endowment for International Peace: Sada*, November 3.
Gall, Carlotta. 2013a. "A Political Deal in a Deeply Divided Tunisia As Islamists Agree to Yield Power," *New York Times*, December 16.
———. 2013b. "Tunisia Faces More Anger After an Ambush Kills Soldiers," *New York Times*, July 29.
———. 2014a. "Tunisian Discontent Reflected in Protests That Have Idled Mines," *New York Times*, May 13.
———. 2014b. "Despite Signs of Progress, Security Issues Rise in Tunisia," *New York Times*, February 7.
Gargarella, Roberto. 2004. "Too Far Removed from the People: Access to Justice for the Poor: The Case of Latin America." Universidad Torcuato di Tella, Buenos Aires. http://www.gsdrc.org/go/display&type=Document&id=1124.
Gassner, Robert J. 1987. "Transition in Tunisia," *Harvard International Review* vol. 9, no. 5 (May/June): 29–30.
Gaub, Florence. 2010. *Military Integration After Civil Wars: Multiethnic Armies, Identity and Post-Conflict Reconstruction*. New York: Routledge.
———. 2011. *Rebuilding Armed Forces: Learning from Iraq and Lebanon*. Carlisle, PA: Strategic Studies Institute Monographs.
Gelvin, James. 2012. *The Arab Uprising: What Everyone Needs to Know*. Oxford: Oxford University Press.

al-Gharini, Khaled, Inas Ali Al-Rashidi, and May Al-Gamal. 2009. "The Report of the National Survey of the Citizens' Opinions on Corruption, the Judicial System and the Quality of Governmental Services in Egypt," *The Social Contract Center.* http://siteresources.worldbank.org/INTLAWJUSTINST/Resources/Egypt_Corruption_JudicialSystem_Government_Services_Report.pdf.

el-Ghobashy, Mona. 2012. "Egyptian Politics Upended," *Middle East Report,* August 20.

Ghribi, Asma. 2013. "Minister of Defense Resigns Amidst Lagging Cabinet Reshuffle Talks," *Tunisia Live,* March 7.

Global Integrity Report. 2011. https://www.globalintegrity.org/global-year/2011.

———. 2012. https://www.globalintegrity.org/global-year/2012.

Goldstein, Eric. 2011. "Dismantling the Machinery of Oppression," *Wall Street Journal,* February 16.

Golub, Stephen. 2006. "A House Without a Foundation," in Thomas Carothers, ed., *Promoting the Rule of Law Abroad: In Search of Knowledge.* Washington, DC: Carnegie Endowment for International Peace.

González-Ocantos, Ezequiel. 2013. "Legal Preferences, Capabilities Diffusion and Judicial Activism: Explaining the Prosecution of Human Rights Violations After Peru's Internal Armed Conflict." Unpublished manuscript on file with the author.

Goodin, Robert E. 2004. "Democracy, Justice, and Impartiality," in Keith Dowding, Robert E. Goodin, and Carole Pateman, eds., *Justice and Democracy: Essays for Brian Barry.* Cambridge: Cambridge University Press.

Government of Tunisia, Law 69-4 of January 24, 1969, Regulating Public Meetings, Processions, Parades, Demonstrations, and Large Gatherings.

Guarnieri, Carlo, and Patrizia Pederzoli. 2002. *The Power of Judges.* London: Oxford University Press.

Guarnieri, Carlo, and Daniela Piana. 2012. "Judicial Independence and the Rule of Law: Exploring the European Experience," in Shimon Shetreet and Christopher Forsyth, eds., *The Culture of Judicial Independence: Conceptual Foundations and Practical Challenges,* 113–124. Leiden, Netherlands: Martinus Nijhoff.

Guelke, Adrian. 2012. *Politics in Deeply Divided Societies.* Cambridge, UK: Polity.

Gümüşçü, Sebnem. 2010. "Class, Status, and Party: The Changing Face of Political Islam in Turkey and Egypt," *Comparative Political Studies* vol. 43, no. 7 (July): 835–861.

———. 2012. "Egypt Can't Replicate the Turkish Model: But It Can Learn from It," *Carnegie Endowment for International Peace: Sada,* January 12.

Gürsoy, Yaprak. 2011. "The Changing Role of the Military in Turkish Politics: Democratization Through Coup Plots?" *Democratization* vol. 1, no. 26: 735–760.

Hammergren, Linn. 2002. *Do Judicial Councils Further Judicial Reform? Lessons from Latin America.* Working Paper no. 26, Rule of Law Series. Washington, DC: Carnegie Endowment for International Peace.

———. 2007. *Envisioning Reform: Improving Judicial Performance in Latin America.* University Park: Pennsylvania State University Press.

Hamzawy, Amr. 2013. "Why the Muslim Brotherhood Doesn't Want to Hold Elections Right Now," *Atlantic Council–Egypt Source,* June 4.

Hanf, Theodor. 1993. *Coexistence in Wartime Lebanon: Decline of a State and Rise of a Nation.* London: Tauris.

Hänggi, Heiner. 2004. "Conceptualising Security Sector Reform and Reconstruction," in Allan Bryden and Heiner Hänggi, eds., *Reform and Reconstruction of the Security Sector,* 3–18. Münster, Germany: LIT Verlag.

Hanlon, Querine. 2012a. *The Prospects for Security Sector Reform in Tunisia: A Year After the Revolution*, Strategic Studies Institute, US Army War College. Carlisle, PA, Carlisle Barracks.

———. 2012b. "Security Sector Reform in Tunisia: A Year After the Jasmine Revolution." *USIP Special Report* No. 304 (March): 1–14.

Hansen, Suzy. 2012. "The Economic Vision of Egypt's Muslim Brotherhood Millionaires," *Businessweek.com*, April 19.

Hart, John Mason. 1978. *Anarchism and the Mexican Working Class, 1860–1931*. Austin: University of Texas Press.

———. 1987. *Revolutionary Mexico: The Coming and Process of the Mexican Revolution*. Berkeley: University of California Press.

Hartzell, Caroline A., and Matthew Hoddie. 2007. *Crafting Peace: Power-Sharing Institutions and the Negotiated Settlement of Civil Wars*. University Park: Pennsylvania State Press.

Heller, Patrick. 2000. "Degrees of Democracy: Some Comparative Lessons from India," *World Politics* vol. 52, no. 4 (July): 484–519.

Helmke, Gretchen, and Frances Rosenbluth. 2009. "Regimes and the Rule of Law: Judicial Independence in Comparative Perspective," *Annual Review of Political Science* vol. 12: 345–366.

Hendley, Kathleen. 1996. *Trying to Make Law Matter: Legal Reform and Labor Law in the Soviet Union*. Ann Arbor: University of Michigan Press.

Henry, Clement M., and Robert Springborg. 2011. "The Tunisian Army: Defending the Beachhead of Democracy in the Arab World," *HuffingtonPost.com*, January 26.

Hessler, Peter. 2013. "Big Brothers: Where Is the Muslim Brotherhood Leading Egypt?" *New Yorker*, January 14.

Heywood, Paul. 1995. *The Government and Politics of Spain*. London: MacMillan.

Hilbink, Lisa. 2007. *Judges Beyond Politics in Democracy and Dictatorship: Lessons from Chile*. New York: Cambridge University Press.

———. 2008. "Change and Continuity in the Judicial Role in Chile: What Londres Did and Did Not Do." Paper presented at El Efecto Pinochet, Diego Portales University, Santiago, October 8–10.

———. 2009. "The Constituted Nature of Constituents' Interests: Historical and Ideational Factors in Judicial Empowerment," *Political Research Quarterly* vol. 62, no. 4 (December): 781–797.

———. 2012. "The Origins of Positive Judicial Independence," *World Politics* vol. 64, no. 4 (October): 587–621.

Hill, Richard. 1991. "The Policing of Colonial New Zealand: From Informal to Formal Control, 1840–1907," in David Anderson and David Kallingray, eds., *Policing the Empire: Politics, Professionalism, and Public Order, 1850–1940*, 52–71. New York: Greenwood.

Hirst, Derek. 1986. *Authority and Conflict: England, 1603–1658*. Cambridge, MA: Harvard University Press.

Hofstadter, Richard. 1955. *The Age of Reform: From Bryan to FDR*. New York: Alfred A. Knopf.

Hope, Bradley. 2012. "A Towering Reminder of Egypt's Corrupt Decades," *The National*, May 20.

Horowitz, Donald. 1985. *Ethnic Groups in Conflict*. Berkeley: University of California Press.

al-Houdaiby, Ibrahim. 2014. "Judging the Judges. The Present Crisis Facing the Egyptian Judiciary," *Arab Reform Initiative*, December.

Hudson, Michael C. 1968. *The Precarious Republic: Political Modernization in Lebanon*. New York: Random House.

———. 1977. *Arab Politics: The Search for Legitimacy*. New Haven, CT: Yale University Press.
Huggins, Martha. 1998. *Political Policing: The United States and Latin America*. Durham, NC: Duke University Press.
Human Rights Watch. 2012. "Tunisia: Mass Firings a Blow to Judicial Independence," October 29. www.hrw.org.
Huneeus, Alejandra. 2006. "The Dynamics of Judicial Stasis: Judges, Pinochet-Era Claims, and the Question of Judicial Legitimacy in Chile (1998–2005)." PhD diss., University of California, Berkeley.
———. 2007. *The Pinochet Regime*. Boulder: Lynne Rienner.
Huntington, Samuel P. 1957. *The Soldier and the State: The Theory and Politics of Civil-Military Relations*. Cambridge, MA: Harvard University Press.
———. 1991. *The Third Wave: Democratization in the Late Twentieth Century*. Norman: University of Oklahoma Press.
Husain, Ed. 2012. "Where Are We Heading in Egypt?" *Council on Foreign Relations*, May 24.
Ibrahim, Amirah. 2012a. "A Victory Celebrated," *Al-Ahram Weekly*, October 4–10.
———. 2012b. "All at Sea," *Al-Ahram Weekly*, October 25–November 1.
———. 2012c. "No Foreign Ownership in Sinai," *Al-Ahram Weekly*, October 27.
———. 2012d. "The Military Under Fire," *Al-Ahram Weekly*, December 5.
———. 2012e. "What Lies Beneath," *Al-Ahram Weekly*, December 12.
———. 2013. "Porous Borders," *Al-Ahram Weekly*, January 9–15.
Ibrahim, Saad Eddin. 1998. "Ethnic Conflict and State-Building in the Arab World," *International Social Science Journal* vol. 50, no. 156 (June): 230–242.
IISS (International Institute for Strategic Studies). 2012. "The Middle East and North Africa," in *The Military Balance,* pp. 303–361. London: International Institute for Strategic Studies.
Illades, Carlos, and Ariel Rodríguez Kuri, eds. 1996. *Ciudad de México: Instituciones, Actores Sociales, y Conflictos Políticos, 1774–1931*. Mexico: El Colegio de Michoacan.
Ingram, Matthew. 2012. "Crafting Courts in New Democracies: Ideology and Judicial Council Reforms in Three Mexican States," *Comparative Politics* vol. 44, no. 4 (July): 439–458.
Iñigo, Alejandro. 1994. *Bitácora de un policía, 1500–1982*. Mexico City: Grupo Editorial Siete.
Institute for Integrated Transitions. 2003. *Inside the Transition Bubble: International Expert Assistance in Tunisia*. Barcelona, Spain.
International Bar Association Human Rights Institute. 2014. *Separating Law and Politics: Challenges to the Independence of Judges and Prosecutors in Egypt*, February 2014.
International Crisis Group. 2010. "Loose Ends: Iraq's Security Forces Between U.S. Drawdown and Withdrawal," October 26.
———. 2011. "Popular Protest in North Africa and the Middle East (IV): Tunisia's Way," *Middle East/North Africa Report* no. 106, April 28.
International Federation of Leagues of Human Rights. 2011. "Instrumentalisation de la justice en Tunisie: Ingérence, violations, impunité" [The abuse of justice in Tunisia: Intrusion, violations, impunity], No. 553. Draft-limited edition, FIDH/CNLT-Tunisia/3.
International Foundation for Electoral Systems. 2012. *Elections in Egypt: Implications of Recent Court Decisions on the Electoral Framework*. http://www.ifes.org/~/media/Files/Publications/White%20PaperReport/2012/Egypt_SCC_Decisions_August9.pdf.

Jebnoun, Noureddine. 2014. "In the Shadow of Power: Civil-Military Relations and Tunisian Popular Uprising," *Journal of North African Studies* vol. 19, no. 3: 296–316.
Johnston, Michael. 2005. *Syndromes of Corruption: Wealth, Power, and Democracy.* Cambridge: Cambridge University Press.
———. 2011. *First, Do No Harm—Then, Build Trust: Anti-Corruption Strategies in Fragile Situations.* Background paper for the 2011 World Development Report. Washington, DC: World Bank.
———. 2013. *Corruption, Contention, and Reform: The Power of Deep Democratization.* Cambridge: Cambridge University Press.
Johnston, Michael, and Sahr J. Kpundeh. 2002. *Building a Clean Machine: Anti-Corruption Coalitions and Sustainable Reforms*, World Bank Institute Working Paper no. 37208, December.
Jones, Christopher D. 1981. *Soviet Influence in Eastern Europe: Political Autonomy and the Warsaw Pact.* New York: Praeger.
Journal Officiel de la République Tunisienne. 2012. No. 80, October 19.
Kadlec, Amanda. 2012. "Disarming Libya's Militias," *Carnegie Endowment for International Peace: Sada,* February 16.
Kallander, Amy Aisen. 2011. *Tunisia's Post Ben Ali Challenge: A Primer*, Middle East Research and Information Project (MERIP), January 26.
Kalmanowiecki, Laura. 1995. "Military Power and Policing in Argentina, 1900–1955." PhD diss., New School for Social Research.
———. 2003. "Policing the People, Policing the State: The Police-Military Nexus in Argentina," in Diane Davis and Anthiny Pereira, eds., *Irregular Armed Forces and Their Role in Politics and State Formation.* Cambridge: Cambridge University Press.
Kamm, Henry. 1984. "Tunisia Appears to Halt Wave of Rioting with Show of Troops and Armor," *New York Times,* January 5.
Kandil, Hazem. 2012. *Soldiers, Spies, and Statesmen: Egypt's Road to Revolt.* London: Verso.
———. 2014. *Inside the Brotherhood.* London: Polity.
Katz, Friedrich. 1998. *The Life and Times of Pancho Villa.* Palo Alto, CA: Stanford University Press.
Kerr, K. Austin. 1980. "Organizing for Reform: The Anti-Saloon League and Innovation in Politics," *American Quarterly* vol. 32, no.1 (Spring): 37–53.
Khalidi, Walid. 1979. *Conflict and Violence in Lebanon.* Cambridge: Harvard University Press.
Khanna, Jyoti, and Michael Johnston. 2007. "India's Middlemen: Connecting by Corrupting?" *Crime, Law, and Social Change* vol. 48, no. 3–5 (December): 151–168.
Kier, Elizabeth. 1997. *Imagining War: French and British Military Doctrine Between the Wars.* Princeton, NJ: Princeton University Press.
Kirkpatrick, David D. 2011a. "Protests Spread to Tunisia's Capital and a Curfew Is Decreed," *New York Times,* January 13.
———. 2011b. "In Tunisia, Clashes Continue As Power Shifts a Second Time," *New York Times,* January 15.
———. 2011c. "Military Backs New Leaders in Tunisia," *New York Times,* January 16.
———. 2011d. "In Tunisia, New Leaders Win Support of Military," *New York Times,* January 17.
———. 2011e. "Chief of Tunisian Army Pledges His Support for the Revolution," *New York Times,* January 25.
Kiselycznyk, Michael, and Phillip Charles Saunders. 2010. *Civil-Military Relations*

in China: Assessing the PLA's Role in Elite Politics. Washington, DC: National Defense University Press.

Klaas, Brian. 2013. "The Long Shadow of Ben Ali: How a Decades Old Fake Coup Attempt Is Taking Its Toll on Tunisia," *Foreign Policy,* December 17.

Kleinfeld, Rachel. 2006. "Competing Definitions of the Rule of Law," in Thomas Carothers, ed., *Promoting the Rule of Law Abroad: In Search of Knowledge*, 31–74. Washington, DC: Carnegie Endowment for International Peace.

———. 2012. *Advancing Rule of Law Abroad: The Next Generation of Reform.* Washington, DC: Carnegie Endowment for International Peace.

Knack, S., and Phillip Keefer. 1995. "Institutions and Economic Performance: Cross-Country Tests Using Alternative Institutional Measures," *Economics and Politics Journal* vol. 7, no. 3 (November): 207–227.

Knickmeyer, Ellen. 2011. "Just Whose Side Are Arab Armies On, Anyway?" *Pulitzer Center on Crisis Reporting,* January 28.

Knight, Alan. 1986. *The Mexican Revolution* (Volumes 1 and 2). Lincoln: University of Nebraska Press.

Krauze, Enrique. 1976. *Caudillos culturales en la Revolución Mexicana.* Mexico City: Siglo Veintiuno Editores.

Krebs, Ron. 2006. *Fighting for Rights: Military Service and the Politics of Citizenship.* Ithaca, NY: Cornell University Press.

Krishnasamy, Kabilan. 2003. "Bangladesh and UN Peacekeeping: The Participation of a 'Small' State," *Commonwealth and Comparative Politics* vol. 41, no. 1 (March): 24–47.

Kurer, Oskar. 2005. "Corruption: An Alternative Approach to Its Definition and Measurement," *Political Studies* vol. 53, no. 1 (March): 222–239.

Lacher, Wolfram. 2013. *Bruchlinien der Revolution: Akteure, Lager und Konflikte im neuen Libyen.* Berlin: Stiftung Wissenschaft und Politik.

Lagos, Andrea. 1998. "Revolución en la Corte Suprema," *La Tercera en Internet*, November 1.

Lang, Anthony, ed. 2004. *Political Theory and International Affairs: Hans J. Morgenthau on Aristotle's* The Politics. Westport, CT: Praeger.

Langer, Máximo. 2007. "Revolution in Latin American Criminal Procedure: Diffusion of Legal Ideas from the Periphery," *American Journal of Comparative Law* vol. 55: 617–676.

Law, David. 2011. "Judicial Independence," in Bertrand Badie, Dirk Berg-Schlosser, and Leonardo Morlino, eds., *International Encyclopedia of Political Science*, vol. 5. Washington, DC: Sage.

Lear, John. 2001. *Workers, Neighbors, and Citizens: The Revolution in Mexico City.* Lincoln: University of Nebraska Press.

Lee, Dongmin. 2006. "Chinese Civil-Military Relations: Divestiture of People's Liberation Army Business Holdings," *Armed Forces and Society* vol. 32, no. 3 (April): 437–453.

Lehmbruch, Gerhard. 1974. "A Non-Competitive Pattern of Conflict Management in Liberal Democracies: The Case of Switzerland, Austria and Lebanon," in Kenneth Mcrae, ed., *Consociational Democrac.* Toronto: McClelland and Stewart.

Levin, Nadia, Kindiza Ngubeni, and Graeme Simpson. 1994. "Meeting the Challenge of Change? Notes on Policing and Transition in South Africa." Occasional paper written for the Centre for the Study of Violence and Reconciliation, Johannesburg, May.

Li, Nan. 2010. "Chinese Civil-Military Relations in the Post-Deng Era," *China Maritime Studies*, no. 4. Center for Naval Warfare Studies, U.S. Naval War College.

Lijphart, Arend. 1968. *The Politics of Accommodation: Pluralism and Democracy in the Netherlands*. Berkeley: University of California Press.
———. 1977. *Democracy in Plural Societies*. New Haven, CT: Yale University Press.
———. 2004. "Constitutional Design for Divided Societies," *Journal of Democracy* vol. 15, no. 2 (April): 96–109.
Lustick, Ian. 1979. "Stability in Deeply Divided Societies: Consociationalism Versus Control," *World Politics* vol. 31, no. 3 (April): 325–344.
Lutterbeck, Derek. 2012. "After the Fall: Security Sector Reform in Post–Ben Ali Tunisia," *Arab Reform Initiative*, September.
———. 2013. "Arab Uprisings, Armed Forces, and Civil-Military Relations," *Armed Forces and Society* vol. 39, no. 1 (January): 28–52.
Luttwak, Edward N. 2013. "Keep Syria in a Stalemate," *International Herald Tribune*, August 24–25.
MacCormick, Neil. 1999. "Rhetoric and the Rule of Law," in David Dyzenhaus, ed., *Recrafting the Rule of Law: The Limits of Legal Order*, 163–177. Portland, OR: Hart.
Macías, Ricardo Córdova. 1999. *El Salvador: Reforma militar y relaciones civico-militares*. San Salvador: Fundación Dr. Guillermo Manuel Ungo.
Maghreb Confidential. 2011a. "Has Ben Ali Played His Last Cards," January 6.
———. 2011b. "Army Serves as Ben Ali's Last Rampart," January 13.
Malleson, Kate, and Peter H. Russell. 2006. *Appointing Judges in an Age of Judicial Power: Critical Perspectives from Around the World*. Toronto: University of Toronto Press.
Marks, Jon. 2013. "Tunisia: Lack of Trust and Murderous Rivalries," *Chatham House*, February 12. http://allafrica.com/stories/201302130958.html?viewall=1.
Marshall, Shana. 2012. "Egypt's Other Revolution: Modernizing the Military-Industrial Complex," *Jadaliyaa*, February 10.
Marshall, Shana, and Joshua Stacher. 2012. "Egypt's Generals and Transnational Capital," *Middle East Report* no. 262 (Spring).
Masetti, Oliver, Kevin Korner, Magdalena Forster, and Jacob Friedman. 2013. *Two Years After the Arab Spring*. Frankfurt: Deutsche Bank.
Maslow, Aaron. 1943. "A Theory of Human Motivation," *Psychological Review* vol. 50, no. 4: 370–396.
Masrour, Amira. 2013. "Salafist Security Patrols Divide Tunisians," *Tunisia Live*, February 13.
Al Masry al Youm. 2013a. "Lawyer Held for Allegedly Possessing Classified Military Information," *Egypt Independent*, January 2.
———. 2013b. "Ministry Announces Governor Reshuffle: Islamists to Gain Eight Posts," *Egypt Independent*, January 7.
———. 2013c. "US to Send Fighter Planes, Tanks to Egypt on Monday," *Egypt Independent*, January 17.
———. 2013d. "Army Ready to Protect Country, but Not Involved in Politics, Says Military Source," *Egypt Independent*, January 24.
McCulloch, Allison. 2014. *Power-Sharing and Political Stability in Deeply Divided Societies*. London: Routledge.
McEldowney, John F. 1991. "Policing and the Administration of Justice in Nineteenth-Century Ireland," in Clive Emsley and Barbara Weinberger, eds., *Policing Western Europe: Politics, Professionalism, and Public Order, 1850–1940*, 18–37. New York: Greenwood.
McFate, Sean. 2008. "Securing the Future: A Primer on Security Sector Reform in Conflict Countries," *Special Report*, no. 209, US Institute of Peace.

McGeough, Paul. 2012. "Authoritarian Habits Prove Hard to Break," *Sydney Morning Herald,* April 8.
McGrath, Cam. 2012. "Egypt: Mubarak Still Has His Billions." *AllAfrica.com,* May 8. http://allafrica.com/stories/201205080105.html.
McLauchlin, Theodore. 2010. "Loyalty and Military Defection in Rebellion," *Comparative Politics* vol. 42, no. 3 (April): 333–350.
McLaurin, Ronald. 1991. "From Professional to Political: The Redecline of the Lebanese Army," *Armed Forces and Society* vol. 17, no. 4 (Summer): 545–568.
Mechiche, Said. 2013. "Post-Revolution Police Reform: Current State and Challenges." Paper presented at the Tunisian Institutional Reform Regional Conference on Police Reform, Tunis, Tunisia, January 25.
Meierhenrich, Jens. 2010. *The Legacies of Law: Long-Run Consequences of Legal Development in South Africa.* New York: Cambridge University Press.
Merryman, J. H., and Rogelio Pérez-Perdomo. 2007. *The Civil Law Tradition,* 3rd ed. Stanford, CA: Stanford University Press.
Merton, Robert K. 1957. *Social Theory and Social Structure.* New York: Free Press.
Michel, Veronica. 2012. "Access to Justice, Victims' Rights and Private Prosecution in Latin America: The Cases of Chile, Guatemala, and Mexico." PhD diss., University of Minnesota.
Mietzner, Marcus. 1999. *Military Politics, Islam, and the State in Indonesia.* Singapore: Institute of Southeast Asian Studies.
Miliha, Ihab Muhammad. 2010. *Al simat al nafsiyya li dubbat al shurta.* Cairo: Anglo Egyptian Library Press.
Moller, Jorgen, and Svend-Erik Skaaning. 2014. *The Rule of Law: Definitions, Measures, Patterns, and Causes.* New York: Palgrave MacMillan.
Moten, Matthew. 2010. "Out of Order: Strengthening the Political-Military Relationship," *Foreign Affairs* vol. 89, no. 5 (September/October): 2–8.
Moussa, Abdessatar. 2013. Speech at the Tunisian Institutional Reform Regional Conference on Police Reform, "Post-Revolution Police Reform: Current State and Challenges," Tunis, Tunisia, January 25.
Moustafa, Tamir. 2003. "Law Versus the State: The Judicialization of Politics in Egypt," *Law and Social Inquiry,* vol. 28: 883–930.
———. 2008. "The Political Role of the Supreme Constitutional Court: Between Principles and Practice," in Nathalie Bernard-Maugiron, ed., *Judges and Political Reform in Egypt,* 91–110. Cairo: American University in Cairo Press.
Mungiu-Pippidi, Alina. 2006. "Corruption: Diagnosis and Treatment," *Journal of Democracy* vol. 17, no. 3 (July): 86–99.
———. 2014. "Of Virtuous Circles: Modeling Control of Corruption Beyond Modernization." http://papers.ssrn.com/sol3/papers.cfm?abstract_id=2452615.
Murphy, Emma. 1999. *Economic and Political Change in Tunisia: from Bourguiba to Ben Ali.* New York: Palgrave Macmillan.
———. 2002. "The Foreign Policy of Tunisia," in Raymond Hinnebusch and Anoushiravan Ehteshami, eds., *The Foreign Policies of Middle East States,* 235–256. Boulder, CO: Lynne Rienner.
———. 2011. "Exit Ben Ali—But Can Tunisia Change," *BBC News Africa,* January 15.
El Nacional. 1996. "Dio posesión al nuevo jefe de la SSP," September 6.
Najjar, Yasmine, and Monia Ghanmi. 2013. "Tunisia: Nation Studies Police Reform," *Magharebia,* April 26.
Nasr, Vali. 2004. "Military Rule, Islamism and Democracy in Pakistan," *Middle East Journal* vol. 58: 195–209.
Nerguizian, Aram. 2009. *The Lebanese Armed Forces: Challenges and Opportuni-*

ties in Post-Syria Lebanon. Washington, DC: Center for Strategic and International Studies.
New York Times. 2005. "Mexico Says Drug Cartel Had Spy in President's Office," February 7.
———. 2014. "Mixed Results for Mideast Democracy," January 15.
New Zealand Herald. 2013. "Thousands Protest Government at Tunisia Funeral," July 28.
Nordlinger, Eric. 1977. *Soldiers in Politics: Military Coups and Governments.* Englewood Cliffs, NJ: Prentice Hall.
Nunes, Rodrigo. 2010. "Ideational Origins of Progressive Judicial Activism," *Latin American Politics and Society* vol. 52, no. 3 (Fall): 67–97.
O'Donnell, Guillermo. 1999. "Horizontal Accountability in New Democracies," in Andreas Schedler, Larry Diamond, and Marc F. Plattner, eds., *The Self Restraining State: Power and Accountability in New Democracie.* Boulder, CO: Lynne Rienner.
Okrent, Daniel. 2010. *Last Call: The Rise and Fall of Prohibition.* New York: Scribner.
Oldenburg, Philip. 1987. "Middlemen in Third-World Corruption: Implications of an Indian Case," *World Politics,* vol. 39, no. 4 (October): 508–535.
O'Leary, Brendan. 2013. "Power Sharing in Deeply Divided Places: An Advocate's Introduction," in Joanne McEvoy and Brendan O'Leary, eds., *Power Sharing in Deeply Divided Places,* 1–66. Philadelphia: University of Pennsylvania Press.
Owen, Roger. 2000. *State, Power, and Politics in the Making of the Modern Middle East,* 2nd ed. London: Routledge.
Pacheco Miranda, S. 1998. *Historia de las desaparecíon del Municipio en el Distrito Federal.* Mexico City: El Colegio de Mexico.
Pachon, Alejandro. 2014. "Loyalty and Defection: Misunderstanding Civil-Military Relations in Tunisia During the Arab Spring," *Journal of Strategic Studies,* vol. 34, no. 4 (April): 508–531.
Peck, Linda Levy. 1990. *Court Patronage and Corruption in Early Stuart England.* Boston: Unwin Hyman.
Peled, Alon. 1998. *A Question of Loyalty: Military Manpower Policy in Multiethnic States.* Ithaca, NY: Cornell University Press.
Penner Angrist, Michele. 2007. "Whither the Ben Ali Regime in Tunisia?" in Bruce Maddy-Weitzman and Daniel Zisenwine, eds., *The Maghrib in the New Century: Identity, Religion and Politics,* 122–149. Gainesville: University Press of Florida.
———. 2013. "Understanding the Success of Mass Civic Protest in Tunisia," *Middle East Journal* vol. 67, no. 4 (Autumn): 547–564.
Perito, Robert. 2009. "The Interior Ministry's Role in Security Sector Reform," *USIP Special Report* no. 223 (May): 1–15.
———. 2012a. "USIP Hosts Discussion on Security Sector in Arab World," *C-Span,* November 5.
———. 2012b. "Reforming the Security Sector in Tunisia and Libya," *USIP,* February 7.
Perrot, Roger. 2006. *Institutions judiciaires,* 2nd ed. Paris: Montchrestien.
Peruzzotti, Enrique, and Catalina Smulovitz. 2006. *Enforcing Rule of Law: Social Accountability in the New Latin American Democracies.* Pittsburgh: University of Pittsburgh Press.
Pew Global. 2013. "Tunisians Disaffected with Leaders As Conditions Worsen," December 12.

———. 2014. "Tunisian Confidence in Democracy Wanes," 15 October.
Picard, Elizabeth. 1990. "Arab Military in Politics: From Revolutionary Plot to Authoritarian State," in Giacomo Luciani, ed., *The Arab State*. Berkeley: University of California Press.
———. 1996. *Lebanon: A Shattered Country*. New York: Holmes and Meier.
Picatto, Pablo. 2001. *City of Suspects: Crime in Mexico City, 1900–1931*. Durham, NC: Duke University Press.
Pion-Berlin, David. 1997. *Through Corridors of Power: Institutions and Civil-Military Relations in Argentina*. University Park: Pennsylvania State Press.
Pion-Berlin, David, Diego Esparza, and Kevin Grisham. 2014. "Staying Quartered: Civilian Uprisings and Military Disobedience in the Twenty-First Century," *Comparative Political Studies* vol. 47, no. 2 (February): 230–259.
Popova, Maria. 2012. *Politicized Justice in Emerging Democracies: A Study of Courts in Russia and Ukraine*. New York: Cambridge University Press.
Procuraduría General de la República. 1994. *Reseña histórica de la policía auxiliar del Distrito Federal*. Mexico City: Departamento del Distrito Federal.
Al Quds al Arabi. 2013. "The MB and the Iranian Card in the Face of the Gulf," *Mideastwire.com*, January 17.
Quinlivan, James. 1999. "Coup-Proofing: Its Practice and Consequences in the Middle East," *International Security* vol. 24, no. 2 (Fall): 131–165.
Rabbani, Mouin. 2011. "The Securitization of Political Rule: Security Domination of Arab Regimes and the Prospects for Democratization," *Perspectives* vol. 2 (May): 258–262.
Rabinovich, Itamar. 1985. *The War for Lebanon*. Ithaca, NY: Cornell University Press.
Raghavan, Sudarasan. 2011. "In Tunisia, Luxurious Lifestyles of a Corrupt Government," *Washington Post*, 28 January.
Raz, Joseph. 1979. "The Rule of Law and Its Virtue," in Robert L. Cunningham, ed., *Liberty and the Rule of Law*, 13–27. College Station: Texas A&M University Press.
Republic of Tunisia Ministry of Interior. 2011. *Security and Development: A White Paper for Democratic Security in Tunisia*. Trans. Graeme Carroll and Winnie Tsang.
Ricard, Thierry. 1990. *Le conseil supérieur de la magistrature [The high council of justice]*. Paris: Presses universitaires de France.
Ríos-Figueroa, Julio. 2012. "Justice System Institutions and Corruption Control: Evidence from Latin America," *Justice System Journal* vol. 33, no. 2: 195–214.
Roach, Kent. 2013. "Security Forces Reform in Tunisia," *IDEA and the Center for Constitutional Transitions at NYU—Consolidating the Arab Spring: Constitutional Transition in Egypt and Tunisia*, no. 7, June. http://constitutionaltransitions.org/wpcontent/uploads/2013/06/7_Roach_Security_Sector.pdf.
Roberts, Clayton. 1980. *The Growth of Responsible Government in Stuart England*. Cambridge: Cambridge University Press.
Rodrigo, Fernando. 1991. "A Democratic Strategy Toward the Military: Spain, 1975–1979," in Constantine Danopoulos, ed., *From Military to Civilian Rule*. London: Routledge.
Rodríguez Kuri, Ariel. 1996a. *La experiencia olvidada. El ayuntamiento de México: Política y gobierno, 1876–1912*. Mexico City: El Colegio de Mexico.
———. 1996b. "El ano cero: El ayuntamiento de México y las facciones revolucionarias (agosto 1914–agosto 1915)," in Carlos Illades and Rodriguez Kuri, eds., *Ciudad de México: Instituciones, actores sociales, y conflictos políticos, 1774–1931*. Mexico City: El Colegio de Michoacan.

Rodrik, Dani, Arvind Subramanian, and Francesco Trebbi. 2004. "Institutions Rule: The Primacy of Institutions over Geography and Integration in Economic Development," *Journal of Economic Growth* vol. 9, no. 2: 131–165.

Roeder, Philip G., and Donald Rothchild, eds. 2005. *Sustainable Peace: Power and Democracy After Civil Wars*. Ithaca, NY: Cornell University Press.

Ron, James. 2003. *Frontiers and Ghettos: State Violence in Serbia and Israel*. Berkeley: University of California Press.

Rothstein, Bo. 2011. *The Quality of Government: The Political Economy of Corruption, Social Trust and Inequality in an International Comparative Perspective*. Chicago: University of Chicago Press.

Russell, Peter, and David O'Brien, eds. 2001. *Judicial Independence in the Age of Democracy: Critical Perspectives from Around the World*. Charlottesville: University Press of Virginia.

Said, Atef Shahat. 2008. "The Role of the Judges' Club in Enhancing the Independence of the Judiciary and Spurring Political Reform," in Nathalie Bernard-Maugiron, ed., *Judges and Political Reform in Egypt*, 111–132. Cairo: American University in Cairo Press.

———. 2012. "A New Judicial Moment in Egypt," *Jadaliyya*, December 25.

Salas, Luis. 2001. "From Law and Development to Rule of Law: New and Old Issues in Justice Reform in Latin America," in Pilar Domingo and Rachel Sieder, eds., *Rule of Law in Latin America: The International Promotion of Judicial Reform*. London: ILAS.

Salem, Elie. 1993. *Violence and Diplomacy in Lebanon*. London: Tauris.

Salibi, Kamal. 1976. *Crossroads to Civil War*. New York: Caravan.

Samti, Farah. 2013a. "Tunisian Civil Society Lambasts Police Reform Process," *Tunisia Live*, January 25.

———. 2013b. "Deadlock over Controversial Group Delays National Dialogue Agreement," *Tunisia Live*, May 15.

Sanhueza, Ana Maria. 2011. "La Regelión de los Jueces." *Qué Pasa* (November 4): 38–43.

Sayigh, Yezid. 2011. "The Tunisian Army—A New Political Role?" *Cairo Review*, October 31.

———. 2012. "Above the State: The Officers' Republic in Egypt," *Carnegie Papers–Middle East*. Washington, DC: Carnegie Endowment for International Peace.

———. 2014. "Arab Police Reform: Returning to Square One," *Carnegie Endowment for International Peace*, January 9.

———. 2015. "Missed Opportunities: The Failure of Police Reform in Egypt and Tunisia," *Carnegie Endowment for International Peace*, March 17.

Schedler, Andreas. 1999. "Conceptualizing Accountability," in Andreas Schedler, Larry Diamond, and Marc Plattner, eds., *The Self-Restraining State: Power and Accountability in New Democracies*, 13–28. Boulder, CO: Lynne Rienner.

Schumpeter, Joseph. 1912. *The Theory of Economic Development*. Cambridge, MA: Harvard University Press.

Scott, James C. 1972. *Comparative Political Corruption*. Englewood Cliffs, NJ: Prentice Hall.

Sedra, Mark. 2010. "Introduction: The Future of Security Sector Reform," in Mark Sedra, ed., *The Future of Security Sector Reform*, 1–23. Waterloo, Ontario: The Centre for International Governance Innovation.

———. 2011. "Security Sector Transformation in North Africa and the Middle East," *USIP Special Report* no. 296: 1–15.

Seghaier, Roua. 2013. "What Are the Leagues for the Protection of the Revolution?" *Tunisia Live*, January 23.

Shapiro, Martin. 1981. *Courts: A Comparative and Political Analysis.* Chicago: University of Chicago Press.
Shelley, Louise. 1995. *Policing Soviet Society: The Evolution of State Control.* New York: Routledge.
Shetreet, Simon. 2011. "Judicial Independence and Accountability," in H. P. Lee, ed., *Judiciaries in Comparative Perspective*, 3–24. New York: Cambridge University Press.
al Shubaki, Amr. 2013. Open discussion at the seminar organized by the Arab Reform Initiative and Arab Forum Alternatives, Cairo, June 10.
Siavelis, Peter M. 2008. "Chile: The End of the Unfinished Transition," in Jorge Domínguez and Michael Shifter, eds., *Constructing Democratic Governance in Latin America*, 3rd ed., 177–208. Baltimore, MD: Johns Hopkins University Press.
Siddiqa, Ayesha. 2007. *Military Inc.: Inside Pakistan's Military Economy.* London: Pluto.
Silva, Patricio. 2002. "Searching for Civilian Supremacy: The Concertación Governments and the Military in Chile," *Bulletin of Latin American Research* vol. 21, no. 3 (July): 375–395.
al-Sirgany, Khalid. 2008. "Khaskhasa aksa'am a'shurta," Arabic Network for Human Rights Information, November 9.
Sirrs, Owen L. 2010. *The Egyptian Intelligence Service: A History of the Mukhabarat, 1910–2009.* London: Palgrave Macmillan.
el-Sisi, Abdel Fattah. 2006. "Democracy in the Middle East." Unpublished thesis, Army War College. www.nytimes.com/interactive/2014/05/24/world/mideast/sisi-doc.html.
Sisk, Timothy. 1996. *Power Sharing and International Mediation in Ethnic Conflicts.* Washington, DC: US Institute of Peace.
Smock, David R., and Audrey C. Smock. 1975. *The Politics of Pluralism: A Comparative Study of Lebanon and Ghana.* New York: Elsevier.
Springborg, Robert. 2013. "Learning from Failure: Egypt," in Thomas C. Bruneau and Florina Cristiana Matei, eds., *The Routledge Handbook of Civil-Military Relations*, 93–109. London: Routledge.
Stacher, Joshua. 2012. *Adaptable Autocrats: Regime Power in Egypt and Syria.* Stanford, CA: Stanford University Press.
Staton, Jeffrey K. 2010. *Judicial Power and Strategic Communication in Mexico.* New York: Cambridge University Press.
Stepan, Alfred. 1988. *Re-Thinking Military Politics.* Princeton, NJ: Princeton University Press.
———. 2011. "Tunisia's Election: Counter-Revolution or Democratic Transition?" *Social Science Research Council: The Immanent Frame*, December 17.
———. 2012. "Tunisia's Transition and the Twin Tolerations," *Journal of Democracy* vol. 23, no. 2 (April): 89–103.
Stotsky, Irwin P., ed. 1993. *Transition to Democracy in Latin America.* Boulder, CO: Westview.
Strayer, Joseph. 1970. *On the Medieval Origins of the Modern State.* Princeton, NJ: Princeton University Press.
Strömberg, Håka. 2000. *Allmän Förvaltningsrätt.* Malmö, Sweden: Liber.
Sultan, Amer. 2013. "Iran's Intelligence Leader Suleimani Never Entered Egypt, Morsi Aide Asserts," *Ahram Online*, January 12.
Svolik, Milan. 2012. *The Politics of Authoritarian Rule.* Cambridge: Cambridge University Press.
Tajine, Synde. 2014. Trans. Rani Geha. "Tunisia Suffers Bloodiest Day in 50 Years as Terror Strikes," *Al Monitor*, July 16.

Tamanaha, Brian. 2004. *On the Rule of Law: History, Politics, Theory*. New York: Cambridge University Press.
Taylor, Brian. 2003. *Politics and the Russian Army: Civil-Military Relations 1689–2000*. Cambridge: Cambridge University Press.
Telegraph. 2012. "Egypt: Protesters Vent Anger After Hosni Mubarak's Sons Are Acquitted," June 2.
Thorne, John. 2012. "In Tunisia's Sentencing of a Dictator, a Model for Bringing Justice?" *Christian Science Monitor*, June 14.
Tilly, Charles. 1985. "War Making and State Making as Organized Crime," in Peter B. Evans, Dietrich Rueschemeyer, and Theda Skocpol, eds., *Bringing the State Back In*, 169–191. New York: Cambridge University Press.
Toronto, Nathan W. 2011. "Egypt's Coup-volution," *Middle East Insight* no. 6, February 16. http://blog.nus.edu.sg/middleeastinstitute/2011/02/16/egypts-coup-volution/.
Trablesi, Houda. 2012. "Tunisian Salafists Suspend Hunger Strike," *Magharebia*, November 21.
Trager, Eric. 2013. "What Every American Should Know About Egypt's Muslim Brotherhood" (Lecture Transcript E Notes), *Foreign Policy Research Institute*, January.
Trinkunas, Harold A. 2005. *Crafting Civilian Control of the Military in Venezuela: A Comparative Perspective*. Chapel Hill: University of North Carolina Press.
Tusa, Felix. 2014. "Security Sector Reform and the Democratic Transition in Tunisia." Speech presented at the Third International Conference of the Center for the Study of Islam and Democracy, Tunis, Tunisia, March 28–29.
Tu Thanh Ha. 2012. "Tunisian Fugitive Ready to Face Trial at Home," *Globe and Mail*, May 8.
UN Department of Economic and Social Affairs. 2010. *Reconstructing Public Administration After Conflict: Challenges, Practices, and Lessons Learned*. New York: UN Department of Economic and Social Affairs.
UN Development Programme. 2009. *Arab Human Development Report*. www.arab-hdr.org.
UN News Centre. 2012. "UN Rights Chief Urges Tunisia to Stop Use of Excessive Force Against Demonstrators in Siliana," November 30.
UN Security Council. 2004. "The Rule of Law and Transitional Justice in Conflict and Post-Conflict Societies," August 23. http://www.unrol.org/files/2004%20report.pdf.
US Central Intelligence Agency. 2012. "The World Factbook." https://www.cia.gov/library/publications/the-world-factbook/.
———. 2015. "The World Factbook." https://www.cia.gov/library/publications/the-world-factbook/.
US Embassy Tunisia. 2008. "Africom Visit Strong U.S. Tunisian Relations," May 30.
US Institute of Peace. 2008. "Securing the Future: A Primer on Security Sector Reform in Conflict Countries," *USIP Special Report* no. 209.
USAID. 2003. *Conseils pour promouvoir l'indépendance et l'impartialité judiciaires [Recommendations for the promotion of judicial independence and impartiality]*, May. http://pdf.usaid.gov/pdf_docs/pnacp333.pdf.
Valenzuela, Arturo. 1995. "The Military in Power: The Consolidation of One-Man Rule," in Paul W. Drake and Ivan Jaksic, eds., *The Struggle for Democracy in Chile*. Lincoln: University of Nebraska Press.
Vargas, Juan Enrique. 2007. "Alternativas para estructurar el gobierno judicial res-

petando la independencia de los jueces," in Javier Couso and Fernando Atria, eds., *La judicatura como organización*, 97–124. Santiago, Chile: Expansiva e Instituto de Estudios Judiciales.

Waller, J. Michael. 1994. *Secret Empire: The KGB in Russia Today*. San Francisco: Westview.

Walt, Vivienne. 2011. "Chaos Threatens Tunisia's Revolution," *Time,* January 16.

———. 2012. "Political Battles in Tunisia Shade Attacks on U.S. Embassy," *Time*, September 16.

Ware, L. B. 1985. "The Role of the Tunisian Military in the Post-Bourguiba Era," *Middle East Journal* vol. 39, no. 1 (Winter): 27–47.

Weber, Max. 2003. *The Essential Weber: A Reader*. London: Routledge.

Wolf, Anne. 2013. "The Salafist Temptation: The Radicalization of Tunisia's Post-Revolution Youth," *CTC Sentinel*, April 29.

Wong, Edward. 2006. "U.S. Is Seeking Better Balance in Iraqi Police," *New York Times*, March 7.

Woo, Jongseok. 2011. *Security Challenges and Military Politics in East Asia: From State-Building to Post-Democratization*. New York: Continuum.

Worboys, Katherine J. 2007. "The Traumatic Journey from Dictatorship to Democracy: Peacekeeping Operations and Civil-Military Relations in Argentina, 1989–1999," *Armed Forces and Society*, vol. 33, no. 2 (January): 149–168.

World Bank. 2003. *Better Governance for Development in the Middle East and North Africa: Enhancing Inclusiveness and Accountability*. Washington, DC: World Bank.

———. 2004. *World Development Report: Making Services Work for Poor People*. Washington, DC: World Bank.

———. 2009. *From Privilege to Competition: Unlocking Private-Led Growth in the Middle East and North Africa*. Washington, DC: World Bank.

———. 2011. *MENA Regional Strategy Update: Sustaining Recovery and Enhancing Prospects for Inclusive Growth*. Washington, DC: World Bank.

———. 2012. *Governance and Accountability Updated Strategy*. Washington, DC: World Bank.

World Justice Project. 2014. "The Rule of Law Index 2014 Report." http://world justiceproject.org/publication/rule-of-law-indexreports/rule-law-index-2014 -report.

Yasm. 2013. "Tunisia: Jebel Chaambi Terrorists Claim More Lives," *Magharebia,* June 7. http://allafrica.com/stories/201306101414.html.

Young, Thomas-Durrell. 2006. "Military Professionalism in a Democracy," in Bruneau and Scott Tollefson, eds., *Who Guards the Guardians and How*. Austin: University of Texas Press.

Youssef, Nariman. 2012. "Egypt's Draft Constitution Translated," *Egypt Independent*, December 2.

Zapata, Maria Francisca. 2009. Interviewed by Lisa Helbink. Santiago, Chile, January 5.

Zepeda, Felipe Victoria. 1994. *"Perro rabioso": La corrupción policiaca*. Mexico City: EDAMEX.

The Contributors

Tewfiq Aclimandos is a lecturer at Cairo University and the French University of Cairo and a columnist for Al-Tahrir.

Oren Barak is associate professor of political science and international relations at the Hebrew University of Jerusalem.

Zoltan Barany is Frank C. Erwin, Jr., Centennial Professor of Government at the University of Texas, Austin.

Eva Bellin is Myra and Robert Kraft Professor of Arab Politics at Brandeis University.

Mohamed Salah Ben Aissa is Tunisia's minister of justice and professor emeritus of public law at the University of Tunis.

Nathalie Bernard-Maugiron is a senior researcher at the Institute of Research and Development, Paris.

Risa A. Brooks is associate professor of political science at Marquette University.

Lida Bteddini is a public sector specialist at the World Bank.

Diane E. Davis is Charles Dyer Norton Professor of Regional Planning and Urbanism at Harvard University's Graduate School of Design.

Querine Hanlon is president and executive director of the Strategic Capacity Group.

Günter Heidenhof is practice manager of Governance Global Practice at the World Bank.

Lisa Hilbink is associate professor of political science at the University of Minnesota.

Michael Johnston is Charles Dana Professor Emeritus of Political Science at Colgate University.

Heidi Lane is associate professor of strategy and policy and director of the Greater Middle East Research Group at the US Naval War College.

Robert Springborg is visiting professor in the Department of War Studies at King's College, London. Previously he was professor of national security affairs at the Naval Postgraduate School.

Index

Abd Al Hadi Badawi, 174
Abd al Halim Musa, 176
'Abd al-Jawwad family, 180
Abdel-Malek, Anouar, 90
Abu Basha, 187*n*8
Abu Ghazala, Abd al Halim, 91
Accountability: in Egypt, 42–43; in Europe, 3–4; horizontal, 9–10, 262; importance of, 241; in MENA, 251–253, 252*fig*; of police force, 258; public, 111, 245–247, 246*fig*; vertical, 9, 261
Active-duty military personnel, 68
el-Adly Habib, 177
Age of retirement, 41–42, 51*n*24
Agriculture, 228–229
Ahmadinejad, Mahmoud, 100
Akhwanat, 97–98
al-Alfi, Hassan, 176
Alawites, 145
Algeria, 249*fig*
Amer, Abdel Hakim, 91
Amin Shurta, 98
Ammar, Rachid, 119
Antiprotest laws, 44
Anticorruption: crusaders for, 2–3; hazards to, 234–235; policies for, 236; in rule of law, 259; for safe space, 233; UNCAC, 254–255; World Bank strategy for, 255. *See also* Corruption

Anti-Saloon League, 220
Aoun, Michel, 143
Appointment rules: in Egypt, 32–34, 47–48, 50*n*14; in reforms, 12–13
Arab Human Development Report, 245–247, 246*fig*
Arab Spring: armed forces before, 86; government functions in, 255–256; optimism in, 192; police force in, 152–153; role of, 5; security sectors before, 132
Arab world: defense reform in, 80–86; intercommunal relations in, 132–135, 134*tab*; judicial independence in, 245–246, 246*fig*; judicial reform in, 23–24; optimism in, 273; polarization in, 272; police reform in, 169; rule of law in, 2, 257–259, 269–274; security sectors in, 131–132; specialists in, 2; stocktaking in, 264–269; in transition, 10
Arab-Israeli War, 100
Arbitrary rule, 1
Argentina: armies in, 74–75; Supreme Court in, 26*n*26
Armed forces: before Arab Spring, 86; in Argentina/Chile, 74–75; in Bangladesh, 75; bringing society in, 73; in China, 83; command in, 68–69; decree, 99; democratic control of, 110–111; in economy, 71–72;

301

302   Index

eliminating domestic missions of, 70–71; expertise of, 73–74; gradualism/compromise in, 77–78; having clear roles in, 76–77; in Libya, 83–84; marginalization of, 74; in Mexico, 159; Morale Affairs Department, 100; in national economy, 71–72; new missions for, 74–75; in postsocialist states, 70; in post–civil war environments, 84–85; retired generals in, 75–76; role of, 67; Royal Thai, 80; sequencing/interference in, 78–80, 274n6–275n6; in socialism, 70; strengthening legislative involvement with, 72–73; in Tunisia, 81, 110, 126, 197; understanding of, 69; in Yemen, 83–84. *See also* Lebanese Armed Forces; Supreme Council of the Armed Forces

Association of Tunisian Judges (ATJ): important acts of, 64n6; with Ministry of Justice, 65n17; role of, 54

Authoritarian police force, 154–155

Autocratic regime: attachments to, 123; control of, 127; protection from, 124

Autonomy: institutional, 265–266; of judges, 33–34, 46, 266, 274n4; of military, 267; of police force, 154, 266–267

Aylwin, Patricio, 18

Aziz, Sahar, 45, 47

Badie, Mohammed, 97, 107n26

Bady, Azad, 190

Bangladesh Armed Forces, 75

Banking, 234

Barraket Essahel Affair, 123

al-Batran, Hamdi, 175

Beirut, 145

Belaid, Chokri: assassination of, 194, 211–212; role of, 190–191

Ben Achour, Iyadh, 193

Ben Ali, Zine El Abidine: control under, 117–119; corruption under, 191; defense minister under, 130n19; dismantling security after, 210; family wealth of, 226–227; first year after, 193; history of, 116–117; Interior Ministry under, 118; judges under, 54; looting under, 128n10; military estrangement from, 123; protests against, 114, 118, 201; violence under, 129n15; wealth of, 226

Bird Shot, 202

Bosses, in US cities, 220–221

Bou Nassif, Hicham, 129n14

Bourguiba Legacy, 115–116, 225–226

Bribery, 167

Brown, Nathan, 45, 89

Budget process: legislative oversight of, 252*fig*; in MENA, 249*fig*

Buscaglia, Edgardo, 16

Cairo Court of Appeal, 33

Caribbean, 249*fig*

Carothers, Thomas, 5

Carranza, Venustiano, 159–160, 165

Carranza regime, 161–162

Central Asia, 249*fig*

Central Europe, 3

Central Security Forces, 98, 174

Chaambi Mountains, 196

Checks and balances, government conflict-of-interest safeguards and, 252*fig*

Chile: armies in, 74–75; conflict resolution in, 10–11; corruption scandal in, 19; judges in, 19; legal academy in, 20, 26n31; lessons from, 18–23; Supreme Court in, 19–20, 26n32

China, armed forces in, 83

Christian army, 140

Christian law, 4

Church, 3–4

Citizens: armed, in Mexico, 159; of Egypt, 227; engagement, self-interest based, 217; groups, 231; judicial reforms for, 11, 14–15; life quality of, 240; militias, Mexican, 159; Ministry of Interior grip on, 182–183; in public services, 231–232; trust, in police force, 158, 183; as voters, 27n38

City bosses, 220–221

Civil law, 25n13

Civil society: engagement, in MENA, 253–254, 254*fig*; groups, 195; rule of law in, 260–261; in Tunisia, 192, 200

Civil war: in divided societies, 147*tab*; in Lebanon, 138–139; reformers, 220

Civil-military relations, democratic: components of, 68–69; French, 116; gradualism/compromise in, 77–78;

implementation of, 76–77; privileges of, 69; role of, 67–68; sequencing/interference in, 78–80, 274n6–275n6; teaching of, 73
Clans, 223
Colonial policing, 154–155
Community dispute resolution, 195
Conflict resolution, 10–11
Congress of the Union, 171n18
Constituent Assembly: in Egypt, 36–37; National, 193; in Tunisia, 54–55, 63n2
Constitution of 2014, 46
Constitutional Convention, 171n18
"Constitutional Declaration," 36–37
Constitutional Tribunal, 21
Control model: in divided societies, 133–134, 134tab, 139–140; in Lebanon, 140–141; legitimacy of, 147tab; in security sectors, 139–140, 146; in Tunisia, 215
Corporate ethos, 120–121
Corruption: under Ben Ali, 191; change and, 224–225; in Chile, 19; contrasting syndromes of, 222–224; in Egypt, 227–228; fighting of, 217; impunity and, 224–225; infant mortality and, 242–243, 243fig; in Mexico, 167–168; under Mubarak, 229; new ideas against, 218; in Parliament, 218; in police force, 168–169, 183; during reform, 216–217; solutions to, 229–231; under specific moguls, 230; in Tunisia, 215, 225–227; UNCAC, 254–255; violence in, 216. See also Anticorruption
"Coup-volution," 89
Court of Administrative Litigation, 49n8
Court of Appeals: in Cairo, 22; in Tunisia, 56–57
Court of Cassation: role of, 32–33, 39; in Tunisia, 58–59
Couso, Javier, 21
Cultural homogeneity, 4
"Culture of compliance," 22

al Dawla, Majlis, 49n7
Death sentences, 44
Deep democratization: in England, 219–220; role of, 217; in rule of law, 260–261; strategies for, 232
Defense minister: under Ben Ali, 130n19; in defense reform, 68

Defense reform: in Arab republics, 80–86; clarity in, 76; components of, 68–76; defense minister role in, 68; gradualism/compromise in, 77–78; implementation of, 76–80; objectives of, 67; sequencing/interference in, 78–80, 274n6–275n6; of Tunisian military, 109–111
Democracy: building rule of law in, 261–263; "deep," 217, 219–220, 232, 260–261; Egyptian military nonacceptance of, 103–104; el-Sisi views of, 105n8; "formal," 148n4; freedom in, 262–263; human rights in, 69–70; Islam-based, 105n8; after Mexican Revolution, 161–163; "pacted" agreement of, 104; police force in, 151–152, 154–155; in police reform, 161–163; qualities of, 261–262; reform of, 124–126; religion in, 104; security sectors vs., 168–169; in Tunisia, 53
Democratic control: through exclusion, 112–115; prospects for, 111–112; in rule of law, 110–111; of Tunisian military, 109–111
DF. See Distrito Federal
Díaz, Porfirio, 156–157
El Din, Gamal, 106n19
Distrito Federal (DF): formation of, 162–163; politicization of, 166
Divided societies: Arab world as, 132–133; civil wars in, 147tab; control model in, 133–134, 134tab, 139–140; intercommunal relations in, 132–135, 134tab; military role in, 135–136; power sharing in, 144–146; regime change in, 156–157; repression/stalemate model in, 134, 134tab, 141–143; security sectors in, 135–136, 147tab; violence in, 133, 134tab
Domestic missions, 70–71
Druze militia, 142–143, 148n14

Eastern Europe, 249fig
Economy: armed forces influencing, 71–72; in Egypt, 178; government responsible for, 239–240, 242; growth of, 232; in Mexico, 157, 170n6; space, 233
Egypt: accountability/justice in, 42–43;

agriculture in, 228–229; antiprotest laws in, 39, 44; armed forces in, 81–82; budget process in, 249*fig*; building rule of law in, 264–265; citizens of, 227; Constituent Assembly in, 36–37; constitution in, 126; "Constitutional Declaration" in, 36–37; corruption in, 227–228; death sentences in, 44; economy in, 178; elections in, 30; executive branches in, 39; general prosecutor in, 33, 39–40; investigative services in, 175; Islamism in, 47; Islamist threats in, 175–176, 267; judges in, 29–33, 45–47; judicial appointment in, 32–34, 47–48, 50*n*14; judicial independence in, 30–32, 264–265; judicial reforms in, 32–34, 47–48, 50*n*14; judicial screening in, 275*n*7; justice system in, selective, 44–46; legislative branches in, 39; modern, 186; Muslim Brotherhood in, 177–178, 182; National Defense Council in, 105*n*13–106*n*13; National Security Council in, 105*n*13; NGOs in, 31; obstacles in, 185–186; official moguls in, 227–228; open government in, 254*fig*; Parliament in, 36–67; police academy in, 178–181, 199; police force in, 175, 177; police reform in, 169, 266–267; political isolation law in, 35–36; politics in, 30; reform ideas for, 235–237; religion in, 104; retirement age in, 41–42, 51*n*24; security sectors reform in, 173; specialists in, 2; State Council in, 36–37, 49*n*7; Supreme Constitutional Court in, 34–35, 42; transition process in, 34

Egyptian military: challenges to, 92; civilian protection from, 105*n*12; drawing partition line for, 93–97; under kings, 90; Muslim Brotherhood cohabiting with, 89–93, 267–268; reform ideas of, 107*n*29; rule of law not accepted by, 103–104; strengths of, 90–91; tension in, 97–103; weakness of, 94

Egyptian Republic of Retired Generals, 227

Elite cartels, 223

Energy sector, 102

England: deep democratization in, 219–220; during Stuart monarchy, 218

Ennahda-led government: elections for, 212*n*12; judicial system in, 70; role of, 190, 193–194

Ertman, Thomas, 3

Esparza, Diego, 113

Ethical universalism, 4

Europe: accountable government in, 3–4; Central, 3; Eastern, budget process in, 249*fig*; governance functions in, 3–4; rule of law success in, 3–4; Western, 3

Exclusion: democratic control through, 112–115; in military, 271

Executive branches: in Egypt, 39; of HCJ, 56–57

Executive power, 32–34

Exports, 233–234

Federalist 78, 12

Financial police, 182–183

Fitch, Samuel J., 113

Fouda, Khaled Aly, 227

Free Officers, 90

Frei, Eduardo, 18

French civil-military relations, 116

From Privilege to Competition, 242

Gas companies, 102

el-Gebaly, Tahany, 42, 51*n*25

Gender, of judges, 42, 51*n*25, 51*n*29

General Council for Judicial Affairs, 58–59

General prosecutor: appointment of, 32–33; removal of, 39–40

Ghonim, Wael, 274

Governance functions: in Arab Spring, 255–256; dividends of, 242–243, 243*fig*; for economy, 239–240, 242; in Europe, 3–4; principles of, 241–242; qualities of, 240–241; selected issues in, 250–255, 252*fig*, 254*fig*; types of, 195

Government conflict-of-interest safeguards, checks and balances, 252*fig*

Gradualism: in democratic civil-military relations, 77–78; in post–civil war environments, 85

Grand coalition, 133

Grisham, Kevin, 113

Hamilton, Alexander, 12
Hammad, Talaat, 187n13
Hariri, Rafic, 145
HCJ. *See* High Council of Justice
High Council of Justice (HCJ): executive branches of, 56–57; formation of, 54; reform of, 58; reorganization of, 58–59; reshuffling by, 62
Horizontal accountability, 9–10, 262
al Houdaiby, Ibrahim, 45
Human rights: defenders of, 44–45; in democracy, 69–70; International Federation of Leagues of, 63n1; laws, 26n31; National Council for, 32; NGOs, 31; in police force, 168–169, 185–186, 199; Tunisian League of, 211; watch, 66n26
Huneeus, Alejandra, 20
Huntington, Samuel P., 74–75

Impeachments, 219
Impunity: in corruption, 224–225; institutionalized, 168
"Independent Current," 30
Infant mortality, 242–243, 243*fig*
Influence markets, 223
Informal justice, 195
Institution building, 250–251
Institutional autonomy, 265–266
Institutional culture, 209–212
Institutionalized impunity, 168
Intercommunal relations: in divided societies, 132–135, 134*tab*; examples of, 137–139; in LAF, 140–143; models of, 139–143; in security sectors, 132–135, 134*tab*, 137–139
Internal Security Forces, 149n18, 196–206
International Federation of Leagues of Human Rights, 63n1
International Monetary Fund, 102
Investigative services: in Egypt, 173–174, 175
Iranian Revolutionary Guard Corps, 100
Iraq, 135
Islamists: Badie views of, 97; based democracy, 105n8; el-Sisi views of, 96, 100, 110; Ennahda views of, 70; judicial control by, 35, 37, 46–49; Morsi views of, 107n25; police screening for, 179–180; threats by, 175–176, 267; in Turkey, 83

Israel's Security Agency, 148n15

al-Jabouri, Najim Abed, 135
al-Jahir family, 180
Jebnoun, 129n15
Jordan, 249*fig*
Judges: autonomy of, 33–34, 46, 266, 274n4; behavior of, 16–17; under Ben Ali, 54; caveats/cautions for, 15–16; in Chile, 19; Club, 30, 48n2, 49n9; distancing from state, 45–47; in Egypt, 29–33, 45–47; executive power in, 32–34; gender of, 42, 51n25, 51n29; in Latin America, 25n16; legal requirements for, 13; new generation of, 20; politics influence on, 46; removal of, 12, 42, 60–61, 66n26; reshuffling of, 62–63; retirement age of, 41–42, 51n24; salaries of, 20–21; Syndicate, 54; training of, 12–13, 20, 26n31; in transition process, 34, 45–47. *See also* Association of Tunisian Judges
Judicial Academy, 20, 26n31
Judicial appointment: in Egypt, 32–34, 47–48, 50n14; rules of, 12–13; in Tunisia, 56–57
Judicial Authority Law: amendments to, 52n30; retirement age under, 51n24
Judicial councils, national, 12–13
Judicial independence: in Arab world, 245–246, 246*fig*; caveats/cautions for, 15–16; in Chile, 18–23; concept of, 10–11; conditions for, 258; consequences of, 271; in Egypt, 30–32, 264–265; institutional mechanisms of, 12–15; before Mubarak, 30–32; perceived laws in, 24n5; political science in, 16–17; rule of law in, 9, 264; transition process for, 45–47; in Tunisia, 62–63
Judicial Inspection Department, 33
Judicial police force, 163–165, 167
Judicial reforms: appointment rules in, 12–13; in Arab world, 23–24; for average citizens, 11, 14–15; caveats/cautions for, 15–16; challenges in, 11; in Chile, 18–23; conflict resolution in, 10–11; constitutional-level guarantees for, 12; for criminal justice institutions, 14; in Egypt, 32–34, 47–48, 50n14;

long-term strategies for, 21–22; police force in, 163–165, 167; political science in, 16–17, 260; rule of law in, 11, 23–24; in Tunisia, 53–54

Kennou, Kalthoum, 66*n*31
Kilani family, 179
King John, 218
Kissinger, Henry, 91
Kleinfeld, Rachel, 6, 7*n*1
Kurtzer, Daniel, 7

LAF. *See* Lebanese Armed Forces
Latin America: budget process strength in, 249*fig*; checks and balances in, 252*fig*; criminal procedures in, 25*n*18; judges in, 25*n*16. *See also Specific country*
Lebanese Armed Forces (LAF): intercommunal relations in, 140–143; Muslims in, 148*n*16; no peace in, 145–146; reforms of, 145; violent examples of, 138, 140–141
Lebanon: Christians in, 142–143; civil war in, 138–139; control model in, 140–141; Muslims in, 148*n*16; political system reform in, 138; post-civil war, 144; security sectors in, 133, 137–138; Syria connections with, 143–145
Legislative action, 15–16, 72–73, 252*fig*
Legislative branches, 39
Libya: armed forces in, 83–84; security sector in, 85–86
"Local stakeholders," 6, 271–272
Locke, John, 4
Looting, 128*n*10

MacCormick, Neil, 10
Madero, Gustavo, 158–159
Magna Carta, 218
Marginalization: of armed forces, 74; beliefs in, 113; control through, 127; in military, 271; strategies for, 112
Maronites, 141
Marzouki, Moncef, 189
Material interests: in autocratic regime, 123; in Tunisian military, 114–115
Meierhenrich, Jens, 23
MENA. *See* Middle East and North Africa
Mexican National Archives, 169*n*2

Mexican Revolution: democracy after, 161–163; police reform after, 164–165; politicization after, 164–168; regime change after, 153
Mexico: bribery in, 167; citizens armed in, 159; constitutional rule in, 161–162; corruption in, 167–168; economic model in, 157, 170*n*6; establishing order in, 158–159; military in, 158–163; police force in, 151–154, 157, 170*n*7, 172*n*23; police power in, 163–165; police reform in, 168–169; regime change in, 153, 157–159; security sectors in, 158–159; before war, 171*n*13
Mexico City: corruption in, 167; economic model in, 157, 170*n*6; Historical Archives, 169*n*2; postrevolutionary police in, 172*n*23; during regime change, 153
Middle East and North Africa (MENA): accessing information in, 247–250, 248*fig*–249*fig*; business environment in, 247; civil society engagement in, 253–254, 254*fig*; government accountability in, 251–253, 252*fig*; ongoing transitions in, 246*fig*, 248*fig*–249*fig*; open-government reforms in, 253–254, 254*fig*; poor governance in, 247; public engagement in, 247–250, 248*fig*–249*fig*; rule of law in, 246*fig*, 254–255; selected governance issues in, 250–255, 252*fig*, 254*fig*; transparency in, 247–250, 248*fig*–249*fig*; World Bank strategy for, 239–240
Military: autonomy of, 267; building rule of law, 258–259, 268–269; in divided societies, 135–136; estrangement, from Ben Ali, 123; in Iraq, 135; marginalization/exclusion in, 271; in Mexico, 158–163; during Mubarak, 90–91; in police reform, 161–162. *See also Specific military*
Militia: Druze, 142–143, 148*n*14; Mexican citizen, 159; Shiite, 142–143; Sunni, 143–144
Ministry of Interior: under Ben Ali, 118; changes in, 174–175; changing image of, 192–193; in citizens' lives, 182–183; critique of, 106*n*21;

organizational structure of, 207; reform of, 125, 187n6, 206–209; restructuring of, 210; role of, 97–99, 174; security sectors under, 176
Ministry of Justice: ATJ involvement with, 65n17; removing judges by, 60–61; reshuffling judges in 2012 by, 62–63
Modern state, 3
Moller, Jorgen, 3, 7n1
Money laundering, 233
Morgenthau, Hans, 68
Morocco, 249*fig*
Morsi, Mohamed: cabinet changes led by, 98; in first days elected, 39; islamist views of, 107n25; power of, 40–41; presidency of, 29; regime of, 188n17; removal of, 42–43; tensions with, 102–103
Mubarak, Gamal, 178
Mubarak, Hosni: challenges to, 92; corruption under, 229; fall of, 173; interference of, 32–34; judicial independence before, 30–32; judiciary history of, 29–30; military during, 90–91; politics of, 30; prime minister for, 36; retirement laws under, 51n24; rule of law under, 90, 181; three decades of, 227–229
Municipal police, 159
Municipio Libre, 161, 164
Muslim Brotherhood: drawing partition line for, 93–97; members of, 30, 44, 97; military cohabiting with, 89–93, 267–268; Obama support of, 105n6; police relationship with, 177–178, 182; power of, 93; recruitment of, 98; tensions in, 98–103

Nabih Berri, Amal Movement, 142–143
Nahas, Safwat al, 101
Nahda party, 65n18
Nasser, Gamal Abdul, 90–91
National Constituent Assembly, 193
National Council for Human Rights, 32
National Defense Council, 105n13–106n13
National Guard: pay of, 203–204; schools for, 199; security by, 202–203
National Security Council, 105n13–106n13

NATO. *See* North Atlantic Treaty Organization
NGO. *See* Nongovernmental organization
Nongovernmental organization (NGO), 31
Nonstatutory forces, 195
North Atlantic Treaty Organization (NATO), 72–73
Nusayr, Shadin, 181

Obama, Barack, 105n6
Obregón, Álvaro, 170n9
O'Donnell, Guillermo, 261
Official moguls: corruption under, 230; in Egypt, 227–228; in model, 223–225; pressure on, 235
Oil companies, private, 102
Oligarchs, 223
Open Budget index, 249*fig*
Organizational culture, 112
"Overachievers," 7n5

Parliament: corruption in, 218; in Egypt, 36–67; Supreme Constitutional Court with, 38–39; in Tunisia, 225
Partition plan, 94–95
Perceived laws, 24n5
Pew Global Survey, 125
Pinochet, General Augusto, 18
Pluralists, 230–231
Polarization, 272
Police academy, 178–181, 199
Police chiefs, 171n16
Police force: accountability of, 258; in Arab Spring, 152–153; authoritarian, 154–155; autonomy of, 154, 266–267; avoiding corruption in, 168–169, 183; citizens' trust in, 158, 183; in democracy, 151–152, 154–155; in Egypt, 175, 177; equipment for, 203–204; financial, 182–183; human rights in, 168–169, 185–186, 199; judicial, 163–165, 167; in Mexico, 151–154, 157, 170n7, 172n23; municipal, 159; Muslim Brotherhood relationship with, 177–178, 182; oversight of, 258; pay of, 203–204; politicization of, 164–168; in postrevolutionary Mexico City, 172n23; preventative, 164–165, 167; during regime change, 153–154, 158–159; rule of law in,

258; threats to, 189–191; transparency of, 258; violence in, 155, 162
Police officers: having beards, 98; interviews of, 213n30–214n65; killing of, 39, 44, 190
Police reform: in Arab world, 169; democratic legitimacy in, 161–163; in Egypt, 169, 266–267; in Mexico, 164–165, 168–169; military role in, 161–163; in Tunisia, 169, 189–191, 198–199, 202–203
Political isolation law, 35–36
Political settlements, 217, 221–222
Political space, 232–233, 260–261
Political will, 267, 272, 274
Postsocialist states, 70
Power-sharing system, 144–146, 147*tab*, 148n8
Presidential Guard, 118–119, 197
Preventative police, 164–165, 167
Private oil companies, 102
Professionalism, 121–124, 127–128
Promotion rules, 12–13
Protestant Reformation, 4
Protests: against Ben Ali, 114, 118, 201; of police killings, 39, 44; against SCAF, 93, 105n5; in Tunisia, 121–122, 190
Provisional Council of Justice, 59
Public debate, 186n1
Public funds, 2
Public information, 248*fig*
Public sectors: accountability of, 111, 245–247, 246*fig*; employment of, 244–245

Qaddafi, Muammar, 83–84
Quds Brigade, 100
Qurashi family, 179

Real Estate Court, 58–59
Repression/Stalemate model: in divided societies, 134, 134*tab*, 141–143; in security sectors, 141–143
Retired generals, 75–76
Retirement age, 41–42, 51n24
Role beliefs: emphasis of, 113; in Tunisian military, 120–122
Roman republicanism, 4
Royal Thai Armed Forces, 80

Rule of law: anticorruption in, 259; in Arab world, 2, 257–259, 269–274; case studies of, 2, 271–274; in civil societies, 260–261; convergence to, 221–222; in deep democratization, 260–261; defining of, 2–3; in democracy, 261–263; in democratic control, 110–111; in Egypt, 103–104, 264–265; European success building, 3–4; future of, 1; future research in, 271–274; general lessons in, 271–274; good governance dividends of, 242–243, 243*fig*; hope for, 273–274; in judicial independence, 9, 264; in judicial reforms, 11, 23–24; in MENA, 246*fig*, 254–255; military in, 258–259, 268–269; under Mubarak, 90, 181; in police force, 258; political settlements giving rise to, 217; political will in, 267, 272, 274; in politics, 5–6, 259–261; reform ideas for, 235–237; second generation thinking of, 5; sequencing of, 261–263, 274n6–275n6; timing of, 261–263, 274n6; toolkit for, comparative lessons, 257–261; underpinnings of, 1; unintended consequences of, 271; World Bank building, 269
Rutherford, Bruce, 272

Sadat, Anwar, 91, 187n7
Saleh, Ali Abdullah, 83–84
Salehi, Akbar, 100
Salem, Hussein, 227
Sawt al-Umma, 179
SCAF. *See* Supreme Council of the Armed Forces
Schumpeter, Joseph, 5
Secularists, 100; as activists, 44–45; armies of, 86; against el-Sisi, 100; political will of, 267; revolutionaries, 92, 94; Salafists *vs.*, 193–194; Wafd party, 36, 90
Security and Development: A White Paper for Democratic Security in Tunisia, 212n11
Security forces: central, 98, 174; internal, 149n18, 196–206
Security sector reform (SSR): agenda of, 194–195; importance of, 194;

reforming of, 206–209; role of, 192; in Tunisia, 191–196; two categories of, 210
Security sectors: agencies in, 147n1; before Arab Spring, 132; in Arab world, 131–132; control model in, 139–140, 146; culture of, 178–182; democracy vs., 168–169; in divided societies, 135–136, 147*tab*; in Egypt, 173; historical overview of, 173–178; ideological identity of, 148n11; intercommunal relations in, 132–135, 134*tab*, 137–139; in Israel, 148n15; in Lebanon, 133, 137–138; in Libya/Yemen, 85–86; in Mexico, 158–159; under Ministry of Interior, 176; obstacles of, 184–185; professionalism in, 183; reform of, 182–186; reorienting institutional culture of, 209–212; repression/ Stalemate model in, 141–143; role of, 131–132; training of, 178–182; in Tunisia, 118, 191–192
Serbian Army, 149n17
Shafiq, Ahmed, 36
Shiite militia, 142–143
Shinawatra, Thaksin, 80
Shura Council, 101
Sinai Peninsula, 91, 99, 187n10
al-Sirgany, Khalid, 187n14
el-Sisi, Abdel Fattah: democracy views of, 105n8; embarrassment of, 100; as Islamist, 96, 100, 110; meeting called by, 106n25; virginity tests ordered by, 101
Skaaning, Svend-Erick, 3, 7n1
Socialism: in armed forces, 70; Walid Jumblatt's Progressive Socialist Party, 142–143
South Africa, 170n4
South Asia, 252*fig*
South Korea, 236
SSI. *See* State Security Investigations Service
SSR. *See* Security sector reform
Stakeholders: in decisionmaking, 241–242; local, 6, 271–272; reliance on, 15–16, 260
Stalemate model, 134, 134*tab*, 141–143
State: building, 250–251; Council, 36–37, 49n7; investigative services, 173–174; judges distancing themselves from, 45–47; modern, 3; -ness, 233; postsocialist, 70. *See also* United States
State Security Investigations Service (SSI), 173–174
Statutory forces, 194
Stocktaking, 264–269
Strayer, Joseph, 3
Suleimani, Qassem, 100
Sunni militia, 143–144
Sunni Muslim, 149n18
Supreme Constitutional Court: constituent assembly rulings in, 36–37; members of, removal, 42; new speaker in, 48n1; parliamentary elections in, 38–39; political isolation law in, 35–36; rulings of, 34–35
Supreme Council of the Armed Forces (SCAF): decline of, 95; formation of, 36–37; protests against, 93, 105n5; provisions made by, 95; in reform, 185–186; role of, 93
Supreme Court: in Argentina, 26n26; in Chile, 19–20, 26n32
Supreme Judicial Council, 32–33
Svolik, Milan, 112
Syria, Lebanon connections with, 143–145

Tantawi, Muhammed Hussein: during cabinet reshuffle, 99; rejection of, 94; role of, 91; successor of, 96
Task reform, 235
Tax extraction, 3
Taxation, 233
Taylor, Brian, 113
Telephone justice, 275n7
Territorial power sharing, 148n8
Tilly, Charles, 3
Tlatelolco, 167–168
Torture, 201
Trager, Eric, 99
Transparency: importance of, 2, 241; in MENA, 247–250, 248*fig*–249*fig*; of police force, 258; in Tunisia, 60, 65n19, 210–211
Tripoli, 145
Tunisia: armed forces in, 81, 110, 126, 197; authoritarian practices in, 58–59; after Ben Ali, 193; benefits in, 203–

204; civil society in, 192, 200; civilian control in, 122–123; constitution in, 125–126, 130n26; control in, 215; corruption in, 215, 225–227; Court of Cassation in, 58–59; democracy transition in, 53; dictatorship in, 53; equipment in, 203–204; judge removal in, 60–61, 66n26; Judges' Syndicate in, 54; judicial appointment in, 56–57; judicial independence in, 62–63; judicial power in, 56; judicial revolution in, 53–54; judiciary management in, 60; Ministry of Interior reform in, 207–209; modern foundation of, 225–226; open government in, 254*fig*; parliament in, 225; past judicial system in, 55; pay in, 203–204; police law reform in, 204–206; police officer interviews in, 213n30–214n65; police reform in, 169, 189–191, 198–199, 202–203; political control in, 115–119; Presidential Guard in, 118–119, 197; procedures in, 200–203; protests in, 121–122, 190; recruitment in, 198–200; reform failure/rejection in, 58–59; reform ideas for, 235–237; reorienting institutional culture in, 209–212; revolution in, aftermath, 57–58; *Security and Development: A White Paper for Democratic Security in*, 212n11; security challenges in, 191–192; security sectors in, 118, 191–192; SSR in, 191–196; third transition government in, 193; torture in, 201; training in, 198–200; transparency in, 60, 65n19, 210–211; US Embassy attack in, 189–190; violence in, 190. *See also* Association of Tunisian Judges

Tunisian Constituent Assembly, 54–55, 63n2

Tunisian League of Human Rights, 211

Tunisian military: as apolitical, 121–124, 129n13; civilian control over, 111, 122–123; control of, 127; corporate ethos of, 120–121; defense reform of, 110–111; democratic control of, 109–111; democratic reform of, 124–126; funding for, 129n12; limitations of, 117; marginalization strategies in, 112; material interests in, 114–115; political control implications in, 115–119; professionalism in, 121–124, 127–128; role beliefs in, 120–122; role of, 117–118; social esteem of, 124; social standing in, 115; socialization in, 122–123

Turkey, 83

Tyranny, 9

UN Convention Against Corruption (UNCAC), 254–255

UN Security Council, 2–3

UNCAC. *See* UN Convention Against Corruption

"Underachievers," 7n4

United States: Embassy, 189; fighting bosses in, 220–221; nation-building project led by, 146

Unity government, 194

Vertical accountability, 9, 261

Villa, Pancho, 161

Violence: under Ben Ali, 129n15; in corruption, 216; in divided societies, 133, 134*tab*; in LAF, 143; in police force, 155, 162; in Tunisia, 190

Virginity tests, 96, 101

Voters, 27n38

Wafd Party, 36, 90

Walid Jumblatt, Progressive Socialist Party, 142–143

Wasat Party, 41

Weapons, 196

West Bank, 249*fig*

Western Europe, 3

Whigs and Tories, 219

Women's rights movement, 220

World Bank strategy: for anticorruption, 255; breakdown of, 240–243, 243*fig*; building rule of law, 269; for MENA, general, 239–240; for public services, 253–254, 254*fig*

Yemen: armed forces in, 83–84; budget process in, 249*fig*; security sector in, 85–86

Zapata, Emiliano, 161

About the Book

How might Arab countries build the foundations for rule of law in the wake of prolonged authoritarian rule? What specific challenges do they confront? Are there insights to be gained from comparative analysis beyond the region? Exploring these questions, the authors of *Building Rule of Law in the Arab World* provide a theoretically informed, empirically rich account of key issues facing the countries at the forefront of political change since the Arab Spring as governments seek to develop effective and responsible judiciaries, security sectors, and anticorruption agencies.

Eva Bellin is Myra and Robert Kraft Professor of Arab Politics at Brandeis University. **Heidi E. Lane** is associate professor of strategy and policy and director of the Greater Middle East Research Study Group at the US Naval War College.